CIVILITY AND SAVAGERY

Frontispiece A Prince (Cao Müang) of Nan, probably early nineteenth century

CIVILITY AND SAVAGERY

Social Identity in Tai States

Edited by
Andrew Turton

CURZON

First Published in 2000
by Curzon Press
Richmond, Surrey
http://www.curzonpress.co.uk

Editorial Matter © 2000 Andrew Turton

Typeset in Bembo by LaserScript Ltd, Mitcham, Surrey
Printed and bound in Great Britain by
Biddles Ltd, Guildford and King's Lynn

British Library Cataloguing in Publication Data
A catalogue record of this book is available from the British Library

Library of Congress Cataloguing in Publication Data
A catalogue record for this book has been requested

ISBN 0–7007–1173–2

Contents

Preface and Acknowledgements

This book has grown from initial contributions and discussions at the 5th International Conference on Thai Studies. Nearly half the chapters have been written since then, and all have benefited from a further round of reflection and editing by the authors. The contributors comprise a great many of the most well-known scholars in ethnographic and historical studies of peoples of the Tai speaking region of mainland South East Asia. The chapters build on intensive scholarship over many years and many also strike out in new directions. The collective endeavour was made all the more exciting by the involvement of a large number scholars either from the Tai region, or living and working in the neighbouring Asian region, together with scholars from Europe and the USA.

This volume is already sufficiently framed not to need a lengthy Introduction. My own first chapter partly serves this function as do the section introductions which I have written. I am immensely grateful to Nicholas Tapp who has provided a postscript that reflects on the project as a whole, and its implications for Thai studies, Tai studies, and other regional studies. He brings to bear his role as informal rapporteur of the original discussions and his considerable experience in the region in its widest sense, to emphasise our purpose to enlarge thinking about the Tai speaking region and overcome some of the intellectual and political limitations of essentialist, and in the end often racialising consequences of some – arguably the predominant style of – previous scholarship and its influence on public policies and attitudes. At the same we are concerned to recognise the important contributions of distinguished predecessors in this field. It is terribly difficult to mention these without offence to any who may be omitted but I would especially like to refer to the work – other than that of the authors of this volume – of certain regional scholars who have influenced my own work: Charles Archaimbault, Jit Phumisak, Georges Condominas, E.R. Leach, and F.K. Lehman. I would also like to mention the pioneering scholarship of many Thai scholars – most of them not academics – of earlier generations whose work deserves critical, and appreciative appraisal, among whom I will only mention Phya Anuman

Rajadhon and Sanguan Chottisukharat both of whom I had the privilege to meet personally.

At the 1993 conference at SOAS, London, there was a large attendance at the two 'minority' sessions as they were colloquially called: 'Minorities within Tai/Thai political systems: historical and theoretical perspectives' and 'Minorities policy and practice in the Tai speaking region'. Among those who took a prominent part then who are not represented here I would particularly like to thank Georges Condominas, Gehan Wijeye-wardene, Craig Reynolds, Ananda Rajah, and other participants in the two panels: Amara Pongsapich, Jean Berlie, Scott Bamber, Chupinit Kesmanee, He Shengda, Shih-chung Hsieh, Jean Michaud, Jan Ovesen, Srisak Vallibhotama, Nguyen Duy Thieu, Ing-Britt Trankell, and all the many other colleagues who joined in. We missed the company of Jacques Lemoine who was to have attended but was prevented at the last minute. As convenor I take full responsibility for the absence of other scholars who should have been invited or more assiduously and generously encouraged; these include especially Hjorliefur Jonsson and F.K. Lehman.

I would like to express my deep appreciation to all contributors to this book for their patience, and my hope that they – as well as our readers – will both enjoy what follows and be generous in forgiving the Editor's inevitable errors of fact or judgement.

There are many people who have contributed their time, professional skills, and personal support to producing this book: SOAS colleagues Rachel Harrison, Manas Chitakasem, Ian Brown and Irene Cummings; Catherine Lawrence SOAS cartographer who prepared the maps so professionally, and so as to include just about every place name referred to in the text; Nicholas Tapp for personal encouragement, advice and assistance of every sort with editing, and scholarly conversation; Henry Ginsburg of the British Library Department of Ancient Books and Manuscripts, Jonathan Price of Curzon Press, and Muang Boran Publishing House for permission to reproduce our cover image and others.

I would finally like to thank members of my family for more than they know they have given me: Joan Turton, Antonia Benedek, Polly Benedek Turton, Clio Benedek Turton.

Andrew Turton

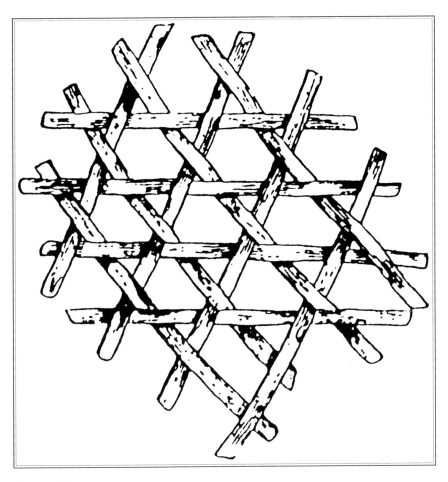

Plate 1 'Talio, or charm'

List of Contributors

Leo Alting von Geusau is Senior Researcher of the South East Asian Mountain Peoples Culture and Development Research Documentation and Information services in Thailand (SEAMP-CD-RDI) linked with SEAMP International Foundation, Netherlands. He is also Vice-Chair of the International Hani/Akha Culture Studies Committee, UNESCO Expert, and consultant regarding ethnic minorities in the region. He has carried out extensive research among the Akha in Northern Thailand since 1977 and has extended this to Southern China, Northern Laos and Eastern Burma since 1993. Together with Deuleu Dzoebaw, his spouse and her Akha family, he has been at the origin of several minority NGOs. The best known of his many articles on Akha culture and minority problems is 'Dialectics of Akhazang' in *Highlanders of Thailand* (John McKinnon and Wanat Bhruksasri eds. OUP, 1981).

Katherine Bowie is Associate Professor of Anthropology and Southeast Asian Studies at the University of Wisconsin-Madison. She first travelled to Thailand in 1974 where she initially worked as a freelance journalist. Since then she has carried out extensive field research (totalling over 8 years) primarily in northern Thailand. Her work has focused broadly on issues regarding the political economy of peasant society. Her books include *Rituals of national loyalty: an anthropology of the state and the Village Scout movement in Thailand* (New York, Columbia University Press, 1997) and *Voices from the Thai countryside: 'The Necklace' and other short stories of Samruam Singh* (University of Wisconsin Center of Southeast Asia Publications Series 1991, revised edition 1998).

Claes Corlin is Associate Professor in the Department of Social Anthropology at Göteborg University, Gothenburg, Sweden. He has carried out two years of field research among Tibetan refugees in Nepal and in Switzerland, and shorter field missions among highland minorities in Northern Thailand. He has participated in a number of field studies in Vietnam since 1986 in connection with development programmes, and is currently the co-ordinator of a capacity-building project in Social Anthropology in Vietnam. His publications include *The nation in your mind: continuity and change among Tibetan refugees* (Gothenburg, 1975), *Common origins and present inequality: ethnic origin myths among highland populations of mainland Southeast Asia* (Copenhagen, 1994, 2nd edition 1995). He also co-edited *On the meaning of death: essays on mortuary practices and eschatological beliefs* (Uppsala, 1983).

Grant Evans is Reader in Anthropology at the University of Hong Kong. His numerous publications include *The politics of ritual and remembrance: Laos since 1975* (Silkworm Books, Chiang Mai, University of Hawaii Press, Allen and Unwin, Australia, 1998); *Lao peasants under socialism and post-socialism* (Silkworm Books, 1995); and with Kelvin Rowley *Red brotherhood at war: Cambodia, Vietnam and Laos since 1975* (Verso, London, 1990, revised edition). He also edited *Lao culture and society* (Silkworm Books, 1998). He is General Editor of the 'Anthropology of Asia' series for Curzon Press. He has acted as a consultant to UNESCO, the World Bank and the World Wildlife Fund on issues of minority rights, heritage and sustainable development in Vietnam and Laos.

Charles F. Keyes is Professor of Anthropology and International Studies at the University of Washington. He has carried out extensive field research (totalling over eight years since 1962) primarily in Thailand, but also in Burma, Laos, Cambodia, and Vietnam. He is the author of three books and the editor of seven, including *The golden peninsula: culture and adaptation in mainland Southeast Asia* (1977; reissued 1995), *Asian visions of authority: religion and the modern states of East and Southeast Asia* (1994), *Thailand: Buddhist kingdom as modern nation-state* (1987, 2nd edition 1995), and *Ethnic adaptation and identity: the Karen on the Thai frontier with Burma* (1979). His research interests include the study of ethnicity, especially with reference to indigenous minorities in mainland South East Asia, religion (especially Buddhism) and modernity, the politics of history and state-society relations, especially in Thailand, Laos, and Vietnam.

Igor Kossikov is a Director of Research at the Institute of Ethnology, Russian Academy of Sciences. He holds a doctorate in historical sciences. He is currently leads two research projects: 'Federalism in contemporary Russia' and 'Monitoring the social and economic situation in the Russian regions and CIS states'. He lectures widely in Europe and also in Taiwan. He has published especially on issues of ethnicity, nationalism, regionalization and federalism. He acts as a policy analyst for the Federation Council (Upper House of the Russian Parliament) and is Editor-in-Chief of the Moscow journal *Business and politics*.

Mayoury Ngaosyvathn is General Manager of Mayoury, Pheuiphanh and Sons Legal Council Office (Laos) consulting on gender issues, socio-legal matters and real estate. She has lectured at the University of Paris from which she obtained a PhD in Law (with *'mention excellent'*). She served in the High Court of the Kingdom of Laos and after 1975 worked as Deputy Director at the Ministry of Justice, and subsequently at the Ministry of Foreign Affairs. She has been a Fulbright Senior Scholar at Harvard University and has held Fellowships at the East-West Centre (Hawaii), the Institute of Southeast Asian Studies (Singapore),the Criminology Research Council (Canberra) and the Centre for the Study of Australia–Asia Relations (Griffith University, Queensland). She has written and co-authored twenty seven articles and books. Her book *Lao women yesterday and today* (1993) has been reissued twice; her latest publication (co-authored with Pheuiphanh Ngaosyvathn) is *Paths to conflagration: fifty years of diplomacy and warfare in Laos, Thailand, and Vietnam, 1778–1828* (Cornell Southeast Asia Programs, 1998).

Ryoko Nishii is Associate Professor at the Institute for the Study of the Languages and Cultures of Asia and Africa, Tokyo University of Foreign Studies. She obtained her PhD degree from the Graduate University of Advanced Studies. She has carried out fieldwork in the border area between Thailand and Malaysia where Muslims and Buddhists are co-resident. This research has resulted in several publications in Japanese and English, the latest of which is 'Social memory as it emerges: consideration of the death of a young convert on the West Coast of Southern Thailand' in S. Tanabe and C.F. Keyes eds. *Cultural crisis and social memory: politics of the past in the Thai world* (Curzon Press, London, and University of Hawaii Press, forthcoming).

Ronald Renard specialises in the study of small groups in upper Mainland South East Asia. He has lived in Chiang Mai for some twenty years, teaching history at Payap University for fifteen years. More recently he has managed the UNDP Indochina Sub-regional Highland People's Pro-gramme and worked as consultant for various agencies and projects in the region. He has written on the Karen and Tai Lue peoples and the dynamics of upland-lowland relations. He has written a number of books including *The Burmese connection: illegal drugs and the making of the Golden Triangle* (L. Rienner, Boulder, Colorado 1996). In a turn away from vice, as he puts it, he is currently editing a CD on *The life and teachings of the Buddha* which is being produced by the Mae Fa Luang Foundation in Bangkok.

Ratanaporn Sethakul is a History Faculty Member in the Graduate School of Payap University, Chiang Mai. Since her doctoral research (*Political, social and economic changes in the Northern States of Thailand resulting* *from the Chiang Mai treaties of 1874 and 1886*, Northern Illinois, 1989) she has continued to research and publish on the history of Tai peoples, especially Lanna history, the social and cultural history of Sipsongpanna and the Mekong corridor. She has conducted research in Burma, China, Laos and Cambodia, as well as in Thailand.

Kobkua Suwannathat-Pian is Senior Lecturer in the School of Liberal Studies, Universiti Tenaga Nasional, Malaysia. A historian by training, she has lectured on Thai and Southeast Asian History at Chiang Mai University, Thailand, and the National University of Malaysia. For the past decade she has conducted extensive research both in Thailand and Malaysia focusing on socio-political aspects of both countries. Her books include *Thai-Malay relations: traditional intra-regional relations from the seventeenth to early twentieth centuries* (OUP, 1988) and *Thailand's durable Premier: Phibun through three decades 1932–1957* (OUP, 1994).

Shigeharu Tanabe is Professor of Anthropology at the National Museum of Ethnology and the School of Cultural Studies, Graduate University for Advanced Studies, Osaka. His area of research interest covers especially Thailand, Laos, Vietnam and Southwestern Yunnan. Thematic concerns include: anthropological theory of practice, spirit mediumship, Buddhism, and peasant farming. His publications include *Religious renewals in Asia: politics of religious experience* (Kyoto University Press, 1995, in Japanese), *Ecology and practical technology: peasant farming systems in Thailand* (Bangkok, Lotus, 1994), *Wearing the yellow robe, wearing the black garb: a story of a peasant leader in Northern Thailand* (Bangkok, Sangsan, 1989, in Thai). He co-edited with Andrew Turton *History and peasant consciousness in South East Asia* (Osaka, National Museum of Ethnology, 1984).

Nicholas Tapp is Senior Fellow, Department of Anthropology, Research School of Pacific and Asian Studies, Australian National University. He has spent nearly four years in Thailand, first teaching English in the South, and later researching the Hmong in the North. His first book *Sovereignty and rebellion* (1989) dealt with the Hmong of Thailand. He has recently researched in Laos and Vietnam. He also lectured at Edinburgh University and at the Chinese University of Hong Kong for six years, during which time he undertook major research on the Hmong of China. A second major volume on the Hmong *Reconstructions: Hmong agents in varied contexts* is forthcoming (University of Washington Press).

Andrew Turton is Reader in Anthropology at the School of Oriental and African Studies, University of London, Chair of Anthropology and former Chair of the Centre of South East Asian Studies at SOAS. He has spent several years living and researching in Thailand, especially the northern region, since 1962 when he spent two years as British Council Assistant Representative based in Bangkok but travelling widely. He has visited minority regions in the area and all neighbouring countries, and has conducted limited research in Laos and in Yunnan province of China. His publications since 1972 have challenged existing paradigms on such issues as matriliny and gender, class and ideology, state and local powers, discourse and knowledge. He is currently working on the 'ethnography of diplomatic mission' in relation to Tai states.

Thongchai Winichakul is Associate Professor in the History Department, and Director of the Center for Southeast Asian Studies at the University of Wisconsin-Madison. He is the author of *Siam mapped: a history of the geo-body of a nation* (1994) which was awarded the Harry Benda prize in 1995, and 'The changing landscape of the past: new histories in Thailand since 1973' in the *Journal of Southeast Asian Studies* (1995). He was Guggenheim Fellow in 1995, and Chair of the Southeast Asia Council, Association for Asian Studies 1996–97. He is currently working on a book on a history of Thai historical knowledge. He also writes occasionally for Thai magazines and newspapers.

Plate 2 'A meal offered by the king of Muong You'

List of Maps

List of Illustrations

[Note: Sources and detailed captions are given in the Appendix p. 360. Short captions in quotation marks are original.]

Map 1 – Mainland South East Asia

Map 2 – Laos and Thailand

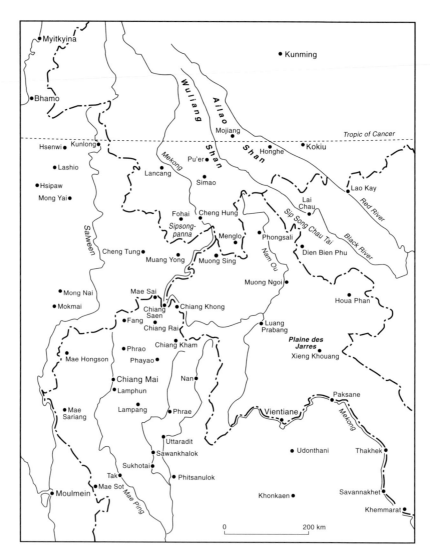

Map 3 – Tai States (detail)

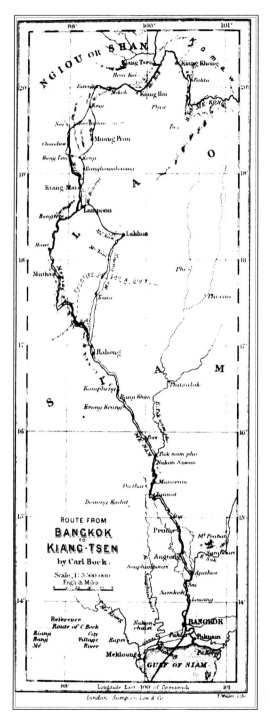

Plate 3 'Route from Bangkok to Kiang-Tsen [Chiangsaen]'

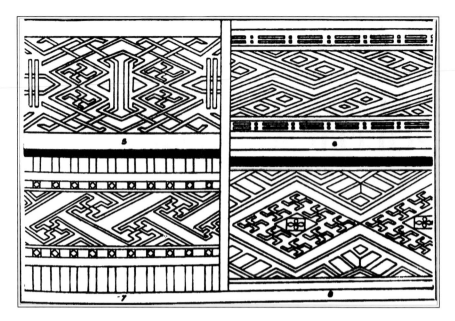

Plate 4. 'Designs on the borders of [Shan] turbans'

Part I

INTER-ETHNIC RELATIONS IN TAI POLITICAL DOMAINS

Introduction to *Civility and Savagery*

Andrew Turton

I

Social identity in Tai political domains

Thailand – the country, the nation – has considerable prominence in the world to-day. Contemporary global currents of movement of people take millions of visitors annually to Thailand as tourists and business people, and Thai people are increasingly present in the societies of North America, Western Europe, Australia, the Middle East and the more well-to-do countries of East Asia and elsewhere, as economic migrants, entrepreneurs, 'guest workers', students and so on. It is a late twentieth century diaspora of considerable scale, in the weaker sense of voluntary dispersal with continuing contact with the homeland, rather than the collective and forced movement of a permanent and often tragic kind historically associated with diaspora. It is too soon to have much idea of what separate and distinct cultural traditions and memories these expatriate or settled communities may be developing inside their various new host countries, which are themselves increasingly conscious of their ethnic plurality.

Outside Thailand and its immediate region, there is less general awareness that the Thai people are 'members' of a 'language family' and cultural area, indeed a regionally defined diaspora of a thousand years and more, comparable in some respects say to that of Romance languages in Europe or even Turkic languages in Western and Central Asia. This Asian region stretches from Assam in North East India eastwards to Guangdong Province of China, southwards to the northern parts of the Malay Peninsula and northwards through eastern Burma. It contains several large ethnic groupings which are quite well-known, in the West at least, as the Shan in Burma, the Lao of Laos (the Lao People's Democratic Republic), and of course the Thai of Thailand. There are also several groupings of considerable size within the borders of China (the Zhuang and the Dai for

Plate 5 'The library of a Laotian pagoda'

example) and Vietnam. All these peoples are also to be found in one or more of their neighbouring countries (see Map 1).

The English and Western language academic term commonly used to designate this cultural space is 'Tai' [ไท]. This is an awkward usage in being barely distinguishable from 'Thai' [ไทย] in look as well as in speech, both being pronounced similarly with an aspirated /t/, and each transcribing a Thai/Tai word of similar sound but – also only slightly – different orthography. Some dialects have an unaspirated /t/ [ไต]. It is also a problematic term for many of the people living in the area; for example, the Lao do not generally like to be referred to as even generically Tai. The Chinese give great emphasis to the distinction between the 'Dai' (a Chinese pronunciation) of Yunnan province and any neighbouring Tai/ Thai. It is possible that, once again, we are seeing the effects of outsiders' views of other people, constructing a questionable entity, whether in terms of scientific or phenomenological validity, and not one entirely welcome to all those involved.

There is however a growing tendency for people in Thailand, at the end of the twentieth century, to think of themselves as a more pluralistic society, in ethnic and cultural senses, and less in terms of the official monocultural nationalism of earlier years, especially after 1910 and up to the watershed 1973–76 period. There is a greater awareness and appreciation of a variety of Thai and Tai traditions both within and beyond the national frontiers. And there is a greater knowledge and acceptance of the co-existence with them of many non-Tai identities and communities. A particular case in point are the Sino-Thai, many of whom are once again celebrating and enjoying their 'double' or mixed identity. Another example and minor encouragement of this tendency has been the way in which the International Thai Studies Conference – held every three years since 1981 – has become increasingly focused on the 'Tai' region and associated problematics, alongside admittedly still preponderant national 'Thai' (Thailand) themes. Studies of non-Tai (here also non-Thai) peoples which had formerly been treated, to a culpable degree, as discrete cultures and which had therefore proved awkward to integrate within earlier notions of a *Thai Studies* conference, began to be included. Also indicative is recent sponsorship by the *Thai* National Culture Commission of research on *Tai* cultures. Finally, the First International Conference on Tai Studies (albeit mainly linguistic in scope) was held in Thailand in July 1998. At the same time several of the non-Tai minorities of the region, notably the Akha, Hmong, and Mien (Yao), have inaugurated their own *trans-national* 'Cultural Studies Conferences'.

Ironically however, it was precisely at the height of Thailand's ultra-nationalism in the 1930s, that the Thai state asserted ideas of 'Pan-Thai' commonality (for a recent use of the notion of 'a pan-Tai cultural complex', see Terwiel 1992: 133, 157). Maps were issued showing territories which had 'originally been Thai', and which extended far beyond the limits either of the Thai 'empire', as I would call it, as it was constituted, for example, in the early nineteenth century, or even at its fullest extent in the Ayutthaya period. This was more than an anti-colonial irredentism, and it was partly based on a knowledge produced by modern scholarship of the time. Arguably recent interest in Tai cultures beyond the borders of Thailand is a continuing element of Thai cultural nationalism and not a move away from it. It was at the end of the 1930s that the international name of the country was decreed to be Thailand, no longer Siam, a centuries old outsider's term. 'Thailand' translates approximately the Thai modernism *Prathet Thai* (literally 'sacred territory [of the] Thai'). It can also gloss the Thai words *Müang Thai* (political domain or polity [of the] Thai) a term which had long been used of themselves by the Thai of the kingdoms or empires based on the cities of Ayutthaya and later Bangkok.

Ayutthaya and Bangkok – both as port cities and their eponymous kingdoms and empires [Ayutthaya 1350–1767; Bangkok from 1782] – have always had highly diverse and differentiated populations, though as we shall see, it may be anachronistic to call them uniformly 'multi-ethnic' over a period of some seven centuries. We may expect demographic, political and cultural diversity to be generally true of empires and port cities anywhere. What is of particular interest for this case and for this volume is that wherever, and whenever, there have been Tai political domains – whether these have been what we might loosely refer to at this stage as chiefdoms, federations of chiefdoms, principalities, or kingdoms – these have been referred to as *müang*; indeed the term in one form or another seems to be even more constant than the term *tai*. As a comparative orientation we could say that *müang* has many of the senses of the Greek *polis* and Roman *civis*. And wherever we find *müang*, we find a situation of relationship, interdependence, and domination between Tai and non-Tai populations. Moreover this is in many ways a systematic relationship distinguished by linguistic, cultural, and social classification. The most important and frequent classifications are the 'pairs' *tai : kha* and *müang : pa;* where provisionally: *kha* = both a generic ethnonym for non-Tai, and a generic social status of servant, slave etc.; and *pa* = forest, the wild, savage (from Latin *silva* = forest) etc. The diacritics involved are often of a binary kind, but by no means always, thus a formulation *tai : müang :: kha : pa* would capture only part of the historically changing realities. However, at this stage in the argument it may already be more appropriate to say that the socially dominant people are classified as Tai, rather than that some 'ethnic Tai' are everywhere socially dominant.

This volume is dedicated to a large extent to examining the relations between people in terms of *müang, thai, tai,* and *kha* in changing historical situations, contexts, and discourses. Hence the title *Civility and Savagery*. In this chapter I attempt to draw together and develop some common themes which contributors have introduced. However, I feel it more than usually necessary to advise the reader of the richness and originality of the chapters which follow and therefore of the number of themes and arguments which I do not take up here.

Discourses of social differentiation

Most oral cultures have textualised peoples' experience and perception of social difference, of differences between human groupings, in narratives (myths, cosmogonies etc.) of human unity and differentiation, often combined with themes of inequality and conflict, loss and decline, of memory and regret, but also pride and hope. Like royal chronicles and genealogies they retain accounts of origins, selectively collapse intervening episodes, and come up-to-date to deal with current concerns. Thus the indigenous people of Central Borneo relate in a single story the origins of laughter and literacy, and the characteristics of Chinese and Europeans (Rousseau, 1990).

The interlocked destinies, to use a poetic metaphor, of Tai and Kha peoples is inscribed in archaic oral texts, or myths which are widespread in the region, especially among the Kha peoples (see Corlin, 1994 and this volume; Condominas, 1980, 1990; and see also Rousseau, 1990 for cognate ideas among quite separate peoples of Central Borneo). After some primordial catastrophe on a global scale (a flood) an incestuous couple procreate a gourd from which spring out of one clean hole cut with sharp metal tools, the Tai people, while out of another hole pierced and blackened by red hot iron, come the Kha peoples of darker complexion. Following some original unity there is marked but complementary differentiation. This immediately forms the basis of hierarchies in terms of birth order, ritual superiority, and political domination. In a Black Tai version, the Tai princely clans are direct descendants of a heavenly lord, while everyone else, Tai and Kha, emerges from a different hole in the gourd. Historical and ethnographic accounts document continuing, apparently long-standing ritual practices in which non-Tai peoples are, at least temporarily, accorded some ritual seniority and recognition of prior occupancy of land and associated ritual powers (see Tanabe, this volume; and Archaimbault, 1971, 1973). But the political domination is uniformly one-sided.

Great literate civilizations, especially in their formative periods, have sought to address issues of social differentiation. Thus early Buddhist writing treats of distinction and unity in moral and natural orders, of what it is to be fully human and what men may become *bhikku* ('ordained' disciples of the Buddha; see Tanabe this volume, also Rhum 1987). Great empires or *oikumene*, which combine collective experience and interests over extensive social spaces, have given rise to texts which document, evaluate, and redefine social and cultural differences (or more geographi-cal, human-physical ones), sometimes as a matter of policy. Herodotus does this in *The Histories* for the peoples on the fringes of the Hellenistic world of the Mediterranean and Black Sea in the fifth century BC, an undertaking which is regarded as the first European work of literary art in prose. From the Chinese empire we have the *Shan Hai Jing* in the second century BC (Mathieu, 1983).

European discourses of social differentiation are far from cumulative or uniform. For example we may discern and contrast a late medieval world view in which peoples beyond Christendom are represented above all as pagan; an enlightenment view of 'natural man', as virtuous and noble; a post-Darwinian account of backwardness and difficult evolution; and a contemporary more pluralistic state of affairs in which versions of older discourses linger on and contend with post-colonial, post-national, and indigenist theories and social movements.

Early accounts, even though they may have been independently produced in different times and circumstances, nonetheless have many features in common, and contacts and exchanges over the centuries have resulted in mutual influences. Owing to the recentness of European imperial expansion overseas – albeit relatively short-lived when seen in a longer perspective – the influence of Western ideas on non-Western thought (Dikötter, 1992; Thongchai this volume) has probably been studied more extensively than reverse influences or influences between non-Western bodies of thought. This is a limitation which the present study acknowledges.

This volume examines discourses of differentiation within a civilization or politico-cultural region of middling scale – compared with, for example, Chinese, or Persian, or Roman empires – namely that of Tai political domains. These are no more uniform or continuous than 'European' counterparts, but the chapters nonetheless argue that they constitute a valid and rewarding context of study, even if we may at the same time want critically to deconstruct it. On the one hand we are dealing with a local, idiosyncratic set of phenomena, with some discreteness of historical development over the past millennium or so. On the other hand, from early times, if not the earliest knowable or imaginable, there have been influences from Hindu, Buddhist, and Chinese sources and their more local manifestations and refractions (via Cham, Khmer, Mon, Vietnamese amongst others; cf. Tanabe, Renard, Tapp, this volume). In the modern era we must add the influences of Christian and European thought (Corlin, Thongchai, this volume).

As already anticipated, this volume examines issues of social identification of people living in areas of South East Asia which have for centuries been under the political dominance of Tai-speaking ruling élites. These Tai political domains include contemporary Thailand which incorporates parts of several former tributary Tai states in the South, North East and the North, notably the Lanna Kingdom centred on Chiang Mai. They also include contemporary Laos, formed out of parts of several former Tai states tributary to Thailand, Vietnam, and, to a lesser extent, China; areas of contemporary northern Vietnam (the Sipsong Chao Tai area), China (especially the former Tai Lue kingdom of Sipsongpanna in Yunnan Province) and Burma (Shan State). In some of these areas the Tai domains were themselves under Chinese, Burmese or Vietnamese overlordship for longer or shorter periods.

One of the chief methodological guiding threads of the volume is precisely the contextualization of 'ethnic' differentiation within Tai political domains, and within this to think of Tai identities, ethnicities if you will, in the same spirit as non-Tai. Despite much originality of focus and approach, the contributors are aware of many intellectual debts to indigenous, western, and other scholars, among whom I might especially mention Coedès' work of synthesis (Coedès, 1949), Leach on 'Kachin'-Shan relations (Leach, 1954), Condominas on the 'evolution' of Tai political systems (Condominas, 1976, 1990), Archaimbault on Lao political and ritual structures and practices (Archaimbault, 1971, 1973, n.d.), and the work of Keyes (1979), Lehman (1963, 1967, 1979), Wijeyewardene (1990), and others who have combined a broad focus, a critical analytical method, historiography, and ethnography. The present study's attempt to address an even wider context risks some loss of focus when compared with say *Political systems of Highland Burma* (Leach, 1954), *Ethnic adaptation and identity: the Karen on the Thai frontier with Burma* (Keyes, 1979), or *Essai sur l'évolution des systèmes politiques thaïs* [sc. *tai* Ed.] (Condominas, 1976). We can only hope that there is some gain in the scope of this pioneering effort that will outweigh the disadvantages, and provoke further work (important recent work includes Lemoine (1997), Proschan (1998), Spangemächer (1997) and Grabowsky (1994)).

The volume deals with experiences of various Tai and non-Tai people(s) within these Tai political domains and the ways in which they were constituted in, by, and for these domains – both by their own agency and also by that of dominant others – and ways in which they represented themselves and were represented by others. These people include: (i) some who have come to have convenient, apparently 'ethnic' names with contemporary recognizability (Akha, Karen, Khamu, Hmong etc.); (ii) Tai peoples who have variously been predominant or minoritarian at different times and places (Lao, Khon Müang, Tai Lue, Tai Dam etc.); and (iii) others whose identity, as such, is no longer, or, who knows, perhaps not-yet-again, likely to secure them political recognition or even a place in the tourist brochure (Kha, Lawa, Sam Sam, Sing Moon etc.).

These are mostly people of peripheries and borderlands, and so by geographical definition often *nowadays* people of the hills and forests. But despite the quite recently introduced official generic term *chao khao* (mountain people, though in English 'translation' the awkward sounding neologism 'hilltribe' – sometimes Hill Tribe, hill-tribe etc. – is almost universal) for 'tribal minorities' in Thailand it would be a mistake, at the end of the twentieth century, to think of all marginal ethnicities as either

9

'tribal' or as geographically remote, as much as to think of the populations of mountains and borders as predominantly non-Tai or non-Thai. The same economic pressures that enlist provincial Thai labour into the metropolis also entice and entrap the kingdom's 'hilltribe' subjects. And even as Bangkok is wired and beamed into global networks, physical expansion threatens long-settled urban and peri-urban communities of people identifying as Cham, Mon, Vietnamese, Lao, Malay, and so on, whose community mobilizations and protests gain occasional new political and media prominence and publicity.

More importantly, geographically peripheral identities are no longer necessarily socially marginal. They, may form new nuclei in newly (re)configured transnational regions, for example in the 'Golden Triangle', the 'Mekong Quadrangle' or economic Mekong corridor between Chengrung and Vientiane, or in the renewal of Buddhist solidarities across the frontiers of Thailand, Laos, Burma, and the Dai autonomous region in China. I have already mentioned the mediation of social and academic conferences and exchanges which have begun to (re-)unite peoples across the frontiers of several countries. Moreover, marginalized personal and collective identities, variously fractured, hyphenated, discriminated and so on, whether primarily of 'ethnicity', or of gender, class, or other status, may as likely be experienced in the metropolis itself as at any other point within or outside the country of residence.

II

The perspectives offered here, in so far as they are not primarily external-academic, or 'etic' (Corlin, Kossikov), are from Tai state or societal viewpoints: Thai (Thongchai, Renard, Keyes), Lao (Mayoury), Lanna (Tanabe, Bowie), Nan (Ratanaporn), Tai Dam (Evans)) and/or from those of a Tai or non-Tai minority: Akha (Alting von Geusau), Hmong (Tapp), Lue (Ratanaporn), Sing Moon (Evans), Thai-Islam or Sam Sam (Kobkua, Nishii). Two chapters attempt a strict methodology of critically juxtaposing 'internal' and 'external' accounts: Alting von Geusau for the Akha and Nishii for the Sam Sam.

The principal historical breaks or periodizations are between an early – and admittedly somewhat mythical-hypothetical – period before say AD 1296, the date of the founding of the Tai state of Chiang Mai; then a long period in which Müang Thai (Siam) was an 'empire' of varying dimensions (*prathet ratchathirat* in Prince Damrong's terms), with dominion over a great many other Tai and non-Tai peoples and states; and finally the period of modern nation-state building which we might date from Prince Damrong's own administrative reforms of the 1890s, though it had its roots in King Mongkut's reign (1851–1868).

Tai and Kha: social and ethnic statuses

One current Thai-English dictionary gives the following entries for Tai and Thai:

> 'Tai – a lord, boss; Thai – 1. free [a free man, freedom-loving] . . .; 2. Thai, pertaining to the Thai *or* Thailand; . . . the Thai race (chat Thai) originally came from Yunnan in China' (Sethaputra, 1972).

An older Thai-English dictionary, which has no entry for Tai, gives:

> 'Thai: tai, the Siamese nation. The Tai race probably originated in south-western China . . .; adj. independent; free' (McFarland, 1944).

One of the most sustained and compelling studies of the etymology or rather the discursive history of the terms Tai, Thai, Kha etc. is still that by Jit Phumisak (1976). He finds evidence in some Tai family languages that Tai (T'ai depending on whether the local language aspirates the /t/ or not) has had the sense of 'person', as indeed in so many instances of self-ascribed ethnonyms, but his strongest hypothesis is that Tai emerged in a specific sense of 'social(ized)' person/people (*khon thang sangkhom*) as opposed to a mere human, or 'natural' person/people (*khon thang thammachat*) hypothetically also reacting to the undifferentiated Chinese term *man* (savage, fierce, uncivilized) for all non-Han peoples of the South and South West China (and so including Tai in the same category as Kha).

I mentioned earlier that the historical assertion of a Tai identity has been in the context of a particular kind of social and political development, namely that of the *müang*. One might even speak of this development as *müang*-ization, by analogy with civil-ization (from Latin *civis*) or even politic-ization (from Greek *polis*). 'People of society' then is identical with 'people of (the) *müang*' (*khon müang*). This last term, which I should now write Khon Müang, is one which has been adopted by one particular Tai grouping, the people of the Lanna kingdoms based on Chiang Mai, Lamphun, and Lampang, perhaps as a distinction, Jit argues, not only from *kha* but also from both Burmese (called *Man* by Khon Müang) *and* T(h)ai oppressors. So they rejected 'Tai' despite their ancestral links with the Tai Lue of Sipsongpanna, and also rejected the ethnonym 'Lao' frequently given to them by the Thai of Ayutthaya and Bangkok. Lao on the other hand have long distinguished themselves as Lao against Tai of various sorts (Tai Khoen of Cheng Tung, Tai Lue of Sipsongpanna [Cheng Hung], the Tai Dam, Tai Daeng, and Tai Khao of Sipsong Chao Tai etc.) and of course the Thai.

Jit shows how the orthography 'Thai' is a consequence of the translation of Tai into Pali [ไท > เทยย > ไทย] after the early fourteenth century, and back again into the written language of the Ayutthaya kingdom, thus contributing to the emergence, among various other identities including other 'Tai', of a distinct new identity namely 'Thai'. In common with many national ideologies, and especially since the Compulsory Education Act of 1923, 'Thai' has become an unquestioned and increasingly homogenous and homogenising term, an essential identity, even a 'national' trans–historical agency. It has become the name for citizens, or at least 'nationals', of a nation-state in contra-distinction from citizens – regardless of 'ethnicity' – of other nation-states such as Chinese, Indonesian, Malaysian, Vietnamese, etc.

In pre-modern times however 'Tai' – and more specific groups within this general category, such as Lao – has been an identity paired more significantly with subordinate peoples with whom Tai were in what Keyes and Lehman (in Keyes, 1979: 30, 231) call a 'symbiotic' relationship. The most widespread paired category throughout the Tai region has been *kha*, which is present in some form in all the Tai languages, especially as a prefix for a more specific name. It could also be regarded as a generic term, although Keyes argues there are other inclusive categories with a similar function, notably Yang in the Southern Shan States and Lanna, and Lua' in Lanna (Keyes, 1979: 30). However both these terms can themselves in turn also be prefixed with Kha-. While both these terms have become fixed as ethnonyms in current usage, it is clear that Lua' and Yang were used to include other than Mon-Khmer-speaking or Karennic/Tibeto-Burman populations respectively. Kha however seems to be capable of much greater inclusiveness, so that for instance it can be used, grammatically so to speak, though the usage is probably not common, to prefix even Meo (Hmong, cf. Miao; see Thongchai this volume) a people with less of a history of contact, let alone symbiosis with Tai. Tapp reminds us that the term 'Miao' itself was formerly used 'extremely loosely to refer to a variety of southwestern minority groups [in China] even after 1200 AD'.

The Kha peoples had their own distinct ways of life and to some extent locally autonomous existence as communities, but by definition – not only a Tai definition but to a large extent their own too – they were part of a Tai social order. They were involved in ritual relations, trading relations, and as subordinate peoples were liable to provide labour and services to the Tai, or at least the *cao* (a generic Tai term for lord; other historical lordly titles (of variable usage in terms of seniority etc.) include: Lao, Khun, Thao, (Cao)Phaya etc.).

The Tai too had their own internal categories and statuses of freedom and unfreedom of various sorts. The chief of these, in the sense of the most widespread in occurrence and probably the most numerous social class, is that of *phrai* (commonly *phai* or *pai*, since the /r/, aspiration, and double consonants are easily lost in Tai languages in contrast to Khmer). *Phrai* has the sense of commoner or servant but usually of 'freeman' status. It often doubles up with *tai*, in a doublet or double doublet, which are Tai language forms commonly used for added subtlety of sound and meaning (*phrai tai*) and is sometimes identical with it, or can substitute for it. For example in phrases for population in general in the Mengraisat (customary Lanna law) '*phrai fa kha müang*', or in the inscription of King Ramkhamhaeng (reigned ca. 1275 – ca. 1317) '*phrai fa kha tai*'. The phrase in the Mengraisat occurs in a passage characterizing, in conventional fashion, the characteristics of the good and the bad ruler. The bad ruler among other things does not hold to the five or eight basic Buddhist moral principles (*sin ha, sin paet*) and as a consequence *yorm mak hy* [C. Thai *hai*] *phrai chiphai, bo rak phrai fa kha müang*. (He) will tend to cause misery for the common people, and (he) will not love his freemen (*phrai*) or his *kha müang*.

So, like the chicken and the egg, the doll that can be turned inside out, or indeed the cosmogonic gourd and its contents, *tai* and *kha* go together, irreducibly. And what is particularly important for this study, is that they are terms denoting both ethnic and social status. Jit Phumisak summarizes the two meanings of Tai as: (i) *chü chon chat trakun phasa tai/thai:* ethnonym for an ancestrally related Tai speaking people, and (ii) *chü wanna ru thanando'n thang sangkhom:* a cultural or social status ((Jit, 1976: 590) my translation).

The terms 'ethnic', 'ethnos', and 'ethnicity' are notoriously unstable and unreliable, and anthropologists would often like to avoid their use altogether, while recognizing their extreme importance in 'non-scientific' discourse, in the same way as 'race' which has been almost entirely disavowed by academic social anthropologists. I use 'ethnic' loosely here to refer to groupings of people usually speaking the same or a similar language *who recognize among themselves* some more or less long standing ancestral commonality, usually expressed in some kind of 'genetic' metaphors, often doubled up (e.g. Thai *chüa, chat, wong, trakun, phao, phan*) together with words with a basic meaning of people or group (e.g. Thai *chao, chon, khon, klum, mu, phak, phuak*). This can only ever be a provisional, initial orientation however. Although genetic-linguistic criteria are probably the most constant and compelling, I agree with Lehman's point '. . . that ethnic labels have no a priori systematic connection at all with the usual dimensions of ethnic differentiation.' And that a given ethnonym '. . . may simply mean any set of local populations that relate to the primary user of the label in a certain ecological and political way' (Lehman, 1979: 231–32).

The identity, complementarity, or dual nature of terms of the same order as *tai* and *kha* are found in many historical situations, for example the naming of darker skinned, aboriginal Veddoid peoples of India by 'Aryan', 'civilized' peoples (Thai: *ariyachon*) from the North as *dasa* (Sanskrit; Thai: *that*, slave or servant), and the comparable naming of certain eastern, trans-Danubian European peoples by the Romans as Slav.

Many scholars have noted the more recent parallel with the term Frank or Franc. The locus classicus is Coèdes who remarks that under or after King Ramkhamhaeng '. . . the ethnic term Thai took on the meaning of "free man" in Siamese, thus differentiating the Thai from the natives encompassed in Thai society as serfs'. To which he adds the footnote: 'This is the same semantic evolution that the word "Frank" underwent at the beginning of the feudal era. Since only free men composed the "populus Francorum", the legal status and the national name became synonymous' (Coèdes, 1949: 330). Coèdes' footnote in turns refers us to, but does not quote, the historian Marc Bloch in his *La Société Féodale*. 'That the *populus francorum* was composed only of free men, independently of any ethnic distinction, is proved by the fact that the national name and legal status came in the end to be synonymous. *Libre* or *franc* – the two words became interchangeable' (Bloch, 1965, Vol. 1: 255). Note that Bloch's original proposition is both less evolutionary than Coèdes, and explicitly denies any idea of an original or preferential ethnicity.

It is an entertaining irony that following the identification of Western European, or Mediterranean Christian peoples generically as 'Francs' by Arabic or Muslim peoples (cf. *lingua franca*) and the transfer of this term, within various languages (see entry under Firinghee in Yule and Burnell, 1994: 352–354), across the Indian ocean into Thai as *farang* for any European (or later American, Australian, 'white' non-Asian etc.), one of the strongest contemporary social distinctions namely Thai/Farang should be of two terms with a similar history, and a certain identity. In contemporary political rhetoric the opposition Thai (free) / slave or servile, is also sometimes still made.

The *tai/kha* distinction is clearly both ancient but also of changing import and valency. Tanabe (this volume) writes of the production and reproduction of the category Lawa (Kha Lawa, Lua') in and for the Lanna Tai polity, and the continuous nature of the category *kha* despite all manner of transformations and assimilations of particular people over space and time. We find Pai (*phrai*) as an ethnonym for some non-Tai peoples. Somewhat Tai-ized or Buddhicized 'Wa' people of Chengtung state have been called Tai Loi (hill Tai). This is almost a contradiction in terms, at best an exception that tests the rule, but it operates according to the logic of civilization or closeness to *müang*. Another instance of greater undifferentiatedness, fusion, or confusion is the occurrence of what appears to be the Tai word *phuak* (a group of people, one might say an ethnos!) as an ethnonym in Laos for some groups of Tai, *and* non-Tai, *and* Tai-ized non-Tai (Tai Phwak, Phwak, Tai Pak, Puok). The current (semi-)official term Thai Chao Khao (perhaps by analogy with Thai-Isan, Thai-Islam etc.) has, to say the least, an ironic overtone since it simultaneously 'civilizes' and naturalizes, both negates and retains the hill-forest-wild connotations of the non-Tai peoples of northern Thailand. But then the official dual identities required for administrative purposes precisely combine the principles of origin (*chüa chat*: a naturalizing notion, *chüa* = strain as in breeding) and citizenship (*san chat*: a more contractual notion).

The Akha (Alting von Geusau this volume) are of exceptional interest in this discussion because their most 'significant other(s)' appear to have been

Tai of various *müang* for many centuries, more consistently so than any other single grouping it seems. They can potentially reveal much about the encapsulating Tai systems, as well as their own, and the interrelation between them. They also seem to have one of the most 'continuist' versions of history of any of the non-Tai peoples of the region. The recent (re-)discovery by some Akha of their cultural affinity and, in a rather strict sense, common lineage with Hani peoples of China from whom they have been separated by geography and politics for as many as six centuries, and new awareness of the consistency of their shared cultural inheritance, is remarkable and perhaps exceptional. They are a limiting case in the region of a people with an oral culture who so strongly and compellingly claim such a long and distinct memory of past experience or history *as* a people. However, as (re-)presented and interpreted by Alting von Geusau, Akha *zang* ('tradition', cultural 'heritage', authoritative knowledge etc.) contains is own dialectics and apologetics which enable it to deal with the complexities and contradictions of experience (Alting von Geusau, 1983). Despite the emphasis on continuity, this is presented as the outcome of continuous struggle and tendencies towards differentiation, dispersal, and 'interspersal' (Alting von Geusau this volume). As such it is only minimally totalizing. *Zang* is as much a set of principles for understanding and remembering as it is a set of contents of knowledge. Thus even this limiting case does not contradict Lehman's proposition '. . . that what counts in the cultural definition of an ethnic category is not the possession of a unique common cultural "heritage" but the use of a set of cultural elements (language included, possibly) in a claim to membership of the category' (Lehman, 1979: 233).

Despite this apparently strongly substantiated claim to the persistence of their 'cultural heritage', Akha internal accounts record the assimilation or adoption of 'Mon-Khmer' hill peoples, and Tai, and some Han Chinese people, events which are memorialized in the clan system. We are left to surmise from this account that some Akha may have been absorbed by Tai communities, just as Christianized Akha are regarded by those Akha who still perform 'ancestor service' – the core practice of Akha collective memory and memorializing – as no longer being fully part of Akha *zang* or tradition. But despite experience of oppression and exploitation at the hands of Tai, Akha did not attempt to leave the Tai zones of domination altogether, preferring a middle position, a middle distance between Tai and some other 'mountain' peoples, from whom they distance themselves in turn and in a hierarchizing idiom. Alting von Geusau's account is of the greatest importance in giving us a detailed Akha perspective. Akha (known as Kha Ko in some areas) is no mere externally generated structural category, but – albeit partly defined within the generalized category and relation *kha* – an identity of self-generated strength and considerable scope within the Akha/Hani's own diaspora and unity.

The proposition that Kha was no mere accidental or peripheral category for the Tai, is represented nicely in a memorable (Lanna) Tai saying which three contributors quote (and I have retained their different translations in the chapters that follow) *kep phak sai sa kep kha sai müang* (see also Kraisri, 1965). The most literal translation might be 'gather vegetables (and/to) put into basket(s), gather *kha* (and/to) put into *müang*'. At this stage we have a sufficient sense of how we might gloss *kha* and *müang* so that 'non-Tai people into Tai domains' has a more appropriate resonance than say 'slaves into cities'. The fact that *kha* may be pronounced *sa* in some Tai (e.g. Tai Khao) languages would conceivably make the saying even more euphonious to some Tai ears. A standard means of 'putting people into *müang*' over the centuries has been to conduct warfare or raids and carry off whole civilian populations from one *müang* to another. This would have primarily affected Tai populations. Ratanaporn (this volume) gives a detailed account of the (re-)settlement of Tai Lue people from a number of *müang* into Müang Nan in the nineteenth century. This might have given some hill-dwelling people periods and spaces of respite and refuge (see Alting von Geusau, this volume, for the concept of 'regions of refuge'), but it is clear that *kha* as well were caught up in this practice of *kwat to'n* ('sweeping' raids). The saying however adopts the usually milder and at the same time naturalizing term *kep* – denoting the gathering of forest or garden produce – instead of the harsher, perhaps more realistic, military image of 'sweeping people up' into *müang*. Ratanaporn records for us the telling phrase *kha lak pai tai lak ma* (Kha leave furtively, Tai arrive furtively, or unnoticed) used in the chronicles to indicate spontaneous population movement within and between *müang* which is uncontrolled by and confusing to the authorities.

The exhortatory saying *kep phak sai sa kep kha sai müang* suggests a *müang* level policy or recommended practice; and it might also refer to practices refracted at lower social levels. There are a number of studies of labour management in pre-modern Tai economies, fewer on the place of unfree labour or forms of 'slavery' within this (see Turton, 1980), and relatively little attention at all to the specific role of the non-Tai peoples, especially as seen from their perspective. Bowie (this volume) by means partly of documentary analysis but more especially of ethnographic fieldwork, argues a strong case for deliberate 'ethnic [labour] management policies' in the Lanna Tai state in the nineteenth century, at least in the economically and military-strategically high priority area of elephant management. The senior *cao* made use of specialized labour of various 'ethnicity', Tai and Kha [here: Khamu] over whom they had sovereignty; and Bowie refers to this as an example of relative 'ethnic blindness'. The lower status Tai *cao noi* and *phrai* in the villages engaged in monetized exchange with available non-Tai labour (especially Khamu and Karen). The study again prompts the question of whether it is appropriate or whether it is anachronistic to call this 'ethnic' management or indifference to 'ethnic' criteria.

Jit Phumisak (1976) demonstrates, uncontroversially, that the distinction currently made in the Thai language between *kha* (low tone) as an ethnonym and *kha* (falling tone) as 'slave', servant' etc. is due to the Thai taking on the ethnonym from the southern Lao where it had undergone a sound shift. By that time Thai already had alternative words for categories of 'slave' from Sanskrit (*that*) and Khmer (*chaloei*) and *kha* took on a variety of senses of 'servant' even in the least servile usages (Turton, 1980: 289). By contrast, in the Tai Lue language *kha* combines all these several meanings of slave, war captive, servant etc., together with its use as ethnonym. In some ways, for a European at least, the fortunes of *kha* resemble those of the Latin *hospes* (foreigner, stranger, guest, friend, and also the reciprocal term host) and *hostis* (stranger, foreigner, armed foreign enemy) – a hostage being somewhere in-between – and their Greek equivalents, namely someone who is not a member of one's own family group, ethnos etc., but with whom one is engaged in a relationship which may involve either positive obligations (hospitality) or negative duties (hostility) or both.

This ambiguity or tension is expressed in other ways. Is the other person or group fully social and human, or animal, demon, or spirit? Do they have powers or rights which supersede our own? Is relationship inevitable and with what advantages? Is 'our' conquest and domination of them fully secure; or, from the other point of view, despite 'our' subordination, is some relative autonomy adequately ensured? The initial historical situations of contact of Tai and non-Tai peoples clearly varied. Archaimbault (1973) has shown in fine detail the differences in relationships in different parts of Laos, depending on for example demographic balance and extent of conquest, leading to varying amount and type of intermarriage and subsequent ritual relations and practices. The initial contrast may not have been so much between *pa* and *müang*, but between autocthony and recentness of arrival, rights of occupancy and use versus rights of domination.

The concept autocthony adds to the notion of indigenousness and even to aboriginality a stronger dimension of connectedness to the land, the ground, the earth itself and associated mystical powers. This connectedness is recognized in rituals of respect by Tai for indigenous 'spirits' or powers of the land and places of the non-Tai. Tanabe (this volume) suggests that the spread of 'Buddhist missionary discourse' in the fifteenth century (in Lanna Tai) may have consolidated the idea of '. . . non-Buddhist aborigines as living in a state of nature close to animality, but as being capable of being civilized through Buddhist moral precepts and practices'. The ancestors of the (Kha) Lawa are represented in Tai myth and ritual practices as *ñak* (N. Thai; Pali *yakkha*) fearsome, cannibalistic demons (Tanabe). Renard, who glosses *yakkha* as 'beast', speculates that in the early Sinhalese Buddhist text Mahavamsa, pre-Aryan aborigines were regarded as animals in human form who were ineligible in Buddhist law to be ordained as monks (along with criminals, slaves, and others).

17

The notion of animality as a contrast with human needs to be considered carefully. Condominas discusses the status of 'slave' (*kuong ñok*) for members of the White Tai (Tay), commenting 'However, their membership in the Tay ethnic group keeps them fully within the domain of humanity; whereas, the Sa', non-Tay slaves, remain midway between animality and humanity'. And he adds a footnote 'Father Antoine Bourlet, among others, reports the popular saying which was common among the Tay of the Hôi Xuân region of Vietnam: "A Kha is as different from a monkey as a Tay is from a Kha"' (Condominas, 1990: 69). Logically of course this does not imply that Kha are intermediate; and it does imply that the closer a Kha is to a monkey the closer also are the Tay. Ethnologically it can be taken to imply that while Kha are not monkeys (and are even perhaps far from that status), they are indeed intermediate, or somewhere in-between, in a hierarchy of Tai, Kha, and monkeys. Nonetheless, it is necessary to recall that humans and non-humans in Tai mythology engage in marriage, and that non-humans are given many exalted human and social attributes, including statehood and kingship (monkeys and nagas, notably). *Yakkhini* (female *yakkha*) were held to have intermarried and given rise to 'a semi-human hybrid race' (Rhum, 1987: 101). One might even note the Buddhist respect for larger animals in a hierarchy of size and assumed sentience; when the Lawa ancestors Pu Sae Ña Sae ask to be allowed just one human sacrifice a year after their 'conversion' to Buddhism, they are granted a buffalo sacrifice (Tanabe). Tai offerings to 'spirits' are much more likely to be of pigs or chickens, and in some cases to exclude the meat of larger animals such as buffalo or cows altogether.

More extreme forms of classification are sometimes applied to members of hunter-gatherer groups who were perhaps historically 'beyond' the category *kha*. Thongchai reviews Thai representations of the Senoi people as Ngo' Pa (wild rambutan) and also as 'half-monkey half-human'. Despite or because of this status, King Chulalongkorn ordered a member of this group to live at court in Bangkok. Thongchai's Siamese ethnographers are likely to have been somewhat influenced by late nineteenth century European notions of human evolution. Another, and possibly less 'contaminated' Tai representation is use of the classifier *phi* ('spirit') for the Mrabri people, also hunter-gatherers: as in *phi pa* ('forest spirits'), *phi to'ng lüang* ('spirits of the yellow leaves', another vegetable metaphor, referring to their transient shelters in the forest). As often it is hard to determine whether a usage indicates a long-standing classification or a looser, more half-hearted or self-conscious metaphor, such as the Akha self-attribution of monkey-like behaviour as a tactic in their dealings with Tai. We might note too that monkey-like behaviour can connote clever duplicity as well as stupidity in common Thai usage.

III

Discourses of transformation of inter-ethnic relations

The foregoing discussion of social distinctions has focused particularly on classifications. Inevitably, at the same time it has begun to examine the social and economic 'content', or rather the practices and representations that constitute the relations. I now turn to another major theme of this volume, discourses of transformation of 'inter-ethnic' relations, ways in which social distinctions and relations *become* ethnicized, racialized, and nationalized. Contributors offer a rich variety of contexts of transformation, and of processes in which the two – or it may be more – entities merge and mix, or resist and re-emphasise distinction, whether by state policy, popular movement, or gradual process, and whether more or less voluntarily on the part of the subordinate.

Unsurprisingly no single paradigm holds across the region. Evans argues that Leach's 'oscillation' model, of the processes by which Kachin élite adopt Tai (Shan) political idioms, works better for a region where the power differential between 'Kachin' (a generalizing term rather like Yang and Lua', called by Shan variously *Kha*-pok, *Kha*-nung, *Kha*-ng etc.; Leach, 1954: 222) was not as uniformly great as in the 'northern Indo-China' area, where Condominas' argument for the 'irreversibility' of 'Tai-ization' is more appropriate. However, if no general models of systemic structural transformation are proposed in this volume, there are nonetheless some generalizable approaches. First, there is a broad consensus that there is something distinctive about social identification and classification within this Tai region. This is indeed the rationale for this volume and why I have given so much attention to the *tai-kha* and *müang-pa* relations.

Secondly, there is agreement to beware of what Evans calls 'the assumption of pre-modernity' in many studies. This is related to the tendency of many anthropologists to use an 'ethnographic present' tense when giving an account of a 'culture' or a 'society'. In contrast, there is a concern here to deal with contemporary realities, contemporary political dilemmas and debates. Linked with this, if to a more varying extent among the authors, is the need to avoid anachronistic use of the notion of ethnic perceptions, and to consider historical processes of *ethnicization*.

Thirdly, again reflecting the theoretical pre-occupations of the moment, there is an emphasis on 'agency', and away from systems. This has had the effect not only of encouraging an extra effort to represent in a balanced way the positions of non-Tai minorities within an academic as well as state-political T(h)ai hegemony, but has lead to detailed accounts in which local voices and non-Tai histories are put centre-stage. This can lead both to more 'continuist' and collectivist accounts of ethnic distinctiveness and survival (Akha), and to highly localised and fragmentary accounts (Sing

Moon). One interesting consequence has been to give greater weight to the more voluntary nature of certain kinds of social emulation, linkage, integration, and even assimilation. This has great relevance to continuing projects of 'nation-building' which are still underway while at the very same time they are located within a globalizing, 'post-national' world context in which all parties are to some extent involved. Thus there are themes of multiple identity, multi-lingualism, of localism co-existing with national identification (Evans, Kobkua, Nishii, Renard, Tapp), of consumers active in redefining and recontextualizing external, hegemonizing influences.

A key question when dealing with integration or assimilation is whether we are talking of the aspirations and projects of an élite, or a people as a whole, or of some more specific social movement. The Akha, with their egalitarian ethos and dialectical strategy of a middle position, clearly memorialize a collective interest in trading with, adopting cultural elements from, and generally treating with the Tai. We must note however that this is a world view or societal view more or less unknown to Tai, except perhaps very locally. Groupings characterized by a greater degree of social inequality, and helped by stronger shamanic leadership roles and more organized clan systems, such as the Hmong and Mien (Yao) seem to have a historical tendency to more autonomous and extensive social formations, and to be able to provide the leadership and organization for larger scale uprisings and rebellions (Evans, Tapp). Many non-Tai groups have historically been prepared to accept the role of tributary chieftainship or 'indirect rule' positions under alien states (Burmese, Chinese, Tai, Vietnamese; Alting von Geusau, Renard, Evans). Almost all the larger groupings memorialize some past period or episode when they did have some state-like existence, notably the Lawa (Tanabe) and Hmong (Tapp), and some Tai groups after experiencing dislocation and exile from their homeland (Ratanaporn). The Akha remember such a period as a kind of 'cautionary tale' of over-reaching themselves (Alting von Geusau). The Karen of Thailand under King Chulalongkorn had the status almost of a tributary state, and then in the early years of administrative modernization, began to have a formal standing within the provincial government, even enjoying some favourable tax discrimination (Renard). But while some wealthier and more powerful non-Tai élites have attempted to pursue maximum emulation with retained autonomy (the classic Kachin *gumsa* mode), others have sometimes adopted the strategy of avoiding the social costs of emulation (a *gumlao* strategy). Evans provides instances of both. The leader of a Sam Sam district in Southern Thailand at the turn of the century, To Nai Sim, provides an instance of, indeed a generalizable type of charismatic, personally feared and powerful 'bandit' style chief, whose criminality and semi-outlaw status was itself almost a badge of ethnicity (Kobkua), and whose political competence seems to have been exploited by the Thai state (Nishii; cf. Onghokham, 1984).

Inevitably numbers of ordinary people re-classify themselves voluntarily so to speak, not as a societal shift or as a result of coercion: the Kachin who 'become Tai' (*sam tai*) through marriage and adoption of Buddhism and lowland agricultural practices (Leach, 1954: 221); the Sing Moon, and other minorities in contemporary Laos who repudiate their less 'civilized' kinsmen; the Khamu and Karen who settled in Thai villages where they worked with elephants. During my own fieldwork in Mae Sruay district, Chiang Rai, in the late 1960s, I would occasionally hear casual mention of generationally fairly recent Khamu, Karen, or Chinese and Farang members of apparently thoroughly Khon Müang households. One village had, within living memory, had a Karen village as a close neighbour just in the foothills on a tributary of the Mae Lao river. This had become, though intermarriage and other social movement, a fully Khon Müang village with a school if not yet a *wat* (or any monastic building) and yet another smaller Khon Müang settlement had been founded further upstream, which in turn had been recognized by the administration. Yet further uphill there was a Karen (Yang) village. This was a micro-process of both absorption and repulsion that must have many counterparts. Leach reports that perhaps half of the valley 'Shan' in northern Burma had derived from 'Kachin'. This takes us back again to the idea that the identities Khon Müang and Tai themselves are more social than ethnic, or genetic, in any primordialist sense.

Perhaps formerly it may have been easier for some Karen, Khamu, Lua' etc. to remain quite distinct while living on or near the valley floor. Here I need to introduce another deceptively simple little term *ban*. I hesitate to gloss this immediately as 'village', given the spirited debate about the status of such units in colonial or modernizing administrative discourse, in Thai known as *mu ban* or administrative groupings of *ban* under a state-appointed 'headman' (see Breman, 1980, 1987; Kemp, 1988). *Ban* are the constituent settlements of *müang*, other than the main place or capital (the French *chef lieu* captures this nicely, see Condominas, 1990) of the *müang*. This 'capital' or *chef lieu* may be prefixed with the term Müang, Chiang, Wiang, and other variants, some of which also connote 'walled town'. *Ban* has long had a meaning of 'home' and is paired with *müang* to connote 'homeland': *ban müang, ban koet müang no'n (kert* = be born; *norn* = sleep), or closely related homelands: *ban phi müang nong* (sibling, or just closely related homelands; Ratanaporn, referring to Lanna and Sipsongpanna; cf. English: home, hamlet, homeland; German: Heim, -heim, Heimat). While it increasingly denotes an individual residential 'house' in the Thai language, it probably has a longer historical sense of settlement, even if only a very small one, or multi-house compound, neighbourhood, or even 'long-house' (for the latter among Tai Lue, see Moerman, 1968). In a sense *ban* occupies a domestic space between *müang* and *pa*, but it can be ambiguously positioned closer to or further from either. In a more adjectival sense *ban* denotes domestication and *cultivation* (an important term I have not yet used) and is also opposed to *pa*: wild (see Turton, 1978). Thus the names of many animals and plants have one suffix or the other to distinguish whether they are wild or cultivated: mangoes, rambutans, bananas; cattle, pigs, chickens, cats etc. In these terms various Kha could also be further differentiated, for example Kariang Pa or Kariang Ban (or Piang = plain), Khamu Pa or Khamu Ban (Bowie) and so on. This can be seen as evidence of both a synchronic classification and a slow diachronic process.

An unduly strict structuralist interpretation needs to avoided here, however. It is important to emphasise that there is a gradation of classification within Tai speech usage and specific historical discourses. In other words, and once again, at the local level there is much overlap and similarity between Tai and non-Tai cultural forms. Thongchai shows how late nineteenth century Siamese ethnographers distinguished not just between *chao pa* and *chao ban*, but introduced a category of *chao ban no'k* (*no'k* = outside, external) to sub-divide the Tai category. These were Tai primitives and peasants, perceived especially as distant, regional, and what we might anachronistically term 'minority' Tai, who were often grouped together by Siamese Thai as Lao (Khon Müang, Lao, Lao Isan, or Thai Lao etc.). This 'pseudo-ethnic' classification, as Thongchai calls it, was apparently influenced by evolutionary ideas in which Kha had become *khon doem* (original, aboriginal people) and (Tai) 'peasants' (in a popular, modern, and largely disparaging sense) had become a new semi-ethnicized class category. The temporal evolutionary difference becomes further extended, cartographically laid out, in geographic, national space. *Khon doem* is not quite the same as the old Tai notion of autocthony as respected in rituals of mutuality and subordination. This new distinction between 'civilized' and 'uncivilized' Tai, in practice often between 'Lao' (of the North and Northeast) and 'Thai', received greater emphasis under the modernizing nationalism of King Vajirawudh (r. 1910–1925) and its subsequent transformations. The English language 'civilized' became a Thai term (romanized as *siwilai*), which was to be largely replaced by the notion of 'development' (*kan patthana*) in the 1960s. Keyes discusses the importance of the trope of the Lao (and the country Laos) perceived as needing the civilizing influence of the Thai/ Siamese in what he calls Siamese 'colonial' discourse.

In Thongchai's account, aristocratic and royal 'ethnographic' writers of the 1880s saw these *chao ban no'k* as 'docile' others in contrast with the unmanageable 'wild' *khon pa*. But for King Vajiravudh it was precisely the (Tai) people of the North who needed to be 'tamed' (*chüang*, see Renard). As if in some political game of Snakes and Ladders, it was as if the Karen, and perhaps others, having reached higher levels of political status on the hierarchical stairway within Müang T(h)ai, were to slide down not the socialized Naga of autocthony but a reptilian representative of lower evolutionary orders. This shift is a strong instance of 'discontinuity' unsettling the discourse of unilinear progress.

The Thai word *chüang*, to tame and train, especially of animals, is used in the title of Shakespeare's 'The Taming of the Shrew' which King Vajiravudh translated. This prompts an important reminder of the related theme of gender differentiation which is largely beyond the scope of this volume (but see Mayoury, this volume). A nearly synonymous term to *chüang*, is *prap*, which has the meaning subjugate, suppress (a rebellion), and also to clear forest. In practice there have been episodes of rebellion, as well as lesser acts of political violence, of both non-Tai (Renard, Kossikov) and Tai-speaking people against their Tai rulers from the late nineteenth to late twentieth century, and some of them involved coalitions with non-Tai groups (Turton and Tanabe, 1984). Millenarian ideas and imagery are common to both traditions of memory, hope, and resistance (Corlin, Tapp, Keyes, Mayoury; and see Turton, 1991).

Possibly the distinctions recorded by Thongchai have a longer history but within different pre-modern political discourses. My own fieldwork provided evidence that Tai have long made distinctions within the Tai category. The term *khon nok wiang* was current during my early fieldwork (1968–70), for Tai who are *chao ban*, *chao hai* (upland forest field or swidden farmers; C. Thai *rai*), *chao na* (irrigated rice-field farmers), indeed Khon Müang, but not *chao wiang*, or *khon nai wiang* 'city people'. Also current were expressions by some villagers that they lived in a *ban pa* – a striking oxymoron (cf. *tai loi* [N. Thai *tai do'i*] – a settlement both far from and distinct from not only the *müang*, here denoting 'towns', but other villages closer to towns. Even *ban pa* – as a rather general category of remote, unmodernized village – were distinguished more specifically from 'forest', and usually further upland *Thai* settlements such as *ban hai*, settlements in upland swiddens, and *ban pa miang*, upland tea growing villages. Many Thai village proper names indicate a close relation with the forest or some particular kind of forest (Ban Dong, Ban Pa Daed, Ban Hai, Ban Lao [here = abandoned swidden], Ban Pa Miang, Ban San Pu Leui, Ban Dorn Salii etc.).

IV

Ethnicizing practices and policies

Several contributors discuss state policy concerning 'ethnic minorities', 'nationalities' or whatever the locally, and currently correct political term may be. As I have mentioned earlier, it is inappropriate and misleading to ethnicize, even racialize historical discourses out of context. Similarly use of the word 'policy' (Bowie) may suggest a too deliberate, systematic, corporate, and hierarchical notion of the planning, promulgation, and implementation of a course of action. Laos (currently the Lao Peoples' Democratic Republic, LPDR) provides one of the most dramatic and troubled examples. Let us recall some of the social complexity (Kossikov, Mayoury, Evans). There are officially at least 47 'ethnic groups' or 'nationalities' (*son phao*) in Laos – or up to 820 depending on how economically and pragmatically various academic conventions and people's self-identifications are treated. Virtually none of these groups of people are exclusive to the territory of the country. By some reckonings the 'ethnic' 'Lao' may not be a majority. And ethnic relations have been radically affected by political events which make Laos, from the early nineteenth century until the late twentieth century, one of the most disputed and fought over places. Kossikov writes '. . . the national [this also has the sense of 'nationalities'] policy of the LPDR leadership was an attempt to accomplish rapid cultural and ethnic assimilation of the whole non-Lao population of the country, that is, to realize an objective that none of the previous rulers of Laos could realize'.

As can be seen this totalizing project never had a long life either as policy or practice. But the point I wish to underline, and which has already become a major theme is that this is to assume that pre-modern 'rulers' did indeed want to, need to, or try to realize such a social project. The evidence seems to point to something different. That while Tai *cao* did want to attract, and did if need be forcibly settle *phrai* and *kha* into their *müang*, their social status was more important than any 'ethnic', or other cultural status in senses which modern 'ethnicizing' discourses have largely themselves created. Renard argues strikingly, and with deliberate paradox and irony – that it has been such processes, such 'non-Tai ideology' adopted by 'a non-Tai Thai nation', that have given rise to perceived 'hilltribe' problems in Thailand, and have made the Karen, for instance, 'aliens in their own land'.

It is important to recall that these Tai/non-Tai relations began before the large scale influence of Theravada Buddhism on Tai societies. The idiom of political relations, of the relations of the *cao müang* with the constituent social units of the *müang*, was predominantly 'ritual', and within these especially practices which expressed a mutual sense of relative power, control, occupation, and ownership of land in all the senses of territory, earth, and agriculturally exploitable land. These ideas and practices – of ancestral or aristocratic 'spirits', and of posts or columns set up in the ground – and their attendant myths and imagery linked the various parties to larger ancestral memories, and cosmic influences. Tanabe gives a detailed and carefully argued account of such rituals in the Lanna kingdom, and their transformations, and refers to the exceptional ethnography of Archaimbault on the cognate Lao/Kha rituals.

Tapp (this volume and Tapp, 1989) has established the significance of ritual practices that can be generically termed 'geomantic' and which constitute a kind of common ritual (and therefore social and political) idiom in the region. Alting von Geusau also highlights some commonalities between Akha and Tai, based on a long co-presence in a Chinese influenced world, rather than in a dichotomized valley/hill, or Hinduized/Sinicized world (see Leach, 1960; Lehman, 1967). Some of these might also be called locality cults, territorial cults, practised both according to a calendrical system and also ad hoc. In Tai systems the cults are often practised within a hierarchical encapsulation, which allows for a degree of variation and autonomy for local, and ethnically distinct practices, as in the Müang Nan case studied by Ratanaporn (see also Condominas, 1975; Turton, 1972, 1978). Alting von Geusau instances an Akha ritual offering to the 'owners of the land, the mountain, and the water' which is 'performed in a Thai way', with Thai gestures. Comparable practices which recognize a local owner of the land in a Tai idiom (commonly *cao thi* or similar, meaning 'lord or owner of the place') and often using invocations wholly in a Tai language, are recorded from many parts of the region. The occurrence seems to be associated with non-Tai peoples who are becoming more settled (e.g. Iijima, 1965, 1970, for the Karen of Thailand), and who are also perhaps wealthier and claiming higher social status (e.g. Izikowitz, 1951, for the Lamet of Laos).

I would hypothesise that these cults of non-Tai peoples recognizing Tai categories of ownership and control, are probably more widespread than those of Tai acknowledging non-Tai local powers. Variations and discontinuities may occur due to early differences in relative size and power of the two sides (cf. Archaimbault, mentioned above), gradual historical drift in favour of 'Tai', and perhaps the reserving of recognition of autocthony for less frequent but higher level rituals of royal installation etc. (Tanabe). However, in the late 1960s in Khon Müang villages in Mae Sruay district, Chiang Rai, I several times noticed the presence of non-Tai visitors (in this locality usually Lahu) on auspicious occasions, especially when entering a new house. All strangers, I was told, perhaps politely since I, a Farang, was present, are auspicious but especially *khon do'i* (hill people). The local exception to this seems to have been the Mrabri people (locally referred to as *phi to'ng lüang*) who I was told were not invited 'up' into Khon Müang houses on any occasion when they came into a village. Only later did I come across a reference by the Thai writer Bunchuay Srisawat to the Governor of Müang Wiangpapao (a district neighbouring Mae Sruay) inviting Lawa to enter his new house first as an auspicious practice (cited in Jit, 1976: 465; the date of the event is not certain; cf. Tanabe regarding Lawa 'first-footing' the city of Chiang Mai).

Assimilation and the exchange of powers: reversibilities and discontinuities

It is clear that there is a process of mutual attraction and to some extent respect between Tai and Kha. The 'centre' or *müang*, desires the resources, the potency and potentiality, the 'alien power(s)' (Tapp) of the periphery, the wild, the forest. Both centre and periphery seek to restore 'vitality', in an exchange of powers. Messianic forms of ritual action, often seen as only a form of 'resistance' to power, Tapp argues, are a strong form of the process of absorption, ingestion, and incorporation – all metaphors of the most intimate, indeed metabolic, transformation – of such powers. But we also have many examples of orthodox, legitimate powers at the 'centre' seeking strength from fringe practitioners, 'forest saints' (Tambiah, 1984), magical virtuosi (Mendelson, 1961; Turton, 1991) and so on. The pre-Buddhist hermits (rysi) in the Haripunjaya Kingdom (Renard) possibly exemplify both tendencies at once, seeking out an external ruler from another (and perhaps regardless of whether 'ethnically' different) high centre, and being used in the subsequent élite record to legitimise the new dynasty.

Tapp writes: 'This absorption of alien power is accomplished through the dissolution of the normal boundaries of the self and cultural identity; identity is submerged in a chaos of differences. The boundaries are then constituted in a new way, not merely reconstituted in a replicatory way, and this I would see as the creative dynamism inherent in popular rituals such as those of shamanism and messianism.' (this volume)

An element of 'dissolution of the normal boundaries of the self and cultural identity' is perhaps a normal condition of 'inter-ethnic' exchange, and not without its risks and uncertainties of outcome. But what seems clear from many instances examined in this volume is that there is a multiplicity of outcomes, with no guarantee of the amount or quality of change, or gain and loss of 'self and cultural identity'. Processes of 'assimilation' and the like – often referred to in the harsh and inappropriate imagery of metallurgy: melting pot, amalgam etc. – almost always remain incomplete, or are subverted, characterised by discontinuity, reversibility, contradiction between local or more intimate practice and experience, and behaviour at more public and national levels.

Tapp's account and argument combine the exceptional with more everyday practices, hegemony with resistance, apparently irreversible with non-linear processes, in a way which suggests a broad theoretical approach of great value to this field of study, within both Tai and Chinese zones of influence. It recognises that '. . . Chinese influences on the Hmong mark a long process of violent subordination to which consent has largely been won' (p. 99); and that these rituals can all be 'subsumed under the category of such general hegemonic processes as Indianization or Sinicization which have considerable similarities to those of Sanskritization' (p. 97), to which we could add Tai-ization. But at the same time he argues that 'Incorporation of the ideology of the dominant group . . . does not represent a triumph of hegemonic discourse but rather a successful challenge mounted on the centre by the periphery.'

'Ritual' – and perhaps stylised public 'performance' more generally – remains a highly significant medium of inter-ethnic relations. This is dramatically demonstrated by Keyes in his account of the way in which a Thai royal visitor to Laos, gave 'ritual recognition' to that country's independent and neighbourly status as a Tai state, by an itinerary of religious and political pilgrimage. Nonetheless, an arguably even more powerful medium than ritual is *writing*. The theme of writing is common to inter-ethnic discourse throughout this China border region (Tapp, Nishii, Kossikov). Writing arguably exists on the margin between magic and material resource. Along with the asset of the *müang*, it is probably true to say that the possession of one of several Tai languages *and* one of several scripts for writing it, is a more common denominator of Tai than Buddhism. Indeed becoming Christian or Malay may be one way to remain a Thai citizen, and at the same time to avoid some of the hegemonic implications of such religious incorporation (Kobkua, Corlin). It is probably also the case that 'Buddhism' has become, or reverted again to being, less monolithic, and currently co-exists with new, non-religious philosophies and world views. And while Tai may use the lack of knowledge of (Buddhist) morality and teaching (Kham Müang = *bo hu sin, bo hu tham*) as the (negative) mark of the non-Tai, the internal histories and traditions of non-Tai peoples are virtually unanimous in their self-deprecation or self-commiseration for their lack of, or loss of a written script. Hence the political importance of establishing scripts for 'minority' languages, problems of the hegemonic 'roman' scripts, missionary interventions, difficulties of keeping revolutionary promises and so on (Kossikov).

Of course it is the use of the script that matters most. One of the oldest means of literal 'incorporation' of the alien script has undoubtedly been through the tattooing of often unintelligible magical words on usually male bodies. But in the late twentieth century it is not mere literacy but education, largely secular and which, though still often 'ideological', has a tendency to become more practical and critical than doctrinal and hierophantic in content and potentiality (Mayoury, Alting von Geusau), that is the new medium of orthodoxy/subversion, of the dialectical homogenizing-differentiating process. It was therefore highly significant, as Keyes elucidates, that the royal Thai visitor to Laos – along with the televised ritual gestures and selective diplomatic amnesia of past events – should have written her 'authoritative counter-narrative' to the prevailing Siamese contemptuous view of Lao in a book which has a 'Lao' title and makes a point of treating the Lao language with particular respect.

Keyes emphasises that this event, though a 'watershed' in Thai-Lao relations, does not mark the supercession of the old Siamese 'colonial' narratives. It foregrounds the old historical theme of the encapsulation (what Condominas calls *emboîtement*) of Tai *müang*, and the predominance of hierarchy over federation. It also shows the continuing or re-invented importance of Tai ('ethnic' Lao here of course) cultural elements in the making of a post-monarchical 'Laotian' national culture (Kossikov) in what Kossikov, Mayoury, and Evans all call a 'poly-ethnic state'. The evidence that the Lao state has swung this way and that between policies variously favouring minorities, favouring Buddhism or not, tolerating local non-Buddhist customs and identities or not, shows again the non-inevitability of any uniform Tai-ization or Lao-ization. This is a theme and an argument made by many contributors to this volume. On the other hand in spite of the contrasts in treatment of nationalism and nationality as between the six or seven countries of the region in terms of constitution, policies, social attitudes, and political practice, several contributors argue that it has been the establishment of the modernizing, expanding (that is to say within its own territory) state that has been most influential in dismantling those 'intermediate' social spaces and borderlands (Condominas, 1976) which formerly allowed for what Nishii calls the play in relations between *müang* and periphery, Tai and Kha.

By and large we are still in the era of expansion and consolidation of the national state administrative system, the national market and infrastructure. In Thailand there is near completion of modernizing expansion ('penetration' in contrast with pre-modern 'radiation' as the processes have been called; cf. Walker, 1997) as a task of 'nation-building'. This is truest in terms of those modern requirements of electrification, road construction and so on, though the bottle-neck of secondary education remains a surprising piece of unfinished business on the agenda of the national project. But even elsewhere, in Burma, Yunnan, and Laos, where crude indices of infrastructure, primary health care, basic literacy, not to mention GDP etc. still characterize largely pre-modern situations (Mayoury) some effects are already being felt or at least messages getting through, of post-national, globalizing tendencies in other parts of the world. These harbingers include a re-positioning, a re-spatializing of 'minority' and 'indigenous' peoples – through diaspora, regionalism, marginality within urban centres, temporary movement of labour, more pluralistic visions of citizenship and so on. They also include a greater, more appreciative hearing for their voices and narratives, which they have struggled to make heard, and greater respect for their identities, however newly (re-)created these may be. The (re-)discovery and (re-)presentation by these peoples – and, to be sure, their other biographers and advocates – of their 'internal' historical memories, of their continuities and concentrations, discontinuities and dispersals, their re-groupings and coalitions, their willing abandonment in part or whole of old identities and willing re-fashioning or acceptance of transformed identities, these are the themes of this collection of historiography and ethnography.

28

References

Archaimbault, Charles. 1971. *The new year ceremony at Basak (South Laos)*. Ithaca: Cornell University, (Data Paper 78, Southeast Asia Program).

—— 1973. 'Le cycle de Nang Oua – Nang Malong et son substrat sociologique'. in his *Structures religieuses Lao (rites et mythes)*. Vientiane: Vithagna, pp. 131–54.

—— 1973. *Structures religieuses Lao (Rites et mythes)*. Vientiane: Vithagna.

—— n.d. *La fête du T'at (Trois essais sur les rites Laotiens)*. Vientiane: Mission Française d'enseignement et de coopération culturelle au Laos (Série documents sur le Laos 1)

Breman, Jan C. 1980. *The village on Java and the early colonial state*. CASP 1, Rotterdam: Comparative Asian Studies Programme, Erasmus University.

—— 1987. *The shattered image: construction and deconstruction of the village in colonial Asia*. Comparative Asian Studies 2, Amsterdam: Centre for Asian Studies Amsterdam.

Bloch, Marc. 1965. [1939–40]. *Feudal society*. London: Routledge and Kegan Paul, 2 volumes.

Coedès, Georges. 1949. *Les états hindouisés de l'Indochine et d'Indonésie*. Paris.

Condominas, Georges. 1975. 'Phiban cults in rural Laos.' *In* G.W. Skinner and A.T. Kirsch (eds.) *Change and persistence in Thai society: essays in honour of Lauriston Sharp*. Ithaca: Cornell University Press, 252–73.

—— 1976. 'Introduction.' In his *L'espace social à propos de l'Asie du Sud-Est*. Paris: Flammarion.

——. 1976. 'Essai sur l'évolution des systèmes politiques thaïs.' In his *L'espace social à propos de l'Asie du Sud-Est*. Paris: Flammarion, 259–316.

—— 1990. 'Essay on the evolution of Thai political systems.' *In his From Lawa to Mon, from Saa' to Thai: historical and anthropological aspects of Southeast Asian social spaces*. Canberra: Research School of Pacific Studies (Occasional Paper of the Department of Anthropology), 28–91.

Dikötter, Frank. 1992. *The discourse of race in modern China*. London: Hurst.

Grabowsky, Volker. 1994. 'Forced re-settlement campaigns in Northern Thailand during the early Bangkok period', *Oriens Extremus*, 37(1), pp. 45–107.

Iijima, Shigeru. 1965. 'Cultural change among the Hill Karens in northern Thailand.' *Asian Survey*. 5 417–23.

—— 1970. 'Socio-cultural change among the shifting cultivators through the introduction of wet rice culture: a case study of the Karens in northern Thailand.' *Memoirs of the College of Agriculture*, Kyoto University (Agricultural Economics Series 3) 97 1–41.

Izikowitz, Karl Gustav. 1951. *Lamet: hill peasants in French Indochina*. Göteborg: Etnografiska Museet, (Etnografiska Studier 17).

Jit Phumisak. 1976. *khwampenma khong kham sayam thai lao lae khom lae laksana thangkansangkhom khong chüchat* [Etymology of the terms Siam, Thai, Lao and Khom, and the social characteristics of ethnonyms], Bangkok: Social Sciences Association of Thailand.

Kemp, Jeremy. 1988. *Seductive mirage: the search for the village community in Southeast Asia*. Comparative Asian Studies 3, Amsterdam: Centre for Asian Studies Amsterdam.

Keyes, Charles F. (ed.) 1979. *Ethnic adaptation and identity: the Karen on the Thai frontier with Burma*. Philadelphia: ISHI.

Kraisri Nimmanahaeminda. 1965. 'Put vegetables into baskets, and people into towns'. in Lucien M. Hanks, Jane R. Hanks and Lauriston Sharp (eds.), *Ethnographic notes on Northern Thailand*, Ithaca, N.Y.: Cornell University, Souheast Asia Pogram, Data Paper No. 58, pp. 6–9.

Leach, Edmund R. 1954. *Political systems of Highland Burma*. London: Athlone.

—— 1960. 'The frontiers of "Burma".' *Comparative Studies in Society and History.* 3 (1) 49–68.

Lehman, F.K. 1963. *The structure of Chin society.* (Illinois Studies in Anthropology 3) Urbana: University of Illinois.

—— 'Ethnic categories and the theory of social structures.' In P. Kunstadter (ed.). *Southeast Asian tribes, minorities and nations.*

—— 1979. 'Who are the Karen, and if so, why?' In C.F. Keyes (ed.). *Ethnic adaptation and identity: the Karen on the Thai frontier with Burma.* Philadelphia, ISHI.

Lemoine, Jacques. 1997. 'Féodalité Taï chez les Lü des Sipsong Panna et les Taï Blancs, Noirs et Rouges du Nord-Ouest du Viêt-Nam', *Péninsule*, 35(2), pp. 171–217.

Mathieu, Rémi. 1983. *Etude sur mythologie at l'ethnographie de la Chine ancienne: traduction annotée du Shanhai jiang.* Paris: Collège de France, Institut des Hautes Etudes Chinoises (Mémoires de l'Institut des Hautes Etudes Chinoises XXII), 2 vols.

McFarland, George Bradley. 1944. *Thai-English dictionary.* Stanford: Stanford University Press.

Mendelson, E.M. 1961. 'A messianic Buddhist association in Upper Burma.' *Bulletin of the School of Oriental and African Studies.* 24, 500–580.

Moerman, Michael. 1968. *Agricultural change and peasant choice in a Thai village.* Berkeley: University of California Press.

Onghokham. 1984. 'The *jago* in colonial Java: ambivalent champion of the people.' In A. Turton and S. Tanabe (eds.). *History and peasant consciousness in South East Asia.* Osaka: National Museum of Ethnology (Senri Ethnological Studies 13), 327–343.

Proschan, Frank. 1998. 'Cheuang in Kmhmu foklore, history and memory', in Sumitr Pitiphat (ed.), *Tamnan keowkap thao hung thao chuang: miti thang prawattisat lae wattanatham*, Bangkok: Thai Khadi Research Institute, pp. 174–209.

Rhum, Michael R. 1994. *The ancestral lords: gender, descent, and spirits in a northern Thai village.* Northern Illinois University, Center for Southeast Asian Studies, (Special Report 29).

—— 1987. 'The cosmology of power in Lanna.' *Journal of the Siam Society.* 75, 91–107.

Rousseau, J. 1990. *Central Borneo: ethnic identity and social life in a stratified society.* Oxford: Clarendon Press.

Sethaputra, S. 1972. *New model Thai-English dictionary.* Bangkok: Thai Wattana Panich, 2 volumes.

Spangemächer, Anne. 1997. 'Les systêmes politiques des Plang dans le contexte de la société féodale Taï aux Sipsong Panna (Chine du Sud-Ouest)', *Péninsule*, (35)2, pp. 117–131.

Tambiah, Stanley. J. 1984. *The Buddhist saints of the forest and the cult of amulets.* Cambridge: Cambridge University Press.

Tapp, Nicholas. 1989. *Sovereignty and rebellion: the White Hmong of northern Thailand.* Singapore: Oxford University Press.

Terwiel, B.J. 1992. 'Laupani and Ahom identity: an ethnohistorical exercise', in Gehan Wijeyewardene and E.C.Chapman (eds.) *Patterns and illusions: Thai history and thought – in memory of Richard B. Davis*, Singapore: Institute of Southeast Asian Studies and Department of Anthropology, Research School of Pacific Studies, The Australian National University, pp. 127–166.

Thongchai Winichakul. 1994. *Siam mapped: a history of the geo-body of a nation.* Honolulu: University of Hawaii Press.

Turton, Andrew. 1972. 'Matrilineal descent groups and spirit cults of the Thai-Yuan in northern Thailand'. *Journal of the Siam Society.* 60 (2) 217–256.

—— 1978. 'Architectural and political space in Thailand.' In G. Milner (ed.). *Natural symbols in South East Asia.* London: SOAS.

—— 1980. 'Thai institutions of slavery.' In J.L. Watson (ed.). *Asian and African systems of slavery.* Oxford: Blackwell, 251–292.

—— 1991. 'Invulnerability and local knowledge.' In Manas Chitakasem and A. Turton (eds.) *Thai constructions of knowledge.* London: SOAS, 155–182.

Turton, Andrew and Tanabe, Shigeharu. (eds.). 1984. *History and peasant consciousness in South East Asia.* Osaka: National Museum of Ethnology (Senri Ethnological Studies 13).

Walker, Andrew. 1998. *The legend of the golden boat: regulation, trade and traders in the borderlands of Laos, Thailand, Burma and China,* London: Curzon.

Wijeyewardene, Gehan. (ed.) 1990. *Ethnic groups across national boundaries in Southeast Asia.* Singapore: ISEAS.

Yule, Henry and A.C. Burnell. 1994 [1886]. *Hobson-Jobson: a glossary of colloquial Anglo-Indian words and phrases,* Sittingbourne: Linguasia.

Part II

INTERNAL HISTORIES AND COMPARISONS

Introduction

It is highly appropriate that this section should be started off by two historians. Thongchai offers a contribution towards 'a history of ethnographic knowledge in Siam'. He re-examines ethnographic and travel writings in élite literary journals of the 1880s and 1890s and other royal and aristocratic sources from the early twentieth century, and shows how Siamese rulers had a project of ethnographic and ethnic classification parallel to that of Western colonial enterprises. He identifies an 'ethno-spatial discourse', a 'pseudo-ethnic categorization by geography and/or ecology' of Siam's 'Others within', of which the principal were the *chao pa*, the forest, wild people, and the *chao bannok*, the multi-ethnic, 'docile' villagers under the supremacy of Bangkok.

Thongchai's account opens with a story that can serve as an emblem for this collection as a whole. It epitomises much of the relations between Tai states and semi-autonomous peoples on their peripheries, and between concepts of savagery and civilization. It is the story of a young Senoi boy from the forested Siamese territories in the Malay peninsula who was apparently captured, at the will or whim of King Chulalongkorn, domesticated and brought up to be a Page in the court of the King in Bangkok in the late nineteenth century. The boy was part-unfree, part-free; he was both a concrete historical personage and also the fictionalized subject of a verse play by the King. Captured (on photographic film too), taken home, (re-)identified, written up, represented, transformed, and commercialized (he sold photographs of himself), he is a biographical analogue of the ethnographic process itself.

Social classification and representation of minorities (or people as minorities) by the élite is followed through into contemporary Thai society where they have become part of everyday discourse, but where those people who are still not fully 'assimilated' into the national culture and the territorial nation-state are now contradictorily regarded as both exotic and commodifiable, and, at the same time, as the 'health-hazardous' and 'un-environmentalist' 'Other'.

Renard focuses on a single people, the Karen, but broadens the time-scale, starting with early Buddhist definitions of people who are fit to rule and live in cities, or *müang*. He argues that such distinctions were based on values of civility and merit, literacy and urbanity, and not on any 'ethnic' criterion. From the mid-nineteenth century, however, the process began of transforming Karen from subjects into citizens, a process which he shows 'involves many of the problems found in Thai state formation'. Specifically 'the very conceptual basis of Thai civilization changed, so too did the notion of what it meant to be Tai and Kha'.

A detailed analysis of historical records of the period approximately 1895–1910 shows a socially inclusive but not assimilationist policy and Karen retaining, or even gaining, a degree of social autonomy within the new state. But whereas Thongchai's material relates mainly to the fifth reign (1868–1910) Renard has an important additional focus on the sixth reign, of King Vajiravudh (1910–1925), and an altogether different and fiercer spirit of cultural nationalism. King Vajiravudh ignored or down-graded the old distinctions Tai and Kha, and the rituals that both linked and transcended them. Karen, like all other minorities, were now 'foreigners' to be 'tamed'. The forests they lived in were now valued more highly than the people themselves, in a reversal of the values held by King Chulalongkorn. Renard's chapter ends with the challenging paradox of a 'non-Tai Thai nation'.

Tapp's theoretically and empirically wide-ranging essay also addresses practices and representations involved in the ethnicizing and nationalizing of cultural identity. An appropriate epigraph to the volume as a whole might be his sentence 'The seamless web of Thai national identity is in fact a tangled skein of local identities interacting with one another in the context of the formation of the nation-state'. Tapp's main ethnographic referent is Hmong people – in Chinese 'Miao', a term historically as inclusive and protean as Lua', Yang (Karen), and Kha have been – whose most significant state 'other' has historically been Chinese, though they constitute an important minority in contemporary Thailand.

Tapp examines the role of peripheries in the construction of the cultural and political centres, in particular two-way practices of appropriations and incorporations – of the most physical and metabolic kind – of alien powers. He compares Tai absorption of aboriginal Lua' rituals and Hmong absorption of Chinese elements in shamanic practice. His argument that incorporation of elements of dominant culture may constitute 'a successful challenge mounted on the centre by the periphery' rather than 'a triumph of hegemonic discourse' challenges many theories of cultural domination or hegemony. In a similarly provocative manner

Tapp argues strongly against the reification of cultural essences in the construction of ethnic minority identity (see also his Postscript to this volume).

Resistance and anti-state militancy by peripheral minorities are themes that run through several chapters in this volume. Greater prominence is given here to the importance of ritual in the construction and transformation of social identities and their relations. However resistance and ritual combine dramatically in the form of 'millenarian' and 'messianic' ideas and social movements throughout the region, over centuries of recorded history, and involving both Tai and non-Tai peoples, both against each other and on the same side. While shamanic practices deal on the whole with the restitution of health and self-hood for the individual, the millenarian leader typically offers the hope of restoration of collective well-being, self-esteem, and sovereignty after experience or anticipation of social loss and suffering. Corlin provides a valuable survey of the literature on generically millenarian or messianic ideas and practices in the region, referring to numerous instances of such movements and among a variety of peoples. He also reviews some of the classic anthropological theories of such phenomena. Key tropes in the narratives of social distinctiveness are the myth of original unity (inside a gourd, for example) and subsequent disunity following cosmological crises (flood, incest). Corlin examines 'external-political' aspects and conditions of messianic movements as well as their 'internal-cultural' aspects, finding that there are 'cultural propensities' towards messianism among 'non-Tai' peoples especially, but that these are in turn crucially determined by Theravada Buddhist and, later, missionary Christian influences.

Alting von Geusau's intensive ethnographical and historical studies of the Akha have been long in the making, and it has to be signalled that his chapter is work of exceptional originality and virtuosity. One condition of the possibility of approaches taken by many authors in this volume has been the way scholars, indigenous and otherwise, including some of the present company, have looked at issues and populations across many frontiers in the regions, not as border people or in terms of international politics and problems, but as parts of large, historically ancient diasporas within a newly re-defined region.

In this perspective it is indeed a fresh insight that for many centuries the Akha have mainly interacted with Tai states of various sorts, whereas in Thailand they are regarded as relative newcomers. Tai are the principal 'other' for Akha. But only recently have Akha/Hani people themselves become aware of the widest extent of their own unity, despite dispersal and separation in some cases for as long as six hundred years. Alting von Geusau carefully reconstructs both an 'internal' Akha historical account, or mnemesis, of themselves – based crucially on a 64 generation genealogy and other oral texts and forms of traditional knowledge of great complexity

– and an 'external' account which provides corroboration or interleaving commentary on key elements.

At first sight it may seem that this approach to history and cultural identity – shared it seems by both the ethnographer and the Akha – is radically different from Tapp's insistence on the need to avoid 'paradigms of cultural essentialism' and the need to emphasise, on the contrary, 'historical disjunctures and discontinuities'. But the core of Akha culture and identity turns out not to be any essence but paradox and dialectic: 'the history of their political and ecological marginalization and their overcoming this in continuous adaptation constitutes the very heart of [Akha] culture'.

(i)

(ii)

(iii)

Plate 6. Ngo' Pa (i) Mr. Khanang dressed as a Ngo' (ii) Mr. Khanang in full dress for attendance on His Majesty (iii) The Ngo' Pa called 'Khanang': photograph executed by the hand of His Majesty King Chulalongkorn

The Others Within: Travel and Ethno-Spatial Differentiation of Siamese Subjects 1885–1910

Thongchai Winichakul

Introduction

The Thai word *ngo'* in present day usage denotes three things. First, it is an exclusively Thai word for one of the aboriginal (Orang Asli) Senoi peoples of the Malay peninsula. In common Thai perception of their physiognomy they are seen as having relatively dark complexion and thick curly hair; and in terms of habitat they are seen as living in the forest or forest fringes in Patalung and Trang provinces of southern Thailand.

Secondly, it is the Thai word for a hairy, dark-red, thick-skinned fruit originating from the Malay peninsula, and known in Malay – and thence English – as rambutan. The first usage is probably derived from the second by means of a common naturalizing analogy.

Thirdly, Ngo' is a famous character in a classic of Thai literature *Sangthong* (The Golden Conch) composed by Rama II (r.1809–1824) and based on a Thai/Lao folk story. The story is about a prince who never reveals his true identity or true body, first by hiding in a conch shell, becoming known as Phra Sang (Prince Conch), and later by disguising himself as an ugly man known as Ngo'. The King and other princes judge him by his appearance. They expel him from the palace and submit him to various ordeals until he finally proves that his virtue is superior to theirs. Furthermore, in 1906 King Chulalongkorn, Rama V (r.1867–1910) composed a famous poetic story entitled *Ngo' pa* (1969). *Pa* means forest or jungle, with connotations of wilderness, wild, untamed, or uncivilized, and culturally non-Tai (Stott 1991: 146). The title redoubles the connotation of wildness.

The Wild *Ngo'*

Ngo' pa is a tragedy of two Senoi lovers who decide to follow their hearts despite the girl's arranged marriage to another man. The intended groom feels his dignity is damaged beyond repair, takes revenge, and in the end all die in fighting and suicides. It is a rather poor plot, but the story is not significant here. Nor is the prominence of Senoi in itself indispensable to the plot, they could be replaced by any people. Moreover, the origin of the story is not clear: as to whether the King created it, as suggested in his preface, or whether he heard the story when he travelled to southern Siam. The first stanza of the poem reads: 'First of all, *suppose* that we took a trip to the jungle' (*thieo pa*); then the author meets some local officials who tell him the story (1969: preface, 20). Nor is it clear whether King Chulalongkorn really took that trip; or if so, whether he related the story exactly as it had been told.[1] Probably these aspects of the story's creation are not significant either. What does seem clear is that the poetry is merely a stage to put the *ngo'* on display; the *ngo'* show itself is the sole purpose. It demonstrates the King's interest and ability in a new field of knowledge.

The most noteworthy feature of this literary creation is the description of the *ngo'*. In the preface, the King gives a description of the people, their general characteristics, hair, eyes, mouth, colour, language, houses, clothes, food, medicine, weapons, some customs such as marriage, and beliefs. In the verses, he describes again their clothes, decorations, huts, weapons, and daily life. The reader cannot fail to recognize the King's skill in incorporating *ngo'* vocabulary into the Thai verse, with a glossary of about 60 words given in the preface. The whole piece is an ethnographic note about the *ngo'* in literary disguise. The *ngo'* was observed and exhibited in writing by the royal author.

The only verifiable fact about the background of the poem is the circumstance of the act of writing itself. The King was sick and becoming bored because there was nothing to do. He was not strong enough 'to contemplate anything, or to do any good writing'. So, he took a piece of paper, and 'jotted down (*khia*) a nonsensical story', making up an amusing story for his own entertainment (ibid., preface). When he recovered he returned to work. He intended to revise it later, if he had the time. Originally he had no intention to turn it into a piece for the theatre. He was not sure if it was a good enough story, precisely because it was about forest people. In brief, the '*ngo'* show' seems to have been conceived casually and perhaps not fully intentionally. Despite that, the King later thought that it was good enough to publish and produce as a play.

The King acquired a real *ngo'* boy as his servant. His name was Khanang, which happens also to be the name of a character in the verse play. It is well known that most people in the palace treated him well, and gave him special treatment, not because he was the King's favourite, but because he was an orphan from the far-away jungle. The boy had more freedom to wander in the palace, even to behave improperly, because he was regarded as a wild person (*khon pa*), 'half-monkey, half-human', a category beyond the court's conventions (Sadap 1984: 27).[2] Little known is the fact that he had been captured (on the capture and enslavement of non-Tai peoples see Turton, 1980). During one of his tours to the South, the King had wanted to see a *ngo'* and to have one in his palace. Local officials responded. Out of kindness, they chose an orphan since it would hurt no parents and would be easier for the boy to adjust to a new life. The boy was lured and, as if in some fiction by Rudyard Kipling, was put in a prison at first, before the King released him and gave him clothes. The King later expressed the wish that a girl had been taken as well. But, in kindness, he did not want to hurt a girl (Chulalongkorn 1939: 5, 7; 1969: 121–32; Sadap 1984: 22). The *ngo'* boy was wild, uncivilized; yet once captured, and domesticated, he became a spectacle, an object of leisured curiosity.

On one occasion the King put Khanang in *ngo'* dress. This did not mean Khanang's authentic dress, but the dress of the *ngo'* character in the classical play *Sangthong*. A photo of Khanang in this dress was then taken and reproduced. Khanang himself sold the photo at a temple fair, where the *Ngo' pa* play was first performed. Some three hundred photos produced were sold out, much sought after by the Thai audience. Foreigners (*farang*) preferred another photo of Khanang in the normal dress of a Thai boy (Chulalongkorn 1939: 6, 8; Sadap 1984: 30–31). This incident epitomizes the transgressive identification of the *ngo'*. On the one hand, *Ngo'* are a people, an ethnicity or ethnic group, who had been transformed through writing into a romantic fiction by the head of the Siamese nation. On the other hand, *Ngo',* the character of another fiction, was personified (no need for a mask!) by a Senoi or Ngo' boy. Two ethnographic fictions went on display in the same event: the fictionalized ethnography inside the theatre; the ethnicized fictional character outside the theatre in the temple grounds. This transgression generated a poetics of ethnographic identity. The poetics of the *ngo'* was subsequently reproduced. For example a recent edition of *Ngo' pa* has on its cover not a Senoi but the *ngo'* character of *Sangthong*. The seal of the Fine Arts Department, granting official licence, is shown on the same cover (Chulalongkorn 1969).

This story of different Thai representations of *ngo'* points to issues this chapter wants to engage with. Ethnography is an inquiry and a knowledge which seeks to identify, thus differentiate people according to certain 'markers' of identity. The history of ethnographic studies suggests that this has been determined by various kinds of knowledge and sciences, such as biology, linguistics, cultural anthropology, and others. Evidently, most markers attempt to define the 'intrinsic quality', or the essential identity of those peoples or cultures. The results have been known in terms of race, ethnicities, cultures, or peoples, each with particular political and intellectual implications. Ethnographers have enough problems among themselves regarding what an ethnic identity is, since most now agree that all markers of identity are complex or relative. Moreover, ethnography is first and foremost a writing. It exists in writing in order to capture and domesticate [sc. take (down) and bring home Ed.] the observed people into certain forms of narratives which embody facts, discourses, representations, and of course the power relations between the observed and the writers. In other words, ethnographic categories are allegories, formulated by many kinds of knowledge including the effects of narratives (Clifford 1986). This chapter is a preliminary study calling attention to ethnographic differentiation of another sort, namely pseudo-ethnic categorization by geography and/or ecology. It has explicitly nothing to do with the inner quality of any of those peoples. It is, quite explicitly and honestly, a classification by more powerful outsiders, and by superficial observations, without any pretension otherwise.

Ethnographic construction, generally speaking, was part of the colonial project to formulate and control the Others of the West. Alongside the colonial enterprise, the Siamese rulers had a parallel project of their own, concerning their own subjects, a project which reaffirmed their superiority, hence justifying their rule, over the rest of the country within the emerging territorial state. It was a project on the 'Others Within'.[3] In the late nineteenth and early twentieth century (roughly speaking 1885–1910), travels had mediated the construction of an ethnographic classification in the eyes of the Siamese élite. Discursively formulated through travelogues and ethnographic notes, it was an abstract scheme which differentiated Siamese subjects spatially within the geo-body (see Thongchai 1994) in relation to the superior space of Bangkok. The two principal categories of people, of 'Others Within', are the *chao pa*, the forest, wild people, and the *chao bannok*, the multi-ethnic villagers under the supremacy of Bangkok. Arguably, this ethno-spatial discourse has been more influential, on Siam's policies and treatment of ethnic minorities, than scholarly attribution of ethnic identification. It has certainly been more prevalent among Thai people, from those times to the present, than any scholarly discourse. The concept and taxonomy echoed both the indigenous perception of non-Buddhist, primitive peoples, and colonial discourses of tribes and peasants. Probably, the concept was a mixture, a hybrid knowledge, a reworking of traditional concepts by modern sciences as happens in other fields of knowledge at about the same time (Thongchai 1994: 37–61) The result was new indigenous knowledge in a Thai context (Turton 1991: 11–13). More importantly, this ethno–spatial ordering and relationship gave the Siamese élite a sense of its superior place within Siam and in relation to the world beyond. In other words, since its inception Siam has always been a hierarchical domain, differentiated not only by class and status, but by ethno-geography as well. And given the implicit temporal implication of any anthropology,[4] this chapter argues that this Siamese ethnography of Siam was also a temporalizing practice, locating and juxtaposing peoples, including the élite themselves, in a new linear (progressive, temporal) cosmic order called civilization.

Travel

The enjoyment of travel which we yearn for today might not be what people in Siam before the late nineteenth century experienced. Travel was not a desirable activity, and pleasure was not its primary purpose. Not only was travelling rough, tough, and possibly dangerous, but there were also political and social constraints which made travel less enjoyable. The serfs (*phrai*), slaves (*that*), and their lords (*cao*) alike, though for different reasons, were supposed to get permission from their overlords before travelling. The lords and their subjects did indeed travel for war and other business, but travel was not for entertainment or leisure. Only traders enjoyed a certain freedom of movement, though it was primarily for their livelihood. Monks also had the liberty to travel, within certain rules and at certain times of the year, but this was supposed to be a method to encounter spiritual challenges. Religious pilgrimages, solitary travel, were primarily for acquiring inward wisdom and spiritual enlightenment. The wilderness was the ideal site for the search for wisdom not because of any perceived environmental beauty, but because it was the negation of normal life; it was adversarial nature, wild animals and so on, to be subdued by the power of merit (Tambiah 1984: 36, 87–92).

The fact that travel was not undertaken for pleasure, was reflected in travel literature. There are two genres: *chotmaihet raiwan* and *nirat*. The former is usually a diary or prose travelogue, the chronological record of activities and happenings during a journey. Since the expeditions were mostly for war and public works, records were informative and concerned only business. The latter genre is a poetic expression of love-separation melancholy with the chronology or excursion in the background. *Nirat* literally means separation, departing from something which is dearly desired. Travelling automatically implies leaving behind someone, somewhere. A traditional *nirat* assumes that the author has left his loved-one(s) behind. Sadness on love-separation is the core, the 'flesh' of the genre. Travel betokened sadness, not pleasure. The journey itself was mere background; indeed in old *nirat*, a journey can be imaginary, simply providing a framework for the poet to show his literary ability (Manas 1972: 138–45).

A transformation in the *nirat* genre took place when fictional excursions became actual journeys in historical times and places (ibid: 147). A famous Thai poet, Sunthonphu (1786–1855), added his personal experience, social criticism, and other content, to the male-voiced complaint of love-separation. His lovers were real (ibid: 152–56). In following generations *nirat* became accounts of actual events, activities, places, times, and people the travellers had encountered, without significant cries of love-longing (ibid: 165–68). In other words 'a word map of the route . . . a travelogue in verse' (Reynolds 1991: 20). It was a break, a shift, a new genre in the old

name. The old *nirat* was pre-occupied with separation or the departure and
'leaving from'. Modern *nirat* pays attention to the journey, the 'going to'.
The old *nirat* was overwhelmed by sadness; modern *nirat* can be mundane
travelogue, or an account of a tragic military expedition, an eye-opening
trip to the world's metropolis, or an entertaining tour. *Nirat* became 'a
source of historical geography' (Terwiel 1989: 25). The old core was
abandoned.

This shift did not occur in literature alone. It also took place in a wider
discourse and practice of travelling itself. Rapid socio-economic change in
Siam from the mid-nineteenth century provided new contexts for travel:
the market oriented agrarian sector, internal migrations, modern
commerce, and social activities in the new economy. Canals were opened
up for trade and transport. The demand for labour loosened social
constraints. By the late nineteenth century, Prince Damrong wrote that the
two aims of travel were pleasure and knowledge (Damrong 1961: 1–5).
Place-names, flora and fauna were no longer poetic signifiers triggering a
traveller's longing for the beloved, they became food for curiosity,
knowledge, and satisfaction. A traveller's desire was to get away from old
things, depressing, familiar things and to visit, to see, to have contact with
the unfamiliar, exotic world. King Chulalongkorn loved travelling, and was
advised to travel by his doctor in order to get away from the stress of work.
For that reason he travelled widely in Asia and Europe. Travel was for
leisure, relaxation, and temporary freedom.

The newly emerging conception and desire to create the geo-body of
Siam in the same period, resulted in a new provincial administration on a
territorial basis (Thongchai 1994: 120). The rulers realized their lack of
knowledge of Siam's interior. While surveyors and mapping technicians
proceeded to mark the limit of Siam's body, Siamese rulers travelled the
interior continuously throughout the reign. Travel, a physical movement in
space, was rendered into narratives, producing a knowledge of Siam's
spatial Self. Just as the Europeans' 'new planetary consciousness' led to the
exploration of the 'contents' of earth's surface (Pratt 1992: 25, 30), so too,
the 'new nationhood consciousness' in Siam resulted in travels to the
interior, mapping, and knowledge of peoples within the Siamese Self.

Travellers and Ethnographers

The reform of provincial administration was first and foremost the
integration of former tributaries by tightening Bangkok's control over
them, no longer relying on hierarchical networks of overlordship. The
system was later applied to Siam's entire geo-body, to all provinces in Siam-
proper. For the first time in history, Siamese rulers, including the King
himself, travelled extensively throughout the country to implement and

oversee the new territorial-based state. A considerable number of princes and administrators from Bangkok were assigned to the most senior posts throughout the country. Many of them wrote about their experiences, missions, and travels, about peoples and places, in the forms of monographs, commentaries, articles, reports, and travelogues. Many contributed regularly to the journals of literary societies in Bangkok which had become popular among the Siamese upper class and foreigners resident in the country. These writings, especially those published in the journal *Wachirayanwiset,* form the materials of this study.[5]

Unlike the participant-observer approach of a modern anthropologist, these travellers were admittedly interrogators/rulers. Like the early European travellers or colonial visitors, the distance between rulers and their subjects was probably due not so much to differences in ethnic cultures, as to power relations and class. They did not even attempt or pretend intimacy; the distance was obvious and in most cases maintained throughout the contacts and subsequent accounts. Ethnographic data were acquired through formal inquiries, by interrogations of local officials by Bangkok rulers, and of local people by local officials, or by questionnaires from Bangkok. While the superiority of Western travellers over native informants was assumed by the supposedly advanced race, the superiority of the Siamese travellers was established and confirmed by their actual power relations. The author-object relationship in the inquiries was hierarchical, and rarely pretended to be otherwise.

Royal journeys, the *sadet praphatton,* have been celebrated as the rulers' attempts to overcome or suspend social distance and hierarchy by travelling in disguise.[6] The original trips were King Chulalongkorn's initiative to see his country in 'normal' circumstance without any preparation as for royal visits (Chulalongkorn 1939: 78–79; Damrong 1976: 6). It was expected that secrecy and camouflage would produce authentic knowledge in contrast with the formal encounter. Unfortunately, these trips seem to have been pretentious, a self-entertaining imposture, with half-hearted disguise. Even in disguise, the King and entourage appeared to be a troupe of nobility or wealthy people from Bangkok, which was indeed the true identity of most of them. From time to time, their true identity was revealed and the ruler/subject relation was resumed (Damrong 1976: 4, 5, 11, 14, 16). The travellers experienced pleasure rather than regret. The more successful the disguise, the more excited they became when the truth was revealed. In the most popular instance, a villager boasted that he had seen the King, whose picture was inside his house, but that he had not recognized the King who sat next to him. The disguise seemed so fully successful that the King was eager to hint at his identity to his village host. The monarch/subject relationship was immediately resumed with great joyfulness, providing perhaps the maximum amusement the travellers could have expected (Damrong 1976: 28–30). Such half-hearted suspension of hierarchy may have been what they really wanted. They derived pleasure from travelling not because it enabled them to see the real life of their subjects, but because their disguise released them from their social status for a while for their amusement (Damrong 1976: 12–13). The suspension of identity gave them freedom. It was an élitist carnival, not a fact-finding mission, though the travelogues and stories were published shortly afterward in a journal. It was a self-entertaining show which failed to produce a similar success on the second trip undertaken two years later; notably because the story of the first trip had already been publicized and people eagerly awaited the King-in-disguise (Damrong 1976: 34). Not surprisingly, the practice has been praised as evidence of the King's self-denial and concern for the well being of his subjects (Prayut 1980).

The travellers/rulers maintained their distance and authority in the inquiry as well as in writing. It is interesting to compare the authors' positions and perspectives as described above with those adopted when they travelled to the world's metropolis, Europe. There the Siamese travellers, the Orientals, became students of civilization observing the West with astonished and absorbent minds (Chulalongkorn 1984). But that is beyond the scope of this chapter.

It goes without saying that all the interrogator/rulers whose accounts I have consulted were men; their perspectives and interests were those of the male rulers. This might have some effects on the 'Orientalizing' project and its outcomes: what they chose to itemize or categorize, and how they did it. The constructed ethno-body of Siam was, thereby, a male Siam.

The 'Wild' Others

'Until the 1960s, there was essentially no tradition of ethnography within Thai scholarship' announced Charles Keyes in 1978 (17). While this is correct if the statement means academic ethnography by professional ethnographers, the production of ethnic knowledge in the Thai language had begun long before.[7]

In 1886, a two page article by Khun Prachakhadikit (later Phraya Prachakitkorachak[8] appeared in the journal *Wachirayanwiset*, titled 'Waduai praphet khon pa ru kha fai nua' (On the varieties of the forest people – literally 'forest people or *kha*' – in the North). The article describes the peoples in the northernmost border areas of Siam's sphere of power who were unknown to general Thai readers. The author states clearly that the article 'intends to tell of the kinds of *khon doem* (native people, autochthonous people, original inhabitants) who still live in the jungles and mountains there, to entertain your ears' (164). The author does not include the Lue or the Shan because 'actually they are like the Lao or Thai people like us' (164).

The description proceeds from one people to another, seemingly without order, from the Lawa (Lua') and Yang (Karen) to the varieties of the Khamu and other Kha peoples, then the Hmong (Kha Meo in the article), the Musser (Lahu), and finally those whom the Lao called Phi Pa (spirits of the forest), that is, the Mrabri who were known in Thai as Phi Tong Luang (spirits of yellow leaves). In each case, just a few sentences of description are given on features such as: clothes, appearance (hair), house, plants, food, weapons, and other special characteristics.

On closer inspection, the narrative order is always there. The article begins with the Lawa and the Yang who are 'superior to the Kha', and similar to the Karen. Then there are varieties of the Khamu and Kha: Lamet, Lamang, Khahet, and so on. Among the Khamu, there are Khamu Ban (settled or village Khamu) and Khamu Pa (forest Khamu). The village Khamu live and work with the timber traders. The forest Khamu, on the contrary, have strange hair and live separately. Both are able to speak a language similar to Lao or Thai, but have no script. Some Kha customs are similar to Lao or Thai. But they, and the Meo, the Ko (Akha) and the Kui look similar to the Yunnanese Chinese (Ho) in dress, hairstyle, and language. The Musser have a place of worship for ancestors and spirits, but not for monks. They are filthy, dirty, and never clean their body. The Phi Pa smear their bodies with animal blood, and live without houses. Their ancestors are said to have been banished criminals and so they dare not to return to town. The list of *khon pa* from the Lawa to the Phi Pa ranged from the most to the least civilized ones. The author weighs up the features of each people and somehow measures their overall degree of civilization. But the list does not include Lue or Shan because they are as civilized as the Thai and Lao, and thus beyond the classificatory boundary of the 'Wild People' or *khon pa*.

Features considered worthy of mention are those which are unusual or strange to the readers. That is to say, strangeness (*plaek pralat*) is the trope of the 'Wild People'. The strangeness of the 'Wild People' is even more conspicuous in another article of 1889, 'Waduai chao pa chat tangtang' (On the forest races) by Chaophraya Surasakmontri,[9] who at that time was the commander of the Siamese army in the areas of northern and central Laos today. Like the previous article, it consists of notes from observation, rather than detailed description or extensive research. Nonetheless he describes twenty peoples, and twelve sub-divisions, in five issues of the journal.

'The peoples of this kind', says the introduction, 'live in the jungles on the mountains at the frontiers far away from town (*banmuang*). But they never settle down in any place nor have any homeland, preferring to wander in the jungles. Supposing that any country kindly wished to care for and protect these races, they might not be able to accept civilization anyway. They might avoid contact, or escape and return to their accustomed life in the jungles and mountains' (Surasakmontri 1972: 242). The possibly un-civilizable forest peoples then become objects of interrogation, gaze, and dissected description. It is stated from the outset that the work is going to describe these peoples within nine topics: 1) village and housing; 2) personal characteristics, physical appearance, complexion, spoken language and script; 3) food and clothing; 4) products and special skills; 5) headmen or leaders, and their personal items (probably marks of office or regalia); 6) money or media of exchange; 7) marriage customs, procreation, and childbirth; 8) medicines and death ritual; 9) religion, beliefs, seasonal events, and festivals (1972: 241). The supposedly major characteristics or features within each topic were noted. Those features which are regarded as strange in the eyes of the Siamese élite are given prominence, as signs of primitiveness and hence un-civilizability in the view of the gazing subjects.

The ideas of physical appearance were perhaps influenced by Western knowledge concerning physical or biological anthropology at that time, although no references to Western literature are given (Streckfuss 1993: 126–32, 145–46). In Surasakmontri's writing, colour of skin, curliness of hair, length and quantity of body hair, thickness of lips, are all carefully noted for each people. But their politeness 'compared to town people' (243), their anger, 'hot or cold' temperament (258, 268), and their ability to run 'as fast as a dog' (254) are also noted. Their vernacular languages are discussed in terms of which major languages they resemble, and whether there is a script. Clothing is among the most obvious differences deserving detailed description. On political relations, the issue is whether or not they are egalitarian, or are under simple rule with an uncomplicated headman-ship without title, or whether they have complex rules. However, most chiefs have no regalia. On media of exchange, most of them use any available metal currency which they could weigh and cut for the value they want. Customs and beliefs are the major subjects: courtship, proposal of marriage, requirements for marriage ceremonies, love-making, hygiene concerning the new born baby and the mother, what spirits people believe in and how they are worshipped, and death rituals. Strange customs are favourite subjects. For example, the Phuthai keep dying persons wakeful to delay death, and dress them up in the final hours to prepare them for their new abode (282–83). A Phama (Akha?) couple sleep in the same room, but in separated sections, designed to allow them to signal each other for love-making (246). Some races do not have a rule for parental consent or any other custom, provided lovers agree to live together. One Kha people will not do any work above ground level in the lord's house because they say their humble place is on earth (268), while the Meo people will not stay overnight in the lowlands believing they will fall ill (260). The author does not hesitate to pass judgement as to how dirty, stupid, or ridiculous he considers these people to be.

Similar ethnographic notes with itemized description, appeared on subsequent occasions, such as Chulalongkorn's notes on the 'Ngo" people in the preface of his book already mentioned (1969: 1–16), Sommot-amornphan on the Karen (1890), the description of the Phuthai and Yo (?) people's life and customs by Phothiwongsachan (1972). The 'Wild People' seem to be a 'marginal subject' in every sense of the word. *Pa* was the marginal space and *khon pa* the marginal peoples in it; and they were different to the Bangkok élite at the centre. They did not receive any further attention from the Bangkok rulers. As Surasakmontri reflected, they were seen as wild people who refused civilization and whom it seemed not worth trying 'to care for and protect'. *Chao pa* or *khon pa* is a category of Other who should be left alone as constituting a polar contrast to civilization.

The 'Docile' Others

Was there a particular narrative for describing the non-*chao pa* subjects? An answer is hinted at in another essay by Prachakitkorachak (1904). It is a description of the land, places, products, and history of people, mostly the Lao, in the Mun and Chi valleys, in what is the North-East of Thailand today. The description is plain and dry; it looks objective and scientific, perhaps since it was written for the Siam Society. People live a normal, though not uninteresting, life in a vast and rich land. Furthermore, half of the article is the history of that region. Unlike the 'Wild People', these valley people have history, no matter how mythical it may sound. The main part of history as related here, however, is the benevolence of Bangkok rulers towards those people, indicating that they have been a part of Siam for a long time. The people, the landscape, and everything on that part of Siam's geo-body became the objects of Bangkok's gaze. They are represented as normal villagers who had lived peacefully under the rule of Siam in ways that are familiar to the author and his readers. They deserve a particular representation, a specific style of description which, among other things, confirm that they are and always have been a part of Siam. They were the *chao bannok* (the people of the outer villages) of Bangkok.

Most travel accounts in the period under review (1885–1910) are chronologies of travels by Bangkok administrators to the provinces, the domain of *chao bannok*, whether for business, leisure, or for religious purposes. The mode of narrative is detailed and rather tedious description. It does not try to represent the people and their societies comprehensively or by itemizating and cataloguing their characteristics. The events described are often the receptions held for the travellers/administrators by local authorities. Therefore, the writers were participants, but superior ones whose visits and appearances were the very occasions of the events described. In Chulalongkorn's words, they were not 'normal' events since they were not part of people's daily life.

These travelogues conspicuously take note of the following elements: first, the towns and the villages, and the individuals whom the travellers met (their livelihood, crops, crafts, customs, communal activities, trade, and the human environment, such as rivers, canals, farms, animals, and so on). Secondly, they describe landscape and nature, mostly their beauty, fertility, and value as natural resources. Thirdly, the travellers usually visited temples and historical sites along the way. Unlike the description of the 'Wild People', the *chao bannok* are not held up motionlessly for the gaze of their observers. The participant rulers, 'looking down', are in procession with the people while observing them. The most important contrast to the description of the 'Wild People' is the absence of strangeness (the *plaek pralat* trope) and the presence of familiarity. In describing nature, village life, or temples, the travelogues contain mostly the least unexpected things, rendering many of them boring and unexciting. Many customs are so familiar that the authors could tell the nuances of difference from ones practised elsewhere, nuances that might not be recognizable by complete strangers.

The reason for the distinction between the two kinds of narratives, I would argue, is not that the *chao bannok* were Thai while the *chao pa* were not. The heartland of either Lanna or Siam, that is, the Mae Ping and the Chao Phraya valleys respectively, were full of multi-ethnic migrants or settlers and war captives (Terwiel 1989: 58–59, 85–86, 91–92, 115–16, 150–51, 174–75; Bowie 1996 and in this volume). Whether or not Siam had ever been more homogeneous, by the nineteenth century it was a heterogeneous 'melting pot'. Ethnic minorities formed two circles around Bangkok for defending the capital (Terwiel 1989: 253–54). The Bangkok overlords were aware of this fact. Their travelogues of journeys to the space of *chao bannok* often make clear whether the people were what we might call 'ethnic Thai' or not. Some distinctive customs might then be mentioned. But the narrative mode is the same. In fact, in the traditional polity, the more diverse the peoples under his suzerainty, the more powerful the overlord would be acknowledged to be.

The distinctive representation of these multi-ethnic *chao bannok* contrasted with the 'Wild People' indicates the discursive differentiation of Siamese subjects. The *chao bannok* were people of whatever race or language who, according to the traditional (Siamese) imperial discourse, begged to live 'under the shadow of protection of the enlightened Siamese overlord'. They 'fled from the heat to live in [literally 'depend on'] the cool' (*ni ron ma phung yen*). Of course, this is the conqueror's discourse. Yet the point is that these people are capable of domestication. They are docile. The marked difference from the 'Wild People' is not race, but the tamed/untamed, 'civilizable/uncivilizable' differentiation. They might not be Thai; it did not matter, as long as they were 'subjects'.

The formation of the new territorial state – the geo-body consciousness and the integration of the peripheries into the body of Siam – and the open economy under the influence of colonialism since the mid-nineteenth century, radically changed the ways Bangkok ruled over the space of *chao bannok*. The Siamese court could no longer sit at the apex of the hierarchy, expecting labour, tribute, and tax from their subjects under fragmented and often antagonistic lords in return for Bangkok's self-proclaimed benevolent protection. They had to engage in running the economy, especially commodity production for the world market, and governing the integrated state. New demands required new inquiries and new curiosity, and in turn these produced new knowledge and new government. In the new state, knowing the space of *chao bannok* more analytically, and being able to exploit information under specific demands, projects, or agenda, are equivalent to 'governing' them. A new territorial management was required. Data and knowledge about Siam's interior had been limited under the *ancien régime*. Travel brought the space of Siam under investigation, note-taking, recording, and description. The towns, lands, and localities throughout the realm were observed, and in many cases quite thoroughly investigated and documented in the form of travelogues. The data were later put on charts and tables, into exhibitions and statistical yearbooks. What landscape, nature, and village life had in common in the eyes of the modernized rulers was value in terms of productivity and economic potential. The space of *chao bannok* was becoming administratively domesticated, economically exploitable as natural and human resources. The trope of the narratives of the 'Docile People' is that of state-territorial exploration, for production, for civilization.

Differentiated Space and the Temporality of Civilization

The absence of strangeness does not necessarily mean that the *chao bannok* must always be tedious. Besides natural and human resources, official functions, and temple visits, Siam's interior space of *chao bannok* is never short of intriguing stories. For the sake of discussion here, strangeness may be defined as unusual elements beyond normal expectation, which the readers would never expect to encounter in their own lives. The strangeness belongs to a far-away domain, almost beyond imagination, but just within the bounds of what is plausible and understandable. Perhaps the reader might have just heard of it, acquired some slight knowledge of it, and be able to relate the story to their background store of knowledge or compare it with familiar experience.

The favourite stories from travels to the domain of *chao bannok*, are about magic, superstition, spirits, local customs, and beliefs. Rare occupations, unusual individuals and their skills are also included. The stories are told merely as entertaining side issues, not as the main items. The authors seldom dare dismiss these tales, nor show disrespect, nor interrupt what they saw at the time, yet they usually express scepticism. They comment as non-believers, especially those who considered themselves men of science, such as King Chulalongkorn and his royal associates. For example, Prince Damrong's *Nithan borankhadi*, his recollections of travels to Siam's interior space of *chao bannok*, are full of stories of superstition and rural life which he had witnessed himself or gathered at first hand. Phadungkhwaenprachan (1918), in his account of the Lao in Siam's North-East, considers them to be an inferior, superstitious, and uncivilized people, and throughout the work offers his ideas as to more correct understandings of phenomena.

Our ethnographers were born and grew up in the middle of the nineteenth century when the intellectual atmosphere among the Siamese élite was overwhelmed by curiosity in modern sciences. In their fascination for science they wrote off many traditional beliefs (Thipakorawong 1971; Reynolds 1976). For them, superstitions belonged to the domain of simplicity, of less civilized, unsophisticated, and uneducated people (Sathiankoset 1978: 222–25, 238–54). The space of the *chao bannok* was permeated by superstition, ignorance, uneducatedness, and the like, which belong to the past of science, modernity, and civilization. By the end of the century, the literature on old customs, such as Chulalongkorn's *Phraratchaphithi sipsong duan* (Royal rituals of the twelve month cycle) was a conscious effort to record things of the past (1966). This might be called 'nostalgia production', a longing for the past by those who live, enjoy, and commit themselves to the future-oriented present. A number of publications which blossomed during this period are instances of this 'nostalgia production', including the famous journal *Wachirayan* by the élitist literati club, and the notorious journal by a commoner *Sayam praphet* (1897–1908) by K.S.R. Kulap and many others of his works (Chai-anan 1979; Kulap 1995). The explosion of interest and writing on history, myth, and legend, from the end of the nineteenth century were also part of this phenomenon (Winai 1983: chap 4).

In this context, the ethnography of the *chao pa* and *chao bannok* was regarded as writing about the past. Surasakmontri's *Chao pa* was reprinted in 1920 with an introduction by Prince Damrong extolling it as a source for inquiry into the remote past of the country since the *chao pa* were the oldest inhabitants (Surasakmontri 1972: 238). Despite their contemporaneity, the 'Wild People' were captive in a remote past. The entire collection of *Latthi thamniam tangtang* was classified in 1918 by the royal Vajiranana library as 'history' (Phadungkhwaenprachan 1918: 1–2; Phothiwongsachan 1972: 355). Anuman Rajadhon, a famous ethnographer, considered his works as both ethnography and history (Sathiankoset 1978: 257, 263). For the modernized élite, the *chao bannok* characteristically belonged to the domain of pre-modernity, and would soon become the past. Travels had taken the modern élite to the realm of a by-gone age and nostalgia. Unmistakably, representations of these 'Others' indicate that the travellers and writers were culturally in the domain of modernity and the future-oriented present. While Siam's rural areas were contemporaneous with the space of Bangkok, they were temporally distant from it, as is suggested by the title of Prince Damrong's book, *Stories of the Past*.[10] Fabian has commented on the tendency for some anthropologists to create a distance between themselves and the observed by the 'denial of coevalness, . . . a persistent and systematic tendency to place the referent(s) of anthropology in a Time other than the present of the producer of anthropological discourse' (Fabian 1983: 31). The Siamese rulers employed the same device in order to place themselves in a superior, gazing position over the observed. They were cultural as well as temporal 'Others Within'.

There emerged a discourse of comparative ethnographic space. Ethno-spatial categories were conceptually juxtaposed, thanks to the mediation of travels and travelogues. This produced a spatial and temporal tabulation of civilization. Those categories of Others Within, – and the domains of neighbouring Others and the West which lie outside the present discussion – can be plotted on different positions in the cultural and temporal scheme of civilization. It is true that the notion of civilization, an ideological weapon of colonialism, has never been clearly defined. Siamese intellectuals were aware of this and had debated the notions of modernity and civilization since the late nineteenth century. The opposing ideas underscored political ideologies, and vice versa. For example, the visions and agenda for a civilized Siam held respectively by Thianwan, a commoner, and strongly pro-Western, and the modernizing monarchs, Chulalongkorn and Vajiravudh, were irreconcilable (Chai-anan and Kattiya 1989: 108–35, 150–55). However, the tabulation needs no clear definition of civilization. On the contrary, the discursive juxtaposition of peoples in places, in ethno-space, with implications as to various levels of civilization, could help to form concrete ideas of progress and levels of civilization in the Thai context. The Thai discourse of *siwilai* was not necessarily the same as the Western notion of civilization.

Under the colonial project, civilization, *siwilai* in Thai, became a new cosmic order determining the spatio-temporal relations of cultures and peoples. On the one hand, the Siamese élite had always been and desired to remain superior to their subjects and peripheries. On the other hand, Siam might be among the Others of Western civilization. The Siamese élite adamantly refused to be placed at the opposite end of un-civilization. Actually the élite constituted the socio-cultural 'contact zone' in which the transculturation and indigenization took place (Pratt 1992: 6–7). Consequently, they saw themselves moving ahead on the train of civilization, rather than staying with their subjects in the boat of tradition. Unfortunately, the undeniable fact was that the Bangkok élite was also the tug-boat pulling a huge ship filled with its own Others Within.

As a result, the élite created a scheme to negotiate a position of its own. There were two intellectual strategies to negotiate a desirable position in the scale of civilization. The first was to situate oneself at a desirable position in the comparative, cultural space of civilization. The second was to measure the great distance one had covered so far, from an uncivilized past, thus ensuring one's place towards the more civilized end of the temporal scale. Neither strategy operated to the exclusion of the other. The major discourses of civilization in Siam embodied both strategies, and both were well served by the ethno-spatial trope.

The discourse on civilization has been institutionalized in many ways. For example, it found its visual representation in the rising popularity of the exhibit culture of the time. Between 1890–1930, exhibitions and museums, both domestic and international, were parts of Siamese projects of modernity and civilization. Each particular domain of *chao pa, chao bannok*, and of the Bangkok rulers was proposed to be represented in three kinds of museum, namely, the ethnological, the historical and the 'museum of commerce and commodities'. The competition between these contenders to be *the* national museum and the eventual success of the historical museum in the 1920s reflected shifts and development in the discourse on civilization in Siam in the twentieth century. This is a subject I intend to deal with in a separate publication.

The ethnography of differentiated space/time remained nonetheless, and was developed further. The early years of the Siam Society, an Orientalist club of foreign and Thai élitist scholars, was significantly devoted to ethnography. Ethnology was a major part of its foundation programme in 1904. From the first general meeting of the Society, several projects were urged, such as anthropometric measurement, study of the blue spot of Mongoloid children, and the need for an ethnological museum (*Journal of the Siam Society* 1, 1904: III, 1–6, 211–16). In subsequent decades, ethnography was a major component of the Society's journal. Much of the foundation of ethnographic knowledge in Siam must be attributed to the efforts of the Society, especially the projects under Major Seidenfaden from the 1910s to 1930s, in close collaboration with Siamese administrative and scholarly institutions. They continued the search for *khon doem* (autochthonous people) such as the Lawa (Seidenfaden 1918, 1919), and the identification and classification of ethnic minorities, applying anthropological concepts from the West. Under Seidenfaden's chairmanship of the sub-committee on Anthropological, Ethnographical, and Linguistic Research, the Society launched a major inquiry in 1920, asking local officials all over the country to investigate the non-Thai 'tribes and races' in their areas. The responses were encouraging, at least succeeding in 'awakening the interest of the Siamese intelligentsia' (*Journal of the Siam Society* 19, 1921: 53–55). Some of the responses were published in the journal (Anonymous 1922; Boriphan 1923).

As Siam moved further along the path of modernity, with Bangkok always representing the most modernized space, the differentiation of cultural space and its temporal implications also shifted. In 1935, Seidenfaden warned that the ethnic 'melting-pot' of Siam was rapidly becoming Thai; the destruction of diverse ethnological characteristics seemed inevitable; therefore 'research work (on various ethnic groups) should be taken up *now* . . . before it becomes too late' (1935: 18; his emphasis). The same trend rendered the anthropology of villages more significant, but territorial exploration was no longer the narrative on villages. It was displaced by the anthropology of authentic Thai culture (kinship, social order, genuine Thai traditions etc.). Not only superstitions, but the entire domain of village and peasant life represented the past. The works of Anuman Rajadhon, for example, paid attention to old customs, gradually disappearing traditions, and to village and peasant life. He had travelled and witnessed them at first-hand, but he nonetheless assumed that what he saw had been true fifty years or even much earlier, and thus 'in former times' (Sathiankoset 1978: 257 and title of the book).

Once again, those observed were captured in the past tense, while those observing were in the future-oriented present, though the two 'times' were separated only by space. Soon after, the Cornell project found its laboratory for the studies of the genuine Thai villages and culture at Bangchan, a village on the outskirts of Bangkok. The site of true Thai-ness could be found in the space of *chao bannok* which was about to be the past due to modernization. Living in yet another space of modernity, those anthropologists knew other futures, and ironically the site of the village has now become an industrial park, a huge amusement park, in a dense residential area of greater Bangkok. The ethnography of *chao bannok* has become the past of the 'Thai-self'. It is a temporal Other, not a culturally alien one (Sathiankoset 1956: 11–13). Once it has been domesticated spatially and temporally, the domain of *chao bannok* can be appropriated, romanticized, or even (re-)invented, for example as a leisure space beside the palace in Bangkok (Chulalongkorn 1939: 89–92), or as a historical utopia (Thongchai 1995: 114–15).

The Differentiated Ethno-body of Siam

Siam's geo-body emerged amidst at least two geo-political forces. First, it was founded upon the pre-territorial state: on the one hand, a hierarchical space of lord/subjects, or 'class' relations; on the other hand, an imperial space where the shadow of protection of the enlightened monarch had boastfully prevailed over peoples of many races and languages. Secondly, the geo-body itself has brought Siam into the global community in which Siam found its humble place. Anderson's imagined national community and my national geo-body may leave the impression that undifferentiated contemporaneity and spatial homogeneity are intrinsic to nationhood (Anderson, 1991; Thongchai: 1994). It is true that nationhood purports to be an integrated Self. Yet it is in fact an organic body within which differentiated but integrated components must work together in an orderly manner. The differentiated ethno-body of Siam emerged in response to, and as a result of, this geo-political context.

Siamese rulers seemed to find minimal difficulty in looking outward, as a strategy for surviving and prospering in the modern world. The élite in the early Bangkok period had already been largely outward-oriented towards overseas trade (Hong 1984). When the centres of the traditional universe, namely China and India, fell to the West, and thereby lost their hold on Thai mentality, Siamese rulers were quick to abandon them (Mongkut 1973: 43–44). The eyes of the élite turned to Singapore, colonial India, and the West. They did so aware of the wealth of their own backyard, the hinterland of Siam. They exploited it; and yet in many respects it was kept as a backyard, a backwoods, a backward ethno-space. This chapter has asked how Siamese rulers saw their relations with their subjects, and has suggested that the rulers saw their own position as far ahead of, or high above their subjects, those under the shadow of their protection. It is difficult to measure the distance; but the extent of the gap was sufficient to enable the élite to 'look back' or 'look down', depending on which metaphors for the relations we choose, on their subjects and the marginal minorities, not as They, yet not as We, but perhaps as Theirs. The 'Their' Otherness is missing in Edward Said's binary opposition of We and They. The 'Their' Otherness as argued here includes not only the alien forest or mountain peoples, but also the familiar *chao bannok*. In this scheme of ethno-space within the geo-body, the élite maintained their privileged position over their Otherness, setting themselves apart from their subjects while associating themselves with the civilized world metropolitan league.

Is it therefore impossible from the inception of the modern Thai state to expect Bangkok to speak for the entire country? The relationship has always been hierarchical. Bangkok can only speak *of*, not speak *for*, the rest. It can speak *for* only Bangkok itself, and always in order to negotiate its privileged space over their Others Within, and always in association with the metropolitan world. One of the most important conditions of survival of these ethno-spatial relations is the discourse which continuously allows Bangkok to speak on behalf of the entire nation. As the differentiated ethno-body was maintained or developed, the politics of nationhood has always deflected the fragmentation, the ethno-spatial heterogeneity, and tension of diversity within the nation. The *chao bannok* have rarely been successful in their negotiations with the Bangkok élite, be they kings, generals, or politicians. As long as Bangkok is allowed to be the voice of the entire nation, the interests of the *chao bannok* or the *chao pa* will be cast as narrow, specific interests.

Recent controversies over dam projects, reforestation, resource management, and environmental issues have brought the tension to the forefront. These are the new sites where the legitimacy of Bangkok's voice is questioned, and Bangkok's parochial interest can be exposed. They are the locations where the political tensions of differentiated 'ethno-spatial' politics is revealed. The contest is fierce; there is more at stake than many would have thought. So far Bangkok maintains its claim to be the privileged voice for the entire nation. Bangkok pretends to speak *for* Others while only speaking for itself. Even the political debate about vote-buying and corrupt 'provincial' politicians in the 1992 and 1995 Thai elections was based on a Bangkok-centric notion of democracy. Speaking in the name of democracy for the entire country, the Bangkok media and educated urbanites accused the *chao bannok*'s practices, so-called 'vote-buying', as being the prime enemy of democracy. Political analysis has ignored the history of power relations among the differentiated ethno-spaces and the consequences for the present Thai political system.

The 'Wild People' remain objects of Bangkok's shifting geo-politics. In recent discourse on ethnic minorities, the category of *chao pa* has been shifted to *chao khao* (mountain people or 'hill tribe'). The terms are closely related but not quite the same.[11] Ethnic minorities in Siam have experienced dramatic socio-cultural changes, including 'Thai-ization' in the past century. But the extent of change among the diverse groups, and the degree of assimilation are uneven. The *chao khao* category and its discursive content has emerged as much through the ethnography of socio-cultural change as by the security paranoia of the Thai state. Since the traditional claim to a multi-ethnic realm had become unnecessary – even dangerous – for the nationalizing Thai state, and since the *chao bannok* are now considered parts of the Thai-self, what have been left on the margin of the Thai geo-ethno-body are the less assimilated *chao khao*. As alleged 'opium producers', the well-being of the mountain peoples is believed to be in contradiction to the well-being of the rest of the people of Thailand. They are the health-hazardous Other, a risk to Thai welfare. On the other hand, tourism has made a large number of them the exotic Other, a friendly, commercializable, exhibited Other. Real life 'hill tribes' are put on display at resorts, hotels, theatres, shopping malls, and even along the highways. And finally at a time when environmentalism is a burning issue, some hill people are charged with being the un-environmentalist Other, in conflict with lowland *chao bannok*. Contradictory embodiments of these forms of representation and commodification, the 'Wild Peoples' remain distant and problematically different from the 'Thai-self'.

Despite the foregoing formal elaboration of ethno-spatial categories, a student of Thailand should not fail to recognize that the scheme is part of everyday life in the country. Thai people may not be familiar with the academic identification of ethnic groups such as the Lue, the Karen, the Kayah, and so on. But they are definitely familiar with the terms *chao khao*, *chao bannok*, *chao krung* (Bangkok), and *farang* (Westerners). The following diagram may represent some relations between these categories:

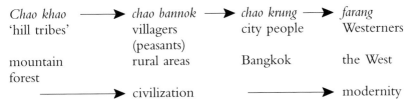

In a way, this chapter does not discover any unknown knowledge at all. On the contrary, it calls attention to a discourse which has become influential popular knowledge, whose significance and impact is far-reaching in more ways than academic ethnography may realize.

Final Remarks

A number of significant topics integral to the theme of this chapter are left unexamined, among them, the Western Other and Siam's neighbours (Burma, Cambodia, Laos, Malaysia, Vietnam, and in a sense China). Without them, perhaps we cannot understand fully the tabulation of all kinds of Otherness. They too are subjects of travel and ethnographic formulations. Furthermore, the chapter does not even mention yet another Other, a very crucial one for the modern Thai state: the Chinese. I realize the complexity of the issue which cannot be dealt with here. Besides, the mediation of travel is not applicable to the discursive construction of the Chinese Other.

Many other issues justify extensive further study; for instance, the contending ideas of *siwilai* and exhibit culture. The programme would amount to no less than a history of ethnographic knowledge in Siam. Regardless of questions some may wish to ask as to who the Thai, the Lue, the Karen, or any other ethnic groups 'really are', we ask how the Others of Bangkok are classified and represented by various kinds of knowledge. What are the effects on the conceptual classification of people, of the development of state power, the agrarian sector, industrialization, and ecological transformation in various domains and regions of the country? Another major issue stems from the fact that the discourse of civilization is both cultural and temporal. While the Orientalizing discourse measures Siam's civilization by comparing it with the Others Within and with the West, the historicizing one measured the distance Siam had travelled through its own past. The Orientalizing discourse has been deeply

Plate 7. 'Lao architecture: the Chow Radjasee's house at Kiang Hai'

implicated in the making of historical knowledge in Siam. We need to address the question which this chapter has begun to formulate: how did ethnography help give birth to Thai history?

Notes

Research for this chapter was supported by the Social Science Research Council and the Graduate School of University of Wisconsin in 1992–93. Thanks for comments from Prasenjit Duara, Paritta C. Ko-anantakul, Charles Keyes, Craig Reynolds, Andrew Turton and several others at presentations in London, Madison, Seattle, Chicago, Ann Arbor and Cambridge, Mass.

1 *Thieo* means travel or tour; *thieo pa*, a trip to jungle or forest, or a remote, uncivilized area. The author also lists the names of his characters, many of whom have both Thai and Senoi names and some with genealogies, implying that they are not fictional (pp. 17–19).
2 See also Yib 1992: 21, a photo of Khanang, dressed in a full princely uniform, standing in line with Chulalongkorn's sons, including the future King Rama VII.
3 Mary Louise Pratt calls this an 'autoethnography', referring to 'instances in which colonized subjects undertake to represent themselves in ways that engage with the colonizer's own terms . . . (It) involves partial collaboration with and appropriation of the idioms of the conqueror' (1992: 7,9). But the notion of 'auto-' and 'themselves' here are problematic. The terms imply undifferentiated power relations among the colonized subjects, between the observers and the observed. An 'autoethnography', thus, could claim an anti-colonial privilege while advancing a hegemonic agenda over its dominated subjects.
4 'Anthropology . . . is a science of other men in another Time. It is a discourse whose referent has been removed from the present of the speaking/writing subject. . . . Anthropology's Other is . . . other people who are our contemporaries' (Fabian 1983: 143). This idea will be elaborated later from Thai cases.
5 *Wachirayanwiset* was published weekly between 1886–1894. A related monthly journal *Wachirayan*, was published from 1884 to 1905. (cf. Sukanya 1977: 41–42 which gives different dates) The journal was arguably the most prestigious one among the élite literati of the time.
6 The adjective '*ton*' signifies the royalty of the noun, in this case a journey. But this is not the reason given by Damrong (1976: 8–9).
7 These earlier writings might be called 'proto-ethnography'. The term 'ethnography' used here is inclusive, however, for I am not trying to argue a distinction between 'proto-' and 'true' ethnography.
8 The author was better known by his later title Phraya Prachakitkorachak (Cham Bunnag), one of the finest provincial commissioners under Chulalongkorn and among the best scholars of that time. His best known book is *Phongsawadan yonok* (1972) which is a compilation of articles in *Wachirayan* and *Wachirayanwiset* during his tenure as the royal commissioner in the north.
9 The term *chat* here should read 'race', not 'people', and certainly not 'nation'. So the title can be, 'On the varieties of the forest races', or 'On the wild races'. After their first appearance in several issues of *Wachirayanwiset*, 5 (1890), the articles were later compiled as Part 5 of *Latthi thamniam tangtang* (On various customs) (Fine Arts Dept 1972), first published in 1920.

10 In today's usage, *nithan* means fables; and *borankhadi* is the specific word for archaeology, the discipline. The book has very little to do with archaeology and none of the accounts are fables. They are true stories from Damrong's travels within Siam about thirty years before the book was first published in 1944. The development of the modern concept of history in Siam was represented by several terms including *nithan* and *borankhadi*. The translation of the title is, thus, difficult because both words are among the loci of the new historical knowledge in the making, hence the unfixed meanings.

11 Terwiel notes that *chao khao* were mentioned in the literature from the early nineteenth century. But in fact those Karen were called *chao pa* (1989: 91–92). Terwiel substitutes the earlier category with the recent one, assuming, like most people, that the two categories are the same.

References

Anonymous (1922), 'Ruang rangkai thamniam prapheni kanliangchip thang phasa chao yangkalo (kariang)' (On the physique, customs, traditions, livelihood, and language of the Yangkalo (Karen) race), *Journal of the Siam Society*, (XVI)1: 47–89.

Boriphanthurarat, Luang (1923), 'Chat meo (The Hmong race)' *Journal of the Siam Society*, (XVII)3: 121–52, 175–200.

Bowie, Katherine (1996), 'Slavery in Nineteenth Century Northern Thailand' in E. Paul Durrenberger (ed.), *State Power and Culture in Thailand,* monograph 44, Yale Southeast Asia Studies.

Chai-anan Samudavanija (1979), *Chiwit lae ngan khong Thianwan lae K.S.R. Kulap,* (Lives and Works of Thianwan and K.S.R. Kulap), Bangkok: Thiranan.

Chai-anan Samudavanija and Kattiya Kannasutr (eds.) (1989), *Ekkasan kanmuang kan pokkhrong thai 2411–2475* (Documents on Thai politics, 1868–1931), Bangkok: Social Science Association of Thailand.

Chulalongkorn, King (1939), *Samnao phraratchahatthalekha suanphraong phrabatsomdet phra chunlachomklao chaoyuhua thung chaophraya Yommarat (Pan Sukhum)* (Copies of private correspondence of King Chulalongkorn to Chaophraya Yommarat (Pan Sukhum)), Bangkok: Bamrungtham.

—— (1966), *Praratchaphithi sipsongduan* (Royal rituals of the twelve month cycle), Bangkok: Phraephitthaya.

—— (1969), *Ngo' pa*, Bangkok: Sinlapabannakarn.

—— (1984), *Klai ban*, 2 vols., Bangkok: Phraephitthaya.

Clifford, James (1986), 'On Ethnographic Allegory' in James Clifford and George Marcus (eds.), *Writing Culture,* Berkeley: University of California Press, 98–121.

Damrong Rajanuphap, Prince (1961), *Athibai ruang thieo,* Bangkok: Khurusapha.

—— (1966), *Nithanborankhadi,* 13th printing, Bangkok: Sinlapabannakarn.

—— (1976), *Sadetpraphatton,* Bangkok: Sinlapabannakarn.

Fine Arts Department (comp.) (1972), *Latthi thamniam tangtang,* 4th printing of the edition, Bangkok: Khlangwitthaya.

Hong Lysa (1984), *Thailand in the Nineteenth Century: Evolution of the Economy and Society,* Singapore: Institute of Southeast Asian Studies.

Journal of the Siam Society, (JSS) 1 (1904).

Keyes, Charles (1978), 'Ethnography and Anthropological Interpretation in the Study of Thailand' in Elizer B. Ayal (ed.), *The Study of Thailand: Analyses of Knowledge, Approaches and Prospects in Anthropology, Art History, Economics, History, and Political Science,* Athens, Ohio: Center for International Studies, Ohio University, 1–60.

Kulap, K.S.R. (1995), *Ayatiwat,* Bangkok: Thailand-Japan Friendship Association, reprint from the original 1911 edition.

Manas Chitakasem (1972), 'The Emergence and Development of the Nirat Genre in Thai Poetry', *Journal of the Siam Society,* (60)2: 135–68.

Mongkut, King (1973), *Prachum phraratchaniphon nai ratchakan thi 4* (Collected writings of King Mongkut), cremation volume for Phra Thammadilok (Thongkham).

Phadungkhwaenprachan, Luang (Chan Uttaranakhon) (1918), 'Latthi thamniam lao' (Lao customs), Part 1 of *Latthi thamniam tangtang* (On various customs), cremation volume for Khun Chenkrabuanhat (Yin Phonnithet).

Phothiwongsachan, Phra (Tisso Uan) (1972), 'Waduai chonchat phuthai lae chat yo lae ruang uen' (On the Phuthai and Yo races and other stories), *Latthi thamniam tangtang,* vol 2, part 18, Bangkok: Khlangwitthaya.

Prachakhadikit, Khun (1885) 'Waduai praphet khonpa ru kha fai nua' (On the varieties of forest people in the north' *Wachirayanwiset* vol. 1(9): 164–6.

Prachakitkorachak, Phraya (1904), 'Waduai maenam mun lae muang tawanok' (On the Mun River and the towns in the east), *Journal of the Siam Society,* I: 175–90.

—— (1972), *Phongsawadan yonok* (Yonok Chronicles), Bangkok: Phraephitthaya.

Pratt, Mary Louise (1992), *Imperial eyes: travel writing and transculturation*, London: Routledge.

Prayuth Sitthaphan (1980), *Prawattisat praphatton* (A history of the royal tour), Bangkok: Siangthai.

Reynolds, Craig J. (1976) 'Buddhist Cosmography in Thai History, with Special Reference to Nineteenth Century Culture Change', *Journal of Asian Studies* 35: 203–20.

—— (1991), 'Sedition in Thai History: a Nineteenth-Century Poem and Its Critics', in Andrew Turton and Manas Chitakasem (eds.), *Thai Constructions of Knowledge*, London: School of Oriental and African Studies, University of London, 15–36.

Sadap Ladawan (1984), 'Ruang khong nai khanang mahatlek' (The story of Mr. Khanang, the royal page) *Sinlapa watthanatham* 5(3): 20–31.

Sathiankoset (Anuman Rajadhon, Phraya) (1956), 'The Application and Potential Values of Cultural Anthropology' in G. William Skinner (ed.), *Sangkhomsat kap prathet thai* (Social sciences and Thailand), Bangkok.

—— (1978), *Kansuksa ruang prapheni thai lae chiwit chaothai samai kon* (A study of Thai traditions and the life of Thai people in former times), 3rd printing, Bangkok: Khlangwitthaya.

Seidenfaden, Erik, Major (1918), 'Some Notes about the Chaubon: a Disappearing Tribe in the Korat Province' *Journal of the Siam Society,* (XII)3: 1–4.

—— (1919), 'Further Notes about the Chaubon, etc.' *Journal of the Siam Society,* (XII)3: 47–53.

—— (1935), 'Anthropological and Ethnographical Research Work in Siam', *Journal of the Siam Society,* (XXVIII)1: 15–18.

Sommot-amornphan, Prince (1890), 'Waduai khonchat kariang khwaeng muang saiyok' (On the Karen in Saiyok province), *Wachirayanwiset,* 5(50): 593–5.

Stott, Philip (1991), 'Mu'ang and Pa: Elite Views of Nature in a Changing Thailand', in Andrew Turton and Manas Chitakasem (eds.), *Thai Constructions of Knowledge,* London: School of Oriental and African Studies, University of London, 142–154.

Streckfuss, David (1993), 'The Mixed Colonial Legacy in Siam: Origins of Thai Racialist Thought, 1890–1910' in Laurie Sears, ed. *Autonomous Histories: Particular Truths,* Essays in honor of John Smail, Monograph no.11, Madison: Center for Southeast Asian Studies, University of Wisconsin-Madison.

Sukanya Tirawanich (1977), *Prawatkan nangsuphim nai prathetthai phaitai rabob somburanaya sitthirat 2325–2475* (A history of newspapers in Thailand under the absolute monarchy 1782–1932), Bangkok: Thai Watthanaphanit.

Surasakmontri, Chaophraya (1972), 'Waduai chaopa chat tangtang' (On the various races of forest peoples), *Latthi thamniam tangtang*, part 5.

Tambiah, Stanley J. (1984), *The Buddhist Saints of the Forest and the Cult of Amulets*, Cambridge: Harvard University Press.

Terwiel, B.J. (1989), *Through Travellers' Eyes*, Bangkok: Duang Kamol.

Thipakorawong, Chaophraya (1971), *Nangsu sadaeng kitchanukit* (A book on miscellaneous things), Bangkok: Khurusapha.

Thongchai Winichakul (1994), *Siam Mapped: A History of the Geo-body of A Nation*, Honolulu: University of Hawaii Press.

—— (1995), 'The Changing Landscape of the Past: New Histories in Thailand since 1973' *Journal of Southeast Asian Studies*, 26, 1: 99–120.

Turton, Andrew (1980) 'Thai Institutions of Slavery' in James L. Watson (ed.) *Asian and African Systems of Slavery*, Oxford, Blackwell, pp. 252–292.

—— (1991) 'State poetics and civil rhetoric' in Andrew Turton and Manas Chitakasem (eds.) *Thai Constructions of Knowledge* London, School of Oriental and African Studies, University of London, 1–14.

Winai Pongsripian (1983), 'Traditional Thai Historiography and its Nineteenth Century Decline', Ph.D. thesis, University of Bristol.

Yib Phanchan (1992), *Chiwit dang fan thi thuakkhao banthat* (A fantasy life in the Banthat range), Bangkok: Sinlapa Wannakam Publishing.

Chapter Three

The Differential Integration of Hill People into the Thai State

Ronald D. Renard

One of King Chulalongkorn's (Rama V) titles was 'King of the Karen'. Inheriting this title from his father, King Chulalongkorn worked during his reign from 1868 until 1910 to integrate his Karen subjects into the Thai state he was then reforming. He considered Karen as citizens with all the rights and obligations of native Tai-speakers and other ethnic groups. This chapter examines the process of transforming Karen from subjects to citizens, which as will be shown, involves many of the problems found in Thai state formation. The chapter also provides a basis for the historical examination of whether the so-called 'hill tribe problem' can be traced to this process of integration.

Civilized and Uncivilized Peoples

Karen in nineteenth-century Thailand lived in a world far removed from the new ways of life emerging in Bangkok. The modes of thinking based on Western civilization then reshaping the Thai capital profoundly challenged the Karen lifestyle. Yet there were civilizing influences arriving in South East Asia much earlier that also profoundly affected life in this region. Evidence of such changes is found in early Tai[1] writings, with references to people who lived in *müang*[2] and to people who did not. Those living in *müang* were seen as having acquired a number of 'civilizing' influences – religious, legal, linguistic, and governmental – that had been imported from India. Those who lived outside *müang* were less affected by these influences.

Despite the early history of the Karen being unwritten, old references to Karen make it seem they were living outside *müang*, living on the fringes of lowland kingdoms. Although some Karen appear to have ruled small kingdoms, at least from the 1660s, most Karen, whether Sgaw or Pwo – the two major Karen sub-groups – seem to have lived in localized groups,

Plate 8. 'Karen packmen'

generally no larger than a *kau* (multi-village cluster). References to peoples living in small rural groups appear in written sources that were based on oral traditions dating to before the formation of Tai kingdoms in the thirteenth century. The *Chamathewiwong*, written in fifteenth-century Chiang Mai by the monk Phothirangsi, refers to persons fit to rule *müang* and persons unfit to do so. In a discussion between two holy men (*rishi*) as to how to find a ruler fit to rule *müang* Hariphunchai[3] which they were creating to honour the Buddha, one observed that 'some people [in the area of Hariphunchai itself] are characterized as denizens of the forest. They are not inclined to know whether "this thing is good, this thing is bad; this thing is meritorious, this things is demeritorious"'. Concluded one *rishi*, 'these are "people not ready to hold royal power"' (Phothirangsi 1973: 74).

To find a proper ruler for *müang* Hariphunchai, they turned to the queen of Lavo (now known as Lopburi) hundreds of kilometres to the South on the Chao Phraya river. Since her husband, the city ruler, had become a monk, she was free to come and rule Hariphunchai. She was pregnant, so a line of descent was ensured. Most important, the text tells that she possessed (Indic) attributes such as *kusalo* (merit), which the holy men believed were needed to rule a *müang*. The use of the Pali word for merit, *kusalo,* indicates that Indic influences played so important a role in Hariphunchai that they determined who was fit to rule *müang*. In a centuries-long process, peoples living along travel routes, usually in valleys, acquired such 'civilizing' influences faster than people in the hills. As valley settlements coalesced into *müang*, the local rulers accepted Indic influences that fostered state authority, such as devotion to individual Hindu deities.

One such influence was the belief that there were people fit and not fit to live in or rule over *müang*. The Sri Lankan Buddhist chronicle, the *Mahavamsa*, refers to a time over two millennia ago when aboriginal, non-Buddhist residents of Sri Lanka were referred to as *yakkha* (beasts) (Kirabamune 1985: 9). These pre-Aryan aborigines seem to have been deemed animals in human form who could not enter the monkhood. This is apparently based on a misinterpretation of a section in the Buddhist *Vinaya* which forbids persons with contagious diseases like tuberculosis, as well as criminals, those in the king's service, debtors, slaves, and animals in human form, from becoming ordained.

Tai Buddhist kingdoms, apparently under the influence of such borrowings, came to use *kusalo* to distinguish the high-ranking from the low-ranking. In this 'inherently unequal' situation, higher-ranking criminals were punished less than the lower-ranking. To what extent such status distinctions had existed in pre-Tai kingdoms is uncertain, although evidence, such as the discussion between the *rishi,* hints at *civilized/non-civilized* distinctions, as does the continued existence of status differentials among contemporary Mon-Khmer hill groups in Thailand.

This inequality in terms of 'civility' and *kusalo*, which was based on Indic learning, was non-ethnic. To the Indic-influenced Mon-Khmer and Tai, who later moved into Mon-Khmer areas, élites lived in cities, were literate, and had acquired Indic religious influences. The non-ethnic nature of this distinction is shown by the *rishi* wanting not just any fellow Lua'-speakers,[4] but a 'civilized' queen to rule Hariphunchai (Renard 1988).

Tai and Kha

The emergence of the Tai as the rulers of kingdoms such as Chiang Rung in what is now southern China to Chiang Mai, Sukhothai, Ayutthaya and Nakhon Si Thammarat on the Malay peninsula, remade the ethnic map of the region. Although the origin of the term 'Tai' is uncertain, it came to denote speakers of a language family which inhabited lowland kingdoms. The fact that there are no Tai 'hill tribes' – in the sense of forest dwelling peoples reliant principally on unirrigated agriculture – indicates the term's non-ethnic nature, although as non-Buddhists, and as 'minorities' vis-à-vis the Lao, the Tai Dam, Tai Daeng, and Tai Khao are sometimes given the epithet 'tribal Tai' or 'Hill Tai (see for example Turton and Mayoury in this volume). As rulers of *müang*, 'Tai' were a 'civilized' people.[5]

Also of unknown origin is the term 'Kha', which indicates the non-Tai, and includes hill and forest peoples who did not rule *müang*. Kha includes Tibeto-Burman-speaking groups, such as *Kha*chin, Mon-Khmer-speakers such as the *Kha*mu,[6] and speakers of other languages, such as the *K(h)a*ren. Although speaking sometimes unrelated languages and practising divergent cultures, they were united by living in the forest surrounding Tai *müang*, with which they were linked ritually, as Leach and others have shown.

Tai kingdoms and Kha forest-dwellers existed in an area of low population. Tai chronicles and Kha oral traditions record perennial warfare, the prizes of which were prisoners-of-war. The frequent marching off of people to be relocated in other *müang* resulted in constant assimilation as the prisoners took on their captors' cultural and ethnic identity. Because Tai *müang* controlled more people than the Kha, Tai armies usually defeated the Kha in battle. Losers generally took on a lower social status. The Tai Lue of Sipsongpanna, for example, gave prisoners little or no land; they became known as *hong hai*, who, even after considerable cultural assimilation were not, according to some contemporary Tai Lue, even considered Tai. *Hong hai* performed menial tasks for higher classes, such as the *tai moeng* (the Tai of the *müang*). The *tai moeng*, because of their higher status, made larger offerings to the king and at religious events.

There were also cases where Tai 'became' non-Tai. Akha folk history tells of one clan, the Akha Aker, formerly being Tai and then becoming Akha (Alting 1986, and in this volume). Izikowitz recorded that Black Tai neighbours of the Lamet had 'lower clans' that seem to be descended from non-Tai, usually Mon-Khmer-speaking Kha (Izikowitz 1951: 29). The nineteenth-century Thai poet, Sunthon Phu, tells of Thai fleeing their masters to live – presumably permanently – with Karen in Suphanburi (Sunthon Phu c.1839).

As among the Tai, latecomers to Kha societies were usually given lower social status. Among the Lolo (Yi), for example, only the highest class was 'really' Lolo. Second were the Pai-i, and the Wa-tzu, recently purchased and poorly-assimilated Chinese slaves who were 'less fully' Lolo (Yoshiro 1966). The Bahnar, a Mon-Khmer-speaking hill group in southern Vietnam, had four status levels: 'freemen', debtors, foreigners, and prisoners who are slaves (Guilleminet 1951–52: 513–15). This pattern, where full membership in Tai and Kha society belonged to the oldest members, pervaded the region well into the 1800s when the Bangkok élite were still buying slaves captured by K(h)ayah raiders.

Leach and others describe groups in upper Burma and southern China who call themselves Tai, but who are not native Tai-speakers. Leach writes that, 'many . . . Hkamti [Shan] would a century ago have been . . . [labelled] Singpho, Lisu, or Nung [that is, Kachin]' (Leach 1964: 40). Condominas cites references linking Kadai and Tai linguistically. These people had passed for Tai and were being called Tai by their neighbours until after World War II when Vietnamese anthropologists observed them speaking a non-Tai language at home (Condominas 1978: 108–9). A Chinese specialist on the Tai, Xie Yuan Zhan, mentions also that 'Tai Doi [or Loi]' (hill Tai) refers to members of groups like Bulang who have 'become Tai' (Xie 1989: 6–9). They were Tai Loi because they possessed 'civilized' attributes such as Buddhism or literacy. They sometimes also held political power, most likely based on their access to widely-sought forest produce such as pharmaceuticals, fragrant woods, spices, and minerals. Condominas, after seeing a Lua' (that is, Tai Doi) burial site southwest of Chiang Mai city, wrote that these Lua' had ruled their own states (Condominas 1974: 143–64). The subsequent discovery of hundreds of other Lua' burial sites, often marked by stone pillars and containing priceless Chinese and Tai porcelains and celadons, only strengthens this argument. A poetic account by a Persian embassy to Ayutthaya – prone, it must be said to literary hyperbole – in 1686 mentions a 'Lavand' (apparently Lua') ruler, who was so wealthy that it took two 'whole buffaloes to feed [his] birds each day' (O'Kane 1972: 156). These places must have been the Lua' *müang* referred to in the Ayutthayan chronicles (Chakraphatiphong 1964: 925–27).

Such references mean, of course, that terms like Tai and Kha were ultimately not racial or ethnic denotations. Rather, they were social indicators that identified groups differently from contemporary Western standards. By these traditional standards, Tai were mostly lowlanders where the flatlands facilitated padi agriculture. By contrast, Kha tended to live in the hills where the topography was more amenable to swiddening.

In the Tai-Kha world, since 'civility' was more important than ethnicity, Tai accounts seem confused in Western terms. Although many Tai knew that Karen differed from Lua' and other Kha, the difference seemed insignificant. When Tai met the two forest groups wearing red and white clothing and speaking languages unintelligible to them, they were seen simply as Kha (or Lua'). There are no central Thai and scarcely any Mon references to Karen as such before the nineteenth century.

Subjects of Tai States

The Tai looked on the most remote Kha as outside the ritual linking them with Tai states, and thus as 'wild' or 'untamed', like 'wild' Wa on the Burma-China border (cf. the 'Moïs indépendents' of Cambodia, as the French called them). 'Wild' Karen, *Kariang pa* (forest, that is, 'wild' Karen), were distinguished from *Kariang ban* (house/village Karen, that is, 'tame' Karen) who lived closer to *müang* centres.[7] Although the Thai may have considered 'untamed' folk as subjects in a general sense, the rulers of Chiang Mai and Bangkok were under no misconception that 'untamed' tribal peoples would provide taxes, tribute, or corvée labour for them in the same way as *Kariang ban*.

Kariang ban were among those groups who resided in Tai polities for so long that they were considered subjects. In Ayutthaya, after royalty, there were two main classes of Tai subjects: *phrai* (commoner, 'freeman'), and *that* (non-free, 'slave'). There were *phrai luang* who were subject directly to the king, and *phrai som* who were under lesser royalty or nobility. Generally, *phrai* fulfilled their obligation by corvée labour, serving in the king's army, and sometimes by making contributions in kind or tribute. The latter were called *phrai suai*. The word *phrai* shares many connotations with the word *tai* (see Turton, this volume). *Phrai luang* were much the same as *tai* of many Tai societies who distinguished themselves from Kha. Just as some Kha became *tai* (although sometimes taking generations), Karen and others subject to Ayutthaya, and later Bangkok, became *phrai*.

Before the fall of Ayutthaya, *Kariang ban* in Si Sawat, a regional centre in Kanchanaburi, paid annual *suai* of elephant tusks, cloth, and valuable woods (Phrachao Uthumphon 1972: 277). Because such forest produce was of value to the Thai courts, and royal traders, and because Karen lived on the kingdom's borders, Karen were well accepted by the Thai rulers. In some cases, Karen leaders, such as the head of Si Sawat who was almost certainly Karen, were named regional rulers in the Ayutthayan administrative structure. They went to regional centres such as Kanchanaburi to vow personal allegiance, just as did rulers of Tai-speaking areas. Karen girls were sometimes offered to royalty, both in Bangkok and in the northern states, as minor wives.[8] However, once Karen became well-integrated into Thai life, they had Tai (or Indic) names, making them indistinguishable from Tai in written records (Renard 1980: 19).

There were written agreements with both Lua' and *Kariang Ban* in the Lanna kingdom. Lua' in Chiang Mai and to the West in Mae Sariang received inscribed silver plates on which it was stated that the Lua' could stay in a certain area, receive the ruler's protection, and send tribute to the Chiang Mai court (Kraisri 1965; Krisana 1989). Karen on Doi Inthanon in Chiang Mai had paper books denoting such agreements (Renard 1980: 148–50).

By 1774, after the fall of Ayutthaya and the restoration of the capital at Thonburi, Thai leaders were in touch with the ruler of Si Sawat (ibid.: 69) about operations to forestall the Burmese. These and other Karen subjects served in the *Krom Atamat* (undercover/spy division). In the ensuing decades of battles with the Burmese, Karen rulers from Si Sawat and elsewhere received royal titles from the king, such as Phra Si Suwanakhiri (Lord of the Golden Mountain).

Some Karen seem to have entered Thai society as *that* (slave), but it is not known to what extent. Karen slaves were prisoners-of-war brought into the midst of Thai society, such as one group mentioned in 1806 as perhaps having been taken to Bangkok (Thailand Prime Minister's Office 1971: 32), or others resettled at about the same time near Wat Phrabat in Saraburi (Carpenter 1876: 13). In such situations, the Karen usually assimilated fully into Thai society, became Buddhist, learnt to read northern Thai or central Thai, and acquired other 'civilized' aspects of Thai culture. As this process was occurring, however, Thailand was itself made to accept the new 'civilized' values of the European West. As the very conceptual basis of Thai civilization changed, so too did the notion of what it meant to be Tai and Kha.

Thai Citizenship

Thailand came to be remade through Europe's power of suggestion, as well as by Thailand's resourceful monarchs in the late nineteenth century. As Thailand was recreating itself as a bureaucratic, capitalistic, liberal-progressive, nineteenth-century nation-state acceptable to the West, the concept of Thai state membership was remade. From the personal subject-hood of the early Bangkok period (and in the northern states), membership in the new bureaucratic nation-state Thailand was 'objectified'.

According to the liberalism so popular in nineteenth-century Europe, each race should have its own nation-state.[9] Old empires were being broken up as German, Italian, Irish, and other liberals sought a nation-state for their own 'race'. The Europeans coming to South East Asia felt each 'race' here needed its own nation-state (although some became colonies first). As such a nation, Thailand was to be ruled by law, with even its absolute monarch being subject to it. King Chulalongkorn accepted the idea of a limited monarchy while at the same time – partly because of the threat from Western imperialism – he came to wield more power than any previous Thai king. But rather than ruling absolute, as a *devaraja* (god king) with Hindu- and Buddhist-influenced codes as guides, King Chulalongkorn used his power to implement the rule of (modern Western-type) law (Engel 1975: 15–20).

These efforts set in motion a process that led to the elimination of the *phrai* system. King Chulalongkorn began this process just after being crowned, by eliminating the practice of prostrating before royalty. In 1874, he put into practice means by which all slaves in Thailand would be freed within twenty-one years. However, in the face of entrenched opposition, the king needed more than twenty-one years to carry out all his social reforms. To raise income for his many projects and to replace the income formerly earned by receiving tribute from *phrai suai* and tributary states, the King implemented a taxation system in 1873 with the establishment of the Revenue Office (after 1887, the Finance Ministry). With the increasingly capitalistic economy of Thailand replacing the traditional subsistence, tributary system, the government had to find new sources of income.

The King's efforts to eliminate forced labour began with the recruiting of *phrai* without masters to build a modern army. By doing so the King had access to a large body of manpower that would not directly threaten existing interests and thus enhanced his own power. Later he pushed through the 1888 Military Act that allowed *phrai* to become free after ten years of military service. But it was not until 1896 that the King abolished the *phrai* system altogether, substituting a head tax for forced labour. All former *phrai* (including *phrai suai*) were required to pay the new 6 baht annual head tax while being except from all corvée and *suai* obligations (this lasted until 1933, when income tax was instituted) (Kajorn 1976: 121–22).

To organize the people within the kingdom, the King set up means by which the country was divided into *monthon* (circles), provinces, districts, *tambon,* and villages. All citizens were registered as residents of a particular village. They elected headmen who in turn picked one of their own number to be the *kamnan*, head of the *tambon*. Talented local leaders were usually integrated into the new administration. For Karen on the borders of lowland society, the government usually had to make a special effort to reach them.

Despite these reforms, the threat of British or French intervention remained. Towards the end of the nineteenth century, King Mongkut and King Chulalongkorn had been integrating tributary states, such as Chiang Mai, Vientiane, and the southern Malay sultanates, to strengthen Thailand

and to enact the changes called for by the West, so that Thailand might escape being colonized. When, despite King Chulalongkorn's efforts, France seized what is now Laos in 1893 over a minor pretext, Thai leaders recognized the need fully to integrate the northern states. Even before this incident, boundaries were being surveyed on all of Thailand's borders. Since many border areas, such as almost the entire western border with Burma which was inhabited by Karen, were in non-Tai-speaking areas, the King became concerned with ways to integrate these peoples – as also the northern states – into the new Thai nation-state.

To do this, and reflecting the centuries-old non-ethnic Tai-Kha ritual relationships, King Chulalongkorn sought to bring all indigenous peoples, that is, all the peoples who had been subjects, whether as *phrai* or as slaves, whether they were Tai or Kha, into the Thai state. This included the wild forest groups, such as the *Kariang pa* and Semang ('Negrito', on the Malay peninsula), so as to strengthen the country's population and territory in which they lived.

Three years after the French accession of Laos, in 1896, the government set up the Royal Forest Department. The Department's purpose was to control the teak trade which had given rise to disputes between the rulers of the northern states, who controlled the forest, and the mainly British logging companies. Fearing that a logging dispute might result in the British annexing northern Thailand, the King asked a British Indian forester, Mr. H. Slade, to serve as the first Director-General. Slade was imbued with the teachings of German forestry popular in British India, which sought to exploit forests 'scientifically', that is, as effectively as possible. The German and British foresters came from a tradition where because villagers were excluded from forests (which, like parks, were royal preserves), farming never impinged on forests. The type of agriculture practised in the Thai hills was abhorrent to these foresters who were convinced that huge sums of money were lost every year when swiddeners burned the forest. A modern forester, Zinke, has shown to the contrary that soil loss and other degradation is minimal if shifting cultivation is practised carefully (Zinke 1978: 134–59), Slade, however, wanted to reforest the swiddens, exploit them commercially, and introduce permanent agriculture. Commercial logging dovetailed with European conceptions of the new world order, in which tribute and offerings were to be phased out. Logging the forest for profit was the direction in which Thailand was heading.

Such steps, however, brought the government into conflict with the uplanders who had been farming the hill forests for centuries, usually causing little damage to the forest. Nonetheless, forest policy followed the British lead, and the Royal Forest Department was to gain control over upland land use, thus impinging on hill-tribe practices. During the early twentieth century, however, forests were so extensive that when the Royal

Forest Department came into conflict with the Karen, they had ample forests into which to flee the government's reach. In any case, during the reign of King Chulalongkorn the Department had little authority outside teak forests where shifting cultivation was rare.

Recruiting Citizens

By 1899, the King's reforms were being implemented throughout central Thailand. The King and Prince Damrong – his brother and Minister of the Interior – sought to bring all the natives of Thailand into the new Thai state as citizens. The government's efforts to integrate Karen in Phetburi, Ratburi, and Kanchanaburi provinces into this state demonstrate a determination to treat Karen fairly and equally as Thai-speaking subjects. King Chulalongkorn was determined that the reforms would benefit the common people. In 1895, when he had begun extending his programme to Ratburi, he ordered a census and asked for reports on living conditions throughout the *Monthon*. He gave his officials new titles and ranks, and directed new headmen to rule justly.

Patterns of Integration in Central Thailand

The government's strong desire that Karen become citizens is shown in accounts by the Ratburi Commissioner, Phraya Woradet Sakdawut (Chek Charuchinda), who in 1900 and 1901 visited Pwo Karen areas of Kanchanaburi. He went to Kanchanaburi, up the Khwae Noi river to Sai Yok, and then to Ban Kuiyaplo, the Pwo village of 62 individuals, on 18 December 1990 (NA R5 M55/16, Prince Woradet 1901: 10). There Phraya Woradet arranged for the installation as headman of Luang Attsakhiri, whom the Karen had elected but the local governor had not installed. The governor promised to install other Karen headmen-designate.

Phraya Woradet then went to Wang Khan, near Sangkhlaburi. Si Sawat had declined in power, while Sangkhlaburi had grown because of its strategic location near the Three Pagodas Pass. There Phra Si Suwanna-khiri, the newly-appointed *Nai Amphoe* (District Officer) had organized the Karen build a police station which they gave to the government. Under the King's reforms, the *Krom Mon* (the Mon Department responsible for border matters on the central western border), in which Karen had assisted, had been incorporated into the new police department. Five Thai police had moved to Wang Kha from Ratburi to supervise police work where they were assisted by seven Karen; all twelve operating under the supervision of Phra Si Suwannakhiri. The Karen had also started building district office and a three-room rest-house which could also serve as a courthouse, all of which were to be handed over to the government (ibid.: 10).

In an effort aimed at building the population, which was a priority for the country, the King told the police to detain individuals entering the kingdom without passports and make them apply for Thai documents before moving on. Since, as Phra Si Suwannakhiri told Woradet, there were no slaves here, all the Karen were free, and newcomers could be sure of a good reception (NA R5 M55/16, Prince Woradet 1901: 10–12).

Phraya Woradet noted that Phra Si Suwannakhiri had many children, nephews and nieces, who could neither read nor write Thai. Woradet wanted to send them to the school in Ratburi, after which the brightest could attend the Royal Pages' School in the capital (ibid.: 10). Phra Si Suwannakhiri concurred, and at least one son reached the Royal Pages' School (Somchit Setaphan 1976; Somsak Setaphan 1977).

When Woradet explained to the people in another Karen village that King Chulalongkorn aimed to help all the kingdom's citizens, the residents showed their appreciation by staging a Karen dance. Woradet showed his position as a proponent of the modern, capitalist government by noting that the forests seemed a good place to plant teak, presumably commercially. Phra Si Suwannakhiri agreed to co-operate, although it seems the government did not follow up on the proposal (NA R5 M55/16 Report by Phraya Phichai Sunthon 1898: 18–19). Woradet next headed for Si Sawat where he found that the ruler, Phra Phichai Songkhram, had moved to a place called Si Loe which was down-river from Kanchanaburi. Most of the Karen had also left, resettling just East of Si Sawat at Na Suan. At Na Suan, Woradet met the Karen leader, Phra Phitakphonkhun, who had built a shelter and a jail. One Karen Buddhist monk who resided at Wat Na Suan, told that the Karen supported him well (NA R5 M55/16 Prince Woradet 1901: 10–12).

On 1 January 1901, Phraya Woradet launched another inspection tour, this time to Ratburi and Phetburi. Heading up the Phetburi river, he passed through several Pwo Karen settlements interspersed with those of Lao prisoners-of-war resettled after the Thai sacking of Vientiane in 1826. At Lin Chang, Woradet met Luang Si Raksa the *nai kong* in charge of the 100 Pwo Karen and 125 Lao in the village (ibid.: 19).[10]

Woradet became frustrated when he found several Pwo villages which had not yet selected a headman, and scolded the Phetburi governor, Phraya Surinruchai, for failing to select headmen or survey the Karen areas. Woradet reported that he had not done so himself because he wished the provincial authorities to do so.

Near the Ratburi border, at Ban Yanghak, though, Woradet did preside over the selection of Karen headmen. After the Pwo *nai kong*, Luang Wiset Sirirak, summoned the villagers, all agreed that Luang Wiset should be headman. Woradet, impressed by the village site, elevated it to *tambon* (sub-district) status and called a second meeting, this time inviting Karen from the six villages in the new sub-district. According to Chulalongkorn's plan, the headmen of these villages should have selected one of their own as *kamnan* (head of a *tambon*). Even though the other villages had not yet picked headmen, Woradet called for all villages to select the *kamnan*. The Karen unanimously chose Luang Wiset. Woradet and Wiset them collaborated on the delineation of the sub-district boundaries. Woradet directed Luang Wiset and his clerk to take a census of the people in the district and report on local conditions (ibid.).

A few days later, Woradet entered the Pwo village of Lampha, where he met a Pwo *Nai Kong* (village headman) named Luang Phithak Khirimat. King Chulalongkorn had some twenty years earlier given the Karen leader of the Suan Phung area, Sau Rau, the noble title of Luang Khirimat (*Luk Sua Chaoban Ban Bo*, 1976; Ra-oen Bunloet 1977). Two other Pwo Karen succeeded him, Sau Htau Di and Nai Wang Kha, and one of these two had served as the first *Nai Amphoe* (district officer) of Fang Tai District of Kanchanaburi (Ra-oen Bunloet 1977; Tri 1967: 159). One of the title-bearers Luang Phithak Khirimat had also served as the *Yokkrabat* (Inspector-General) of Kanchanaburi during the mid 1890s (NA R5 M2/22 Aram Khirirak and Phithak Khirimat: 6).

At the village of Suan Phung, Woradet met representatives of four villages. They consented to Luang Phithak chairing the meeting, and then selected headmen. The four headmen – Nai In Kariang, Nai Thuk, Nai Rit, and Nai Khechong – met privately and selected Luang Phithak to serve as *Kamnan* (sub-district headman). Sub-district boundaries were established and the headmen reported on conditions to Phraya Woradet. On his departure, Woradet returned to Ratburi.

Besides the selection of headmen, the new 6 baht head tax for able-bodied men – which only the richest Pwo could afford – also affected the Karen (NA R5 M2/22 Woradet 1900–01). Woradet must have realized this, but since the Karen were not required to pay the 6 baht until the elections, the censuses, and headmen reports had been completed, and they had officially become citizens, he did nothing. However, Woradet may well have discussed a suggestion to give the Karen tax relief with Prince Damrong.

On 3 January 1901, Damrong ordered the head tax for Karen and Mons to be reduced in Ratburi *Monthon*. Observing that Karen and Mon in the border areas 'resided in wilderness and made only a bare living', Damrong ordered that they be allowed to submit less than 'those living in areas of plenty', by paying only 2 baht per year in 81 localities, including Si Sawat, Sangkhlaburi, and Karen areas on the upper Phetburi river (*Ngoen Kha Ratchakan, PKPS* 18: 53–55). The richest Pwo areas visited by Woradet in and around Suan Phung did not, however, receive the dispensation and were expected to pay the 6 baht tax. Unlike most places listed by Damrong, Suan Phung produced ample padi rice, and Karen there lived on a par with many Thai.

Reductions of taxes on rice fields were also granted for areas outside Kanchanaburi, Ratburi, and Phetburi. In 1904, King Chulalongkorn observed that Thai officials were finding it difficult to survey Karen swidden fields near Mae Sot. The King set aside the standard taxation method and ruled that the Karen be taxed when they asked for permission to cut swiddens at a rate of 32 *at* per *rai* (*Prakat Yok Loek Kep Ngoen Kha Akon PKPS*1 19: 33). In 1919, during the reign of Chulalongkorn's son and successor King Vajiravudh, Pwo in Hat Siao district of Sukhothai Province were granted reductions to 2 baht (*Prakat Phraratchabannyat* 1919: 25).

Pwo Karen in central Thailand responded favourably to Thai overtures for fuller participation in the government. They selected headmen, reported on local conditions, and paid taxes as best they could. Some entered the Thai military and police, while others received Thai primary schooling, or military and police training. Several Pwo leaders found responsible positions in the Thai national administration. Though sometimes unfamiliar with the new system, the Karen tried to understand the changes the government was implementing. Thai leaders found many loyal citizens among the Pwo in Kanchanaburi, Ratburi, and Phetburi.

At the same time, there were Karen, often Sgaw, in remote areas that were not reached by Woradet or other officials. Even though many of them would have been willing to become Thai citizens, and despite the fact that King Chulalongkorn's government clearly wanted to increase its official population by bringing Karen into the system, they remained outside the Thai polity.

Patterns of Integration in Northern Thailand

The reforms which Karen in central Thailand had greeted so enthusias-tically were less well received in the North following the enactment of much the same measures for northern Thailand in 1900 and 1901. On 23 April 1900, King Chulalongkorn struck at the basis of the northern rulers' control of people by decreeing the end of the *phrai* system, by exempting able-bodied men in the North from corvée. The government substituted a 4 baht annual head tax, an amount less than that assessed in central Thailand, apparently because northern Thailand was less affluent than areas further South. The King stated that forest-dwellers and uplanders could, on a case-by-case basis, be taxed as an (extended) family unit, or at a lower rate; in keeping with the King's equal treatment of non-Tai-speaking groups, the proclamation made no mention of ethnic groups (*PKPS* 1900: 231–34). The King's decree abrogated *suai* payments but allowed poor individuals in some cases to perform government work for 20 days in lieu of the tax. In an accompanying legal regulation, the King enjoined local tax officials to take a census of all the peoples in the North as a basis for efficient tax administration.

Response to the new measures was mixed. Although some Karen, such as Kayah near Mae Hong Son and Pwo in Lamphun complied, others resisted (interviews with Kayah headmen Pho Thai, Tip, and Lu Moe). Despite Chulalongkorn's best intentions, abuses of the northerners continued. Though northern subjects appreciated the exemption from corvée, central Thai bureaucrats still called on northerners to work for the state, to build roads and bridges, and dig canals, without giving the compensation required by law, and, apparently, in excess of the 20 days legal maximum.

The principal political take-over in the North took place in 1900 with the 'Ministry of the Interior Order, being the regulations for the governing of Monthon Tawan Tok Chiang Nua [northwest circle]' (*PKPS Kot Senabodi* 1900). The Order reworked civil service positions, salaries, and responsibilities. Although the King employed some northern royalty in the civil service, many were not invited since the King wanted to open positions of responsibility only to the talented.

These reforms disappointed many Karen in the North. They had been loyal to the *Chao* in the same way Karen to the West of Bangkok had been loyal to Bangkok royalty. When the northern *Chao* lost power, many Karen felt betrayed. When central Thai officials tried to collect the tax, or enforce work requirements in lieu of paying the tax, they sometimes met resistance from uplanders who refused to pay (Prani 1963 vol.2: 350–51).

Karen recall that between 1900 and 1910 they and some Thai killed the first Nai Amphoe of Ping Tai (now Hot) District over taxation matters (Hamilton 1976: 34). Yet other northern Thai and Karen recall that they objected to the central Thai officials turning them into *that* (slaves) when they could not pay the tax, which was 4 baht in Tha Pha District of what is now Mae Chaem District of Chiang Mai. Karen and Thai there in 1980 told of local people having killed the Nai Amphoe some 70 years before, causing a Thai armed presence and the moving of the District seat to Chang Khoeng village.[11]

The largest outbreak of violence over alleged central Thai abuses in the North took place in 1902, when Shan miners and some Karen sympathizers near Phrae captured the town and murdered the Siamese commissioner and some other central Thai. A central Thai military expedition, skilful mediation by Westerners in Phrae, and the rebels' disorganization eventually led to the dissipation of the uprising, although scattered resistance continued for months.

Central Thai leaders, dismayed by the resentment their intervention had created, began hiring northern Thai to collect taxes after 1905. One such man was Chao Koson, a part-Karen *Chao* from Huai La. Chao Koson had inherited teak rights in Mae Sariang and entered the logging business, developing contracts with Pwo, Sgaw, and Kayah in Mae Hong Son and Lamphun provinces. He retired to Huai La in Lamphun. In return for often unremunerated Karen help with his logging work, Koson represented the Karen in dealings with the government. After Chao Koson became a tax collector for the central Thai, he further ingratiated himself with the Karen by negotiating a reduction of the tax to 2 baht. So popular was Chao Koson with the Karen, that he persuaded them to help rebuild the famous old Lamphun temple, Wat Phra Yun (Chao Mae Kham 1977; Griswold 1974: 72).

Actions by individuals like Chao Koson helped reduce tax burdens on Karen throughout the Chiang Mai area. In 1906, the padi tax in Doi Tao, in the South of Chiang Mai, an area almost entirely Karen, was lowered from 33 to 16 *at* (*PKPS* 21 *Prakat Ruang* 1907). Sensitive northern Thai played a crucial role in reducing friction between Karen and Siamese administrators who did not always appreciate northern traditions.

The longer central Thai rule in the North continued, however, the fewer opportunities Karen had to participate in government. From 1901, ceremonial contacts with the northern Thai royalty had been declining with the ending of Chiang Mai royal power. Some Sgaw Karen continued though, bringing cloth and forest produce to the last Chiang Mai rulers. As northern Thai royalty left the countryside for new opportunities in Chiang Mai, Karen-*Chao* contacts slid further. Very few *Chao* like Chao Koson stayed outside the major towns. One was the daughter of Chao Mahawong near Saraphi in Chiang Mai. She had once received annual offerings from the Karen, but as they withdrew from Thai life they were replaced by Thai villagers wearing rustic garb and black-faced to simulate Karen (Calavan 1976).

During the years following the 'Shan' rebellion, resentment between central Thai and the minorities simmered. Still, the central government maintained its wish to enlist the support of all the peoples of Thailand. When a police draft was extended to the North, no specific ethnic groups were excluded. Forest and upland peoples were exempted, but King Chulalongkorn sought competent minority group members for enlistment (*PKPS* 21 *Prakat Ruang* 1907: 331–37). By the end of King Chulalongkorn's reign in 1910, Karen near Thai areas were becoming Thai citizens. Government policy aimed at integrating those who had been *phrai, Kariang pa,* and even many across the border in Burma. This was applied to the areas West of Bangkok as well as in the North, where the remoteness of many Karen, as well as the alienation they felt as the *Chao* lost power, meant that the process proceeded more slowly.

King Vajiravudh, Thai Nationalism, and Karen

Into this situation came the new King, Vajiravudh. His stay in England from 1893 to 1903 where he studied at Sandhurst and Oxford, gave Vajiravudh an understanding of European attitudes, and evoked within him the commitment to build national strength. Admiring the sense of nation he found in Britain, he believed a 'national spirit' possessed by the country's citizens would enhance Thailand's strength. To translate the radically new concept of 'Thai race', the King needed an invented phrase, which he found in *chat Thai. Chat* was derived from *Jati*, Sanskrit for 'birth', and also 'caste' (Vella 1978: 177, 308n). The King believed that neither residence, nor birth in Thailand, nor naturalization made a person truly Thai. To Vajiravudh, a true Thai was loyal to *chat* (Thai race), *sasana* (religion), and *mahakasat* (king), a slogan adapted from the British slogan 'God and Country'. More specifically, he believed that a Thai knew and appreciated Thai language, art, history, religion (i.e. Buddhism), love of the King, and a warrior spirit [Vella 1978: 177–78]. King Vajiravudh believed education could build national unity. He was able to build on the existing National Plan of Education that had been adopted in 1902 on the model of Japan. King Chulalongkorn had admired the Japanese system which used education to instil national devotion to the Emperor in the people as a unifying national force (Vachara 1988: 95).

The King hoped that a Thai school system would integrate the Chinese and the other non-Thai-speaking groups. As the first Thai King to have believed in the primacy of ethnicity, Vajiravudh even saw the people of Chiang Mai and Lamphun as not quite Thai, but as people who had to be 'tamed' (*chuang*).[12] He reported this to his father following his visit there as Crown Prince in 1906, adding that schooling would 'tame' them. Education, he believed, would 'form their character and their thoughts while they are still young' (quoted in Vachara 1988: 96–97). The reason for such precautions coming when the threat of imperial invasion of Siam had declined (and all but disappeared by World War I), was the estimated 200,000–300,000 Chinese in the country (Skinner 1957: 193–95). Oriented towards China, having come to Thailand in order to remit money to relatives, the Chinese had remained mainly a-political in the nineteenth century. However, the increasing numbers of Chinese in Thailand, their growing affluence, and the overthrow of the Emperor ushering in the Chinese Republic in 1912, raised fears of Chinese militancy. Strikes and possible rebellion by the Chinese in Thailand now worried the King more than the chance of external invasion. In carrying over such fears of the Chinese and applying them to groups more akin to the central Thai, such as the people of Chiang Mai, Vajiravudh was the first Thai King to look at non-Thai-speakers as peoples apart from Thai-speakers. His acceptance of the nationalistic outlook led him to believe that ethnic groups had immutable cultural traits. This then allowed him to ignore the old Tai-Kha dichotomy, the distinction between people of the *müang* and of the *pa*, and the ritual language uniting them. The spirit of nationalism spread among government officials, most of whom then came from Bangkok and surrounding provinces. When they went to administer the North, they met unfamiliar peoples. The officials were unable to discern that there were old-timers like Karen and relative newcomers such as Hmong, Akha, Lisu, and Yao who had been migrating mainly since the late 1800s. As a result, Thai officials in the North who saw themselves as building a new Thai state along modern (European) lines, came to change the long-standing Tai-Kha dichotomy to a new Thai-alien dichotomy. Many believed that Karen were foreigners who had to be 'tamed'. Karen participation in anti-Thai revolts only strengthened the Thai conviction of Karen alienation.

Thailand's Nationality Act of 1913, in which citizenship was related primarily to being the child of a Thai father, reflects this nationalistic spirit. Even though citizenship was accorded to all persons born on Thai soil, the spirit of the Act was that citizenship is inherited from Thai parents.

Such attitudes changed Thai policy towards the Karen and other groups. Although the Karen and others were subject to the draft, taxation, and other obligations of Thai citizens, this too changed after conflicts between some hill peoples and officials. One group of Hmong and Yao grew angry over efforts to draft them, leading to their revolting in 1921. A Thai official recommended chasing them out of the country by burning the villages since they were not Thai. When higher authorities suggested that it would be more appropriate to leave them alone, they and other hill tribes not already enrolled as citizens came to be largely ignored. And such attitudes were made easier to maintain with the decline in strategic importance of Karen frontier areas and the reduced value of Karen goods for Thai royalty. Karen in the forests began to be seen as less important than the forests themselves. With the Forest Conservation Act of 1913, the Director-General of the Royal Forest Department gained authority over the use and gathering of produce in the forest.[13]Although it would be decades before their way of life was to be threatened, laws and attitudes dating from the 1910s provided the means. Although some Karen had been integrated into Thai life, and a number of these people's descendants now seem completely 'Thai', most Karen stayed in forests and other marginal areas and outside the Thai nation. Thus, when the last Phra Suwannakhiri died near the end of Vajiravudh's reign in 1923, the posting of a Thai to replace him in Sangkhlaburi symbolized the decline in Karen fortunes after the death of King Chulalongkorn.

Karen as Aliens in Thailand

When Karen either withdrew from or assimilated into the new Thai state, most Thai came to see Karen as similar to recent upland immigrants to Thailand. Although rural Thai near Karen settlements stayed on good terms with Karen for decades, younger generations of nationally-educated Thai in northern and central Thailand came to see Karen as a 'race apart'. In common with other *Chao Khao* Karen came to be seen as opium-using, potentially rebellious forest destroyers who were immoral, unclean, and backward. Even when a more sympathetic portrait of Karen was painted, such as the famous Thai epic *phu chana sip thit* (Victor of the Ten Directions), Karen are shown to be a fantastic blend of Ayutthayan romance, Western medievalism, and rural curiosity. More typical, but not less erroneous, was the 1950s film *daen Kariang* (Karen Frontier), in which the Karen are shown as notorious opium-smuggling brigands.

That Karen and other Kha could be so misconstrued represents a perversion of the nationalist process. By the forced adoption of nationalism, itself alien to Thailand, Thai leaders embraced the idea of *chat Thai* so fully that most have forgotten the Tai-Kha, *müang*-forest tradition. Instead, as noted by anthropologist Lief Jonnson, Thai nationalists have so enlarged the *müang* that it has enveloped the forest, making the Karen aliens on their own land. Thai nationalists, having adopted a non-Tai ideology (admittedly under duress), implemented it in a non-Tai way resulting in a 'hill tribe problem' whereby these people took on the identity of 'non-Thai', and have often been severely disadvantaged. With their position marginalized, Karen now face being declared aliens in a land they have inhabited for centuries, lack of rights over forest they once protected (and are now wrongly blamed for destroying), lack of access to their own land, and to the school system intended to assimilate them, and the mistaken idea that they engage in illegal narcotics marketing. King Chulalongkorn would surely find their plight appalling, all the more so because of the lack of alternatives in this non-Tai Thai nation.

Notes

1 In this paper, Tai refers to such groups as Thai, Lao, Shan, Lue, and Ahom. Thai refers to both Tai living in Thailand and members of other linguistic groups who have become Thai subjects or citizens.

2 Usually meaning 'city', the term refers to a political entity at least nominally independent and spatially contiguous. The smallest *müang* might number only a few villages, the largest comprise an entire country. Thailand can thus be called Muang Thai.

3 Now known as Lamphun, 25 kilometres southeast of Chiang Mai.

4 Lua' is today defined as a Mon-Khmer dialect and the term refers to the people who speak the dialect. Prior to the nineteenth century, however, the term had a much broader meaning, referring in general to rural Mon-Khmer, and sometimes other linguistic groups in what is now Thailand and Upper Burma [see Tanabe, this volume Ed.].

5 Non-Buddhist Tai, such as the Black Tai, rule *müang* and otherwise live like Buddhist Tai. They do not live in small groups like Karen or Lua'.
6 Sgaw Karen refer to Lua' and Wa as 'Kawoe', that is, Kha Wa. References cited below to the Kha Wa indicate that in the past it was not just Karen who used this term.
7 Kariang is the Thai term for Karen, that is, Kha Yang.
8 Sometimes they were seized. Karen in Chiang Mai tell stories of attractive girls hiding from visiting Thai princes, and of girls committing suicide to avoid being taken. Yet others went through with it, both willingly and unwillingly.
9 Derived from the Latin *natio*, meaning 'race', itself derived from *nasci*, 'to be born'.
10 An official government position in charge of a small segment of the population.
11 The two accounts may in fact represent the same story, distorted by frequent telling.
12 *Chuang* means to tame, and is conventionally used when training animals.
13 Forest is 'land on which no royal permission has been given to issue a title deed for anyone to reside or engage in agriculture'.

References

Abbreviations:

NA   Thailand National Archives
PKPS   Prachum Kotmai Pracham Sok (Collected Laws, Listed Chronologically) Bangkok, 1935–53, edited by Sathian Lailat.

Alting von Geusau, Leo (1986), Personal conversation.
Calavan, Sharon Kay. Interviewed 1976. Anthropologist who conducted field research in Saraphi.
Carpenter, C.H. (1876), 'A tour among the Karens of Siam', *Baptist Missionary Magazine*, 53, 9–16.
Chakraphatiphong, Phra (Chak) (1964), 'Phraratchaphongsawadan Krung Si Ayut-thaya' (Royal Chronicle of Ayutthaya), in *Phraratchaphongsawadan Krung Si Ayutthaya Chabap Phan Chanthanumat (Choem) kap Phra Chakraphatiphong (Chak)* (The Phan Chanthanumat (Choem) and the Phra Chakraphatiphong (Chak) recensions of the Royal Chronicle of Ayutthaya, Bangkok: Khlang Withaya, ca. early nineteenth century, 1–592.
Chao Mae Kham. Interviewed 1977. Widow of Chao Koson.
Condominas, Georges (1974), 'Notes sur l'histoire lawa à propos d'un lieu-dit lua' [Lawa] en pays karen' (Amphoe Chom Thong, Changwat Chiengmai) en Thailand, in Thai Fine Arts Department, *Art and Archaeology in Thailand*, Bangkok: Fine Arts Department, 143–64.
—— (1976), 'Essai sur l'évolution des systèmes politiques thais', In his, *L'Espace social à propos de l'Asie du Sud-Est*, Paris: Flammarion, 259–316.
Engel, David (1975), *Law and Kingship in Thailand during the Reign of King Chulalongkorn*, Ann Arbor: University of Michigan Centre for South and Southeast Asian Studies, Paper no.9.
Griswold, A. D. (1975), *Wat Pra Yun Reconsidered*, Bangkok: Siam Society.
Guilleminat, Paul (1951–52), 'La tribu Bahnar du Kontum', *Bulletin de l'Ecole Française d'Extrême-Orient*, 45, 393–561.
Hamilton, James W. (1976), *Pwo Karen: at the edge of mountain and plain*, St. Paul.
Izikowitz, Karl (1951), *Lamet: hill peasants in French Indochina*, Göteborg: Etnografiska Museet, (Etnografiska Studier 17).

Kajorn Sukpanich (1976), 'The freeman status', Chatpridi Chattrabhuti, (trans.), *Social Science Review*, 95–122.

Kayah, elder (1977), Headman of Huai Phung village, Muang District, Mae Hong Son Province.

Kraisri Nimmanamaehinda (1965), 'An Inscribed Silver-Plate Grant to the Lawa of Bo Luang', in *Felicitation volumes of South-east Asian Studies presented to His Highness Prince Dhaninivat Kromamun Bidyalaph Bridhayakorn*. 2, Bangkok: Siam Society.

Krisana Charoenwong (1989), *Khwamsamphan Rawang Klumchon Lua Kap Chao Phuchrong Nakhon Chiang Mai* (Relations between the Lua' and the Ruler of Chiang Mai), Bangkok: Payap University Research and Development Centre, Research Report no.49.

Leach, E. R. (1964,) *Political Systems of Highland Burma*, Boston: Beacon.

Lu Moe (1976), Karen elder in Huai La village, Ban Hong District, Lamphun province.

Luk Sua Chaoban Bo (Ban Bo Village Scouts) (1976), Ban Bo: n.p.

NA R5 M2/14, 'Report by Phraya Phichai Sunthon', 15 November 1898, 18–19.

NA R5 M2/22, 'Aram Khirirak and Phithak Khirimat to Sommot Amaraphan'.

NA R5 M55/16, Prince Woradet Sakdawut, *Raingan Chatkanpokrong Huamuang Ratburi Lae Kanchanaburi* (Report on Governing the Provinces of Ratburi and Kanchanaburi), 24 March 1901.

O'Kane, John (1972), *The Ship of Sulaiman*, New York: Columbia, (ca.1686).

Phao Thao Tip (1977), Karen elder in San Pa Tong District, Chiang Mai Province.

Phothirangsi (1973), *Khamplae Chamathewiwong Phongsawadan Muang Hariphunchai* (Translation of the Chamathewiwong, the Chronicle of Hariphunchai), Bangkok: Rungwatana.

PKPS 17, *Khobangkhap Kankep Ngoen Akon Kha Thidin Monthon Tawantok Chiangnua* (Regulation on Collecting head and Land Taxes in the Northwestern monthon), 2 May 1900, Bangkok, 1935–53, 319–26.

—— *Kot Senabodi Krasuang Mahatthai Pen Khobangkhap Samrap Pokkhrong Monthon Tawantok Chiangnua* (Ministerial Regulation Regarding the Administration of the Northwest Monthon), 16 July 1900, Bangkok, 1935–53, 389–427.

—— *Prhraratchabannyat Kankep Ngoen Kha Raeng Thaen Ken Monthon Tawantok Chiangnua* (Royal Act on Collecting Silver Instead of Corvée Labour in the Northwestern Monthon), 1900, Bangkok, 1935–53.

PKPS 18, *Ngoen Kha Ratchakan Khun Muang Lae Phrai Luang* (Government Tax on Khun Muang and Phrai Luang), 1901, Bangkok, 1935–53, 53–5.

PKPS 19, *Ruang Kep Ngoen Kha Akon Somphak Law Akon Khana Kae Phuak Kariang Soeng Tang Tham Rai Yu Ban Khao Nai Amphoe Mae Sot Khwaeng Muang Tak Plian Pen Withi Anuyat Fan Rai* (On the Subject of Changing the Method of Revenue Collection from Karen permanent swiddeners in Ban Khao, Mae Sot District, Tak Province to the method used for shifting swiddeners), 30 August 1904, Bangkok, 1935–53, 53–5.

PKPS 20, *Prakat Nai Lot Yon Kankep Khana Nai Tambon Khwaen Doi Tao, Khwaen Umkoi, Khwaen Muang Tun Longkhon Kep Tae Piang Rai La at At* (Announcement Reducing the Tax Rate in Doi Tao, will be reduced to only 16 *at* District, Omkoi District, Muang Tun, to only 15 *at* per *rai*), 1906, Bangkok, 1935–53.

PKPS 21, *Prakat Ruang Kanriak Khon Pen Tamruat Phuthon Nai Monthon Phayap Monthon, Udon Monthon, Isan Monthon Petchabun, Monthon Pattani, Monthon Nakhon Si Thammarat, monthon Chumphon Phuket* (Announcement on the Police Draft in Phayap Monthon, Udon Monthon, Isan Monthon, Petchabun Monthon, Pattani Monthon, Nakhon Si Thammarat Monthon, Chumphon Phuket Monthon), 1907, Bangkok, 1935–53.

Prakat Phraratchabannyat lae Phraratchakamnot Ratchakan Thi 6, 1919, Bangkok: Nugoolkakit.

Prani Sirithon Na Phattalung, *Phet Lanna* (Northern Thai Jewels) (Chiang Mai: Suriwong), 2 vols.

Ra-oen Bunloet. Interviewed 1977. Former Pwo Karen *Kamnan*, resident of Ban Bo, Suan Phung Sub-district, Ratburi (son-in-law of Luang Phithak Khirimat).

Renard, Ronald D. (1980), 'The role of the Karens in Thai society during the early Bangkok period, 1782–1873', *Contributions to Asian Studies*, 15, 15–28.

——— (1988), 'Minorities in Burmese history', in Silva, et al., *Ethnic Conflict in Buddhist Societies: Sir Lanka, Thailand and Burma*, London: Pinter, 77–91.

Shiratori, Yoshiro (1966), 'Ethnic configurations in southern China', *Monumenta Nipponica Monographs*, no.25 (Folk Cultures of Japan and East Asia).

Skinner, G. William (1956), *Chinese Society in Thailand: an analytical study*, Ithaca: Cornell University Press.

Somchit Setaphan. Interviewed 1976. Son of Somsak Setaphan.

Somsak Setaphan. Interviewed 1977. Son of Phra Si Suwannakhiri.

Sunthon Phu (1967), *Nirat Suphan* (Poetic Account of a Trip to Suphanburi, Bangkok: Fine Arts Department.

Thailand, Prime Minister's Office (1971), 'Message to Chiang Mai Accompanying the Presentation of a Royal Title to the Chao Chiang Mai', in *Ruang Tang Chao Prathetsarat Krung Ratanakosin Ratchakan Thi 1* (Accounts of Establishing Tributary States during the Reign of King Rama I), Bangkok: Prime Minister's Office.

Tri Amatyakul (1967), *Phutthasankhati Lae Ruam Ruang Muang Kanchanaburi*, (Buddhist Writings and Collected Accounts of Kanchanaburi), Bangkok: Cremation Volume.

Uthumphon, Phrachao (1972), *Kham Hai Kan Chao Krung Kao* (Testimony on the people of the Old Capital [Ayutthaya]), *Kham Hai Kan Chao Krung Kao, Kham Hai Kan Khun Luang Ha Wat, Lae Phraratchaphongsawadan Krung Kao Chabap Luang Prasoet Akson* (Testimony on the People of the Old Capital [Ayutthaya], Testimony on the *Khun Luang* [Prince] Who Sought the Monastery, and the Luang Prasoet Recension of the Royal Chronicle of Ayutthaya), Bangkok: Khlang Withaya. *Kham Hai Kan Chao Krung Kao*, ca.1778.

Vella, Walter (1978), *Chaiyo! King Vajiravudh and the Development of Thai nationalism*, Honolulu: University of Hawaii Press.

Xie Yuan Zhang (1989), 'Tai names', in *Thai-Yunnan project Newsletter* 5 June, 6–7.

Zinke, Paul, et al. (1978), 'Soil fertility aspects of the Lua' forest fallow system of shifting cultivation', in Peter Kunstadter, et al., *Farmers in the Forest: economic development and marginal agriculture in northern Thailand*, Honolulu: East-West Centre, 134–59.

Chapter Four

Ritual Relations and Identity: Hmong and Others

Nicholas Tapp

Cultural Unification

Reynolds (1992) has recently suggested the potential for 'local history' in Thailand to provide a challenge to 'the conclusions of the general history of the centre', and I should like to locate the following analysis of ritual forms among an ethnic minority within the context of such a potential. Increasingly, 'strong arguments against the idea of a unitary, essential "Thai" culture and the presupposition of fundamental cultural axioms or principles' (Turton 1991: 1) have led to a concern with the construction of national identity out of diverse representations as a process requiring investigation. Clearly such a process of national construction is at once 'mental' as it is 'material', and involves aspects of both practice and representation. Much of the interest of studies of Northern Thai society lies in their capacity to illuminate a process of state formation through the incorporation of local practices and traditions.

Keyes' (1971) examination of the significance of millenarian activities among ethnic minorities in Northern Thailand as a response to the growing centralization of the Sangha and its suppression of local traditions showed that local identity was not merely a matter of ethnic difference where the imposition of national authority threatened traditional autonomies. At the same time, the investigation of ritual in Northern Thailand made it clear that Yuan (Khon Müang) identity itself (in North Thailand) was not reducible to any simple cultural essence, but was composed of a complex variety of inter-weaving strands (Davis 1984). The annual rituals at which the rulers of Tai states propitiated Lua' spirits as aboriginal holders of the land, or in which their conversion to a non-cannibal Buddhism was celebrated, pointed to a long historical process of the absorption and assimilation of non-Tai ethnic groups into Tai political structures [see especially Tanabe in this volume Ed.]. Similar relations were replicated in other Tai states, whose founding legends often pointed to the influence of other ethnic groups. This 'apparently irreversible expansion of Tai-ization of the non-Tai groups' led to historical speculation about the existence of Austroasiatic states in the region before the Indianized civilizations of Angkor and Pagan, and the transformation thereby of inter-ethnic relations into relations of class (Condominas 1990). Meanwhile the work on domestic spirit-cults in Northern Thailand showed that ancestral possessing spirits, like the spirits of professional mediums, could be of Mon or Burmese origin, while also involving the spirits of other ethnic groups.[1]

The concern here is not with the probable non-Tai ancestry of present-day Thai citizens or the establishment of great Austroasiatic kingdoms in the region prior to 'Tai-ization', but with processes of the construction of national identity and the role of ritual in these constructions.

Cultural unification presupposes the formation of a discursive ideology which establishes a coherence out of that 'unsystematicness' which it has been suggested is the normal condition of popular knowledge (Turton 1991: 157). The seamless web of Thai national identity is in fact a tangled skein of local identities interacting with one another in the context of the formation of the nation-state.

It has been these interests which have led to the increasing dissatisfaction with cultural essentialist theorems in Thai studies and a growing concern with the peripheral areas of the Thai state where ethnic minorities are located. It is unfortunate, then, that much of the research on Thai ethnic minorities in the past has tended to reify the cultural essences of ethnic minority identity and replicate the same cultural essentialist paradigms whose shortcomings had largely led to the need for such studies. It was Lehman (1979) who first drew attention to this problem among the Karen (cf. Keyes 1976). But it has been the case that most ethnographers of ethnic minorities in Thailand have emphasised their cultural distinctiveness and ethnic particularity in an artificial isolation which has disguised both their practical interconnectedness with neighbouring groups and the extent of their common histories, backgrounds, orientations, or features with other groups including the Thai.

The problem of cultural essentialism was raised by Moerman in an early debate regarding a Tai minority, the Tai Lue of Northern Thailand and the Indochinese periphery (Moerman 1965; 1968; Naroll 1964; 1968). Moerman's (1968) point was that the Lue themselves 'seem to be . . . cultural relativists' in the timeless and discrete way they categorized their relations with and differences from neighbouring ethnic groups. It was all too easy for ethnographers specializing on the societies of particular ethnic groups and working within their own paradigms of cultural relativism to replicate these essentially folk notions of identity and thereby lend them a spurious validity.

It has become common to criticise the artificial isolation attributed to the societies of 'tribal' minorities as an aspect of the colonial necessity to divide and rule. In retrospect, both the academic tendency to isolate specific 'cultural units' for study, and the deep implication of this process in the requirements of colonial administration, were clearly apparent in Leach's (1954) work on the Kachin of Burma despite its specific reference to broader political systems. Tanaka (1991) aptly remarks with reference to Indian ethnography that the structuralist enterprise merely succeeded in elevating the holistic methodology of culture of an earlier functionalism onto an ideal plane. Similarly, Leach can be seen as having dealt with the complexities of local situations in highland Burma by simply transposing culturally reified notions of 'Kachin' and 'Shan' onto an idealized plane. The fluid passage of groups and individuals across these reified ethnic boundaries which so concerned later regional ethnographers was then made to appear paradoxical in terms of a mode of analysis which continued to reify cultural essences, albeit at an ideal level. The needs of specialized academic study, then, coincided rather too perfectly with the requirements of neo-colonial control and nationalist expansion into the peripheral areas of South East Asia.

Tambiah's work on the Buddhist 'saints of the forest' (1984) was particularly important in showing how, within a Buddhist cultural tradition, centralized moral authority is constantly authenticated through incorporating the charismatic power of the forest-saints of the periphery derived from their conquest and assimilation of the wild forest world and its fierce animals. A similar appeal to the power of the wild can be seen in the incorporation of aboriginal spirits into Tai territorial rituals. The importance of the forest-saint in both representing and subduing an amoral and contingent sphere of erratic spirits, dangerous beasts, and subversive ethnic minorities, is shown in the current appeal of movements such as the Dhamanaat Foundation to precisely these images. The processes which Tambiah describes may be seen as exemplifying the dependence of the centre on its own peripheries, and the ritual recognition of this.

This is essentially a process of incorporation and assimilation of forces and elements felt to be beyond the confines of Thai society. The continuing nature of this process, and its contribution to the constitution of forms of national cultural identity through the absorption of local variations, has brought the role of the peripheries in the constitution of a centre into increasing prominence.

The question of cultural variation, related to the transmission of traditional forms of knowledge, within what Terwiel (1992: 133) has recently referred to as a 'pan-Tai cultural complex', is inherent in the study of sub-ethnic Tai groups within Thailand, and even more so in the study of Tai or Tai-related groups, such as the Zhuang of China, beyond the frontiers of the Thai nation-state and in situations where they are or have become ethnic minority groups. These questions of relation and comparison have not so far confronted researchers on the non-Tai ethnic minorities in Thailand, where cultural identity has seemed relatively unproblematically differentiated in terms of clear-cut contrasts with neighbouring groups and particularly with the majority Thai.

The Hmong for example, have been generally presented as a group whose segmentary tribal organization presents an inherent challenge to the authority of the state, whose traditional practice of shifting cultivation clearly demarcates them as an ethnic group from the practitioners of irrigated cultivation, and who are particularly remarkable for their strong sense of cultural homogeneity, defined by a series of clear contrasts with that of the Chinese, and maintained over extraordinary spatial distances and lengths of historical time. The model conforms closely to the actual model presented by themselves of themselves in South East Asia. Yet in the light of comparative research on the great variety of Hmong and related groups in China, this model requires serious modification.

It has been clear for some time that the Hmong have practised irrigated rice cultivation wherever practicable, and that a variety of subsistence crops such as maize and buckwheat have been grown by different Hmong groups at different times under different ecological circumstances. In Sichuan I have worked in a wet-rice and maize cultivating area where permanent villages had been settled by the Hmong for several hundreds of years. Regarding the question of cultural homogeneity, although there is a strong sense of Hmong ethnic unity among Hmong groups in China, the clear coincidence of colour-coded cultural division with linguistic differences and patterns of costume, housing-structure, and custom which one finds between the 'White' and 'Green' Hmong in South East Asia is not replicated in China. There a much greater variety of dialects and local cultural distinctions has existed between different Hmong groups, and the identity of other groups who refer to themselves as 'Hmu' or 'Hmo' also has to be taken into account.

It may therefore be more valid to view the Hmong as a peasant farming population, a part of whom were broken off owing to the expansion of the Han population and dispersed into inaccessible settlements at high altitudes where, by comparison with their lowland neighbours, they took on an artificial appearance of segmentary solidarity and autonomy (Tapp 1990). In comparison with the dramatic processes of cultural variegation and reunification which appear to have taken place among Hmong populations in China, South East Asia might be seen as a kind of cultural 'relic area' – for the Hmong at least, whose culture in South East Asia seems not to have undergone the rapid transformations characteristic of China. The need not to indulge in paradigms of cultural essentialism thus leads away from models of historical continuity towards an emphasis on historical disjunctures and discontinuities.

Having set the context for a problematic concerning the constitution of ethnic minority identities, it is now possible to raise the question of whether the incorporation of for example Lua' spirits into Tai rituals can in any way be compared with the incorporation of Chinese spirits into Hmong, particularly shamanic, rituals. Both reflect historical processes of conquest, domination, and assimilation which we can associate in the one case with Buddhicization, in the other with the Sinicization of the Hmong.

Views of Ritual

The way in which these sorts of ritual incorporation are analysed must depend on our view of ritual. We might say that these rituals represent the ingestion of alien power in a way that is generatively transformative of ethnic relations and constitutive of cultural boundaries. Yet there is a conceptual problem to do with the adoption of dominant modes of ritual discourse by minority or disadvantaged groups (as in the adoption of central religio-political cosmological designs by millennial Buddhist cults challenging the power of the centre, or in the use of symbols of Chinese sovereignty by Hmong messianic movements similarly directed against the imperial bureaucratic state). Is this to be seen as a genuinely subversive attempt to appropriate the symbols of a dominant cultural discourse, or as the replication of imposed beliefs and values, the continuous subsumption of forms of local knowledge into a universalizing and homogenous discourse?

Bloch's (1992) analysis of ritual in terms of 'rebounding violence' concludes like functionalist theories that the full tripartite structure of ritual ultimately legitimates domination and violence, but he has achieved this conclusion (from which he exempts millenarianism) through an over-rigorous separation of ritual from practical knowledge. The endeavour to demonstrate that the central point of ritual is the 'creation of the ordered transcendental by devaluation of the value of human experience and action' (1986) has arisen out of the difficulties he has experienced in accounting for the apparent plasticity of ritual functions in comparison to the similarity of their forms. The same problem confronts the analysis of Hmong messianic movements, whose long span and repetition of apparently similar forms contrasts with the very different historical circumstances under which they have occurred. Bloch's solution to this problem, that since rituals combine the properties of actions and statements (so that functionalist and structuralist explanations are alike inadequate) 'the ritual can legitimate any authority', is notably unsatisfactory. At the same time, Bloch's call for more historically situated analyses of ritual (1986) and descriptions of the consumption of external vitality in ritual (1992) are important, as is his argument about millenarianism which we shall consider below.

Turner's (1969) emphasis on the liminal phase of rituals and their 'ludic' aspects is still crucial I think, both in clarifying Bloch's own emphasis on the refusal of the second phase of rebounding violence characteristic of millenarian movements and in leading towards a more creative and generative view of rituals as *playing* with external boundaries and differentiations.[2] In a recent collection Ananda Rajah reminds us of Richard Davis' use of *paidia*, 'the playful emphasis of spontaneity, uncontrolled fantasy, and carefree gaiety' which Davis contrasted in myth to the need for order found in ritual (Davis 1984; Rajah 1992). While the distinction Davis drew (and Bloch, 1992, also draws) between myth and ritual in this sense may not be tenable, the contrast between order and play and, I would say, the location of ritual at the nexus of order, play, and chaos, is important to the discussion of Hmong rituals below.

Appropriations of Power

Millenarian movements, which generally create their own rituals, can only be treated as 'ritual' in the very broadest sense, which is why Bloch and others are forced to treat them separately from other 'ritual' activities. Both myth and ritual can here be seen as part of a wider cultural discourse involving fundamental notions of identity, difference, distinction, and transformation. The legends which implicate Mon and Lua' in the founding of Tai kingdoms are myths of origin in a political sense, as the rituals which represent the subjugation of the Lua' or their Buddhicization in forms of physical possession also announce. Legends which depict the saviour of the Hmong as a Chinese sovereign and employ the idioms of Chinese distinction to express his power are importantly implicated, through dream, vision, and spirit-writing, in the messianic uprisings of the Hmong against established forms of political authority, while their own myths of origin are recounted and enacted at rituals for the deceased.

The actual myths of origin which we find among ethnic groups of the region strikingly illustrate a theme of common origin with the members of other ethnic groups. These origin myths, like the widespread stories of the origins of literacy, simultaneously account for the origins of ethnic differentiation, but it is important that differentiation is expressed within the terms of a common (cultural) system.

This can be seen particularly clearly in the case of the Chinese system of geomancy (*feng shui*) used by the Hmong, which they share with the Han Chinese, Yao, Lisu, Lahu, and many other ethnic minority groups of the region, as a common system for the articulation of differences, importantly related to the cult of patrilineal ancestors and the system of burial (Tapp 1989). *Feng shui* acts as an incorporating system of cultural discourse in which differentiations and oppositions can be articulated, and it is significant that messianic myths should be phrased in terms of this system. In this respect, as a ritual system of distinction legitimating an imperial state power, although of course without any institutional establishment, it may be compared to Theravada Buddhism as a cosmological design which can also be appropriated by local and peripheral interests.

Since ritual is fundamental to the construction of cultural identities, the constitution of cultural identity may also be partly demonstrated through the analysis of rituals. It needs to be emphasized, though, that the constitution of identities is a continuous process and that whatever part rituals may play in this process, it is a *present-day* one; that is, although in theory it is possible to 'read' ritual incorporations as illustrating historical processes of domination and subordination, we cannot expect to arrive at an understanding of the *historical* process of formation of cultural identities through an analysis of current ritual, but should be concerned with the present-day processes of domination and subordination, incorporation and appropriation, which actually take place and may be accomplished through the medium of the rituals themselves. So there is a clear need to investigate the nature of these ritual incorporations and adoptions more carefully than has been done in the past, in order to see how the discourse of local, ethnic, regional, and national identity is actually, literally, and currently rather than historically constituted.

Explanations of the legions of Taoist spirit-soldiers invoked by the Hmong shaman, or his recourse to Chinese chants, either in purely historical terms of the Chinese influences upon the Hmong, or in terms of the mystifying effects of the use of unintelligible languages as in Pali or Latin rituals, are inadequate to illuminate the significance of the phenomenon in the construction of cultural identities and the constitution of discourse.

The sort of questions we have to deal with are, therefore, whether the control of 'Chinese' spirits by the Hmong shaman represents the permeation of Hmong shamanic practices by Sinitic values and ethics, or an attempt to internalize or subvert the power and might of a sovereign state by a minority group appropriating the discourse appropriate to that state; and whether the subjugation of Wa spirits expressed in certain Tai rituals represents an incontestable process of Tai-icization, or whether such rituals in some way express an appeal for legitimacy and support to the members of dispossessed and excluded groups. It is clear that the mechanisms of displacement and condensation, suppression, and sublimation, which Freud (1974) described so well for the dream-work, are powerfully at work in these rituals, and that their interpretation depends on an understanding of these processes of censorship.

Hmong Messianism

The messianic cults which have periodically united sections of the Hmong in armed confrontation with the representatives of state authority perfectly illustrate the stability of form which Bloch contrasts to the plasticity of functions with regard to Merina rituals. Chinese chronicles refer to and record instances of 'Miao' rebellions over a period of some 2,000 years, since the legendary defeat of the Miao leader, Ch'ih-yu, by the Yellow Emperor Huang Di, the founder of the Chinese state. However, the term 'Miao' was used extremely loosely to refer to a variety of southwestern minority groups, even after 1200 AD which Ruey Yih-Fu (1962) identifies as the beginning of the 'modern' historical period of the 'Miao', and here the dangers of cultural essentialism in producing continuist histories become apparent. The great Miao rebellions of the eighteenth and nineteenth centuries which convulsed areas of Guizhou and Hunan, on the other hand, almost certainly involved Hmong as well as other groups and adopted a messianic form in which the advent of a *Miao Wang* (Miao King) promised salvation and liberation from oppression (Lemoine 1972). From the initiation of Protestant Christian missionary work among the Hmong of northeast Yunnan at the turn of the century, the Hmong messianic movements reported until the present day in China, Laos, Vietnam, and Thailand, have been of two forms. In one, Hmong individuals prophesying the return of the Messiah have identified with Biblical characters such as Christ, Mary, and the Holy Trinity, in a form of hypostatic possession; in the other the prophet has been possessed by the spirit of the legendary Hmong *Huab Tais* (Huang Di) or Emperor, and the movement has adopted a more nativistic form.

A very approximate periodization, then, would distinguish traditional rebellions from those which occurred after the administrative measures introduced into Guizhou in 1413, which adopted a messianic form; and both of these from those which began to occur in the period of modern colonialization and the introduction of Christianity. A more specific periodization of the modern movements would distinguish between pre-colonial, colonial, and post-colonial movements. Whether one agrees with Bloch that it is the *functions* of these rituals which will have varied under changing political and social systems or would see the meaning and analyses of these phenomena as requiring different interpretations in varying historical contexts, one is nevertheless still confronted by the apparent paradoxicality of their similarity (I would not say stability) of form, particularly the similarity of ritual symbols and discourse mobilized by and appealed to by these modern movements.

The similarities between the actions and accounts of major messianic prophets such as Yaj Soob Lwj who led the messianic movement among the refugees in Laos from 1967 (Lemoine 1972; Chia Koua Vang et. al. 1990), Paj Cai (Pachay) who led the 1918 revolt against French colonial authority (Savina 1930; Allton 1978; Yaj 1972), and the rebellion of Sung Choen-Tien in Vietnam in 1860 (De La Jonquière 1906) are remarkable. The most prominent formal similarity of modern Hmong messianic movements, however, has been the significance accorded by them to revelations of a mystic writing. The significance of a specifically Hmong form of writing is also apparent in messianic cults which have adopted a more conventionally Christian form, where missionary scriptures or romanized orthographies have been taken to represent the mystic script, but is particularly evident in the more indigenous movements in which prophets have been inspired by the *Huab Tais*. In these movements the prophet typically bases his claim to legitimacy on a visionary revelation of the sacred script which assures his followers of 'invulnerability'.[3] In the case of the recent Yaj Soob Lwj movement these claims have been rationally manifested in the form of a highly effective and unique orthography.[4]

Equally remarkable as a defining feature of modern Hmong messianic movements has been the characteristically Chinese idiom of geomantic divination in which legends of the Hmong Emperor whose anticipated return inspires messianic movements are phrased. It should be emphasized here that these legends are frequently recounted in everyday village interactions which occur *outside* the context of messianic cults, and sometimes with no manifestly messianic meaning; that is, they do not invariably or necessarily refer to the prospective return of the hero. But they do nevertheless, as I have argued (Tapp 1989), employ the cosmological symbols and idiom of Chinese sovereign power to authenticate the claims embodied in these legends to a cultural and ethnic autonomy which is defined by contrast to Han Chinese identity and opposition to the Chinese state.

Similar accounts occur in legends of Hmong heroes collected in China today. Typically the claim to sovereignty is validated with reference to the siting of the hero's patrilineal ancestor's grave according to Chinese geomantic terms. I have already raised the question of whether this should be seen as a form of oppositional ideology or the triumph of the hegemonic discourse in a process of Sinicization, and clearly there are resemblances here to the Kayah adoption of the *iyluw* cult (Lehman 1967) and to the appropriation of dominant and centralizing Hindu-Buddhist cosmologies by local religious leaders within the Theravada Buddhist tradition.

Returning to what I have referred to as Hmong 'messianic myths', I have been concerned to draw out the implications of the associations, in the Hmong discourse of rebellion and authority, between the sovereign, writing, and territory. In legend and oral history the Hmong attribute the loss of their writing to Chinese oppression, while Chinese (geomantic) trickery and deviousness (skill) is given as the reason for the downfall of the Hmong Emperor of China and the loss of his Kingdom. In the indigenous messianic movements of the modern period, the prophet promises the restoration of the Hmong state with the return of the Hmong Emperor, and guarantees this promise through the rediscovery of the lost form of writing. In the light of Foucault's work (1979; 1980), it is now possible to see, in these ritual and mythological representations, a clear expression of the unity of power/knowledge which here however is an aspect of *sovereign* rather than disciplinary power. The unique manner in which Chinese ideographs succeeeded in enabling communications across cultural and linguistic boundaries and the early bureaucratic institutionalization of privileged forms of knowledge as part of an 'ideological state apparatus' in China which incorporated and negated local differences, might partly explain the strength of the association between political power and knowledge in Hmong ritual representations. Of course, it is this original power/knowledge which Hmong ritual representations depict as having been misappropriated. The Hmong themselves have, in myth and legend, been *disinvested* of a form of power/knowledge which it is a task of ritual to restore. The messianic movements seek to do precisely this; to restore a source of power/knowledge which is mythically represented as having been purloined. It may now be possible to show that shamanic rituals perform similar functions.

The loss of 'repute' described for the Lisu by Hutheesing (1990) has close parallels with this process of the denial of self-worth and sovereign power in mythic Hmong representations. Cultural identity is therefore constituted in terms of an encompassing discourse of sovereign power which determines both the forms of local knowledge and the possibilities of resistance. To understand how this occurs one has to investigate the actual transmission of traditional and 'indigenous' knowledge.[5] In common with many other peoples of the region (and elsewhere), the Hmong often have recourse to a theory of epistemological entropy, or 'deteriorating knowledge', which is predicated on the assumption that knowledge is a form of property. Specialized forms of knowledge – of shamanism, of blacksmithing, of herbal healing, of hunting – are ritually transmitted along initiatory lines of discipline and instruction, and therefore also from senior to junior generations. Since such knowledge is an invaluable resource, individuals are assumed to be reluctant to transmit the full extent of their knowledge to their younger disciples, and therefore the total sum of knowledge available to the society is steadily diminishing, generation by generation. Although this theory is often given as an elaboration for the occasional failures of shamanic cures, it also has a more general application in accounting for the lack of sovereign power among the Hmong which, as we saw, it is the peculiar task of messianic movements to restore. While the loss of sovereignty, territorial autonomy, and knowledge, therefore, is on the one hand directly and historically attributed to the oppression of the Chinese, on the other hand and in more general terms, it is also accountable for in terms of a general theory of (deteriorating) knowledge.

Hmong Shamanism

While shamanic rituals contrast markedly with the messianic movements we have considered, both messianism and shamanism implicate theories of the loss of an original source of knowledge and power, and both involve supernatural communication through trance and possession. That both are importantly marked by the invocation of elements of a dominantly Chinese form of ritual discourse is a further reason for their comparison here. If the shaman is concerned with the health and well-being of individual patients and their families, however, the messianic prophet is ultimately concerned with the salvation of Hmong society as a whole. Although a variety of functions may be performed by shamans in individual village communities, s/he is typically concerned to retrieve the self or selves of a patient whose affliction is attributed to the loss of self. As Lemoine (1987) has argued, this the shaman primarily does by attributing affliction to external agencies in the form of spirits, contrasting sharply with the techniques of psychoanalysis which attribute disorientation to *internal* agencies. Yet perhaps the picture is still more complex. For the shaman himself must undergo a certain loss of self in order to accomplish his effects, and arguably shamanism is important for the loss of self it *licences*, both for shaman and for patient, rather than for the loss of self it redeems (for the patient) or controls (for the shaman). However, while the messianic prophet restores an original condition of power and knowledge through his identification with the legendary Emperor of the Hmong, the shaman's purpose, through identification with the premier shaman, is to restore a self which has also been robbed, plundered, misappropriated by an external agency. It is the nature of this self which is crucial, however, for it is not a unitary self which is either lost or restored, but a self which partakes of and acts as a representation of social and cosmic elements. In common speech, these are the chicken, bamboo, and bull selves, but also a self which integrates the domestic family, its animals and gardens, and (Lemoine 1987) other elements such as the reindeer and sun–and–moon selves, which together form a shamanic 'system' of selves.

It is possible to differentiate between the types of occasion to which shamanism is appropriate, and to distinguish the shamanic session into its main constituent parts of diagnosis (*ua neeb saib*) and healing (*ua neeb kho*) as Moréchand (1968) has done; or the five parts of the healing seance distinguished by Mottin (1984): the entry of the shaman into trance and invocation of his auxiliary spirits; the search of the patient's house for the source of affliction; the pursuit of the errant self; the return of the self to its physical home; and the return of the shaman and his spirits. But analysis also needs to take into account the nature both of the spirits encountered by the shaman on his adventure into the spiritual world, and the auxiliary spirits summoned by him and yet possessing him in trance (the *neeb*). While figures encountered in the spiritual world by the shaman such as the malevolent Ntxwj Nyug and the Original Couple appear to be of local origin, other prominent figures encountered include Nyuj Vaj whom Lemoine (1972b) identified as derived from the Chinese Jade Emperor (Yu Huang), and Yaj Xeeb Txheeb and Xyooj Xeeb Txheeb, Chinese officials who have the power to issue licences for children (Lemoine 1987). Indeed as I have noted (1989, 1991) much of the world which the shaman traverses is modelled on the Chinese state bureaucracy, where divinities are depicted as celestial officials seated behind gigantic writing-desks issuing, extending, and remanding licences for life and health in a Kafka-esque cosmology of control and terror. If these are 'mediating' symbols, as Taussig (1980) argues for the Devil in South America, what are the processes which are being mediated?

The auxiliary spirits which possess the Hmong shaman are also partly of Chinese provenance (and one must remember that shamanic chants may take place in a vernacular Chinese invoking Chinese spirits although no trace of a similar Chinese tradition has been found). A number of shamanic invocations have now been recorded and transcribed.[6] Mottin's (1982) account lists 111 kinds of auxiliary spirits, although the numbers vary. The spirits invoked include the all-important ancestral spirits of the shaman and the spirits of shamanic masters, of the shaman's dragon-horse and his equipment, and the special spirit of shamanism usually translated as the spirit of the parakeet, domestic, animal, and divine spirits as well as the spirits of natural phenomena such as clouds and winds, the sun, moon and stars, thunder and lightning. The spirits of the Chinese and Yi are also invoked, together with the Chinese gods of blacksmithing and other Chinese spirits identified by Lemoine (1987) as those of the Fourth Mandarin, the Guardian of Wealth, the King of Medicine, and the legions of Chinese cavalry and soldiers.

In effect, then, the shaman is possessed by a kind of primordial chaos of natural, cultural, and spiritual essences which destroys the boundaries of cultural identity and in which his own sense of personal identity and self is submerged. Yet, although in the initial stages of possession the *neeb* are presented as aggressive and threatening, in trance the shaman is presented as *controlling* and mastering all these forces: his own ancestral spirits and those of his teachers, the forces of the cosmos, and of those of other ethnic groups. For the shaman is seen as the master or 'father' of his auxiliary spirits (including the Chinese armies) (*txiv neeb*) and his journey is represented as a celestial flight in which, preceded by the swallow and parakeet, the shaman leads the troupe of *neeb* to retrieve the lost self of the patient.[7]

The Resoration of Vitality

Can we say, following Bloch, that Hmong shamanic rituals function ultimately to reinforce the position of elder males and particularly shamans

95

in society, or that the shaman (and his clients) return regenerated and with a new vitality to the everyday world they negated?[8] The answer to this would depend on an analysis of the shaman's position in Hmong society, but the historical evidence on this is somewhat contradictory. The shaman has no formal political authority; he (or, more rarely, she) is typically a villager and a farmer like other villagers, and the position is not hereditary. On the other hand, it is usually men of some standing in the lineage and local community – married and with children – who tend to become shamans, although again it is not necessary to be a shaman to achieve such standing, and at least some shamans are openly disrespected. Shamanism is, and is seen as, very much an individual vocation, the specialization of certain members of the community, as others specialize in knowledge of funeral rituals or wedding songs. But yet again, it is clear that the mystic authority which the shaman obtains over the supernatural and his power to intervene altruistically on behalf of the health and well-being of others, is a formidable one which lends the shaman a unique status within the community. It is probable, then, that in times of historical crisis it has been the shamans who are above all trusted for their guidance and advice, and that shamans have become political figures and war leaders for this reason.

We might conclude, then, that the capacity for possession which the shaman *shares* with the leaders of messianic movements enables both shamanic and messianic ritual to play a constitutive part in the construction of a Hmong cultural discourse. The shaman is conceptually carefully separated from the patrilineal descent system, both by his exclusion from the important rituals of death and rebirth, and by the seeking of Masters outside the descent group (although the possessing spirits are believed to be ancestrally inherited) and the prohibition on healing members of the immediate family. It is similarly crucial that the messsianic prophet and the Messiah himself is typically conceived of as an orphan, or as the child of a remarried mother whose clan status is ambiguous. Hmong villagers themselves frequently criticise the patrilineal descent system expressed in burial rituals and the *feng shui* system as a cause of social disunity, which they consciously feel is necessary to transcend, and it would be possible to replicate this view at a theoretical level and argue that Hmong messianism represents an attempt at political unification and centralization, validated in terms of the adoption of symbols of a centralizing dominant discourse. However, this would be to ignore the capacity of such rituals creatively to express alternatives to an intolerable or insufferable present, and their potential from that point of view to inspire social action.

Although at one level shamanic rituals can be seen to provide a dramatic contrast to the realities of everyday life, in contrast to messianic movements which are spasmodic and sectoral, shamanic rituals do present the appearance of a certain continuity with and conformity to the realities of everyday life in the village. Shamans are normally not concerned with radical alterations of social life, but with ensuring the continuity of wholeness and health, while messianic leaders are concerned to bring about radical changes in the structure of society. While we may see the leaders of messianic movements as promising a restoration of an original form of power and knowledge denied to the Hmong as a cultural group, the shaman seeks to restore vitality at a personal and domestic level. Though both are forms of ritual action, if messianism can be seen as a type of ritual, forms of power represented as alien ('Other') are absorbed in order to be symbolically controlled. This absorption of alien power is accomplished through the dissolution of the normal boundaries of the self and cultural identity; identity is submerged in a chaos of differences. The boundaries are then constituted in a *new* way, not merely reconstituted in a replicatory way, and this I would see as the creative dynamism inherent in popular rituals such as those of shamanism and messianism. The *manipulation* of rituals to legitimate social hierarchies is an entirely different question, which in fact has nothing to do with the nature of ritual. When we consider Tai rituals involving the Lua' in relation to the actual historical and economic relations of the Tai and Lua', then, we are considering quite different phenomena from the adoption of dominant forms of discourse by messianic movements and local rituals.

Yet clearly all can be subsumed under the category of such general hegemonic processes as Indianization or Sinicization which have considerable similarities to those of Sanskritization. The evidence I have summarised here on Hmong shamanism and messianism should be sufficient to indicate that they can be taken as instances of a general process of the incorporation of Sinitic influences into Hmong society and culture, and the Sinicization of an ethnic minority group at the fringes of the Han Empire.

Conclusion

While not tending towards any Grand Theory in conclusion, nevertheless it seems clear that the processes of Sinicization described here among the Hmong have general similarities with such other processes as Indianization or Sanskritization and that therefore they may be assimilable to a general theory of manners (Elias 1982; Bourdieu 1986). This also does have relevance for general theories of ideology and discourse. Elias describes a process of the adoption of courtly models of behaviour by non-élite sectors whose successful emulation of the manners and customs of the élite led to changes of the model being initiated by the élite in order to maintain their distinction. This model is not only applicable to the development of European manners and etiquette but may have a broader application (Fukushima 1992). If the Sinicization of the Hmong, clearly demonstrated in their rituals and mythology, can be seen in such terms, then the antiquity of the imperial model of Chinese society which is so prominent a feature of their myths and ritual life is explicable in terms of the historic changes of manners and customs which must have been forced upon an élite (here represented by Han Chinese society) by their successful imitation and incorporation by 'savage' outsiders. Here the 'centre' conforms to the 'élite', where change is swifter and more radical than at the periphery, as recognized by diffusionist theory. The culture of the élite, here represented by the culture of a dominant civil group, refuses and denies the validity of its successful replication/adoption by an excluded group.

Incorporation of the ideology of a dominant group, then, does not represent a triumph of hegemonic discourse but rather a successful challenge mounted on the centre by the periphery. Messianism does, therefore, represent a potential challenge to the power of centralizing authority, and its incorporation of the symbols and emblems of that power is similarly a threat to the monopoly of such symbols and emblems by an élite group.[9] Yet the terms on which this confrontation take place are set by the dominant discourse itself. In this process, then, it is impossible to speak of a victory for the individual within the system, since the individual can only function within the terms of the system itself. It is impossible to achieve individual success within the system; in a Chinese context, the Hmong who 'becomes' *hanhuade* or Sinicized is not manipulating ethnic identities or controlling a Han cultural system but a symbol of the triumph of the system over individual attempts to incorporate and master it. What is occurring is a constant process of the search for distinction, and the creation of new distinctions of distinction.

In this process ritual clearly plays an articulatory part, but perhaps not a part which is essentially different from the secular rituals of etiquette and manners, but rather to be distinguished according to its greater degree of formalization, stereotypy, cultural significance, and symbolic content (Davis 1984). There is thus no analytical distinction between ritual and practical communications as Bloch maintains, and the Sinicization of Hmong rituals can be seen as part of the same process as the Sinicization of Hmong daily life. The denial of native vitality and ingestion of alien power which occurs in ritual may then be seen here as part of the attempt to emulate a superior model of manners and custom.

As Kachin become Shan, as Lua' become Tai, and Tai become Thai, as Wa spirits are Buddhicized and in the Sinicization of the Hmong in China, a constant process of absorption and assimilation into more inclusive categories and a permeation of dominant ideas and values takes place which is firmly historically related to the establishment and expansion of the state. It has to be emphasized again that these processes do not take place in a cultural vacuum devoid of power relations. Leach's work succeeded in removing the cultural essentialism and hypothetical holism of functionalist

Plate 9. 'Ecriture des Khâs'

analysis to the level of an ideal realm of structural models from which it has been difficult to detach them. It is clear that Chinese influences on the Hmong mark a long process of violent subordination to which consent has largely been won. But then further questions arise relating to the establishment and extent of this kind of consent which require both a broader appeal to theories of ideology and a more specific attention to the local contexts of shamanic rituals and the emergence of messianic leaders in specific situations than this paper has been able to offer. Yet it is clear that conventional mimetic theories of representation (Hughes-Freeland 1991) are inadequate to explain the power and significance of such processes of encompassment, incorporation, quotation, allusion, reference, annotation, subversion, and adoption.

In conclusion I would emphasize again that if the construction of cultural discourse can be seen in terms of the creation, maintenance, and adoption of distinctions of taste and manners, and therefore notions of cultural essentialism are finally abandoned, then definitions of ethnic minorities are in fact integral to the construction of a Thai national identity – both for the Tai *as* minorities, and for minorities within Tai states. In this sense the periphery defines (or determines) the (changing) centre.

Notes

1 Turton 1972; Davis 1973; Wijeyewardene 1977; Cohen and Wijeyewardene 1984; Irvine 1982; Condominas 1975; Tanabe 1988; 1991; Kraisri 1967; Rhum 1989; also Archaimbault 1973; Swearer 1974; 1987; *et al.*
2 See also Turner (1987). Cohen (1985) pointed out that ritual representations of 'community and its boundaries' increases in significance as the actual 'geo-social boundaries' of the community become weakened.
3 On the notion of invulnerability, see Turton (1984; 1991).
4 See Lemoine (1972) for an early account of these scripts and their messianic significance. Recently two related studies have been published; Smalley et al. (1990) and Chia et al. (1990).
5 I have made a comparison of different forms of traditional Hmong knowledge in Tapp (1991). Cf. Barth (1987).
6 Moréchand 1968; Mottin 1982; Lemoine 1987.
7 A climax of the shamanic session as of other Hmong rituals is the violent sacrifice of an animal by the householder, the 'blooding' of the participants' clothing by the

shaman, and a commensal meal which the shaman shares. The violence of this release of blood and vital energy, and its social ingestion after the shamanic session, might be contrasted with the kind of violence characteristic of millenarian movements, as Bloch's analysis indicates.

8 It is of note that invocations of cosmic and Chinese forces are also attributed to messianic prophets (Yaj 1972).

9 As Chatthip (1984) argues.

10 Much of the background thinking for this paper, which is largely a presentation of previous data in the light of recent theoretical work, emerged in discussions at two conferences at the National Museum of Ethnology in Osaka. I would like to thank Shigeharu Tanabe, Masakazu Tanaka, and Masato Fukushima in particular for their comments on some of the ideas presented in this paper.

References

Allton, I. (1978), 'La guerre du fou: essai d'interprétation', Unpublished M.A. thesis, Paris: CeDRASEMI.

Archaimbault, C. (1973), *Structures Religeuses Lao,* Vientiane: Editions Vithagna.

Asad, T. (ed.) (1973), *Anthropology and the Colonial Encounter,* London: Ithaca Press.

Barth, F. (1967), 'Economic Spheres in Darfur', in R. Firth (ed.), *Themes in Economic Anthropology,* ASA Mons.6, London: Tavistock Publications.

—— (1987), *Cosmologies in the Making: A Generative Approach to Cultural Variation in Inner New Guinea,* (Cambridge Studies in Social Anthropology), Cambridge: Cambridge University Press.

Bloch, M. (1985), 'From Cognition to Ideology', in Richard Fardon (ed.), *Power and Knowledge: Anthropological and Sociological Approaches,* Edinburgh: Scottish Academic Press.

—— (1986), *From Blessing to Violence: history and ideology in the circumcision ritual of the Merina of Madagascar,* (Cambridge Studies in Social Anthropology), Cambridge: Cambridge University Press.

—— (1992), *Prey into Hunter: the Politics of Religious Experience,* Cambridge: Cambridge University Press.

Bourdieu, P. (1986), *Distinction: A Social Critique of the Judgement of taste,* transl. Richard Nice, London and New York: Routledge & Kegan Paul.

Chatthip Nartsupha (1984), 'The Ideology of 'Holy Men's Revolts in North East Thailand', in Andrew Turton and Shigeharu Tanabe (eds.) *History and Peasant Consciousness in South East Asia,* (Senri Ethnological Studies 13), Osaka: National Museum of Ethnology.

Chia Koua Vang, Gnia Yee Yang and William Smalley (1990), 'The Life of Shong Lue Yang: Hmong 'Mother of Writing', (Southeast Asia Refugee Studies Papers 9), Center for Urban & Regional Affairs, Minneapolis: University of Minnesota.

Cohen, A. P. (1985), *The Symbolic Construction of Community,* London: Routledge.

Cohen, P. and Wijeyewardene, G. (eds.) (1984), 'Matrilineal Spirit Cults and the Position of Women in Northern Thailand', (Special Issue 3) *Mankind.*

Condominas, G. (1975), 'Phiban Cults in Rural Laos', in G. Skinner and A. Kirsch (eds.), *Change and Persistence in Thai Society: Essays in Honour of Lauriston Sharp,* Ithaca: Cornell University Press, 252–73.

—— (1990), *From Lawa to Mon, from Saa' to Thai: historical and anthropological aspects of Southeast Asian social spaces,* Occasional Paper, Canberra: Australian National University. (Occasional Paper of the Department of Anthropology).

Cooper, R. (1984), *Resource Scarcity and the Hmong Response: A Study of Settlement and Economy in Northern Thailand,* Singapore: National University of Singapore.

Davis, R. (1973), 'Muang Matrifocality', *Journal of the Siam Society,* 61: 2.

—— (1984), *Muang Metaphysics: A Study of Northern Thai Myth and Ritual,* Bangkok: Pandora.

De La Jonquière, L. (1906), *Ethnographie du Tonkin Septentrional,* Paris: Ernest Leroux.

Diamond, N. (1988), 'The Miao and Poison: Interactions on China's Southwest Frontier', *Ethnology,* XXVII:1.

Elias, N (1982), *The Civilizing Process,* Vol.I, *The History of Manners,* Oxford: Basil Blackwell.

Foucault, M. (1979), *Discipline and Punish,* London: Allen Lane.

—— (1980), *Power/Knowledge,* Colin Gordon, (ed.), New York: Pantheon.

Freud, S. (1974), Symbolism in Dreams', *Introductory Lectures on Psychoanalysis,* Middlesex: Penguin Books.

Fukushima, M. (1992), 'On the Pragmatics of Ritual Order: The Microscopic Constitution of Society and its Transformation in Java', Paper presented at the Symposium on Religious Renewals in Asia, National Museum of Ethnology. Osaka, 24–27 November.

Giddens, A. (1991), *Modernity and Self-Identity: Self and Society in the Late Modern Age,* London: Polity Press.

Hughes-Freeland, F. (1991), 'Classification and Communication in Javanese Palace Performance', *Visual Anthropology,* 4.

Hutheesing, O. (1990), *Emerging Sexual Inequality among the Lisu of North Thailand: The waning of dog and elephant repute,* Leiden: Brill.

Irvine, W. (1982), *The Thai-Yuan 'Madman' and the Modernising, Developing Thai Nation as Bounded Entities Under Threat: A Study in the Replication of a Single Image,* Ph.D. thesis, University of London.

Keyes, C. (1971), 'Buddhism and National Integration in Thailand', *Journal of Asian Studies,* XXX.3.

—— (1976), 'Towards a New Formulation of the Concept of Ethnic Group', *Ethnicity,* 3.

Kraisri Nimmanhaeminda. (1967), 'The Lawa Guardian Spirits of Chiangmai', *Journal of the Siam Society,* LV.2.

La Fontaine, J. (1985), *Initiation,* London: Routledge.

Leach, E. (1954), *Political Systems of Highland Burma,* London: The Athlone Press.

—— (1960–61), 'The Frontiers of "Burma"', *Comparative Studies in Society and History,* III.

Lehman, F. (1967), 'Burma: Kayah Society as a Function of the Shan–Burma–Karen Context', in J. Steward (ed.), *Contemporary Change in Traditional Society,* Vol.II, Urbana: University of Illinois Press.

—— (1979), 'Who Are the Karen, and If So, Why? Karen Ethnohistory and a Formal Theory of Ethnicity', in C. Keyes (ed.), *Ethnic Adaptation and Identity: the Karen on the Thai Frontier with Burma,* Philadelphia: Institute for the Study of Human Issues.

Lemoine, J. (1972), 'L'Initiation du Mort chez les Hmong', *L'Homme,* XII.1–3.

—— (1987), 'Les Ecritures du Hmong', *Bulletin des Amis du Royaume Lao.* 7–8.

—— (1987), *Entre la Maladie et la Mort: le Chamane Hmong sur les Chemins de l'Au-delà,* Bangkok: Pandora.

Moerman, M. (1965), 'Who Are the Lue?', *American Anthropologist,* 67.

—— (1968), 'Being Lue: Uses and Abuses of Ethnic Unit Identification', in J. Helm (ed.), *Essays on the Problem of Tribe,* Seattle: University of Washington.

Moréchand, G. (1968), 'Le Chamanisme des Hmong', *Bulletin de l'Ecole Française d'Extrême-Orient,* LXIV.

Mottin, J. (1982), *Allons Faire le Tour du Ciel et de la Terre: Le Chamanisme des Hmong vu dans les textes*, Bangkok: White Lotus Co.

—— (1984), 'A Hmong Shaman's Seance', *Asian Folklore Studies*, 43.

Naroll, R. (1964), 'On Ethnic Unit Classification', *Current Anthropology*, V.4.

—— (1968), 'Who the Lue Are', in J. Helm (ed.), *Essays on the Problem of Tribe*, Seattle: University of Washington Press.

Rajah, A. (1992), 'Transformations of Karen myths of origin and relations of power', in G. Wijeyewardene and E. Chapman (eds.), *Patterns and Illusions: Thai History and Thought,* Singapore: Australian National University and ISEAS.

Reynolds, C. (1992), 'The plot of Thai history: theory and practice', in G. Wijeyewardene and E. Chapman (eds.), *Patterns and Illusions: Thai History and Thought,* Singapore: Australian National University and ISEAS.

Rhum, M. (1989), 'The Lords of Ava: Spirit Rites in North Thailand', *Crossroads*, 4.2.

Ruey Yih-Fu (1962), 'The Miao: their Origins and Southwards Migrations', *Proceedings of the International Association of Historians of Asia (Second Biennial) Conference*, Taipei.

Savina, F. (1930), *Histoire des Miao*, Hong Kong: Société des Missions Etrangères de Paris.

Smalley, W., Chia Koua Vang and Gnia Yee Yang (1990), *Mother of Writing The Origin and Development of a Hmong Messianic Script*, Chicago and London: University of Chicago Press.

Swearer, D. (1974), 'Myth, Legend and History in the Northern Thai Chronicles', *Journal of the Siam Society*, (62).

—— (1986), 'The Northern Thai City as a Sacred Center', *Journal of Developing Societies,* II.2.

Tambiah, S. (1984), *The Buddhist Saints of the Forest and the Cult of Amulets.* (Cambridge Studies in Social Anthropology), Cambridge: Cambridge University Press.

Tanabe, S. (1988), 'Spirits and Ideological Discourse: The Tai-Lue Guardian Cults in Yunnan', *Sojourn*, 3.1.

—— (1991), 'Spirits, Power and the Discourse of Female Gender: the *phi meng* cult in Northern Thailand', in Manas Chitakasem and Andrew Turton (eds.), *Thai Constructions of Knowledge*, London: School of Oriental and African Studies.

—— (1991), Sacrifice and the Transformation of Ritual: the Pu Sae Ya Sae Spirit Cult in North Thailand', Paper presented at the Symposium on Spirit Cults and Popular Knowledge in South East Asia. National Museum of Ethnology. Osaka, 6–13 November.

Tanaka, M. (1991), *Patrons, Devotees and Goddesses: Ritual and Power among the Tamil Fishermen of Sri Lanka*, Kyoto: Institute for Research in Humanities, Kyoto University.

Tapp, N. (1969), *Sovereignty and Rebellion: The White Hmong of North Thailand,* Singapore: Oxford University Press.

—— (1990), 'Milieu and Context: the Disappearance of the White Hmong', *Proceedings of the 4th. International Conference on Thai Studies*, Institute of Southeast Asian Studies, Kunming, 11–13 May.

—— (1991). 'The Way of Sickness and Death: Practical Understanding among the Hmong', Paper presented at the Symposium on Spirit Cults and Popular Knowledge in South East Asia. National Museum of Ethnology. Osaka, 6–13 November.

Taussig, M. (1980), *The Devil and Commodity Fetishism in South America*, University of North Carolina Press, Chapel Hill 1980.

Terwiel, B. (1992), 'Laupani and Ahom Identity: an ethnohistorical exercise', in G. Wijeyewardene and E. Chapman (eds.) *Patterns and Illusions: Thai History and Thought,* Singapore: Australian National University and ISEAS.

Turner, V. (1980), *The Ritual Process: Structure amd Anti-Structure*, Middlesex: Penguin Books.

Turton, A. (1972), 'Matrilineal Descent Groups and Spirit Cults of the Thai–Yuan in Northern Thailand', *Journal of the Siam Society*, (60)2.

—— (1984), 'Limits of Ideological Domination and the Formation of Social Consciousness', in Andrew Turton and Shigeharu Tanabe (eds.) *History and Peasant Consciousness in South East Asia*, (Senri Ethnological Studies 13), Osaka: National Museum of Ethnology.

—— (1991), 'State Poetics and Civil Rhetoric – an introduction to Thai Constructions of Knowledge' and 'Invulnerability and Local Knowledge', in Manas Chitakasem and Andrew Turton (eds.), *Thai Constructions of Knowledge*, London: School of Oriental and African Studies.

Wijeyewardene, G. (1977), 'Matriclans or Female Cults: A Problem in Northern Thai Ethnography', *Mankind*, 11.

—— (1986), *Place and Emotion in Northern Thai Ritual Behaviour*, Bangkok: Pandora.

Yaj Txoov Tsawb (1972), *Rog Paj Cai.*, mimeo, Sayaboury: Y. Bertrais.

Chapter Five

The Politics of Cosmology: An Introduction to Millenarianism and Ethnicity among Highland Minorities of Northern Thailand

Claes Corlin

Highland ethnic groups of Northern Thailand encompass a range of religious beliefs. Traditional beliefs are often mixed with influences from Buddhism (Theravada and/or Mahayana), Daoism, or missionary Christianity. Frequent messianic and millenarian movements have gathered large numbers of adherents, at times leading to open resistance against majority domination. Several authors have pointed out that the millenarian movements among the highland minorities may be regarded as part of an ethnic profiling against the Thai majority (see for example Hinton 1979; Keyes 1979; Stern 1968; Tapp 1989). In this chapter I suggest that, in addition, there is a cultural propensity towards millenarian movements shown in certain mythical traditions which are common to many of these ethnic minorities. The interrelations between religious belief and political action in an ethnic minority situation are discussed.

My data are obtained from secondary sources as well as from a short field study in Northern Thailand in 1991–92.[1] As these highland cultures spread across national borders, I have included some cases from Burma, Laos, and China (for a wider consideration of messianic and millenarian movements in South East Asia, see Turton and Tanabe, 1984; especially chapters by Tanabe, Chatthip, Shiraishi, and Yasumaru).

Millenarianism

The concept of the *millennium* originates from the Book of Revelation in the Christian New Testament of the Bible (chapter 20, verses 4–6), which envisions a thousand-year messianic kingdom on earth to follow the Christ's second coming as the Messiah. Throughout the Christian world *millenarian* movements have arisen among oppressed strata or among marginal groups in society. Prophets and visionaries have predicted the imminent second coming of Christ and the ensuing liberation of the oppressed. At times these movements have exploded into open rebellion against the political or ecclesiastical authorities. Outside the Christian World, millenarian movements have been reported from several areas. The Ghost Dance among North American Indians and the Cargo Cults of Melanesia are examples of such reactions following culture contact and social change (Worsley 1968; Burridge 1980; La Barre 1970).

A millenarian movement commonly starts with the appearance of a prophet, who claims that he or she is a divine messenger, or being possessed by a spirit. The prophet proclaims that this unjust world will come to an end, and a new and better one will be established. The followers of the prophet abandon their everyday duties in order to wait for the millennium, or for the Cargo of valuables to appear. At times the cult is accompanied by ecstasy, trances, or obsessive dancing. Such behaviour – to outsiders seemingly bizarre – may represent a considerable social and political force. Many millenarian movements have ended in large-scale rebellions against the majority or colonial power. The Taiping Rebellion in China (1851–1864), which was started by the millenarian visionary Hsiu-ch'uan, was one of the bloodiest civil wars on record (Boardman 1962).

The theoretical literature on millenarianism is extensive and cannot be reviewed here. Two major theoretical trends are the *relative deprivation theory* and the *revitalization theory*. The former regards millenarianism as an expression of social discontent. As the gap widens between what individuals perceive to be their legitimate expectations on the one hand and the means of satisfying them on the other, they become progressively discontented. This provides a fertile ground for millenarian prophets or revolutionary agitators to predict a radical transformation of the state of things (Aberle 1966).

A problem with the relative deprivation theory is that it is too wide. Severe relative deprivation may come and go without producing any significant social movement. Also, it does not explain why some societies develop millenarianism and others develop other forms of social movements (see Barkun 1974: 36f.). Anthony Wallace's revitalization theory is an attempt to connect deprivation to millenarianism by introducing an additional variable, *stress*. The essence of revitalization lies in the need of a society under excessive stress to reinforce itself or die.

> 'Wallace postulates a process . . . in which a society moves from homeostasis to crisis to revitalization and back to a 'steady state'. In between the two points of relative stability, mounting stress and the inability of existing cultural mechanisms to relieve it produce a radical resynthesis of existing beliefs and values, in essence the abrupt creation of a new culture.' (Barkun 1974: 39).

This theory takes into account the internal-cultural context as well as external-political factors. Millenarianism is regarded as a stage in the general transformation of culture. A related perspective is assumed by Worsley, who sees the Melanesian Cargo Cults as expressions of proto-nationalism:

> 'These [national groupings] are likely to be conditioned both by the traditional cultural heritage and by the action of new political and economic forces on the societies of this region. Some tribes are breaking up, others are coalescing to form higher social formations. . . . I believe . . . that the activist millenarian movement is typical only of a certain phase in the political and economic development of this region, and that it is destined to disappear or become a minor form of political expression among backward elements.' (Worsley 1968: 254f.).

In the following, I will adopt the revitalization perspective, albeit with special attention to current culture theory. The emergence of millenarianism in highland South East Asia is regarded as an activation of latent cultural traditions, as Tapp (1989: 136) suggested. These become active in a certain historical context of political and economic minority status, as well as by the influence of missionary Christianity.

Ethnic Pluralism in Highland South East Asia

The vast mountainous expanses of mainland South East Asia – Northern Thailand, parts of Burma, Laos, Vietnam, and Yunnan Province in China – are populated by a large number of ethnic groups. Their languages belong to the three great linguistic 'superstocks' of South East Asia (Matisoff 1983): Sino-Tibetan (Chinese, Tibeto-Burman), Austro-Thai (Tai-Kadai, Miao-Yao) and Austro-Asiatic (Mon-Khmer, Karennic). Their customs, religions, and material culture vary widely. Most groups are dry land farmers. The 'typical' traditional community is a mountain village of fewer than a hundred to a few hundred inhabitants who practise shifting cultivation. There are, however, communities who grow irrigated rice on terraced fields or in valleys.

Throughout history these ethnic groups have become more or less incorporated into nations dominated by lowland populations and centralized states. Migrations and wars have forced many minority groups to resettle, often across national borders. Recent refugee contingents from the Vietnam war and from Burma have added to the population. Thousands of highlanders from Laos still live in refugee camps in north-eastern Thailand. Others have migrated on to USA, Canada, or French Guyana, creating an international community-in-exile.

In Thailand the inclusive term *chao khao* (hill tribes) is currently used by the authorities to designate the highlanders. These are then divided into a number of ethnic categories such as: Karen, Meo, Lahu, Lisu, Yao, Akha, and Kammu (Khmu). In addition, the North of Thailand is populated by its lowland majority, the Khon Müang; further by a number of other Tai-speaking groups (Shan, Tai Yai, Tai Lue, Tai Khün, Tai Yong), Austro-Asiatic-speaking lowland groups (Lua', Ht'in), Yunnanese Chinese (Ho), and a tiny number of hunter-gatherers (Mrabri or Phi Thong Luang) (Bhruksasri 1989; Walker 1992a). These designations used by the authorities are not always the same as those used by the minorities themselves. For example, the Meo prefer to call themselves Hmong, and the Yao call themselves Mien. Each category roughly corresponds to a number of culturally and linguistically related groups that may or may not perceive another as associated. For example, the Karen of Thailand possess no term for 'all Karen', but only of the major (linguistic) divisions Pwo, Sgaw, and Kayah (A.B. Jorgensen; personal communication). Subgroups are often distinguished by colour terms, such as Lahu Na (Black), Lahu Nyi (Red) and Lahu Shi (Yellow Lahu). Each sub-group may be further subdivided according to dialect and clan membership. Passing between ethnic categories and groups takes place, and multiple identities are not uncommon.

In northern Thailand until the 1950s, the policy of the state towards the highland minorities was essentially that of non-interference. With increasing immigration of refugees from bordering communist countries, the Government feared that subversive groups among these immigrants would become a threat to national security. The Border Police Patrol was created in 1953 to check potential subversives. In addition, opium growing and armed bands of opium traders (mostly Chinese from the Nationalist ex-army) became increasingly embarrassing to the state and its foreign relations. In 1967 Thai armed forces took action against suspected communists in the hills. Several Hmong and Mien villages were napalmed and large populations were forcibly moved to controlled areas. In the middle 1960s, the Sangha, the national order of Buddhist monks, started sending missionaries to the villages. This was an attempt to incorporate the ethnic minorities into the Thai social order. Some villages converted, but the main consequence of the missions was that the difference between Buddhist Thai and non-Buddhist highlanders became more emphasized. In contrast to Christian missionary activities in Thailand, the Buddhist actions were overtly political.

The authorities' efforts at substituting opium-growing with other crops have met with varying success. Many highland villages now grow vegetables instead, but this requires easy transportation to the markets, which is not always possible. Also, the economic structure is changing. The production requires external investments which often makes the producers dependent on Thai financiers in the cities. To restrain deforestation the state has established large National Parks in the mountains. This has resulted in thousands of highland villagers becoming illegal residents in their habitats. Some have moved to the lowlands. Others find it difficult to survive as they are cut off from economic support and from roads. These and other changes, such as the growing impact of tourism, mean that the highland populations find themselves in an increasingly precarious situation. Not only are their economic resources threatened, but their very way of life is rapidly changing. New values and ideas are being introduced, often in conflict with tradition. Like so many minority cultures in the world, the highlanders are being exposed to a mixture of economic deprivation and cultural over-stimulation. Time-honoured modes of doing and seeing are at odds with the realities of the new situation. The highland cultures try to adapt by putting together bits and pieces of the old and the new. The outcome of this process, strange as it may appear to outside observers, is a renewal of culture.

Local Religion

Among the highland groups of Northern Thailand, the Lua' and Karen are regarded by some authorities, if not generally in popular or official discourse, as native to the area. The other groups probably originated in South China and have migrated through Laos or Burma, some of them in recent centuries. Their cultures have been affected by encounters with other peoples during history. Their religions show influences from Daoism, Chinese folk religion, Confucianism, and Buddhism. Nevertheless, a core of indigenous religious beliefs and practices, myths and rituals may be traced not only among the highlanders of Northern Thailand, but also among related groups in Yunnan, Vietnam, Laos, and Burma.

Among the central elements of this religious heritage one finds a tripartite cosmological scheme of heaven, earth, and underworld. Further there are beliefs in nature spirits, in ancestor spirits, and often in a creator god or goddess. Human beings, and often rice and other entities (see e.g. Izikowitz 1951) are believed to have an individual spirit matter. This spirit matter leaves the human body at death and may leave it during sickness. Certain persons, for example shamans, have the ability to call back the spirit matter of a sick person and hence heal the disease. In addition there is usually a belief in spiritual 'power' or 'blessing' being of importance for an individual's success in life. Finally, most of these cultures share a mythical tradition regarding the origin of the world, the place of mankind and of various ethnic groups in this world. This latter element has not been much considered by Western scholars.[2] I expand on this theme below.

Of course, many of these elements are not unique to the highland minorities. For example, beliefs in spirits are common in Burma, Thailand, and Vietnam, as in Chinese and Tibetan folk religion (see e.g. Spiro 1967; Tambiah 1984; Cadière 1992; Stein 1962). Likewise, concepts of power as an active force in cosmos, man, and society are spread throughout South East Asia (Anderson 1972; Kirsch 1973; Tannenbaum 1989). The general difference is that these majority populations also encompass a 'great tradition' – Buddhism, Confucianism, and in Vietnam also Catholicism and the syncretism of Cao Dai, that more or less incorporates local beliefs and practices into a wider and ordered cosmology. In the highlands there are no centralized societies nor a centralized religion apart from Christianity, which has been introduced in recent times. Each group and each village has a set of religious beliefs and practices that more or less differ from those of other localities. This differentiation can be driven still further. In 1992, the author attended a Hmong New Year celebration at which each *household* had its own way of calling the ancestor spirits, slightly different from others.

Buddhism and Millenarianism

Theravada Buddhism, the world view of the surrounding majority population, may also lend itself to millenarian interpretations. Canonical Buddhist concepts of the *Ariya Maitreya* or future Buddha, as well as the *dharmaraja* (righteous king) or *cakkavatti* (universal king) – the latter titles have been claimed by several Thai and Burmese kings in different historical periods – may be called upon to legitimize political aspirations in millenarian and comparable contexts (Tambiah 1976, 1978). Keyes' detailed investigation of the millenial movement of northeastern Thailand in 1900–02 relates how Buddhist monks or ex-monks claim to be *phu wiset* (men with special powers) who possess extraordinary spiritual powers. The *phu wiset* prophesy an imminent holocaust that will be followed by the coming of a saviour called Lord Righteous Ruler. Similar movements have been reported from Thailand as recently as the 1970s (Keyes 1977: 295ff.).

Highland ethnic groups have been influenced to varying degrees by both Theravada and in some cases Chinese Mahayana Buddhism. There are reports of millenarian and messianic movements of a Buddhist type that have gathered followings of highlanders. One notable case is that of the 'white-robed monk', a defrocked monk claiming supernatural powers, who attracted large numbers of Pwo and Kayah Karen during the 1960s. He urged no radical political action, but promised to lead all the Karen in Thailand back to Burma and their 'blessed ancestral land' (Hinton 1979: 84f.). Although Buddhist concepts may have influenced highland millenarian movements to some extent, it appears that the catalyst for most of these movements since the nineteenth century was provided by another world religion: Christianity. I now turn to the confluence of missionary Christianity and traditional religion in the highlands.

Christianity in the Highlands

Christianity has been quite successful in its missionary activity among highland ethnic groups, while Buddhism has not. The reasons for this difference are complex and not only due to confessional preferences; they are also political, and related to ethnic history (see also Keyes 1993). In Thailand, Theravada Buddhism is inextricably linked with state power and with the Thai majority's value system as a whole. To most highlanders, adopting Buddhism would imply adopting the totality of the majority's way of life – hence, assimilation into the dominant culture (see Tapp 1989). Elements of Buddhist beliefs and rituals have, however, been incorporated into the religions of many highland groups (see e.g. Walker 1992a). Christianity offers a more comprehensive alternative to submission to the values of the majority population. Not only is it associated with the status, riches, and literacy of the West, but there are also elements of the Christian creed that are in tune with fundamental values of these highland cultures. Processed and transformed Christian conceptions unite with age-old beliefs to produce new religious forms and sometimes to motivate social action of an astonishing force. Some of the immigrant ethnic groups established contact with Christian missionaries already while in China. As Tapp has reminded us, in 1904 a large group of Miao (Hmong) in Yunnan approached the Methodist missionary Samuel Pollard, whose account of the event is revealing:

> 'Some days they came in tens and twenties! Some days in sixties and seventies! Then came a hundred! Then came two hundred! Three hundred! Four hundred! At last, on one special occasion, a thousand of these mountain men came in one day! When they came, the snow was on the ground, and terrible had been the snow on the hills they crossed over. What a great crowd it was!' (Pollard 1919: 72; cited in Tapp 1989).

What the good pastor could not know, was that these masses of highlanders were refugees, dispossessed by Yi and Chinese landlords in Guizhou. They were on their way to find new land for swidden cultivation. What had attracted them to the mission station, however, was a rumour that the missionary had *books*, which were specially meant for the Miao. Pollard describes how the Miao converts flooded into his house, eager to devour anything of written matter with which the missionary could provide them. The consequences were unexpected:

> 'We were troubled in yet another way. By some means or other the rumour went abroad that Jesus was coming again very soon. Instead of the teachings of the Second Coming proving a blessing to these simple people, the way in which it was stated by some irresponsible and ignorant people led to disastrous results. Some of the old wizards, and some of the singing women tried the role of prophet, and several dates were announced for the

appearance of Christ. So firmly did some of the people believe these prophecies, that they neglected their farm work and gave themselves up to singing and waiting for Jesus.' (Pollard: 1919: 76; cited in Tapp 1989).

Note two themes in Pollard's account: the Miao's craving for books, and their subsequent giving up everyday activities, waiting for the immediate second coming of Christ. These will recur in other movements.

Among the Karen two millenarian movements, the *Ywa* and the *Telakhon* cults, have been described by Theodore Stern. The Ywa movement, which flourished throughout the nineteenth century, had its origin in a myth about the creator god Ywa:

'In the days after he had created mankind, Ywa set aside the Book of Gold for the Karen. The latter, busy in his swidden, failed to come for it, and it was entrusted to his younger, White Brother. Thereafter . . . the latter built a boat for Ywa and transported him across the ocean, whence Ywa ascended to Heaven. In their sacred songs, the Karen look forward to the return of the White Brother and their Book, as well as to the advent of Ywa.' (Stern 1968: 305; Hinton 1979: 90f.).

The arrival of American Baptist missionaries in the early nineteenth century seemed, to many Karen, to be a fulfilment of this prophecy, for the foreigners were white and brought a book they claimed to be the key to enlightenment. The missionaries won a great many converts, but at the same time some Karen leaders claimed they alone would be able to interpret the contents of the book and lead the Karen in the overthrow of Burmese domination. Large numbers of Karen united behind these prophets in abortive rebellion against the Burmese. The Telakhon is a successor to the Ywa movement and still has adherents. Its leaders promise the overthrow of Burmese authority in the hills but, despite similar references to the Karen origin myth, they see Christianity as a rival to the millennial faith (Hinton 1979: 91).

Among the Tibeto-Burman-speaking Lahu, the cult of G'uisha (living breath) bears resemblance to the Karen cult of Ywa, although with a distinct Buddhist flavour. G'uisha is the creator of the world and of mankind. He is worshipped with prayers, incense, and offerings, but not animal sacrifice. A Buddhist-like morality is governed by G'uisha; only the good may rejoin him after death, while sinners instead go to hell. The return of G'uisha is anticipated, and from time to time prophets arise who claim to be the deity incarnate. Young describes the latest in succession of these 'man-gods', who claims to possess the magical instruments which will enable him to overcome all foes (Stern 1968: 300 n.16; Young 1962: 10f.). Among Christian Lahu, G'uisha is nowadays identified with the Christian God, whose name is pronounced similarly. The Apocalypse in the Bible is interpreted as a prophecy of the imminent coming of G'uisha.

The Hmong of Laos and Northern Thailand likewise embrace messianic elements of faith that may be 'activated' in situations of political resistance. In 1918, the Hmong of Laos rose up in full-scale rebellion against the Thai, Lao and French. The leader of the revolt, Paj Cai, claimed to be possessed by the spirit of the mythical Hmong emperor Huab Tais, and to be endowed with supernatural powers. A Catholic missionary has described how the Hmong presented themselves fearlessly before the rifles of the French, believing that the bullets would not leave their barrels (Savina, cited in Tapp 1989: 95). Although Paj Cai's movement appears more nativistic than Christian, it was influenced by missionary teachings. In 1949, when Protestant missionaries resumed their work after the Second World War, nearly 1,000 Hmong converts were made in a single day, inspired by the prophecy by a female shaman of the imminent coming of Huab Tais. During the 1950s, a movement known as the 'Meo Trinity Cult' grew up. Three Hmong, claiming to represent the Holy Trinity, travelled from village to village winning converts. The movement came to an end when the 'Holy Spirit' killed himself by jumping off a high mountain ledge to prove that he could fly like a dove (Barney 1957, cited in Tapp 1989: 97). Later, during the Vietnam War, an almost 'cargo cult'-like messianism spread among displaced Hmong who were dependent on airlifts of rice from CIA-chartered airlines. A prophet was said to have fallen from the sky to summon all Hmong to form a great independent kingdom. One rumour reported that Christ was to appear in a jeep, wearing American clothes and handing out weapons (Garrett 1974).

Morphology of Millenarianism

The events related above are examples of a phenomenon that seems almost inevitable whenever Christian missionaries begin working among the highland peoples. Conversions start en masse and usually a whole village or a clan are converted at the same time but, despite the continued efforts of the missionaries to preserve the Gospel, its interpretation by the local people starts to change at an increasing momentum. The peaceful message of Christ may end up as its very antithesis. There are several factors that contribute to this process. One aspect I will call *external-political*, another *internal-cultural*.

Messianic and millenarian movements are likely to arise in situations of economic and political inequality. A prophet's vision is embraced by people who feel discriminated against and helpless in the face of oppression, but do not possess the means of changing their situation. The gist of the millenarian message is *change*, the classic 'end of this world' and the creation of another and better world. Political opposition is cosmologized and set in a framework of temporal inevitability – there is no 'maybe' or room for doubt in the millenarian prophet's vision. If the date predicted for the end passes without anything happening, this may be attributed to a mistake in interpreting the signs, but the general framework remains.

Peter Worsley, in his classic study of Melanesian 'cargo cults', identifies three types of situation in which millenarian movements are apt to occur. First, among people living in 'stateless' societies, who have no social means of organization through which they can act politically as a unified force when the occasion arises; secondly, among the underprivileged ranks in agrarian, and especially feudal, states; and thirdly, when a society is fighting for its existence by military-political means, but is meeting with defeat after defeat (Worsley 1968: 227ff.). In fact all of these categories may fit our case. These highland ethnic groups do not possess any centralized authority above the village level. They are increasingly and unwillingly becoming the underdogs of socially stratified, quasi-feudal states where highlanders are discriminated against because of their looks, poverty, illiteracy, 'lack of refinement', and so on. Finally, most groups have a long and bloody past of fighting, and being defeated by the Chinese, then the Lao, the Thai, the French, and most recently the protagonists of the Vietnam war. As we will see, their myths also emphasize their destiny as 'perennial losers'. Small wonder that millenarianism finds a fertile soil in this environment!

Another important external-political aspect of millenarianism is the borrowing or diffusion of ideas and values from majority to minority. Among the highland minorities one may observe similar processes of change. Where formerly ethnic boundaries were defined by tradition and by interaction with other highland groups, 'proto-national' formations are now developing as a result of culture contact and economic change. Millenarian cults articulate such ideas although as yet in a hazy and utopian language. Sometimes, a re-establishment of a past mythical nation is prophesied, such as the return of the legendary emperor Huab Tais among the Hmong (Tapp 1989). Western ideas, transferred by missionaries and colonial officers, have played a part in this process. Maran La Raw shows that the Kachin of Burma were in the past culturally distinctive only in relation to their immediate neighbours, the Shan and the Chin, and the boundary of cultural influence emanating from these neighbours delimited the Kachin's distinctive area. Only with missionary education from about 1880 did a 'national' consciousness arise. When, in 1947, Kachin witnesses gave their approval for a state of some sort within the independent Union of Burma, all but one of the witnesses were products of the Bhamo missionary schools (Maran 1967: 141f.).

I have discussed what I called the external-political aspect of millenarianism in highland South East Asia. However important this may be for the growing-ground of millenarian movements, it is not sufficient as an explanation. An oppressed minority's reaction may take a variety of expressions: passive isolation, assimilation, or revolutionary struggle. So, why millenarianism? In addition to the external-political factors that trigger the process, there must be a prior cultural inclination for this peculiar reaction. In the following sections I discuss this internal-cultural aspect of millenarianism.

Mythical 'History' and Millenarianism

The enormous impact of writing on history is well known. From the time a writing system is established, it serves as a vast collective memory in which the past (or a selection of past events) is stored; writing freezes or reifies history (Goody 1986; Ong 1982). History in this sense becomes an important tool for the legitimation of power; through selecting, and sometimes 'inventing' history, a suitable version of the past is presented to support the political system (Hobsbawm 1993: 2). In this sense history itself becomes a 'restricted code' which is difficult to argue against (Bloch 1974), because the interpretation of the past is largely monopolized by the state and its experts.

Stateless highland societies of South East Asia present a rather different picture of 'history' and 'the past'. In short, where there is no writing system nor a centralized government, it is possible to have *several pasts* (see the discussion on 'real history' in Tapp 1989: 167–79). Here, history is not finished and written down. Instead it is orally transmitted, open-ended, presenting a multitude of potential scenarios that just *may* be realized in a social context. A shaman's or a millenarian prophet's vision is regarded seriously. Although this cognitive orientation may be found in Asian states and stateless societies alike, there is one general difference. In the states, the organized religion can usually handle such alternative worlds by incorporating them with the official religious system (as Buddhism incorporates local beliefs and spirits, see Tambiah 1984). In Berger and Luckmann's terms, the system-transforming potential of such alternatives is neutralized by 'therapy' instead of by 'annihilation' (Berger and Luckmann 1966: 122ff.). Stateless societies usually lack organized religion though people may nominally be Buddhists or Christians. The alternative worlds of shamans, prophets, and visionaries are expressed fully and forcibly in rituals and other public performances. There is no censorship nor standardization by overriding authorities. Many millenarian, revolutionary, or other counter-movements have started from such an alternate world.

The Flood Myth

A pervasive theme in the mythology of most highland peoples, is that present economic and political inequality is explained as being a consequence of events that took place in mythical times. Present shortcomings are attributed either to the group's ancestors being too clumsy or stupid to gain power (and thereby gain wealth and influence), or to the means of power being withheld from them by superior lowlanders, or Westerners.

In the highlands of mainland South East Asia a wide-spread myth is told by itinerant bards and other knowledgeable people (for a fuller analysis of these myths, see Corlin 1994) about a world-wide inundation and two people who saved themselves from the flood. These Asian analogues of the Christian Noah and his wife are a brother and a sister who then marry each other to repopulate the earth. After a pregnancy that lasts for up to several years, the sister/wife gives birth not to a baby but to a gourd. The gourd is placed outside their hut; the couple hear chattering voices from inside the gourd; and overcome with curiosity, the brother/husband pierces a hole in the gourd. Out of it stream the ancestors of the various ethnic groups of the region.

In variants of the flood myth, the number and names of the peoples who emerge from the gourd differ widely, as one might expect with societies that are spread over a vast geographical area. They appear to have two things in common, however. First, the order of emergence from the gourd is connected with a rank order in terms of seniority and authority; secondly, the ancestor of the group relating the myth is usually the elder sibling in the series. The next part of the story concerns the distribution of riches, civilization, and literacy among these groups. Unvaryingly, the group where the myth is told comes out as losers – poorer, illiterate etc – in this distribution. This is often attributed to sheer folly on behalf of their ancestors; for example, they are illiterate because their ancestors have eaten the buffalo hide, the rice cookies, or whatever contained the art of writing. In another variant inequality is attributed to straightforward deception by lowlanders or other outsiders; for example the Karen attribute this sinister role to the white man, who stole their 'Golden Book' in which the secrets of wealth and literacy were written (Stern 1968).

The highlanders' myths thus contrast the normative obligations between brothers with the realities of their economic and political situation. It is a way of stating that, on the one hand, they cannot become as wealthy or educated as the lowlanders or the Europeans, because their ancestors failed to collect what was their due. On the other hand, they should, as siblings, have the right to claim protection and a fair share of the benefits from their 'kin'. The function of the myth in this context is to transform inequality into asymmetric reciprocity. The myth provides an explanation for the present as well as it gives a norm and a course of action for the future.

Let us review the transformations of the mythical story. The pre-flood world is presented as a social order in which the distinctions between spirits, humans, and animals are minimized. A disaster suddenly happens and this harmonious world is destroyed. The couple who are rescued from the calamity must deny culture through an incestuous union to re-create mankind. But with the multiple 'birth' from the gourd, another kind of social order, based on differentiation of languages, cultures, and riches, is created. One may note that the ideology of the millenarian movements appears, as it were, as a mirror image of the flood myth. These movements prophesy that, soon, the world in its present state will come to an end, and a Golden Age will arrive. Through disaster, inequality will be transformed into equality. Thus the transitions between order and disorder, equality and inequality, come full circle. The millenarian myth is the logical supplement to the flood myth. Through the foreshadowed recovery of the Golden Book that was lost in the times of the flood, something akin to the pre-flood world of equality will be restored.

This must have been the dream of the Miao who stormed Pastor Pollard's home searching for books, and of those Karen who, when they saw a Bible 'at the sight of this unspeakable treasure bowed down and worshipped, wept and caressed the sacred book' (Marshall 1922: 298). But as the promised Golden Age did not materialize, their hope turned into frustration and anger. The white man was transformed into a swindler, who had 'ripped out the first page of the Bible in order to withhold the true secret from us'. Or, as a missionary among the Telakhon reported in 1966:

> 'This year [the Phu Chaik] and some of the leaders were more outspoken than ever before, to the point of accusing us, in effect, of withholding the true "Golden Book" from them. As for the Bible, it doesn't even tell how to repair a radio, let alone all the mysteries of western science!' (Dodge, cited in Stern 1968: 324f).

Conclusion

Millenarianism in highland South East Asia is a result of the historical confluence of several factors: first, the cultural idiom of the highland groups; secondly, the economic–political minority situation of these groups during the late nineteenth and the twentieth centuries; thirdly, the influence of the surrounding majority culture, especially Theravada Buddhism; and fourthly, the influence of missionary Christianity.

The cultural idiom 'refers to particular ways of engaging in millenarian activities which, though consistent with the more abstract and general pattern, may be peculiar to the culture concerned' (Burridge 1969: 30). The cultural idioms of these ethnic groups, despite variation, are nevertheless sufficiently alike to be treated as variations on a theme. Basic cosmology, world-view, and a common mythical tradition provide a common repertoire from which the various expressions are formed.

This cultural idiom is not static or timeless, but has been shaped during a long period of time and in interaction with different peoples; hence the Sinitic and Indic elements, for instance. It is a flexible tradition that may be moulded for different contexts. The myths present the highlanders as 'perennial losers', but they also offer the hopeful prospect of a return of a Golden Age. In modern times, the highland cultures have become exposed to culture contact and change at an increasing pace. The impact of the modern Thai nation and Buddhist Sangha threatens to change highland life in a great number of ways, from delimiting their access to habitable land, to cultural assimilation. Being without any centralized agencies to co-ordinate political action, many highlanders look instead for an alternative to adopting the dominant ideology (although at the same time they are adopting concepts from that dominant ideology, and especially from Theravada Buddhism). Christian missionaries happened to provide such an alternative.

The meeting of Christianity and traditional beliefs is not without humorous elements. Initially, both parties were delighted. The highlanders regarded the arrival of white men with their Golden Books as the fulfilment of the prophecy of the return of the Golden Age. The missionaries on their part were happy with the enthusiasm for the Bible they met, and with the great numbers of converts. They were also surprised to find traditional beliefs that seemed to echo those in the Bible, such as the story of the Deluge. One missionary even proclaimed that the Karen must be 'one of the lost tribes of Israel' (see Marshall 1922: 210f.). In this way, mutual misunderstandings produced a consensus about what was desirable. Subsequent developments show that when cultures meet, something new is produced. The highlanders' cultural idiom, their precarious minority situation, and Christian influence united to create political mass movements of a sudden and unexpected nature. Accompanied by a gradual redefinition of ethnicity towards 'proto-nationalism', these movements provide the ideological background of, for example, the Karen Liberation Army in Burma today.

An ironic ingredient in this process is the Thai interpretation of the ideology and rationale underlying the highlanders' social movements. The primary political concern of the state has been to close down communist influence among the highland minorities. The Border Police Patrol was created to this end, and the military campaign of 1967 was launched in order to stop 'Communism' from challenging the state. But there was probably little substantial communist influence among the highland minorities of Thailand at that time. Instead, it was Christianity that, unknown to the missionaries, provided the catalyst to the counter-movements among these minorities.

Today, these highland minorities are subject to rapid economic and culture change. International tourism and trekking, while providing a

Plate 10. 'Village de Khâs Bolovens'

certain income, nevertheless changes life in many ways. 'Exotic' dress and customs are shown off in order to attract tourists, while television sets and T-shirts replace story-telling and traditional dress at home. At the same time, ethnic consciousness is mounting among young educated people. Urban intellectuals of minority background, such as the Hmong Interest Group in Chiang Mai, propagate a new awareness of the rich traditional ethnic culture, as well as political and economic equality with the majority population. Most highland societies are still living under conditions of both deprivation and stress. Hence, it is unlikely that we have met the last of the millenarian prophets. Whether Worsley's prediction, that active millenarianism is a step on the road to nationalism, holds true for these peoples, remains to be seen.

Notes

1 I am grateful to the Swedish Council for Research in the Humanities and Social Sciences for generous support, to Dr Chayan Vaddhanaphuti and his staff at the Social Research Institute, Chiang Mai University, for their co-operation, and to the Nordic Institute of Asian Studies, Copenhagen, for providing research facilities and valuable advice.
2 Fragments of these traditions appear in many monographs on the region. For a reference list, see Corlin (1994: 36–42). Good analyses are Lemoine (1972) and Tapp (1989), both concerning Hmong. A Kammu version is included in Dundes (1988). To my knowledge, no comparative study has been published.

References

Aberle, D. (1966), *The Peyote Religion among the Navaho*, Viking Fund Publications in Anthropology, 42, New York: Wenner-Gren Foundation for Anthropological Research.

Anderson, B. O'G. (1972), 'The Idea of Power in Javanese Culture', in Claire Holt (ed.), *Culture and Politics in Indonesia*, Ithaca and London: Cornell University Press.

Barkun, M. (1974), *Disaster and the Millennium*, New Haven and London: Yale University Press.

Berger, P. and Th. Luckmann (1966), *The Social Construction of Reality*, Harmondsworth: Penguin Books.

Bhruksasri, W. (1989), 'Government Policy: Highland Ethnic Minorities', in J. McKinnon and B. Vienne (eds.), *Hill Tribes Today*, 1–20, Paris: White Lotus-Orstom (Tri-Orstom Project).

Bloch, M. (1974), 'Symbol, Song and Dance or is Religion an Extreme Form of Traditional Authority?', *European Journal of Sociology*, 15, 55–81.

Boardman, E. P. (1962), 'Millenary Aspects of the Taiping Rebellion', in S. Thrupp (ed.), *Millennial Dreams in Action: Essays in Comparative Study*, Comparative Studies in Society and History, suppl.2, 70–79, The Hague: Mouton.

Burridge, K. (1969), *New Heaven, New Earth: A Study of Millenarian Activities*, Oxford: Basil Blackwell.

Cohn, N. (1970), *The Pursuit of the Millennium: Revolutionary Millenarians and Mystical Anarchists of the Middle Ages*, 3rd ed. New York: Oxford University Press.

Corlin, C. (1994), *Common Roots and Present Inequality: Ethnic Myths among Highland Populations of Mainland Southeast Asia*, NIAS Reports, 17, Copenhagen: Nordic Institute of Asian Studies.

Dessaint, W. Y. (1972), 'The Poppies Are Beautiful This Year', *Natural History*, 81(2), 30–7, 92–6.

Dundes, A. (ed.) (1988). *The Flood Myth*, Berkeley: Berkeley University Press.

Ewers Andersen, K. (1981), 'Two Indigenous Karen Religious Denominations', *Folk*, 23, 250–61.

Goody, J. (1986), *The Logic of Writing and the Organization of Society*, Cambridge: Cambridge University Press.

Hinton, P. (1979), 'The Karen, Millenarianism and Accommodation', in C. Keyes (ed.), *Ethnic Adaptation and Identity. The Karen on the Thai Frontier with Burma*, 81–98, Philadelphia: Institute for the Study of Human Issues.

Hobsbawm, E. (1993), 'Introduction', in E. Hobsbawm and T. Ranger (eds), *The Invention of Tradition,* Cambridge: Cambridge University Press.

Izikowitz, K. G. (1951), *Lamet: Hill peasants of Indo-China* (Etnografiska studier 17), Göteborg: Etnografiska museet.

Keyes, C.F. (1977), 'Millenialism, Theravada Buddhism, and Thai Society', *Journal of Asian Studies*, 23 (2), 283–302.

—— (1993) 'Why the Thai are not Christians', in R.J. Hefner (ed.) *Conversion to Christianity: Historical and anthropological perspectives on a great transformation*, Berkeley, University of California Press.

Kirsch, T. (1973), *Feasting and Social Oscillation*, Cornell Southeast Asia Program Data Paper 92, New York: Ithaca.

La Barre, W. (1970), *The Ghost Dance: The Origins of Religion,* New York: Doubleday.

Leach, E. R. (1954), *Political Systems of Highland Burma*, Boston: Beacon Press.

Lemoine, J. (1972), 'L'initiation du mort chez les Hmong', *L'Homme*, 12 (1), 105–134, 12 (2), 85–125, 12 (3), 84–110.

Maran La Raw, (1967), 'Toward a Basis for Understanding the Minorities in Burma: The Kachin Example', in P. Kunstadter (ed.), *Southeast Asian Tribes, Minorities, and Nations,* 125–146, New York: Princeton University Press.

Marshall, H. I. (1922), *The Karen People of Burma*, Ohio State University Bulletin, 26.

Oliver, V. 1976, *Caodai Spiritism: A Study of Religion in Vietnamese Society,* Leiden: Brill.

Ong, W. J. (1982), *Orality and Literacy: The Technologizing of the Word*, London: Methuen and Co.

Pollard, S. (1919), *The Story of the Miao*, London: Henry Hooks.

Shaw, R. and Ch. Stewart (1994), 'Introduction: Problematizing Syncretism', in Rosalind Shaw and Charles Stewart (eds.), *Syncretism/Anti-Syncretism: The Politics of Religious Synthesis,* London and New York: Routledge.

Spiro, M. E. (1967), *Burmese Supernaturalism*, Englewood Cliffs: Prentice Hall.

Stein, R. A. (1962), *Tibetan Civilization*, London: Faber and Faber.

Stern, Th. (1968), 'Ariya and the Golden Book: A Millenarian Buddhist Sect among the Karen', *Journal of Asian Studies*, 27, 297–328.

Tambiah, S. J. (1976), *World Conqueror and World Renouncer: A Study of Buddhism and Polity in Thailand against a Historical Background*, Cambridge: Cambridge University Press.

—— (1978), 'The Buddhist Conception of Kingship and its Historical Manifestations: A Reply to Spiro', *Journal of Asian Studies*, 37 (4), 801–809.

—— (1984), *The Buddhist Saints of the Forest and the Cult of Amulets,* Cambridge: Cambridge University Press.

Tannenbaum, N. (1989), 'Power and its Shan Transformations', in S. D. Russell (ed.), *Ritual, Power & Economy: Upland-Lowland Contrast in Mainland Southeast Asia*, 67–87, (Occasional Paper No. 14.), Northern Illinois University: Center for Southeast Asian Studies.

Tapp, N. (1989), *Sovereignty and Rebellion: The White Hmong of Northern Thailand*, Oxford: Oxford University Press.

Turton, A. and Tanabe, S. (eds.) (1984) *History and Peasant Consciousness in South East Asia*, Osaka, National Museum of Ethnology.

Van Esterik, P. (1982), 'Interpreting a Cosmology: Guardian Spirits in Thai Buddhism', *Anthropos*, 77 (1), 1–15.

Walker, A. R. (1992a), 'North Thailand as Geo-Ethnic Mosaic', in A. R. Walker (ed.), *The Highland Heritage: Collected Essays on Upland North Thailand*, 1–93, Singapore: Suvarnabhumi Books.

—— (1992b) (1986), 'Transformations of Buddhism in the Religious Ideas and Practices of a Non-Buddhist Hill People: the Lahu Nyi of the Northern Thai Uplands', in A. R. Walker (ed.), *The Highland Heritage: Collected Essays on Upland North Thailand*, 381–409, Singapore: Suvarnabhumi Books.

Worsley, P. (1968), *The Trumpet Shall Sound*, New York: Schocken Books.

Young, G. (1962), *The Hill Tribes of Northern Thailand*, Bangkok: The Siam Society.

Chapter Six

Akha Internal History: Marginalization and the Ethnic Alliance System

Leo Alting von Geusau

Introduction

Anthropologists of mainland South East Asia have long debated questions of ethnic identity. In the colonial period anthropologists tended to think in terms of a naturalistic kind of pluralism. Later a more politico-economic and historical approach emerged, for instance in the work of Leach (1954), Lehman (1963), and Keyes (1977). It became clear that an ethnic system or group was not necessarily bound by historically persistent genetic relations, but that ethnic sub-groups could change affiliation and become members of a different ethnic system. These changes tended to be determined by politico-economic variables (Friedman, 1971, 1975). Since the 1970s the concept 'ethnic minority (group)' emerged as that of an ethnic group in a disadvantaged, unequal politico-economic situation, and in a way dependent on a dominant 'majority group' (Geusau, 1986).

Latin American anthropologists, in particular the '*indigenistas*' in Mexico had earlier examined mechanisms of ethnic minority formation and history, in specific ecological contexts. Beltram – in his excellent but unfortunately little known book *Zonas de refugio* (1965) – concluded that certain ethnic groups in mountainous and other inaccessible areas, rich in resources such as wildlife, timber, plants, and minerals, had been marginalized together with these resources. Such peoples, usually 'tribal', and the ecological niches and resource areas to which they had adapted, had formerly covered much larger areas, in which they themselves might have been the politico-economically dominant groups. Expanding outside forces, benefiting from access to international trade routes, came to establish centres of power and population that would gradually 'graze away' those resources, which together with their inhabitants would increasingly be limited to more inaccessible areas. In this process tribal minorities would find themselves identified with 'nature', as the lowest social stratum in the new state systems (Beltram, 1965: 87).

Beltram had Latin America in mind, but his '*zonas de refugio*' (regions of refuge) model seems to fit the South East Asian case, as well as the Himalayan foothills, and has been a guiding thread in my own work for many years in the ethno-analysis of Akha culture. Living with the Akha as their student it became clear to me that the history of their political and ecological marginalization and their overcoming this in continuous adaptation constitutes the very heart of their culture (Geusau, 1983a, 1983b). An effort of intense but sustainable use of ecological resources and adaptation to nearby power centres are reflected in *mnemesis* of traditional knowledge − conceived as continuing historical 'lines' of events − concerning ecology, agriculture, law, life-style, psychology, rituals, kinship, ancestor service, and the genealogical system. Without this dimension a minority culture like that of the Akha cannot possibly be understood. It is part of Akha mechanisms of survival.

In the present study I try to summarise several aspects of the Akha 'internal historical' records, related to the historical process of the marginalization and dispersal of the Akha in the context of ethnic relations. In particular I try to clarify the contradiction as to why Akha (and related Hani peoples) in spite of being interspersed with other ethnic groups, and having many sub-groups, separated geographically for centuries, have been able to maintain a remarkable unity in their *zang*, *yang*, or *yaw-ti* (customary law). The final section concentrates on the Akha genealogical network − their strongest unifying device − and the 'ethnic alliance system' which results from it, especially Hani/Akha ethnic relations with various Tai peoples.

The Akha/Hani Diaspora and Its Historical Context

Geographical Dispersal

The Hani/Akha are a people, an estimated 2.5 million persons, spread over Yunnan province in Southwest China, the northern parts of Laos, Vietnam and Thailand, and eastern Burma. They live in a central part of what is currently called the 'Mekong Quadrangle' between 19 and 24 degrees North, 99 and 105 degrees East, an area of about 500 by 600 km or 30,000 square kilometres, somewhat the size of the European Alps. It is crossed by several major rivers: the Mekong, the Red and Black Rivers, and the Salween, and their many tributaries which cut steep valleys, up to 2,500–3,000m. Of crucial contemporary significance, this border area covers part of the territory of five modern nation-states. The total population of this region, including quickly growing industrial centres, is about 15–20 million. Akha and Hani live mostly in the mountains interspersed with other ethnic groups, but concentrated in certain areas.

Akha/Hani in Yunnan

Those classified as **Hani** by the present Chinese Government are concentrated in the following areas.

(i) The Honghe Autonomous Hani/Yi Prefecture around the Red River, just North of the border between China and Vietnam. Subgroups call themselves by the following names: Xalo, Lopi, Goxo, Piyo, Kato, Ngonu, Xaoni, Pexon, Lami, Gojo, Xiti, Amu, Yicheu. They have mutually intelligible languages and have been classified as Hani by the Chinese (Boucherie, 1995 vol. 1). They are called Dzjha-deh by the Akha, a name unknown to any group among them. Their dialect is different from Akha, but not unintelligible. They live together with Han Chinese in the cities, and with Yi (formerly called Lolo) and smaller numbers of Hmong and Mien. There are also considerable numbers of Tai Dam (Black Tai) and Zhuang in the Red River valley. Yi are the largest minority group in Yunnan, mostly spread along the Ailao Shan mountain range, reaching up to Sichuan Province. Several Hani groups or part-Hani/part-Yi (e.g. the Nisu/Hani) can still be found there (Mao Youquan and Li Qibo, 1989).

(ii) The Simao Prefecture in central southern Yunnan. Akha/Hani are mainly distributed in the Ailao Shan and Wuliang Shan mountains, and in the mountains and valleys of Mojiang, Babianjiang, and Lancangjiang districts. They are concentrated in and around the autonomous city and county of Mojiang where two-thirds of the population of more than 300,000 is Hani. This is the only autonomous Hani County in Yunnan. Hani also live densely in Jiancheng, Puer, Zheng-juan, and Lancang. Hani branches here are: Kadu, Budu, Bukong, Duta, and Biyue. Hani live interspersed with Han Chinese and Dai in the valleys, and with Lisu, Lahu, and Yi in the mountains (Cun Wen Xue 1996).

Peoples calling themselves **Akha** are concentrated in the following areas:

(i) the Xixuangbanna (in Tai: Sipsongpanna) Dai Autonomous Prefecture just North of Laos and the north-eastern Burmese border;
(ii) the Puer Prefecture Southwest of Kunming city;
(iii) the Lancang (Menglangba) Lahu/Wa Autonomous Prefecture near the north-eastern Burmese border.

In these areas Hani/Akha live both in the mountains and with Tai Lue (Dai), or Shan (Tai Yai) in the lowland valleys. In this context they are 'minority peoples'. In the last three areas the Akha are called **Aini** by the contemporary Chinese Government and are lumped together ethnographically with the Hani. They are called Kha Kaw by the Tai-speaking peoples, Akha by the Yunnanese Chinese. The Akha call the Dai and Tai

Yai Bitsm or Atsm, the Chinese Labui, and the Yunnanese Chinese Pehnyoe (green shirts).

The number of Akha (Aini – here excluding Hani) in China, can be safely estimated at about 600,000–700,000 persons, as official statistics only count those in 'areas of concentration' (Stewart Cox and Hall, 1984). The total number of Hani/Akha in China thus can be estimated at nearly 2 million people. The name Aini or A-nyi was given to the Akha by Chinese ethnographers and linguists in the Mao era. It was based on the conviction that the affix *kha* is related to the ancient Tai word for 'serf', 'slave' or minority peoples regarded as such. The Akha themselves believe, however, that it is related to a Tibeto-Burman syllable (low tone, *kha*) meaning 'distance' or 'span'. Akha interpret their name as 'people of the middle'.

Akha in Burma

Peoples calling themselves Akha are concentrated in the mountains of eastern Burma (Myanmar) in Kengtung (Shan) State, interspersed with Lahu, Lisu, and Wa peoples; the lowlanders are Shan. Many Akha have been displaced during the last 30–40 years by incursions of the Burmese army, internecine warfare, including warlords such as Khun Sa (Lintner, 1990). This has concentrated many around Kengtung city and the town of Ho Ki Lek, near the northern Thai border. Many have become Christian, chiefly Catholic, especially the more urbanised. The number of Akha in Burma is difficult to estimate, but is certainly up to 150,000 (Akha Society for Culture and Art, Kengtung, 1996). They are called Kaw by Shan and Burmese. They are the largest highland minority in north-eastern Burma.

Akha in Northern Laos

The Akha in Laos are concentrated in the higher areas of the high plateau of Phongsaly (close to the Black River and Vietnam) and Luang Namtha Province (bordering Sipsongpanna, Burma, and the Mekong River) interspersed with Mien, Hmong, Khmu, Htin, Lisu, and Lahu. Lowlanders are a range of Tai-minority peoples, varying according to different valley and basin locations, and include: Tai Lue (Dai), Tai Dam (Black Tai), Tai Yuang or Yang, Tai Neua, Tai Khao (White Tai) and Tai Doi (Mountain Tai) (Chazee, 1995: 33 ff.). Some were displaced during the Vietnam war, in which they were involved in fighting the Americans or the CIA Hmong groups led by Vang Pao, and in conflicts between the Pathet Lao groups (Dassé, 1976; Cooper and Tapp, 1991). People calling themselves Akha in Laos are called, in Lao, I-ko or Kha Ko. Other names given by outsiders include: Puli, Pussang, Oepa, Oema, and Kopien. Most Tai-speaking lowland groups are called Bitsm by Akha. The number of Akha in Laos can be estimated conservatively to be between 92,000–100,000, but might well be higher (Lao UNESCO Committee, 1996; Duy Thieu, 1996).

Hani-related Peoples in Northern Vietnam

These peoples, related to those in the south-eastern Red River/Honghe Prefecture of Yunnan live in the upper-North of Vietnam near the Chinese border, together with Tai Dam and more recently Vietnamese. Their number is estimated at 20,000–25,000. They are called Xo by the Vietnamese. There are also 2,000–3,000 Akha living near the Lao border, in mountains bordering the Black River (Duy Thieu, 1996).

Akha in Northern Thailand

They are concentrated in the northern border province of Chiang Rai, but some have spread to Chiang Mai, Phrao, Phayao, and Lampang Provinces (Tribal Research Institute, 1995: 52–9). Most have entered Thailand during the last 130–150 years, as a consequence of wars in neighbouring countries. The Akha are interspersed with Lisu, Lahu, Karen, Hmong, and Yao/Mien peoples in the mountains. Until the 1970s the mountains, which make up 35% of Thailand and 65% of its northern 22 provinces, were thinly populated. The mountain peoples were a majority of the population of the mountains. Since the defeat of Chiang Kai Chek in 1949, the northern Thai mountains have been inhabited by a number of Kuomintang refugees known as Haw or Yunnanese Chinese refugees (Hanks, 1975). Lowlanders are Khon Müang Thai. Since the 1970s and 1980s poor Thai peasants have moved into the mountains looking for land, with the result that tribal minority peoples formed a 10% minority in the mountains by the late 1980s (Geusau, 1989), notwithstanding an influx of refugees from Burma, escaping internecine warfare. Since the mid-1980s loss of forest and growing insecurity over land rights and citizenship have encouraged many younger Akha to move to the towns and cities of the North. The Akha are called Ekaw (I-Ko) by the Thai. Unlike any other minority or mountain group it seems, their name has sometimes been prefixed, in northern Thailand at least, by the Tai classifying word *meng* which is used for insects and some other small insect-like animals – and also figuratively as in English 'small fry' – for example as in *meng i-ko*, where the prefix /i/ is itself a diminutive or connotes intermediate status or classificatory oddity of some sort (cf. Wijeyewardene, 1968; Wijeyewardene does not however refer to the usage *i-ko*, but see Cit Phumisak, 1976: 469–70).

The official number of Akha in the mountains of Thailand is now 58,000 persons (Tribal Research Institute, 1995). Given the high number of non-registered Akha and large scale urbanisation, the total number of Akha in Thailand is probably closer to 75,000 persons.

We will from here on call the **Hani** from the Honghe/Red River area, and northern Vietnam by that name; and we shall call **Akha** those related groups living in and around Sipsongpanna in Yunnan, Burma, Laos, and Thailand (the so-called 'Golden Triangle').

Ethno-linguistic Characteristics of Hani/Akha Sub-groups

Hani and Akha are considered to be of the Tibeto-Burman language family, closely related to the Yi (Lolo), also to the Lisu and Lahu in western Yunnan, Burma, and Thailand (Matisoff, 1978, 1983; Bradley, 1979). Yunnan has a larger number of Tibeto-Burman language related minority groups who in earlier centuries were characterised by the Han as 'Man' (barbarians) or Ch'iang (Sainson, 1904; Wiens, 1967). A distinction was made between 'Wu-man' (black bone barbarians – non-sinicized or wild) and 'Pai-man' (white bone barbarians – sinicized). Important amongst these are the Naxi and Bai, who live near the city of Dali and Dali lake and were probably the dominant groups in the Nanchao Kingdom 750–1250 AD (Wiens, 1967; Backus, 1981). Hani speak dialects of a language mutually intelligible with Akha. Chinese linguists have developed a Romanized script, which is in moderate use locally, though Chinese is the language used in school.

Akha – excepting those who have become Christians – use clan names as lineage and family names. They are less often used to identify sub-groups. These are numerous and mostly are not localised, even less so since the 'drifts' of the last 50 years. Clan names are personal, genealogical, names, and not totemic or animal names as with the Lisu. Some of the older, more prestigious clan names, as we shall see later, go back 30–45 generations to a founding ancestor, others 15–25 generations or fewer as a result of fission in the clan. In some cases Akha may use what we might call 'super clan' names, referring to common ancestors of major, older clans of between 45–55 generations, in contradistinction to clans which branched off later but still in very early times. All Akha genealogical names go back to an apical ancestor and common founder of all Akha and Hani tribal groups, Sm-io. For the older clans this is 55–60 generations ago.

There are three main typologies, or criteria for typologizing, used to distinguish major Akha sub-groups which have substantial differences in customary law and dialect. These are used rather promiscuously in the literature and in practice by various parties.

The first criterion is geographic region or even village of concentration, whether this is present-day or from a remembered past; for example

Loimisa Akha (a mountain region in the Burmese Shan states), and Phami Akha and Bala Akha (villages in northern Thailand and Sipsongpanna region of China respectively).

Secondly, distinctions of dress, and most especially women's head-dress. There are many variations in these, and as far as I know no-one has attempted to compile an inventory of them. Note that place names recur as the markers for head-dress styles. They include: Ulo Akha (cone shaped), Loimisa Akha (trapezium shaped), Phami Akha (like a silver veil over the head), Tan-kui Akha (with a tail over the neck shaped like an ant-eater), Law-sang Akha (with a rattan frame and tail of the law-sang flower), Udzang Akha (turban style), U-taw Akha (small, round shape).

Thirdly, and most especially by Akha themselves, genealogical ('super clan' and clan) names may be used to indicate differences in language, customary law, language, and (at least until recently) geographical location. Examples are the Adzjaw Akha and the Akheu (or Akhui), the latter not even wanting to call themselves Akha. These are distinct from descendants of Dzeugh'oe, the Mangpo Akha, and those who claim descent from the Mazeu (or Majeu).

These criteria for classifying sub-groups sometimes overlap in use as the consequence of intermarriage and social and spatial drift. In Thailand until the 1950s most Akha were Ulo Akha from the Dzjeugh'oe and Majeu sub-groups. Subsequently, immigration of refugees from Burma lead to a considerable increase in Loimisa Akha, mostly of the Dzjeugh'oe sub-group. Akha immigrants from China in the same period included a considerable number of Phami Akha of the Mangpo sub-group and a smaller number of Akheu, also known as Udzang Akha.

Historical Context of the Hani and Akha as known from external sources

It is now generally accepted that the Nanchao kingdom which dominated most of Yunnan between the eighth to thirteenth centuries AD was a Tibeto-Burman, rather than a Tai kingdom (Backus, 1981). During this period the ancestors of contemporary Hani and Akha inhabited southern Nanchao – that is the southern part of Yunnan, where the majority still live today – and border areas of contemporary Burma, Laos, and northern Vietnam. Yi/Lolo and related groups, namely southern Yi/Lolo, including Hani/Akha ancestors, had been in the area since at the latest Ch'in (221–207 BC) and Han (206 BC–220 AD) times. Nanchao, as a confederation of tribal chiefdoms or petty states, emerged under the leadership of Ko-lo-feng in the eighth century AD, starting from the chiefdom of Meng-she, or Nanchao, on the Red River, which was already a Yi/Hani area (Backus, 1981: 51; Luce, 1961). Some have speculated that the distant origin of Yi/Hani may have been in eastern Tibet; others have argued that the Sichuan plains would have been a more likely original habitat (Wiens, 1967; Bradley, 1979; Boucherie 1995, Vol. 1). In southern Yunnan these groups had met and partly merged with a Mon-Khmer speaking population. From the beginning of the modern era Han Chinese have considered Hani/Akha ancestors or Heni and Yi/Lolo, in Sichuan, eastern and southern Yunnan, and adjacent parts of Guizhou, as one of the main indigenous groups. They were not limited to the Talian Shan and Ailao Shan mountains, but also cultivated rice in the Red River, Black River, and probably also the Mekong river valleys. They were also identified as Ts'uan (Wiens, 1965: 93; Boucherie, 1995, Vol. 1).

Mon-Khmer language related groups lived to the South of the Tibeto-Burman groups which dominated Yunnan. Tai, as a distinct, valley-based small warrior-state group are not mentioned under that name until the twelfth century AD, just before the Buddhist Mongol invasion, under Kublai Khan, reached southern Yunnan and ended the Nanchao kingdom. By this time most Hani and Akha groups were living in close contact with Tai language groups in nearby valleys. Akha mythologies are in agreement that Tai warrior groups and city states (*müang*) were 'late-comers', and either absorbed them or marginalized them into higher mountain areas (Shi Junchao, 1988, 1991; Mao Youquan, 1989). They were 'late' in the sense that by the twelfth and thirteenth centuries they were able to develop from a 'tribal minority' into a dominant, quickly expanding proto-state system, based in valleys with irrigated rice cultivation. This seems correct historically, as the first twelve Tai *müang* of Sipsongpanna (Xixuangbanna) originated in the twelfth century. Yunnanese records tell of the conquest of the lowland areas by the Tai Lue warrior Ba Zhen in 1180 AD, driving Hani/Akha, Palaung, and others higher into the mountains. This was not long before the Mongol invasions (Li Fuyi, 1946: 7).

Han Chinese were also 'late-comers' in Yunnan, in the sense of colonial administrators. This was largely due to the inability of Han Chinese armies to subdue the rebellious Yi peoples in the Ailao Shan mountains. However the first invasions of Han Chinese certainly pre-date the Christian era. They established tribute obligations, and set up a network of fortified colonial trading centres on trade routes to the south-western border areas. The latter consisted of large walled quadrangular cities, with a core of trading gentry, surrounded by irrigated fields. Irrigation canals were controlled by the rulers or 'owners', those able to dominate the surrounding territory. Fields were tilled by a class of soldier/agriculturists, preferably local tribal peoples. Han Chinese were also appointed to these agricultural garrison cities, but they seem to have 'gone tribal', and were later be called 'Yunnanese Chinese' (Haw) (Backus, 1981: 8; Wiens, 1965: 302).

The Chinese established the *tu'ssu* (vassal) system, of 'faithful' tribal chiefs, who had to re-write their genealogies to fit the Imperial/Confucian system. The local Tibeto-Burman (Yi/Hani/Akha) name for such a tu'ssu was

'Dze-ma', 'Dze-maw', or 'Dzoe-ma' (ruler) signifying that the Chief or his ancestor had received the feudal 'clay tablet' with the Imperial Chinese Seal, conveying the authority to rule. The office was hereditary. The Han Chinese learnt that the Barbarians in the frontier areas were better ruled by the Barbarians themselves (Wiens, 1965: 201 ff.; Boucherie, 1995, Vol. 1: 257 ff.). As in the case of the Tai states, these vassal states could easily develop into oppressive hierarchically structured mini-states or chiefdoms, such as the He-man/Hani chiefdoms in Yunnan (Huang Shirong, 1991).

The Chinese annals relate that when the armies of Kublai Khan invaded, several tribal *tu'ssu*, in particular the Hani or He-man, offered prolonged resistance. In this context the walled city of Mojiang or Ta-lang (Akha: Tm-lang) is mentioned (Mojiang Editorial Committee, 1983). Full occupation of Yunnan and submission of the Wu-man, He-man, and Yung Barbarians was achieved slowly in bloody wars between the sixteenth and nineteenth centuries. This culminated in the Yunnan war between 1855–1873 in which the tribal peoples of the south-western border areas joined a rebellion of the Islamic Haw Chinese against Manchu rule. The rebellion was also triggered by the danger of infiltration by Western colonial powers through China's 'back-door', Yunnan, and its fabulous resources. This is confirmed by French and British sources. The British had occupied Burma. The French had brought the 'miracles' of French 'civilization' to Cochin China in the form of a rigid system of taxation and forced labour. In Yunnan they found an impoverished and desperate population, oppressed by Hani, or Tai tu'ssu and Chinese administrators (Scott and Hardiman, 1900; Bonifacy, 1904; Henry, 1903; Madrolle, 1925; Vial, 1917).

Over many centuries, therefore, the more inaccessible parts of mountainous southern Yunnan, and neighbouring Vietnam, Laos, and Burma became the '*zonas de refugio*' for tribal groups marginalized by the smaller vassal states which occupied the lowland areas. In this process of marginalization, tribal groups such as the Hani and Akha also selected and constructed their habitats – in terms of altitude and surrounding forestation – in such a way that they would not be easily accessible to soldiers, bandits, and tax-collectors. Such processes have been termed 'encapsulation' (Douglas, 1965). They led in this case to differentiation in dialect and forms of dress. In parallel, however, they developed a distinctive unifying social and political structure, which I have called an 'ethnic alliance system'.

Akha Internal Historical Records of Marginalization and Inter-ethnic Relations

Before investigating how far Akha 'internal historical records' correspond with 'external historical data' we must briefly discuss the reliability of the former. This is to raise the question of hermeneutics in a post- and pre-literate society. Akha and Hani societies are 'post-literate' in the sense that they stem from highly developed Yi-Chia groups which possessed a script, as their histories tell us. They are 'pre-literate' in that they had 'lost' their script; they say 'they ate their books of buffalo-hide when they were hungry' (Lewis, 1969, Vol. 1: 35; Yang Wanzhi, 1991).

Mnemesis, the memorising and oral transmission of 'traditional knowledge', including their history of overcoming problems, their use and reproduction of ecological resources, and their reaction to external political pressures, are part of their capacity to survive, their 'survival system'. Not all their 'oral literature' can be considered such, however. Hermeneutic principles, as given by Akha and Hani society itself, have to be used to assess the value of their historical records and stories.

Hermeneutics of Akha Texts and Histories

Hermeneutics means to interpret the meaning and value of historical texts. It is impossible to understand Akha culture and history without knowing a wide range of different oral texts and the value given to each of them by the Akha themselves, that is to say their village leaders (Dzoema), teachers and reciters (Phima or Boemaw) and technicians (Badzji). While Nanga, self-taught lay person, may occasionally be helpful, specialists have been trained over many years to be responsible for the transmission of history and traditional knowledge.

A distinction can be made between the following genres:

(i) Archaic and standardised oral Phima/Dzoema texts, whose wide distribution among Akha and Hani sub-groups indicates antiquity.
(ii) Folk-tales, stories, legends told especially by elders. These may be derived from the historical Phima/Dzoema texts, or be popular stories explaining contemporary phenomena, or have a moral rather than historical intention, deriving perhaps from neighbouring tribal or lowland groups. Examples are stories of the 'twin saved from the flood in a pumpkin', 'the origin of rice', 'the hunting of the ten suns leading to darkness' etc.
(iii) Children's 'fairy tales', of the sort familiar to so many cultures. They have educational value, but cannot be taken seriously as historical records. They include stories about Mawhui and Mawnyi, and several stories about tigers, spirits, and *pehseu* (werewolves and vampires) (Hansson, 1984b).

Older Akha texts start from an image of world and universe different from contemporary Akha conceptions; words and concepts change in content, or have double meanings. In many cases 'flowery' or poetic language is used to describe historical facts. The 'historical kernel' has to be detached from this 'flowery' packaging. A major example of misunderstanding is the common translation of '*neh*' as 'spirit(s)' whereas it means rather 'an invisible/ unobservable (but physical) force or entity'. Ignorance of these principles has lead to ridiculous and misleading descriptions of their cultures and philosophies by outsiders, especially missionaries, but not excluding Western, Thai, and Chinese ethnographers (Scholte, 1975). A younger generation of Akha or Hani, on reading some of the accounts in English or Chinese, often feels highly offended by this discriminatory literature. But they would rather 'make jokes towards the outside' than protest. Errors can in part be explained also by an older generation of Akha teachers who were formerly unwilling to share their knowledge 'to the outside' in what might now be appropriate ways, preferring to conceal, minimise, or distort their knowledge as part of a defensive strategy (Geusau, 1990: 30).

A brief survey is necessary of the more accessible archaic oral Akha texts relating to history, non-territoriality, poverty, and inter-ethnic relations. A fuller account is in preparation. These 'archaic oral texts' are part of a large 'corpus' of pre-literate and maybe partly even 'post-literate' poetic and ritual-related literature. Some texts may go back to a common background with the Yi/Lolo, who had a literate class of *Bemo* (cf. Akha Phima or Boemaw). They are the possession of trained Phima teachers and reciters, trained as Phiza (students) over a period of ten years or more. Phima belong to different Phima schools, of which there are three or four in Thailand. Training of Phizas requires a literal, word-by-word, concentrated, 'meditative' type of memorisation. Before each major recitation 10–20 generations of deceased Phima and ancestors are invoked to witness and check the faithfulness of their memory. Cosmic irregularities are expected to occur in case of incorrect memorisation (Geusau, 1983: 268).

The language of 'archaic oral texts' is not easily understandable by a lay-person. This indicates that 'old language' is being used, although the age of the texts has not been established. What has been established however is that Phima or Boemaw from Akha groups with considerable language differences, nonetheless possess almost identical 'archaic' texts. Even Hani and Akha who separated more than 800 years ago share archaic texts with a high degree of mutual intelligibility. These texts are recited at ceremonial occasions, and other opportunities are taken to recite them in order to teach Akha customary law.

Archaic Oral Texts as Historical Records of Akha Migrations

Gadzangghaeu (Recitations of the roads and origins)

This is frequently used, especially at funerals, as the souls of the deceased have to return by the same road to the original ancestral village. The final parts are thus specific to each village and group, but the roads taken long ago are often similar (Dzoedang, 1979a: 116; Shida and Ahai, 1992; Shi Junchao, 1988a; Dzoebaw, 1980). In the distant past, ancestors came from very high up, moving down and settling in several places. They had conflicts with oppressive Yi/Lolo or related rulers, one of whom was Jabioelang, who initiated the yearly census (*jatjitjieu*). They settled there in Dzadeh Mikh'an, the land of the Hani, near the Red and Black rivers, with the Hani rulers (Abaw Dzadeh) and the Chinese. They grew rice there. It became the Akha's real homeland. Wars, oppression, and the arrival of the Tai forced them to move away from Tm-lang and the Red and Black river areas into south-western Yunnan, crossing the Mekong into Sipsongpanna. There they were driven into the mountains by Tai warriors. From there each group took a different Road.

Sjhazizieu songs and Tjiditjieu ceremony

These describe the history of Dzjawbang, the shamanic, tyrannical Akha ruler of Tm-lang, his death (tyrannicide at the hands of Akha themselves), his succession by two further generations, and the 'loss of the power to rule' (see also Lewis, 1968, Vol. 1: 42 ff.). Because this story describes the violent death of an Akha killed by Akha, it cannot be mentioned in the ritual Phima texts (Dzoebaw, 1980).

The period of the Dzjawbang dynasty about 30 generations ago, is described as a time when the chiefs of the principal older clans, led by the head of Majeu (Mazeu) clan, formed an alliance. It is suggested that Akha customary law (*zang/jang*), specifying detailed rules and regulations for all areas of life, was systematised at this time (Lewis, 1969, Vol. 1: 46).

Guidzuieu

This recounts the (male) ancestor names, from their origin at M-*ma* (Heaven) through Sm-io, the founder, and apical ancestor of all Akha. Genealogical names are the actual names of Akha today who may trace as many as 58–60 generations from Sm-io. Some genealogies are closer to the founder. This genealogical system is like an archive of Akha history. It is used in funeral ceremonies, but also in daily life, to work out the distance between people. The main repository of the genealogies of village clans is the Phima, as they have to be recited at funerals, but most older males know their own genealogy.

The genealogy contains the names of the founding fathers of Akha sub-groups, and affirms their contemporaneity with Dzjawbang. It shows that several originally non-Akha groups entered the Akha 'ethnic alliance system' less than 600 years ago, after they had been marginalized into the mountains. These included poorer marginalized Tai and Chinese, 'mountain people' such as the Lahu, and 'forest people' such as the Wa. These had to become Akha by attaching themselves to the ancestor system and accepting Akha customary law. The Akha call this *padaweu*, or 'adoption' of a group or person into the Akha alliance system by inter-marriage or, in the past, as *jakh'a* (bonded servant). This did not happen in a 'class' context however, but in a 'family' context, leading to integration. There are particular places in the genealogical system where a group or person can attach themselves, and several such groups are aware of this. In the past this led to a ranking of clans and lineage groups, with related marriage prohibitions (Mao Youquan, 1996). I return to this later.

Landlessness, Poverty, Oppression, and Marginalization: References from Archaic Oral texts (Songs and Rituals)

Loss of lowland to the Tai

Loss of lowland, in particular to the Tai, is a recurring theme in Akha and Hani texts.

Euleubieu *and* Latzeubieu songs
These songs accompany the yearly Akha swinging ceremony, held at the end of August, which the Akha say they learnt from Abaw Dzjadeh, a Hani leader, before the splitting of Akha from Hani. Swinging songs explain, among other things, the loss of lowland in Sipsongpanna to the Tai, and thus Akha 'non-territoriality' (Geusau, 1987: 1–2; Lewis, 1968, Vol. 1: 54; Kammerer, 1988: 277 ff.).

Misang laweu
This is the offering to the 'owners of the land, the mountains, and the water' (the specific locality of the village). The ceremony is performed in a Tai way, by bowing with clasped hands (*wai*) – not an Akha gesture – in the four directions of the winds. The ceremony is performed in both Akha and Hani areas, with some variations. In Thailand today it implies the supreme 'Lord of the Land' HM the King of Thailand; in former times other local Tai, Shan, and Tai Lue princes. A related text *Jasang laweu*, is sung in the fields and refers to the 'owner' of that particular field. Many things, besides land, mountains, rivers, and fields, have an 'owner', or *jawsang*. The ceremony is performed outside the village. Akha villages in Thailand do

not have a shrine for an <u>ancestral</u> village owner inside the village, indicating that they do not consider themselves owners of territory (cf. Condominas, 1978: 181; Lehman, 1963, 1980).

Kajehjeheu

This is a ceremony to drive out *neh* or 'invisible evil forces' from the village, by which the lowland majority Tai are intended. It may be noted again here that translating *neh* or *jawsang* as 'spirits' or 'spirit owners' gives a seriously misleading interpretation (Dzoebaw, 1982; Geusau, 1989)

Corvée and slave-trade

Lakhoetoeu, Lanyitoeu, Ladubeu

These are psycho-somatic sickness rituals and their texts intended to retrieve the *sala* ('soul', 'energy parts') of the patient, from the 'underworld'. A journey to this world, with nine layers, is described as a descent from the mountain into the lowlands, where the person's soul has been captured in the 'labyrinth of the dragon' and condemned to perform corvée or slave labour for life. In order to recover the person's soul and strength, they have to offer a pig or other large animal, such as a buffalo (in the case of a family with able-bodied people), in exactly the manner that was usual in the slave-trade (Dzoedang, 1979a; Dzoebaw, 1982; Geusau, 1990).

Themes of hunger, poverty, and loss of irrigated lowland

The lack of food, especially meat, is a recurrent theme, particularly in love-songs, in which the singer is a poor man. Poverty, hunger, loneliness, losing husbands and boyfriends are also expressed in the many forms of *Kajehtsjaeu*, or what we could call Akha 'blues', which are nowadays sung mainly by women (Geusau, 1981).

Akha in northern Thailand have been mostly 'swiddeners'. Most have tried to combine this form of agriculture when possible with irrigated rice-agriculture. In contemporary Thailand we have seen how Akha villages, while trying to occupy lower, irrigable land, have been 'pushed uphill' by Thai lowlanders, and so into swiddening. This seems to be history repeating itself. A striking theme in archaic Phima texts (in particular *Gadzang ghaeu*) is that the Hani and Akha started irrigated wet-terrace agriculture (*dehja*) long ago. Most texts mention three types of rice-fields (Tooker, 1996; Geusau, 1993; Dzoedang, 1979):

(i) *dehma* bigger, flat, (river-fed) irrigated (valley-based) fields, not necessarily needing strong dikes. They are mostly referred to as Tai fields (Dzoedang, 1979: 119).

(ii) *dehja* smaller, flat and terraced, (source-fed) irrigated (up-hill) fields, with strong dikes. Hani and many Akha from the 'Triangle' still have such terraces. They are referred to as Akha fields and the imagery of this field is used in many metaphors (Dzoedang, 1979: 97–8, 100, 120, 142, 149, 166, 206).

(iii) *jagneh* swidden, rain-fed, and steep (non-irrigated) mountain-field. In older Phima texts swiddening is not mentioned as the normal means of production. Swiddening methodology and rules are mentioned as being the knowledge of the Dzoema, or traditional village leader who is more practically oriented. Texts describing swiddening seem to be less archaic, and closer to contemporary Akha language (Dzoedang, 1979: 168; Majeu Takh'ang, 1997).

Stories of oppression and exploitation

These too are numerous, and like the previously mentioned stories, are partly veiled, humorous accounts, in which Akha ridicule powerful others. Two examples of older texts and one more recent are offered here.

(i) Mawhui and Mawnyi, imaginary brothers, descend the nine levels to the underground world with their hunting dog. They are helped by the bamboo-rat and squirrel. They visit the dragon and the 'Akha aunt' who lives in the Dragon's house. The Dragon (*Bjehjang*) is the symbol of oppressive forces and demands impossible tasks, such as collecting 100,000 *tang* of sesame in one day, or collecting 20,000 kilos of ants' brains in a day, and so on. This can be circumvented by fooling the Dragon, thanks to the Akha aunt (*Akh'o*, father's sister). It is not completely clear if the dragon refers to the Naga of the Tai or to the Chinese Empire, in either case not necessarily always unfriendly (Dzoedang, 1981).

(ii) In the story of Dzjawbang he is made to say: 'Even if I tell you to give me each day nine dishes of ants' tears, nine chickens, nine pots of liquor, nine baskets of *smsi* (expensive mushrooms), nine baskets of dried meat, 75 ticals of silver, nine water pots full of brains of flies, you would have to do it. If not I would kill you'. In this way the despotic ruler is ridiculed. Since he was an Akha ruler, he was killed in a plot started by Abaw Majeu head of the principal and oldest clan, who hired another clan to carry out the killing. However, as killing 'inside people' is against the law of non-violence, this clan was ex-communicated (Lewis, 1968, Vol. 1: 68).

(iii) A more contemporary text is the 'Song of the building of the railway'. The French colonial government constructed a railway from Hanoi to Kunming via Jinghong (Chengrung) between 1900 and 1909, with the help of 'coolies'. As many as one million people are said to have died in the building of this railway due to insufficient food, malaria etc. The 'coolies' were predominantly mountain peoples, especially Adzjaw Akha. They still have a song about it: 'If you want to have your iron road, we are happy to ride on it too some day. One day we will ride on it, as you will be far away. Now we die and you ride; one day we will ride and you will die; would you mind, iron road? (Perot, 1909; Adzaw, 1979).

Texts Describing Inter-ethnic Relations

The Akha believe (*gadzang ghaeu*) that in the distant past they were part of a warring group or state system which recognised military leaders, at least until the time of Dzjawbang. They had or participated in *dzoeza* power to rule derived from Heaven, M-ma, through the Chinese. This power is also conceived as a tangible clay tablet, probably with the seal of the Emperor or possibly coming through the Nanchao kings. They lost this after the fall of Tm-lang, during the rule of Dzjui-im, grandson of Dzjawbang. Following this epoch they became 'born losers', committed to non-violence by their customary law (Lewis, 1968). This collapse of power is also the beginning of the marginalization process in which they are dispersed among several other ethnic groups. The texts relate the different roles played by these various groups.

In many archaic texts and ceremonies, Tai Yai (Shan), Tai Lue, and Tai Dam, called Bitsm or Atsm, are mentioned as the main immediate cause of marginalization into the mountains. *Gadzang ghaeu* texts mention that the Akha inhabited fertile land with streams, but the Bitsm came up-stream (meaning also 'from the South'). They liked the land, and they put chips of wood or leaves with messages in the stream, telling their brothers to come up and occupy the land. This led to armed confrontations (they say 'the Tai invented war'). A contest was proposed to settle the matter. The Tai won by a ruse.

A second ethnic group with which the Akha seem clearly to have been in conflict are the Mon-Khmer-speaking peoples of the area. Burmese Akha texts tell us that the Akha, moving up-hill, eventually arrived in *Tangla meu*, literally Donkey City, in Mon-Khmer territory. Mon-Khmer groups are referred to in these texts as Aboe or Kh'aboe by Akha. Particular Mon-Khmer sub-groups are hard to identify since those on the present-day Burmese border (Wa, Palaung or Bulang) are not the same as those on the Lao side of the border (Khmu, Hok). Some texts suggest an initial violent conflict, followed by a victory for the Akha using a ruse which exploited the Aboe's reputed fear of spirits (Lewis, 1968, Vol. 1:55 ff.; Roux, 1924: 380; Boucherie, 1995, Vol. 1: 87). Texts of origin also indicate that the Akha took over several cultural traits from the Aboe (Mon-Khmer) mountain peoples.

Thus, having lost power the Akha become relatively stabilised, relatively impoverished, in the mountains. They become, in their own terms, 'people of the middle', situated between a number of other ethnicities (see Geusau, 1981). It is in this situation that a great many of the Phima and Dzoema texts originated.

Higher up the mountains from the Akha are the Mon-Khmer speaking Wa, Palaung (Bulang), and Khamu. They were feared as head-hunters by Akha until well into the twentieth century. For this reason the principal protective village gate faces up-mountain. The naked standing couple, carved in wood, are intended to frighten away the up-hill people as the village gate foundation text indicates (Dzoebaw, 1981). These people are also described in the texts as dirty, not well dressed, and primitive. Another up-hill people, described in more positive terms, are the (Tibeto-Burman-speaking) Araw or Aghaw (probably Lahu) who are described as a hunting people who have decorated spears.

Lower down the mountain slope are the Sjhehlo, among whom the women wear trousers, and the Lawbi or 'dry Tai', a Tai-related group, possessing elephants, with whom relations seem to have been good (Dzoedang, 1979a: 38, 57–8, 73, 120, 123). The lowland scene is represented as a large river which has to be crossed, a valley, and a market or markets, where the Akha go to buy and sell. The lowland is dominated by the Bitsm or Atsm (Tai) peoples. Several archaic texts recount how poor Akha go to these markets (*lehang ieu*) to buy scrap iron for their blacksmith, a buffalo for a ceremony, or just to look around. On their journey they pass through several different ethnic areas (Majeu Takh'ang, 1979; Dzoedang, 1979a: 54, 154 ff.).

Internal and External History: a Discussion

If we try to see how Akha 'internal' history, or mnemesis, matches up to or fits with the 'external' history of the region, there seems to be no contradiction. In a distant, somewhat mythical past the ancestors of the oldest Akha clans came down from a high mountain area. We have to think in terms of 2,000–3,000 years ago, as these ancestors were part of a Yi-Chai, or Lolo group. The ancestral homeland of the older clans, however, is the Black and Red River area of South-East Yunnan, North of contemporary Vietnam and Laos. There they lived near or were perhaps part of various groups, now called Hani, and belonged to the southern branches of the Yi, in the southern parts of the Nanchao kingdom (Boucherie, 1995, Vol. 1: 82; Wiens, 1976: 95 ff.).

It may be hypothesised that some older Akha clans were originally part of the so-called 'black bone' Yi/Lolo, and were redistributed by the Nanchao rulers to more southerly parts of the kingdom to produce rice (Backus, 1981: 66 ff.). In the story of Jabioelang, or Aiheholo, assigning Akha ancestors to produce rice in the South we find the clan name Ma-jeu or Ma-zeu among the 'black bone' Yi/Lolo clans of the northern Sichuan/Yunnan area (Lewis, 1968, Vol. 1: 33). This seems to be confirmed by the fact that among both the 'black bone' Yi, or Muso, of the Sichuan/Yunnan border areas, and the Akha, some older clan names such as Majeu/Mazeu are identical (Vial, 1917: 45; Boucherie, 1995, Vol. 1: 88 ff.). It is clear too that the Akha belong to the 'Wu-man' groups (independent, non-sinicizing Yi groups), while others, corresponding to contemporary Hani, tended to be 'Pai-man', or more assimilated and intermarried with the Chinese.

In the south-western areas Hani and Akha seem to have been part of the Chinese *tu'ssu* vassal system, in which Han Chinese appointed local tribal chiefs. This is indicated in genealogies which claim descent from Heaven (Wiens, 1976: 208–66; Bai Yu, 1989). As for the Akha, it can be confirmed historically, that a short-lived shamanic Akha chiefdom endured for three generations in Tm-lang, also called Ta-lang, a fortified city close to the watersheds of the Black River. These are Tibeto-Burman names which were later changed to the current Mojiang (Liu Qibyuan, 1989; Huang Shirong, 1991) [for this and other place names mentioned in the text, see Maps pp. xvii–xix, especially Map 3. Ed.].

We have the impression that in a power vacuum in the south-western area between a weakened Nanchao and the Han Chinese during the Sung Dynasty (960–1279 AD) several local vassal states sought greater autonomy (Backus, 1981: 163). In that context we can see the origin of what is here called the Akha 'genealogical and alliance system', and the formative period of a unified Akha customary law system, as we know it now. From ancient Phima texts it is not clear if the name Akha was then already in use, but probably not (Lewis, 1968, Vol. 1: 42 ff.).

What exactly gave rise to this alliance system is not clear. Stories give the impression that Dzjawbang tried to unite the Akha chiefs of several clans in order to gain military power. He married a daughter of Abaw Mazeu, leader of the older Akha clans. He and his son systematise Akha-*zang/jang*, or customary law. He claims a shamanic type of seizure of power, together with claims of direct orders from Heaven. His son Bang Dzjui rides the shamanic horse to Heaven every night. It is a kind of charismatic leadership, looking for direct justification from Heaven; a war-lord phenomenon of a type which still frequently occurs in the region. It was short-lived however, and never lead to state-formation. Dzjawbang was killed by his own people. Bang Dzjui perishes, as his shamanic horse (one broken wing mended with beeswax) fell to the ground, the wax melted by his flying too high, as in the Hellenic story of Icarus. The third generation of Dzjui Im sees the collapse of Tm-lang/Mojiang as the result of wars (Mojiang Editorial Committee, 1983).

The way the story is told, in a 'flowery', exaggerated way, clearly shows an aversion to hierarchical chiefdom and state-formation. The moral is clear, though there is a contradiction between boasting that an Akha once achieved this kind of power, and rejection of unequal division of power. It leads us to conclude that the Akha never had a regular Akha state system. On the contrary, it seems to justify: (i) the fact that Akha live in a diaspora; and (ii) the origin of a non-state-based Akha alliance system.

The Akha have no doubt about the historical basis of the short-lived Dzjawbang dynasty. External history confirms a strong Woni/Hani leadership at Mojiang in that period and its fall to the Mongols (Boucherie, 1995, Vol. 1: 86–90). It is confirmed by Dzjawbang's position in the genealogical 'archive', at about 30 generations ago. It led to the formation of the 'Adzjhaw' Akha clan, as part of the Akha alliance system. This Akha group still has considerable differences of language and customary law from other groups descended from the Dzeugh'oe and Boesoeleh clans. Akha of Thailand think that Adzjhaw Akha is more closely related to Hani languages than to Akha. We could speculate that Dzjawbang and his group were originally more closely related to the Hani lords of the area, who were already well established in the Honghe and Red River terraced highlands. There is an interpretation that the Akha name derives from their being 'refugees of war' in a Hani dominated, class-based corvée system. Being rice-growing agriculturists in and around Mojiang city certainly meant that many would have been both agriculturists and soldiers at some point (Boucherie, 1995, Vol. 1: .87).

The rise and fall of Tm-lang/Mojiang was the beginning of a new stage in the centuries-old process of marginalization. Its fall is described as a war, with the burning of everything, including the 'power to rule' *(dzoe-za)* clay tablet, signifying a total loss of power. Hani and Akha archaic texts agree that loss of power over the (low)land and its irrigation systems, was mostly to the Tai (Tai Lue and/or Black Tai) peoples, coming up through the Black, Red, and later Mekong river valleys. Again this seems correct in terms of external history, since no major Chinese incursions are recorded in the Sung Dynasty (Wiens, 1976: 180–86; Backus, 1981: 159–64).

Tai warriors appear to have laid siege to Tm-lang/Mojiang, cutting off the water supply, and causing the inhabitants to flee. The Tai assumption of power in the valleys of southern Yunnan involved armed conflicts with Hani and Akha and seems to have been a gradual process at first, in which the Hani clearly resisted longer. From Akha texts we know that Akha clans left the Tm-lang/Mojiang area one after another, going into the mountains and adjacent areas.

Another tradition explains the breaking away of the Akha from the Hani as due to earthquakes in the Red River area, which destroyed Akha rice terraces (Tooker, 1996). But Akha traditions in all areas agree that the migrations happened gradually, clan by clan, and over a long period. This notion is expressed in the story of migrants leaving traces in their path, by cutting banana leaves and scattering the carcasses of crabs, in order to indicate the road to be followed by the next party of Akha (Roux, 1924: 381; Dzoebaw, 1981; Boucherie, 1995, Vol. 1: 87). The intervals were too long however, and the traces disappeared, thus providing an explanation for the migration of the Akha in different directions.

Most of them moved South West crossing the Mekong just North of Jinghong (Chengrung), now the capital of the Autonomous Dai (Tai) Prefecture of Xixuangbanna (Sipsongpanna). Some went South, but no further than the East bank of the Mekong, in or near contemporary northern Laos. Local records and Akha seem to agree that this was about 700–800 years ago. Several Akha and some Hani groups can still be found on this migration route, near Puer and Simao. Akha first settled in the more fertile Mekong valley lowlands, but were forced to move into the mountains. They thus spread in the direction of Menghai (southern Sipsongpanna), Menglang (Lancang), and Mengla (Ahai and Liuqia, 1989; Cun Wen Xue, 1996; Gao Wenying, 1986). Akha stories and local records can also be reconciled at a village level. In the mountainous Menghai district of Sipsongpanna there is an old conglomeration of Akha villages known as 'Guilanghui Pu' or 'the village of good fortune'. This has a population of about 10,000 persons living in several villages. The houses are made of brick, and older inhabitants are sure in their knowledge that the principal villages were built 25 generations or some 650 years ago.

The main area in which Akha culture – as we and they know it, as distinct from Hani culture – flourished over the last six or seven centuries, has been south-western Yunnan and its mountainous border areas. Wherever possible Akha groups followed the example of Hani source-fed rice terraces of the Honghe area. Depending on availability of water we see the same patterns, as for example with the Karen in Thailand: source-fed terraces near villages, surrounded by well-tended forests which are managed for forest food, hunting, medicine, and animal fodder. In less well irrigated terraced areas, Akha, like the Hani, have been growing tea, sesame, and cotton as cash-crops in great quantity and over many centuries (Hinton, 1996; Tooker, 1996; Li Qibo, 1996).

The region has long been and still is inhabited by a large number of ethnicities, increasingly scattered and interspersed. Most of the archaic Akha texts, of those which we know, seem to reflect the Akha as 'encapsulated' mid-slope, and in a multi-ethnic situation. This situation is structured, however, in an inverse way to a Thai 'sakdina' type of hierarchy, with the lowest in the class system highest up (Mon–Khmer groups such as Wa, Bulang, Khmu, Htin, and Dulong) and the socially highest situated lowest, in the valleys and plains.

Traditional Knowledge and Unification of the Akha/Hani Diaspora

Given the long-standing geographical separation of Akha and related Hani peoples, and their dispersal among a number of other ethnic groups – notably the Tai – their ability and motivation to maintain such a high degree of unity in their Zang (also *Jang* for the Akha, *Yawti* for the Hani) or customary law, poses questions of the greatest interest.

Akha and Hani had almost no contact for about 800 years until they were linked by Chinese linguists in the 1950s. More frequent contact started after the first International Hani/Akha Culture Studies Conference, held at the Autonomous Hani/Yi Honghe (Red River) Prefecture in 1993. Different Akha sub-groups, spread over 600 kilometres of relatively inaccessible border areas, and with little or no contact over the past 200–700 years, show an even more remarkable unity. Similarities identified to date include: basic village social and political organisation; the calendrical year of festivities etc; archaic texts, songs, and mythology; and customary law systems. Hani and Akha discovered that they belonged to the same genealogical system, with Sm-io as their common founding ancestor and Tang Pang, twelve generations later, as a common point of clan fission. For the Akha, especially those descending from Boesoeleh, about 35 generations ago, it can be said that 'if you know one Akha village well, you know them all'. This cultural and structural unity of Akha groups, and their similarity with several Hani groups, distinguishes them clearly from other mountain groups in the region.

The former existence of some Hani/Akha state system or even united chiefdom has been eliminated as a plausible explanation of this unity. Neither Hani, still less Akha mythology contain stories of past kings or rulers. The history of the Dzjawbang dynasty is rather a warning against strong rulers, and expresses an aversion, still manifest today, from strong chiefs and class stratification. There are signs that Akha and perhaps Hani might have been part of stratified systems prior to the collapse of Nanchao, their breaking away from the Hani, and subsequent marginalization and incorporation into one of the Tai or Chinese class systems. In this respect a main difference between Hani and Akha may be noted. Several Hani sub-groups had, for many centuries, their own Hani *t'u-ssu*, Chinese appointed Hani chiefs. They were also sinicizing to a higher degree. Akha in China, on the contrary, were mainly ruled by Chinese appointed Tai *t'u-ssu* in the border areas (Wiens, 1976: 208 ff.; Bai Yu, 1989; Huang Shirong, 1991).

Indications of Akha forming part of stratified political systems can be found in genealogy and the terminology of village functionaries (Dzoema, Phima, Kh'a-ma). These could be considered remnants of their ancestors having been part of a multi-ethnic Nanchao kingdom or a more stratified Yi society in the distant past.

We thus obtain the strong impression from Akha historical records that Akha *zang*, culture and customary law, as we know it today, originated in and is an adaptation to the Akha diaspora, a multi-ethnic, and 'non-territorial' situation. The structural constant in this situation is that it is primarily Tai dominated.

It could be argued that the Akha have had, and continue to have a strong sense of ethnic identity. Ethnic identity, of which in any definition language is a key index, is not an independent variable however. The anthropological literature of the region shows that ethnic identity in minority groups is the result of structural, economic, political, cultural, and psychological elements that combine to keep groups together as opposed to and in interaction with other groups, especially with a dominant majority. We have to investigate the Akha cultural system itself in order to explain this remarkable cultural unity. Given important differences between Hani and Akha, I shall limit myself here to the Akha.

This chapter has argued that historical mnemesis is part of, and a justification for their identity, their uniqueness as a people, and their ability to survive as a minority group (Geusau, 1983a). Historical mnemesis and interiorisation are insufficient in themselves, however, if they do not serve political-economic, and structural purposes (Tooker, 1992). Akha traditional knowledge, therefore, is extremely pragmatic. The Akha sense of history and identity is not so much based upon descent from gods or heroes, but is rather based upon 'tradition' in its most direct sense, the survival experience of a long line of ancestors, accumulated and transmitted from generation to generation. It is not static; this core of Akha experience is a continuous adaptation to changing circumstances, threats, and challenges. There is no idealisation of heroes or kings. The Akha do, however, display an almost obsessive need for 'the continuation of the lines'; the texts warn 'take care lest the lines break or are interrupted'.

Lines of survival and transmission of traditional knowledge

The more prominent of the many lines of reproduction of accumulated knowledge will now be designated. Fuller treatment of forms of knowledge, selection of specialists and their training will be the subject of another publication.

The Line of Life

The line of life as laid down in the Akha genealogy (*guidzuieu*) continues through sons who maintain the ancestor service (*apoelaweu*). As soon as a child proves able to survive after birth, it receives a genealogical name with a first syllable, identical to the father's name's last syllable. The parents, and a maternal uncle (*aghoe*), are responsible for the child's education. If the child is weak or suffering, but has a good chance of survival, it can be adopted by an uncle (*aghoe*), or the Phima, and the first syllable of the name becomes *ghoe* or *phi* (see Kammerer, 1986: 126 ff.; Tooker, 1988: 85 ff.).

The Line of Alliances

The line of alliances with other lineages (*pha* of seven to nine generations) or clans (*adzjeu/agu*) through marriage should be renewed ideally every three generations by 'clasping and unclasping hands'. To this also belongs the line of the 'carrying of the basket with equal contributions from the bride's family' (*kh'abehdaweu*) to the new husband's house at marriage (Kammerer, 1986: 198 ff.).

The Line of Leadership

The line of leadership is the line of the ideally hereditary head of the village or district, the Dzoema. An annual ceremony (*dzoezanglaweu*) for the ancestors of the Dzoema is held in April. This office requires a long education and unblemished moral record of the leader and his wife and family (Kammerer, 1986: 99).

The Line of Teaching

The line of teaching and reciting oral ritual texts, on several occasions, and containing knowledge of customary law, is that of the Phima (and his students the Phiza). The yearly service for teacher-ancestors (*Khm sjhui Khm milaweu*) is also held in April, at the beginning of the agricultural year. Symbols include a small knife, a bag, a red turban with flowers, and a small fan. This too requires long education with much concentration and meditation, and a 'clean moral record' (Qian Yong, 1996).

The Line of Knowing Customary Law

The line of knowing customary law concerns the rules and rubrics for ceremonies, performed by the Boemaw, who does not recite, but is the ritual officiant. In some Akha traditions the title Boemaw is used for the Phima (Tooker, 1988: 33). This too requires an annual ceremony for his teacher-ancestors.

The Line of Technical Knowledge

The line of technical knowledge is held by the Badzji, the village technician. This comprises the techniques for making iron implements, bamboo working techniques for the construction of houses, village gate, the swing, village boundaries, bridges, water systems etc. Herbal medicinal knowledge and related healing techniques may be included. This requires long education and unselfish attitudes. The Badzji honours his line of teacher-ancestors annually at the Spring Festival (Kammerer, 1986: 99).

The Line of Taking Care of Rice-fields

The line of taking care of rice-fields and related work and rituals is the responsibility of the Yajeh Ama, literally 'the rain field mother'. Women over 45 can be allocated this function. On initiation they receive a white cotton skirt which is used on ritual occasions, when they are often referred to as 'the woman with the white skirt'. Their responsibility for the fields and agricultural knowledge may be exercised through their sons but more especially their daughters-in-law. A wide knowledge of food and medicinal plants from forest and field is included. *Tsjidtsjhieu* in the spring is an important ceremony of the Yajeh Ama, and after the death of her husband she takes charge of all nine annual family ancestor and field ceremonies (Kammerer, 1986: 306 ff.). Associated knowledge of embroidery and handicraft is highly honoured, though the function has changed over the past ten years or so to support production for the tourist market.

The Line of Diagnostics and Healing

The line of diagnostics and healing is the speciality of the Nji-pa or shaman, who may be a man but is more often a woman, and is concentrated in certain families. There is not so much memorising of texts, but some techniques of trance are learned by those who have a clear calling from the custodian Nji-pa who may be a deceased family member. With this generally also goes knowledge of herbal medicine and medical techniques such as bone-setting, acupuncture, massage, blood stimulating techniques etc. It requires much education, concentration and meditation, and again a good moral record.

These rigorously defined and transmitted 'lines' of knowledge, as the Akha call them, collectively referred to as Zang (or Jang) may justifiably be called a *system* of customary law. It is also an educational *network*. To translate Zang as religion is misleading, as Akha insist that they do not worship or adore (*udu tangeu,* literally bow the head) a higher God or being, nor any spirits. Zang as an intricate set of rules and lines of knowledge and education, can explain the unity of the Akha system only in terms of a structural framework that guarantees transmission over generations (Li Ke Zhong, 1996).

Akha Genealogical Practices as an Ethnic Alliance System

We now focus on the hypothesis that it is the (Hani/)Akha genealogical and kinship system (*guidzuieu*) and related ancestor service (*apoelaweu*), underlying so to speak the lines of transfer of knowledge we have just reviewed, which ultimately explain the striking unity of Zang and Jang between Akha groups, and which are at the core of their structural unity and survival.

To conclude my discussion of inter-ethnic relations, I shall examine the characteristics of what I call 'the Akha ethnic alliance system', in terms of (a) its structural characteristics, (b) its ideology as expressed in ancestor service, and (c) its status as an alternative political and economic system for groups marginalized in a 'region of refuge' at the edges of expanding state systems. It is viewed here not so much from an abstract theoretical or academic perspective, but rather in terms of its historic and potential future usefulness for the survival of the Akha and related Hani peoples.

All who have studied and compared this patrilineal descent system have been struck by its consistency. Over many years I have collected, from men of a variety of clans and lineages, their 'counting of generations', and in general they have corresponded well. They are also confirmed by genealogies collected by others (Lewis, 1969–70, Vol. 1; Kammerer, 1986; Boucherie, 1995; Davies, 1909; Tooker, 1988; Dauffes, 1906; Henry, 1903; Duy Thieu, 1996). More striking still has been the (re-)discovery by Akha, and more recently Hani, themselves that their genealogical systems fit together so well (Li Xi Xian, 1996).

The system is patrilineal in the sense that only male successors who continue to have sons are enumerated, together with their genealogical names. As is characteristic of Tibeto-Burman genealogical systems – as opposed to Chinese, Tai, and others – the last syllable of the father's name forms the first syllable of the male children's names (or in the distant past the last two syllables forming the first two).

Characteristically, Hani and Akha genealogies start from *M,* Heaven or 'heaven principle'. It is not counted as an ancestor, but as a kind of original principle. This is followed by *M-Ma* (generation 1) the 'wide, great Heaven', and *M-gh'ang* 'middle of heaven' (generation 2, of whom Akha stories relate that this was an Emperor). There follow eleven generations leading to Sm-io at generation twelve. Most Akha and Hani agree that the first twelve generations are 'mythical' ancestors (neither men nor spirits), and are also ancestors of peoples other than Hani and Akha. Sm-io is the 'apical ancestor' of both Akha and Hani, through whom they (and maybe related ethnic groups) distinguish themselves from others. Sm-io is followed by twelve generations of ancestors with three syllable names, like those known to us from other Tibeto-Burman groups from the Nanchao kingdom: thus Oe-toe-loe (in generation thirteen) is followed by Toe-loe-dzm (in generation fourteen) etc. (Backus, 1981: 58). They end with Dzoe-tang-pang at generation twenty-five. It seems to be some kind of ruler – whether man or woman is not clear. It also refers to a 'fortified high place' on a primordial migration route (Dzoebaw, 1982). It is not clear who these first twelve ancestors after Sm-io are. They are certainly not *neh* (spirits). One hypothesis is that they are Yi/Lolo ancestors, as genealogical lines of some Hani sub-groups originate there (Boucherie, 1995, Vol. 1: 33a).

Akha and Hani believe they can speak of real recognisable people and original named clans (*agu/adzjeu*) only after Tang Pang. Tang Pang is also the place in the genealogy from which to count in order to establish how long a particular clan has been in the system. Today, as in the past, a man marrying an Akha woman can become an Akha, if they have a son. He can then attach himself at Tang Pang as the first generation of a new clan. Further requirements are rigorous. The man has to give up his previous ethnicity, be fluent in the Akha language, accept and have knowledge of Akha customary law. He must start ancestor service and accept related obligations (Mao Youquan, 1996). It rather resembles a change of nationality status in the contemporary world.

After the Tang Pang generation the genealogical system branches into several major directions with long lines of up to forty-five generations (in which case totalling up to seventy since *M* and *M-ma).* Major branches of up to forty-five generations after Tang Pang (fifty-eight generations from Sm-io) are Tang Pang Mang, Tang Pang Ma, Tang Pang Sjang, Tang Pang Ji etc. Tang Pang Mang is seen by the older Akha clans as their link with Sm-io and Tang Pang. Other branches such as those starting from Tang Pang Siang and Tang Pang Sjang clearly lead to Hani groups. There are however also 'mixed' groups (leading to both Hani and Akha groups) derived for instance from the Tang Pang Ji branch (Boucherie, 1995, Vol. 1: 34a). As for people calling themselves Akha, those branches which lead to older clans seem to split into two major branches at Boesoeleh, eight generations after Tang Pang, and twenty-one generations after Sm-io. After this, between the twenty-sixth and twenty-ninth generations after Sm-io, most three syllable names change into two syllable names and the principal older and more prestigious names emerge. Amongst them is Mazeu, in one branch, Mangpo in another, while most others are derived from a branch starting with Dzeugh'oe which includes Dzjawbang. This period of three generations is for most members of the older Akha clans about twenty-eight to thirty generations ago, or about 700–750 years. As we discussed earlier, this was the period of Dzjawbang, the exodus of the Akha to the South-West and their increased marginalization, the unification of customary law, and the formation of alliances between clans, in which Abaw Mazeu or Majeu played a leading role (Lewis, 1969/70, Vol. 1:63).

The case of the ancestor Dzeugh'oe in this period is particularly interesting. This ancestor had so many sons, from whom so many contemporary named clans are derived, that one is tempted to make the hypothesis of an alliance of a number of clans under that name, rather similar to the case of Tang Pang.

Akha history of increased contact with Mon-Khmer groups from this period onwards, finds confirmation in the genealogical system. Of some Akha clans, such as the *Amaw* it is still related that an older clan 'met them in the forest' but that they are Akha now. Another story tells of a first Akha man who was looking for a wife and met a forest woman, who proved to be a *pehseu* or 'vampire' and ate her husband; but a second man was more successful, and this lead to the institution of the custom of separation between men's and women's sleeping spaces. This seems to refer to marriages between 'more civilised Akha men' and women from 'still cannibalistic' Mon-Khmer groups (Aboe, Kh'aboe). It must be emphasised that *pehseu* are not spirits but people in the Akha language (cf. Kammerer, 1986: 32).

There is thus evidence that during their marginalization and encounters with Mon-Khmer-speaking groups in higher areas of southern Yunnan, older Akha clans intermarried with them. In addition some may have been incorporated as *jakh'a* (slave-children, servants, dependants). Two further arguments for this are: first, that there are two current forms of adoption (*padaweu*, to incorporate a lineage), namely (a) incorporation into, or genealogically close to, one's own lineage, and (b) linking with Tang Pang which is a more honorific form; and secondly, the existence, until quite recently, of some remnants of ranking, and a related prohibition of marriage with clans deemed to be 'too low'.

Shorter branches, of fifteen to twenty generations or fewer after Tang Pang (thirty to thirty-five from Sm-io) are thus 'late-comers'. Examples are Tang Pang Bui, Tang Pang Dzju, and Tang Pang Ka, all of about fifteen generations in depth. These are groups which might have entered the Akha system about 375 years ago, as generally one generation (from birth of father to birth of son) is reckoned as twenty-five years. These three cases claim to know that their ancestors entered the system late, and even today are aware of their previous ethnicity. The first claim that they were poor, marginalized Yunnanese Chinese, but are now Akeu-Akha. The second group claims they were Tai-related; and the third group that they were Wa people adopted as Akha.

Akha themselves are thus well aware, thanks to their genealogical system and mnemesis, that the Akha ethnic system is built up of on the one hand much older 'original' Akha groups, and on the other hand clans and lineages which have been adopted, but are fully Akha now.

We can thus hypothesise safely that several stages of the Akha genealogical system seem to coincide with Akha 'internal' historical mnemesis as expressed in oral texts. These are:

(i) a 'mythological period' of earliest beginnings, from a 'heavenly principle';
(ii) a common apical ancestor or founder, Sm-io, not only for all Akha and Hani, but maybe also for other Yi/Lolo related groups;
(iii) a common alliance type of agent/ancestor, Tang Pang, with whom starts the 'real history' of alliances with other Yi/Lolo related groups into one 'system' in southern Yunnan;
(iv) the formation of an alliance between several older clans in a period of three syllable names, coinciding with the Nanchao kingdom into which these groups seem to have been administratively incorporated;
(v) the formative period of the current Akha system of alliance and the unification of customary law, coinciding with the two syllable name period, and followed by the exodus from the eastern parts of central-southern Yunnan towards the south-western borders.
(vi) incorporation of some Aboe or Mon-Khmer groups;
(vii) incorporation of some other marginalized 'lowland' groups as they move up-hill.

It is clear that the Akha ethnic alliance system is not a purely biological one. Nonetheless Akha do not agree with contemporary anthropological wisdom which would suggest that peoples in this region tend to change ethnic identity more easily than elsewhere (Banks, 1976).

One important conclusion to be drawn is that Hani/Akha ancestor service is the ideology and the backbone of the ethnic alliance system. Hani and Akha honour their ancestors nine to twelve times each year in ceremonies (*apoelaweu*) held to mark important occasions. These are performed by each family in the village in honour of its 'line of life'. In addition the Dzoema, Phima, and Badzji honour and remember their ancestors, those lines of people who handed down their knowledge and teachings through 'lines of knowledge'.

These ancestors are not gods or spirits, or devils. They are people who have died but yet can still be present in some way, and on some important occasions. It is clear from the stories about ancestors that they made mistakes, and that learning from these mistakes led, over the centuries, to the building up of Akha Zang.

This ancestor service is not religion, nor superstition. It is the means for the Akha and Hani to recognise their roots, their history, and the manner of their survival. It is also a symbol of their unity, their 'cultural citizenship' in a situation of diaspora (Li Xi Xian, 1995). It is for this reason that a rule of avoidance and non-cohabitation exists in Akha villages between Apoelaw-Akha, who maintain ancestor service and therewith also Zang, and Kali-Akha who have thrown away their ancestor-baskets, and therewith also customary law, morality, and traditional knowledge, as requested by some Christian sects. The latter are considered by those who maintain ancestor service to have destroyed their identity (Kammerer, 1990).

The question of how to maintain and adapt Hani/Akha ancestor service to new situations, such as urban life and modernised agriculture, was discussed extensively at the Second International Hani/Akha Culture Studies Conference in 1996 (Kukeawkasem, 1996).

General Conclusions on Hani and Akha Inter-ethnic Relations

In order to investigate the multi-ethnic, inter-ethnic setting and relations of Hani and Akha with others, we have had to analyse their historical mnemesis, as presented in archaic oral texts, ceremonies, and the genealogical system. We compared it with data known from external sources, concentrating mostly on the Akha. We may now bring together and summarise some conclusions which we have anticipated. It must be emphasised that these do not by any means exhaust the possible conclusions to be drawn from the material outlined above, and that all are provisional and subject to continued research.

1 A number of ethnic sub-groups based in southern Yunnan, historically and linguistically related to the larger Tibeto-Burman Yi/Lolo minority ethnic group, and in modern times lumped together under the name Hani, is now scattered amongst other ethnic groups in the mountainous border areas of contemporary China, Vietnam, Laos, and Burma. Over the past several centuries the Akha, especially – called Aini by the Chinese – have overspilled these borders inside what is now called the 'Mekong Quadrangle' including, over the past 150 years or so, the northern mountains of Thailand.

2 These people are considered part of the indigenous population of southern Yunnan, but some, such as the Akha and Woni, may have moved from more northerly areas in Nanchao times. Hani, and sub-groups derived from them, had been part of several small state systems in the Red River region of East and South-East Yunnan, until they were conquered and incorporated into the Tibeto-Burman Nanchao state in the eighth century AD. To their South and West were Mon-Khmer-speaking groups and other Tibeto-Burman groups such as the Lahu. The region as a whole was an arena of competition for power and resources between larger state systems: Nanchao, the T'ang Dynasty Chinese who had established power in Annam (northern Vietnam), the Pyu kingdom in contemporary Burma, and even Tibet.

3 The Akha as a distinct ethnic group split off from other Hani groups in what Akha regard as a short-lived and unsuccessful Akha chiefdom at Tm-lang (Mojiang) during a power vacuum prior to the Mongol invasions of the mid-thirteenth century. After the collapse of the Hani states under the Mongols, Akha started to move westwards and south-westwards, and over the Mekong River. They tried to occupy lowland valley basins but were successively marginalized at higher altitudes by the expanding Tai states (*müang*). Akha now inhabit the borderlands between the Black River in Vietnam and the Salween River in Burma. The highest concentrations are in Sipsongpanna Yunnan, and the immediately neighbouring parts of Laos (Luang Namtha) and Burma (Kengtung). In all these areas they are interspersed with other ethnic groups. And in all situations and for many centuries their principle dependency has been on one or other of the Tai valley states or chiefdoms. Pressure to move further into Laos, Burma, and Thailand has been generally instigated by violence, warfare, or pressure from lowland states on resources of land, forest, and minerals.

4 Akha experience of inter-ethnic relations has been of three broad types: (i) with a variety of equally marginalized minority groups, (ii) with Chinese, and (iii) most importantly, with Tai.

The second most dominant group in Akha texts, and also psychology, until this today and even in Thailand, are the Chinese (Labui) especially the Islamic or Haw Chinese (Pehnyoe, in Chinese Kui), the latter in most senses a minority themselves. For both Hani and Akha Tibeto-Chinese models rather than Tai have been predominant in many respects, and have been reproduced for example in city and village construction, social organization, educational systems, and in the genealogical system itself, with its origins in M or M-ma, Heaven. Both Taoist, Confucian, and Tibetan models are recognisable in Hani and Akha cultures, but not Buddhist. Some authors have argued that Akha may have been influenced by Indian/Hindu/Theravada Buddhist models derived from contacts with

Plate 11. 'The Hanuman or Hoalaman, from a native drawing'

Tai, for example focusing on sources of power or potency associated with Mount Meru (Tooker, 1996b). But this is to overlook the extent to which Tai have themselves been heavily influenced, as at one time and in places still a 'border minority', by the Chinese, for example in city building as at Chiang Mai and elsewhere in the borderlands. 'Learning from the Chinese' is thus predominant in Akha culture in spite of their experience of exploitative economic relationships of the 'middleman' kind, and in the absence of any desire or need to 'become Chinese'. In all the Tai states the Akha (called by Tai-speakers Ko or I-ko – also romanised as Kaw, I-Kaw, Ekaw) were regarded as being at the lowest level of a strongly hierarchical class system. They were seen as part of (seemingly inexhaustible) natural resources, and to belong to the 'wild, unordered, chaotic' sphere of nature. In Tai/Thai temples they are symbolised by the good-natured but culture-less monkeys of the army of the Ape King Hanuman, from the Indian Ramayana epic.

Thus Akha could be prevailed upon for free, corvée labour, and they could be sold as slaves. We have seen how this relationship is reflected in Akha ceremonies. However, given the need for labour in the smaller Tai states, difficulty of supervising labour, and relative ease of avoidance of

152

compulsory labour, relations between Tai and tribal peoples in practical life appear to have not always been so harsh. Nonetheless, strong ideological mechanisms of almost caste-like discrimination existed and continue to this day.

It is both an intriguing phenomenon and crucial for understanding both Akha and Tai histories including the histories of their mutual relations, that throughout the region the Tai/Akha relation of dominance/dependency and primitive extraction is a historical constant. In Akha ceremonies, texts, and contemporary thinking, the Akha+mountain / Tai (Bitsm)+valley axis is the principle and most contradictory. We have seen that the main responses or adaptations in the face of this contradiction have been those of ecological and psychological 'encapsulation'. In other words the strategy has been on the one hand to maximise economic autonomy and subsistence capacity, and on the other hand to decrease ecological accessibility, and to present to the 'outside', to the dominant extractor, just what he expects, namely an ignorant and stupid monkey, thereby hiding Akha knowledge, wisdom, and cultural treasures (Majeu Takh'ang, 1981).

References

Adzjaw, Alang (1979), 'The Song of the Iron Road', personal communication.

Ahai and Lier, (1996), 'A Survey on Hani Nationality's Medicine', paper presented to the *Second International Hani/Akha Culture Studies Conference*.

Ahai and Liuqia, (1989), *The Anthology of the Sipsongpanna Hani's Legends* (Chinese), National Minority Committee, Jinghong, Yunnan, China.

Akha Society for Culture and Art, Kengtung, (1996), Paper presented to the *Second International Hani/Akha Culture Studies Conference*, Chiang Mai/Chiang Rai 12–18 May, 1996.

Backus, Charles, (1981), *The Nan-chao Kingdom and T'ang China's South Western Frontier*; Cambridge Studies in Chinese History, Literature and Institutions; New York: Cambridge University Press.

Bai Yu, (1989), *The Cultural Drift of the Hani, where Lords (Tu'ssi) Ruled*, Kunming, Nationalities Publishing House, (Chinese).

Banks, David J. (1976), *Changing Identities in modern Southeast Asia*; The Hague: Mouton.

Beltram, Gonzalo A. (1965), *Zonas de Refugio*, Mexico City, Estudios Indigenistas.

Bonifacy, Auguste L.M. (1904), 'Les Groupes Ethniques de la Rivière Claire', *Revue Indochinoise*, n.s. 12, Juin 1904, pp. 813–828, et n.s. II, Juillet 1904, pp. 1–16.

Boucherie, Pascal (1995), *Les Hani: Introduction à l'étude d'une population tibeto-birmane du Yunnan en relation avec la Chine*; PhD thesis, Université de Paris X; UMR 116; Ethnologie et Sociologie Comparative. 3 Vols.

Bradley, David (1979), *Proto-Loloish*, Scandinavian Institute of Asian Studies Monograph Series, nr. 39, London and Malmo: Curzon Press.

Chazee, Laurent (1995), *Atlas des Ethnies et Sous-Ethnies du Laos*, Bangkok, n.p.

Chi Jen Chang (1956), *The Minority of Groups of Yunnan and Chinese Political Expansion into Southeast Asia*; Ph.D. thesis, University of Michigan, UMI Dissertation Service.

Condominas, George (1980) *L'Espace Social à Propos de l'Asie du Sud-Est*, Paris, Flammarion.

Cooper, Robert, Tapp, Nick, et al. (1991) *The Hmong,* Bangkok, Artasia Press Co. Ltd.

Cun, Wen Xue (1996), 'The Minorities of Simao', Paper prepared for the *Second International Hani/Akha Culture Studies Conference*, Chiang Mai/Chiang Rai, 12–18 May, 1996.

Dasseé, Martial (1976) *Montagnards, Revoltes et Guerres Revolutionnaires en Asie Sud-Est Continentale*, Bangkok: D.K. Books.

Dauffes, A.E. (1906) 'Notes Ethnographiques sur les Kos', *Bulletin de l'Ecole Française d'Extrême Orient*, 6, pp. 327–334.

Davies, H.R. (1909) *Yunnan, the link between India and the Yangtse*, Cambridge: Cambridge University Press.

Deal, David Michael (1971), *National Minority Policy in Southwest China, 1911–1965*; Ph.D. Thesis, University of Washington, UMI Dissertation Service, Ann Arbour, Michigan.

Dessaint, Alain, Y. (1980), *Minorities of Southwest China; An Introduction to the Yi (Lolo) and Related Peoples and an Annotated Bibliography*; HRAF Press, New Haven.

Douglas, Mary (1966), *Purity and Danger*, London: Routledge and Kegan Paul.

Duy Thieu, Nguyen (1996) 'Genealogical System of the Akha in Northern Laos', Paper presented to the *Second International Hani/Akha Conference*, Chiang Mai/Chiang Rai, 12–18 May.

Dzoebaw, Assaw and Asseu (1992), *Qoel Nehvq Nyil Nehvq* (Recitations for inside and outside dangers (in Akha) Akha Association for Education and Culture, Chiang Rai, Lawgaw and Lihai (eds.).

Dzoebaw, Phima Assaw (1982), Transcription of several Archaic, Oral Akha Texts, (Geusau, L.A. v. trans).

Dzoedang, Phima Aghaw (1979a), Akha Death Rituals, Ms., Transcribed and translated by Inga Lill Hansson; East Asian Institute, University of Copenhagen.

—— (1979b), Akha Sickness Rituals 1, Ms. idem East Asian Institute, I.L. Hansson University of Copenhagen.

Feng Han Yi and Shyrock, J.K. (1938), 'The historical Origins of the Lolo' *Harvard Journal of Asiatic Studies*. vol. 3., pp. 103–127.

Friedman, Jonathan (1971), *Tribe, Chiefdom, State.*; Ph.D. thesis, Uppsala University; UMI Service, Ann Arbour.

—— (1975), 'Tribes, States and Transformations' in *Marxist Analysis and Social Anthropology*, Maurice Bloch (ed.); Malaby Press, London, 1975, pp. 161–202.

Gao Wenying (1986), 'The Survey of Akha (Branch of Hani) in *Lanchang* Prefecture', in *Nationality Studies*, Nationalities Publishing House, Kunming, pp. 158–170 (in Chinese).

Geusau, Leo, G.M.A(lting) von (1983a) 'Dialectics of Akha Zang: The Interiorisations of a Perennial Minority Group' in *Highlanders of Thailand*, McKinnon, John and Bruksasri, W. (eds.) Oxford University Press, Kuala Lumpur, pp. 243–277.

—— (1983b), 'The Interiorisations of a Perennial Minority Group'. In *Sociology of 'Developing Societies' Southeast Asia*; Taylor, J.G. & Turton, A. (eds.) Basingstoke: Macmillan, pp. 215–229.

—— (1986), 'Ethnic Minorities and the State'; Paper presented to the *Annual Social Scientists of Thailand Meeting*, Chiang Mai, 1986; 6 pp.

—— (1987), 'Swinging for Freedom', *Focus section of the Nation Daily Sunday edition*, Bangkok, November 8. pp. 1–2.

—— (1989), 'The Change in Tribal way of life' in *Chivit Bondoi/Life on the Mountain*, Chiang Mai, pp. 12–21.

—— (1990), '*Studies on Akha Customary Law*': Research report no. 0408/05081, 1986–1990/2529–2533, submitted to the National Research Council of Thailand, Bankhen, Bangkok. 310 pp.

—— (1992a), 'The Akha, Ten Years After', *Pacific Viewpoint*; 33:2 (special edition on *Marginalisation in Thailand*, Lawrence, R., Morrison, P., McKinnon, J. (eds.)), Department of Geography, Victoria University, Wellington, New Zealand, pp. 178–184.

—— (1992b), 'Regional Development in Northern Thailand; Its Impact on Highlanders'. In *Lore: Capturing Environmental Knowledge*; Johnson M. (ed.) IDRC – Ottawa, Canada and Dene Cultural Institute, pp. 141–163.

—— (1992c), 'Documenting and Applying Traditional Environmental Knowledge in Northern Thailand, *ibidem* pp. 164–173.

—— (1993), 'Eco-systems in the Quadrangle Area; Property, Stress, Sustainable Management'. Paper presented at the *Fourth Annual Common Property Conference of IASP*, Manila June 16–19. 15 pp. Forthcoming publication by *Trent University*, Canada, *Native Studies Program*.

—— (1996), 'Avec les Akha du Triangle d'Or', *Grands Reportages*, No. 174, Paris, July, pp. 121–135.

Hanks, Jane (1974), 'Recitation of Patrilineages among the Akha', In *Social Organisation and the Applications of Anthropology: Essays in honour of Lauriston Sharp*. Smith R.J. (ed), Ithaca, Cornell University Press. pp. 114–127.

Hanks, Lucien M, and Jane (1975), 'Reflections on Ban Akha Mae Salong', *Journal of Siam Society*, 63, 1 Bangkok, pp. 72–85.

Hansson, Inga Lill (1983a), A Phonological Comparison of Akha and Hani; *Linguistics of the Tibeto-Burman Area* (7) 1 pg. 63–115.

—— (1983b), Akha Shaman's trance, Ms. (transl.), East Asian Institute, University of Copenhagen.

—— (1984a), Akha Sickness Rituals, 2, Ms. (transl.), East Asian Institute, University of Copenhagen.

—— (1984b), A Folktale of Akha in Northern Thailand, Ms. (transl.), University of Copenhagen.

Henry, A. (1903), 'The Lolos and other Tribes of Western China', *Journal of the Anthropological Institute of Great Britain and Ireland*, vol. 33, pp. 96–107.

Huang Shirong (1991), '*Situo Tusi* [Chinese appointed local chief] was Indigneous Hani', in *Anthology of Studies on the Hani*, Nationality Institute of the Hani/Yi Autonomous Prefecture of Honghe, Yunnan University, Publishing House, Kunming (Chinese).

Imamura Tsutomu (1996), The International Bibliography on Hani-Akha, unpublished Mss.

Jit, Phumisak (1976) *khwampenma khong kham sayam thai lao lae khom lae laksana thangkansangkhom khong chüchat* [Etymology of the terms Siam, Thai, Lao and Khom, and the social characteristics of ethnonyms], Bangkok: Social Sciences Association of Thailand.

Kammerer, Cornelia Ann (1985), *Gateway to the Akha World: Kinship, Ritual and Community among Highlanders of Thailand*; Ph.D. Dissertation Anthropology, University of Chicago.

—— (1988), 'Territorial Imperatives, Akha Ethnic Identity and Thailand's National Integration' in: *Ethnicities and Nations R. Rudieri, F. Pellizzi, S. Tambiah (eds,)* Houston, University of Texas Press, pp. 277–291.

—— (1990), 'Customs and Christian Conversion among Akha Highlanders of Burma and Thailand' *American Ethnologist*, vol. 17(2), pp. 277–291.

Keyes, Charles (1977), *The Golden Peninsula: Cultural Adaptation in Mainland Southeast Asia*, New York, Macmillan.

Kukeawkasem, Aje (1996), Report of the Oral Contributions, *Second International Hani/Akha Culture Studies Conference*, Chiang Mai/Chiang Rai, 12–18 May.

Lao UNESCO Committee (1996), Data-paper, *UNESCO Conference on Safeguarding and promoting the intangible heritage of the Minority Peoples in PDR Laos*, Vientiane, 7–11 Oct. 1996.

Li Fuyi (1946), 'History of the Tai Lue', in *Collection of Studies on South West China* (Series), Kunming, Yunnan University.

Li Ke Zhong (1996), 'Ecology and the original information transfer method', paper given at the *Second International Hani/Akha Culture Studies Conference*, Chiang Mai/Chiang Rai, 12–18 May, 1996.

Liu Qibyuan (1989), 'A Tale of the Hani King', in *Nationality Studies*, Nationalities Publishing House, Year 2, pp. 10–15 (in Chinese).

Li Xi Xian (1995), *Acts of the First International Hani/Akha Culture Studies Conference, February 28–March 6, 1993*; Honghe, Kunming, Nationalities Publishing House (in Chinese).

Leach E. R. (1954), *Political Systems of Highland Burma*, London, Bell.

Lehman, F. K. (1963), *The Structure of Chin Society: A Tribal People of Burma adapted to a Non-Western Civilisation*, Urbana University Press, Illinois.

—— (1980), *Burma: Kayah Society as a Function of the Shan-Karen Context*, Urbana University Press, Illinois.

Lewis, Paul (1969–1970), *Ethnographic notes on the Akhas of Burma*, 4 vols. HRAFlex books; New Haven.

—— (1978), The Introduction of a Family Planning Program to Akhas in Thailand; Ph.D. thesis, University of Oregon.

Lewis, Paul and Lewis Elaine (1973), 'The Fourth Dimension in Thailand' in: *Gospel Tide in Thailand*, American Baptist Mission Studies. Valley Forge, *American Baptist Powers* (pp. 49–54).

Lintner, Bertil (1990), *Land of Jade*, Bangkok/Edinburgh; White Lotus and Kiscadale.

Luce, G.H., and Chen Yee Sein (Transl.) (1961), *The Man shu (Book of the Southern Barbarians)* Ithaca.

Majeu Takh'ang, Pacelo (1979), 'Ghoma law-eu' or the honouring of the big rice stalk, mss. transcribed/translated by Leo A. von Geusau.

—— (1981), 'Yes, we Akha are Monkeys', Taped discourse, transl. Leo A. von Geusau.

Madrolle, Claudius (1908), 'Quelques Peuplades Lo-lo', *T'oung Pao*, Serie II, 9, pp. 529–576.

Mao Youquan (1989), 'Inquiry on the Names, Identity and Migrations of the Hani' *Yunnan Journal of Social Science*, Kunming, Yunnan Peoples' Publishing House (in Chinese).

—— (1996), 'The Core-value of Hani Genealogy', Paper presented to the *Second International Hani/Akha Culture Studies* Conference, Chiang Mai/Chiang Rai, 12–18 May 1996.

Mao Youquan and Li Qibo (1989), *The Hani-People*, Jianshui Nationality Studies Institute, Honghe, Yunnan China (in Chinese).

Mattisoff, James, A. (1978), Variational Semantics in Tibeto Burman; The Organic Approach to Linguistic Comparison; in *Occasional Papers of the Wolfenden Society on Tibeto-Burman Linguistics*, Volume VI; F.K. Lehman (Ed.). Philadelphia, Institute for the Study of Human Issues.

—— (1983), 'Linguistic Diversity and Language Contact', in *Highlanders of Thailand*, McKinnon, John and Bruksasri, W. (eds.) Oxford University Press, Kuala Lumpur, pp. 56–86.

Mojiang Editorial Committee (1983), *Collection of Traditional Stories of the Hani at Mojiang* (in Chinese).

Orleans, Henry Phillipe Marie, Prince d' (1898), *Du Tonkin aux Indes par les Sources de l'Irrawadi, Janvier 1895–Janvier 1896*. Paris: Calmann Lévy.

Perot, Madeleine (1909), 'Histoire du Chemin de Fer du Tonkin à Kunming'. n.p.

Quian Yong (1996), 'Mopi, the Propagator of Hani Traditional Culture', Paper given at the *Second International Hani/Akha Culture Studies Conference*', Chiang Mai/ Chiang Rai, Thailand, 12–18 May 1996.

Roux, Henri (1924), 'Deux Tribus de la Région de Pongsaly' *Bulletin de l'Ecole Française d'Extrême Orient*, 24:373–445.

Sainson, Camille (1904), *Histoire Particulière de Nan-Chao*, 2 vol. Translated from Chinese, Paris, Imprimerie Nationale.

Scholte, Bob (1975), 'Ethnography as Communication', Paper, distributed for the course of Philosophical Anthropology, *New School for Social Research*, New York.

Scott, J.G. and Hardiman, J.P. (1900–1901), *Gazetteer of Upper Burma and the Shan States*, Part 1, Vol. 1, Rangoon.

Shi Junchao (1988a), 'On Ethno-History: Hani Oral History of Migration (Hania-Peizongpopo)', *Nationality Studies*, Nationalities Publishing House, 3 (in Chinese).

—— (1988b), Reflections on Yi and Yue Cultures: Historical Relations between Hani and Zhuang Tai Family of Languages'; Honghe Nationalities Institute, Nr. 2 (in Chinese).

—— (1991), 'Lowland and Highland Civilizations: Research on the Question of Migrations of the Hani' in *Research on Hani History*, pp 30–54; Kunming, Nationalities Publishing House, (in Chinese).

Shida and Ahai, (eds.) (1992), *Yaniya-Gazangga: Oral History of Sipsongpanna Hani's Migrations*, National Minority Committee of Jinghong, Yunnan, China. (in Chinese).

Shiratori, Yoshiro (1966), 'Ethnic Configurations in Southern China' *Folk Culture in South-East Asia* Nr. 25, pp. 147–163. Tokyo University Press.

Stewart-Cox, Belinda and Hall, Margaret (1984), 'The Restructuring of an Ethnic Minority in China', in *Papers of the School of Human Sciences*, Cambridge, 1984.

Telford, James Haxton (1937), 'Animism in Kengtung State' *Journal of Burma Research Society*, 27(2), pp.? 86–238.

Tooker, Deborah E. (1988), Inside and Outside: Schematic Replication at the Level of Village, Household and Person among Akha of Northern Thailand; Ph.D. Dissertation, Harvard University.

—— (1992), 'Identity Systems of Highland Burma: 'Belief', Akha-zang and a Critique of Interiorized Notions of Ethno-Religious Identity' *Man* (N.S.), vol. 27, No. 4 pp. 799–819.

—— (1996a), 'Irrigation Systems in the Ideology and Ritual Practices of Akha Shifting Agriculturists' Paper, given for the *Second International Hani/Akha Culture Studies Conference, Thailand*.

—— (1996b), 'Putting the Mandala in its Place: A practice-based Approach to the Spatialization of Power on the Southeast Asian 'Periphery' – The Case of the Akha', *Journal of Asian Studies* 55, no. 2 (May 1996): 323–358.

Tribal Research Institute (1995), *The Hilltribes of Thailand*, Fourth ed. 30th Anniversary, Tribal Research Institute. Chiang Mai.

Vanicelli, Luigi (1935), *La Religione Dei Lolo*, Publicazioni Dell' Universita del Sacro Cuore, Vol. 2, Milano, Societa Editrice Vita e Pensiero.

Vial, P. (1917), *Chez les Lolos*, Missions Catholiques, Paris.

Wiens, Herold (1967), *Han Chinese Expansion in South China*, The Shoe String Press, Yale University.

Wijeyewardene Gehan (1968), 'Address, abuse and animal categories,' *Man*, 3, 1, 76–93.

Wissman, Hermann von (1943), 'Süd Yunnan als Teilraum Südostasiens, in *Schriften für Geopolitik*, 22, Heidelberg, Kurt Vorwinckler Verlag.

Witfogel, K. (1957), *Oriental Despotism. A Comparative Study of Total Power.* New Haven: Yale University Press.

Yang Wanzhi (1991), 'A Study of Hani Hieroglyphic Symbols', *Nationality-Studies*, Honghe; 3, pp. 43–49. (in Chinese).

Part III

THAI-MALAY BORDERLANDS

Introduction

This section offers two complementary and contrasting studies of the Sam Sam 'Thai-speaking Muslims' who live on either side of the Thai-Malaysian border. Kobkua Suwannathat-Pian, a historian, provides a detailed history from documentary sources of a power-laden discourse on race, culture and nationality. She contributes her own critical commentary and evaluation of three major hypotheses as to the 'origin' of the Sam Sam and the defining characteristics of their identity, largely as this has been constructed by others. Despite differences as to whether the Sam Sam were 'originally' Thai or Malay most European views in the nineteenth century and up to the mid-twentieth century were based on a racial-genetic model in which 'mixture', 'mixed-blood' etc. was usually seen as culturally inferior contributing to low intelligence, propensity to criminality, addiction, untrustworthiness, and so on. The predominant Malay view was that the combination of Thai language (and some other customary practices) with Islam was 'a prohibited infidel mingling' (Nishii). Although most early sources are Western, it is interesting to see senior Thai and Malay rulers and administrators (Prince Damrong and Tunku Abdul Rahman) participating in the same discourse, each to claim these people on the peripheries of new nations as their own, if not fully equal.

Ryoko Nishii, an anthropologist, also reviews 'outside' views or constructions of Sam Sam 'peripheral ethnicity', and leaves aside the 'origin' debate as inconclusive, and in any case favouring a view of Sam Sam as what we might call 'an always-already mixed identity' undergoing transformations. Instead she concentrates on 'the historical memories of Sam Sam regarding a local hero' which she recorded and discussed with Sam Sam from several villages in northern Kedah during ethnographic fieldwork. She spoke to descendants of To Nai Sim (who lived ca. 1840 to ca. 1927–9) who was locally regarded as a '*raja*' appointed by the Sultan of

Kedah, and perhaps the King of Siam (Kedah being formerly under Siamese sovereignty). To Nai Sim has characteristics widely found in instances of local leadership on the peripheries of the power of Tai states, where social and political status counted for more than ethnicity. He was rich, trading in and possessing slaves and elephants. He was physically and magically strong, exercising judicial powers of life and death. He was bilingual, polygamous, and is remembered as a devout Muslim. Locally autonomous he was nonetheless ultimately subject to higher political centres. He was more than a 'social bandit' or an 'enforcer'. Nishii's suggestively anachronistic use of 'provincial boss' nicely links the type with more contemporay political practice.

While the still popular Thai term *khaek* for any Muslim, Thai-speaking or not, may be quite ancient, 'Thai-Islam' is a current neologism that recognises a national identity for non-Buddhists, whereas Malay-izing policy insists on a much closer relation between religion, language, and national identity. Nishii reminds us of the historically shifting valencies atttributed to such criteria: '. . . the boundaries of religion and language were more vague and relaxed in the ambiguous periphery and lacked the strident connotations of the contemporary Malay world'. Intriguingly, while on the Thailand side of the border 'Thai-Muslim' embraces both Thai- and Malay-speaking Muslims, the former no longer being called Sam Sam and apparently becoming 'integrated' while remaining publicly distinct, on the Malaysia side the term Sam Sam continues to be applied, with connotations of shame and old-fashionedness, while the bearers voluntarily commit themselves to rapid 'assimilation' and loss of public differentiation. And yet at the same time locally, concealed from outsiders, a distinct sense of identity persists and memories of the Sam Sam past are 'cherished more profoundly' than in Thailand.

Plate 12. 'Phya Nyak, the king of serpents and dragons'

The Historical Development of Thai-Speaking Muslim Communities in Southern Thailand and Northern Malaysia

Kobkua Suwannathat-Pian

Introduction

Thai-speaking Muslim communities are found in the northwestern Malaysian states of Kedah, Perlis, and Perak, and in the southern Thai provinces of Trang, Phang-nga, Songkhla, and Satun (Setul). In the last-mentioned they form 80 per cent of the inhabitants. They are known among scholars and local people as Sam Sam. Officially there has not been a minority ethnic group known as Sam Sam in Malaysia since the 1911 census. In the 1921 Population Census, the Sam Sam were categorized as Malays. In Thailand, this minority community has long been regarded as religiously wayward Thai who 'have been tainted by Islamic teachings' (Strobel 1908: 172). At the time of the last available statistics there were 15,377 Sam Sam in the States of Kedah and Perlis (Report on the Census, 1911: 5) and approximately 18,000–21,000 in Satun in Thailand (Strobel 1908: 174). Nonetheless, it is apparent from various studies, some as recent as the early 1990s, that this Thai-speaking Muslim community still exists in Kedah and Perlis, Malaysia, and in Satun and the southern part of Songkhla, Thailand. Thai-speaking Muslim communities are unique to the northwestern states of the Malay peninsula. On the eastern seaboard, Kelantan which has the second biggest population of Thai-speakers in Malaysia, and Trengganu have only Thai-speaking Buddhists among their population (Winzeler 1985; Mohamed Yusoff Ismail 1980).

The distinctive features of the Sam Sam are their *bahasa ibunda* the mother tongue which is the old southern Thai dialect interspersed with Malay words; their 'Malay' custom which has been mixed with southern Thai custom and flavour, particularly in their diet and artistic taste and preference; and their Islamic religion. Because of this, Thai-speaking Muslims of Kedah, for example, generally those of thirty years of age and above, are still very much identifiable, at least at the local level. They continue not only to speak the *bahasa Sam Sam*, but also to maintain their other above-mentioned mixed socio-cultural heritage.[1] To the world beyond their village, however, Malaysian Sam Sam cannot be easily detected, and their socio-cultural assimilation appears complete. In South Thailand, however, the Sam Sam are regarded more as a part of the Thai Malay community because of their Islamic faith, regardless of the fact that they do not – and most cannot – speak Malay.

Origin and Ethnicity

There are three main hypotheses concerning the origin and ethnicity of the Sam Sam, which we may name after their principal or first proponents: Crawfurd, Newbold, and Annandale-Robinson.

John Crawfurd observed in 1821 that there were four main indigenous inhabitants in Kedah, namely, Malays, 'Sam-Sam', Siamese, and Samang (Crawfurd 1987: 28). He emphatically points out that the first two mentioned were predominant, 'among whom the second [that is, the Sam Sam] are said to be most numerous' (ibid.: 28–9). Crawfurd explains that the term Sam Sam means 'people of the Siamese race who have adopted the Mohammedan religion, and who speak a language which is a mixed jargon of the language of the two peoples'.[2] After Crawfurd there are many reports on the origin and ethnicity of the Sam Sam; some concur with Crawfurd, and others refute his claim that the Sam Sam were originally of the 'Siamese race'. In 1826, Captain Henry Burney wrote the following in support of the Crawfurd theory:

> 'There is not a respectable and well-informed native of the Queda[Kedah] who will attempt to deny that *previous to the introduction of Mahometanism* [sic] his country was exclusively inhabited by the Siamese race who were worshippers of Boodh [Buddha] or some other Hindoo Deity.' (Burney 1910–1914 vol.II, pt.4: 122–23 emphasis added).

Strobel, an American adviser to the Thai government, wrote in a Memorandum on Satun to the British Minister at Bangkok, that the Sam Sam were the Siamese who 'have become tainted by the Mahommedan [sic] creed'. He also quoted Skinner, former Resident Counsellor of Penang, as describing the Sam Sam as 'Siamese who have embraced Mahommedanism'. Strobel explained that the word Sam Sam itself was a corrupt form of the terms 'Siam Islam', and that 'it is well known that they speak Siamese and are pure Siamese in every respect excepting the one of religion' (Strobel 1908). It is apparent, in retrospect, that the American adviser was well coached by Prince Damrong, then Minister of the Interior. It was Prince Damrong who came across the Sam Sam while on an inspection tour of Perlis and Satun in the early 1900s. From his own study and observation, the Prince came to the conclusion that they were

Siamese who had accepted Islam as their religion, but who otherwise adhered to the Thai socio-cultural way of life, most distinctively in their Thai-speaking habit. The word Sam Sam was the corrupt form of the term 'Siam Islam', which was a name given to them by both the Buddhist Thai, and Malays (Rahmah 1979; Damrong 1962: 642).

Among present-day scholars, Banks is most outspoken in support of the Crawfurd theory, namely that the Thai-speaking Muslims in Kedah were Siamese who changed their religion some time in the distant past. For Banks, this event most likely occurred after the withdrawal of Thai troops from Kedah in 1839–42. He differs from Crawfurd on the Kedah Sam Sam's ancestors. Banks is of the opinion that the bulk of the Sam Sam were descendants of Siamese soldiers who decided to make Kedah their home (Banks 1977: 218, 1980: 100–2). Crawfurd had implied that the Sam Sam and their ancestors must have settled in Kedah long before 1821. If Banks's assumption were to be accepted, he would have to offer historical and socio-cultural evidence to substantiate his hypothesis that, contrary to what had been reported by Crawfurd and Newbold, the bulk of the Sam Sam were relative newcomers to Kedah. There is no apparent reason why these soldiers should change their faith simply because they lived among Malay-speaking Muslims. There were numerous Thai villages within the districts of Kota Setar, Kubang Pasu, and Padang Terap, as well as in Baling, Sik, Kuala Muda, and Langkawi, with which these 'new settlers' could affiliate and relieve any socio-cultural pressure they might have to endure living among Muslim Malays.

From a political perspective, Banks's hypothesis appears porous. From 1842 to 1909, when Kedah was ceded to Great Britain, cordial, harmonious, and intimate relations and rapport existed between Bangkok and Alor Setar (Kobkua 1988: ch.3). There was thus no reason to expect the local authorities to exercise any political or administrative pressure on Siamese communities, either old or new, to force them to conform to Malay-Islamic culture. There is no valid evidence of such policy being conducted throughout this period.[3]

The first account to dispute Crawfurd's findings on the Thai-speaking Muslims of Kedah is that given by Newbold in 1839. Newbold argues conversely that 'the Sam-Sams are a race of Malays who have adopted the religion and language of the Siamese' (Newbold 1971 vol.2: 12).[4] Newbold differs from Crawfurd only on the Sam Sam's origin. He follows Crawfurd's account when describing the component populations of Kedah. Skeat, citing Malay sources on the Sam Sam about sixty years later, also concludes that, 'the Sam-Sams were always Malays who had turned Siamese in everything but their religion' (Skeat 1953: 133–34).[5] Nonetheless, Skeat does not appear to be totally convinced of the information he reports. He makes a pointed observation that, 'There was something distinctive about a Sam-Sam though it was hard to say what – except, of course, the Siamese fashion of wearing the hair with a top knot; the "blacking brush mode"' (ibid.).

From his personal experiences as District Officer in Kuala Nerang in the 1930s, Tunku Abdul Rahman, Malaysia's first Prime Minister, recalls that the Sam Sam were Malays from Siam who spoke Thai. They were not well received by native Malays in Kuala Nerang, most likely because the Sam Sam were then regarded as a crime-oriented community and as Muslims who did not take their religion seriously enough (Abdul Rahman 1978: 23–24).

It seems unreasonable in the light of historical facts available at the time, for Tunku Abdul Rahman to state that the Thai-speaking Muslims were Malays from southern Siam who spoke Thai. It is a well-known socio-political fact that the Malays in southern Siam/Thailand did not (the majority still do not) speak Thai (Omar Farouk 1988: 1–30; McVey 1989: 33–52). Only the Thai Muslims from Satun, Songkhla and Trang spoke Thai, and they could speak Thai by virtue of being Sam Sam, and not Malay. The Malays in southern Thailand took pride in not being assimilated into the Thai Buddhist culture of the majority of their compatriots, and up to the second decade of the twentieth century, the Thai government did little to assimilate its Malay subjects. It was during the reign of King Vajiravudh (1910–25) that the Compulsory Education Act of 1923 was passed which required that all children of school age – regardless of their religion or ethnic affinity – attend state primary schools. This was the first attempt by the central government to force its minorities to learn to speak and read the Thai language. In the South it was not successful, and parents were able to avoid enforcement by the authorities. Thus, generally speaking, only Thai Malays who had the benefit of state education were able to speak and understand Thai; in the 1970s this roughly meant those about fifty years-old and younger. Even then, it would be stretching the imagination to think that these are the Malays who would forsake their mother tongue for a language they had never been comfortable with. Tunku Abdul Rahman's assumption is that Malays in southern Siam were able to speak the Thai language fluently as far back as the nineteenth century. This is glaringly contrary to actual conditions in the region.

The third hypothesis of Sam Sam origin was proposed by Annandale and Robinson around 1901–2 (Annandale and Robinson 1903: 53–4). From his field work in Trang, Annandale discovered that the Sam Sam of Trang, who called themselves *Orang Laut Islam* (Muslim sea people), were 'half-bred Siamese' much looked down upon by their neighbours, the Siamese villagers. The Sam Sam were unwilling to admit that their ancestry was of mixed origin, though they admitted to speaking *bahasa Sam Sam*.[6] Maxwell in his *Annual Report of Adviser*, concurs with Annandale and Robinson when discussing the Sam Sam community in Kubang Pasu and other districts. To Maxwell, the Sam Sams were 'a mixed race of Malay and

Siamese blood, who speak Siamese or the patois and hold the Muhammedan [sic] religion' (Maxwell 1911: 22).

Archaimbault seems to adhere to this school of thought and has made a detailed study of the Sam Sam community The French scholar concludes that the Sam Sam 'are the product of an inter-mixture: an inter-mixture of Malays and Siamese or Malays, Chinese, and Siamese according to some; Siamese and descendants of the aboriginal inhabitants of Langkasuka or Ligor according to others'. In his study, the Sam Sam are also divided by their religion: the Sam Sam Siam (Buddhist) and the Sam Sam Melayu (Muslim). The common denominator between the two is *bahasa Sam Sam* and mixed ancestry, though of different inter-mixtures (Archaimbault 1957: 75–92).[7] Archaimbault considers possible root-words of Sam Sam suggested by his informants: *tcham-tcham* in Hokkien which means 'to mix'; *sama-sama* in Malay which means 'together'; and *sam* (actually it should be *som*) in Thai meaning 'mix' (Archaimbault 1957: 75).

The gist of all this is that, for Archaimbault, Sam Sam by their very name are people of mixed ancestry. It matters little whether they are of the Siamese-Malay, Siamese-Chinese, or even Siamese-Langkasuka/Ligor inhabitant 'inter-mixture'. It is to be expected that the Sam Sam must, like any other ethnic community, have mixed with other ethnic groups through marriage or socio-cultural adjustment and assimilation. However, I am not convinced that by deduction from linguistic evidence alone, one can identify the origin of any ethnic group. Indeed, if these root-word variations are in fact a reliable indication of their origins, why, of all the numerous products of 'inter-mixture' in the region, should Sam Sam be singled out to be called 'mixed'? Moreover, most Siamese 'mixed' communities outside the Kedah/Perlis/Satun belt were, and are non-Muslim. I thus conclude that Sam Sam does not have its semantic origin from either *tcham-tcham*, *sama-sama*, or *som/sam*. Nor does the word necessarily mean 'mixed'.

The hypothesis that the Sam Sam were originally Siamese who at some point in the past were converted to Islam, appears to be the most plausible. The hypothesis not only answers satisfactorily and logically the question of their unswerving adherence to the Thai language and culture, but also makes sense of the earliest written reports on the Sam Sam as one of the predominant components of the population in the northwestern part of the Malay peninsula in the first half of the nineteenth century.

On the origin of the Sam Sam, it is relevant to look into the history of the lower peninsula of present-day Thailand between 7 and 8 degrees North latitude, which forms one of the 'most significant cultural and linguistic frontiers of South East Asia' (Winzeler 1985: 66). Arab and Persian Muslims en route to China and Eastern Asia were active in the ports of Tenasserim and the Isthmus of Kra many centuries before the first independent Thai kingdom of Sukhothai in 1238 AD (Forbes 1989: 168).

By the tenth century, a coastal town existed within this area, probably South of Phuket. The area appears to have been introduced to Islam before the setting up of the Sultanate of Melaka. It is also likely that by the end of the thirteenth century, several small groups of Thai settlers had established communities as far South as Songkhla. Prince Damrong claimed from his researches that the political power-field of Sukhothai-Ayutthaya extended to Songkhla on the eastern seaboard and Satun on the western seaboard. Through interaction with the Arabs and other Muslim merchants who came to trade with the area Satun and other places came under the influence of Islamic teachings (Damrong 1962: 217–18). When Kedah converted to the Islamic faith, Satun found itself drawn more towards its Malay co-religionists than to the Buddhist Thai to the North. Prince Damrong narrated his visit to Satun at the turn of the century when he discovered that the majority of Satun's inhabitants were Sam Sam not Malay, though outwardly the Satun Sam Sam could not be distinguished from Malays. Only when they spoke, would Sam Sam reveal their true identity (see Abdul Rahman 1978: 23–27). It seems probable that the Sam Sam had their origin in the Siamese West coastal area South of Phuket. Most of them lived in the area of present-day Satun, though they could also be found in Trang, Krabi, and the southern part of Songkhla, and the neighbouring Malay states of Kedah, Perlis, and Perak. Because of frequent contact with, and proximity to, the Muslim community of Arab and Persian traders, the Siamese inhabitants of this area embraced Islam, and subsequently felt more at home with their Muslim brothers in the neighbouring state of Kedah.

A Thai origin could certainly explain why Sam Sam continued to speak their original mother tongue, while such Malay language as they commanded was a result of their close proximity with Malay co-religionists. Most Sam Sam villages in the districts under study, namely Kubang Pasu, Kota Setar, and Padang Terap, are surrounded by Malay villages. It would scarcely be possible for the Sam Sam to pick up Thai and discard their supposed Malay mother tongue were they of Malay origin within these geographical confines. Satun, the heartland of the Thai-speaking Muslim community was reported in 1908 to consist of 60 per cent Sam Sam, 25 per cent Malay, and 15 per cent Chinese (Strobel 1908: 174). By 1960, it was reported that 82.9 per cent of Satun's population were Muslim, of whom 81.3 per cent spoke Thai as their mother tongue.[8] Satun represents the southernmost limit of Thai ethnographical expansion on the western seaboard, while Songkhla, with a sizeable proportion of Thai-speaking Muslims, marks the same expansion on the eastern side of the peninsula. Satun could well be the location of the town 'inhabited by Muslims, Indians, and Persians' of the tenth century (Tibbetts, 1957, quoted in Forbes 1989: 168). Historical facts tend to support the hypothesis that Thai-speaking Muslims were Thai in origin who had the opportunity to adopt Islam due to frequent and regular contact with Muslim merchants who visited, and some of whom even 'inhabited' the area.

The linguistic-etymological development of the word Sam Sam, while insufficient on its own, offers further support for the view that Sam Sam were originally Siamese. As I suggested earlier, the proposition that the root-word of Sam Sam might have come from Hokkien *tcham-tcham*, Malay *sama-sama*, or Thai *som* is unconvincing in the context of the Malaysian demographic kaleidoscope, which contains comparable variations of Siamese inter-mixtures outside Kedah and Perlis, none of which are termed Sam Sam. It is the contention of this study that Sam Sam derives from other root-words which do not necessarily mean 'mixed'. Tunku Abdul Rahman states that it derives from 'Siam-Siam' and has been corrupted to Sam Sam with the passage of time (Abdul Rahman 1972: 23). According to Malay usage, repetition of a word carries a connotation of similarity to the single usage, but not identity. For example, *hi jae-hi jauan* means somewhat green, but not really green; *kebudak-budakan*, childish but not a child; or *ker ja-ker ja*, not really having a lot of work, but rather pretending to be working hard. 'Siam-Siam' would thus mean being somewhat Siamese, but not really Siamese because they were not Buddhists. This seems to be the way the Sam Sam were distinguished from Thai-speaking Buddhists who were 'genuine Siamese', or as contemporary jargon would put it: 'hundred per cent Thai' (Arong Suthasasna 1989: 94).

Prince Damrong and Prince Narit, leading Thai scholars of the first half of this century, believed that the term Sam Sam had its origin in *Siam Islam* which was gradually corrupted by southern Thai pronunciation to *Sam Lam*, and eventually by easy lip movement to *Sam Sam* (Rahmah 1972: 217–18, 244).

From the etymological and socio-cultural context, both *Siam Siam* and *Siam Islam* appear to offer a more solid and meaningful explanation of the term Sam Sam than those proposed by Archaimbault in 1957. Both stress the origin of Sam Sam in the context of their socio-cultural development. In short I suggest we can accept the explanations given by Tunku Abdul Rahman, and Prince Damrong and Prince Narit as plausible etymological origins of Sam Sam. This recognizes that present-day Sam Sam are the outcome of the inter-mixture of Siamese/Sam Sam/Malay as much as, or even more than, any original Siamese. The important features of the Sam Sam by the end of the nineteenth century included the Siamese language/*bahasa Sam Sam*, Islamic faith, and certain Siamese cultural practices interspersed with Malay culture, such as their dress and food preferences.

Historical Development

Crawfurd gives a vivid account of the Thai-speaking Muslim community he found in Kedah in 1821, while on his way by sea from Calcutta to the Siamese court at Bangkok. His account, the main thesis of which had not been disputed until recently, distinguished the Sam Sam as an entirely separate ethnic group from Malays and Siamese, and thus underscored their long settlement in the northwestern Malayan peninsula. I proposed above that the Sam Sam began their history most probably as Siamese who inhabited the western coast from Krabi (South of Phuket/Junk Ceylon) to Satun and beyond. By the tenth and eleventh centuries they had converted to Islam. When the Kedah kingdom embraced Islam, most likely in the fourteenth or fifteenth centuries, the Siamese Muslims were naturally attracted to the Kedah socio-religious centre. Intermarriage with Malay-speaking Muslims and other socio-economic and political factors must have led to the migration of the Thai-speaking Muslims from the Trang-Krabi-Satun area to the interior of the old kingdom of Kedah, making them one of the principal ethnic groups in Kedah by the time Crawfurd came upon them.[9]

What has happened since the reports of Crawfurd and Newbold? In 1867, J.R. Logan, in his submission for the setting up of a volunteer police unit in the Muda District, Province Wellesley, had this to say of the Sam Sam who then formed the majority of the people in the frontier areas between southern Kedah and British Province Wellesley:

> 'Some generations back, [the Sam Sam] were converted to Mohammedan-ism, a religion which still sits loosely on them . . . Many of them are more stupid and ignorant even than the Malays in the same condition of life, and many are knavish, thievish, and addicted to gambling and opium-smoking . . . There are among them men habitually predatory, and dangerous from their treachery and ferocity. Their cunning, however, is without the intelligent fore-thought and subtlety of fraud . . .' (Logan 1885: 200).

Logan becomes the first observer to allege very negative features of the Thai-speaking Muslims, features which are repeated by subsequent British writers on the Sam Sam such as Skeat and Maxwell. Skeat, in particular, reports his talk in 1899 with Tuan Kudin, Raja of Satun, on the subject of the Sam Sam and their habits. For example, he claims that they: 'were [not] particular as to their diet. The Sam-Sams generally gave up attendance at the mosque as well as the 'Hours of Prayer' and even ate 'unclean' things such as tortoises (kura-kura)' (Skeat 1953: 133–4). Skeat's report was echoed by Annandale and Robinson writing on the Sam Sam in Trang at about the same time, and by Tunku Abdul Rahman of the Sam Sam in Padang Terap in the 1930s. Annandale and Robinson write:

'Mahommedanism [sic] sits very lightly upon the Sam-Sams . . . [they could easily turn to Buddhism upon encountering some hardships or misfortunes]. This change is not so peculiar as it seems when one understands that the Sam-Sams, like the Malays and many of the Siamese of the eastern Siamese-Malay states believe Buddha Gautama and Moses to have been one and the same person. Thus they regard the status of the Siamese as identical with that of the Jews, whose dispensation . . . was superseded by the dispensation of the Nabi Isa or Prophet Jesus, to give way in its turn to the *agama Islam* or the Mahommedan religion.' (Annandale and Robinson 1903: 59).

In somewhat the same tone, Abdul Rahman reports that:

'In most cases, the so-called Muslims [that is, the Sam Sam] cared very little and knew nothing about religion . . . An incident concerned two young people, the man, a Muslim Sam-Sam and the girl, a Thai Buddhist. They were intent on getting married, and the man was prepared to give up his religion for the girl he loved . . . Then in desperation I asked him to consider the Holy Prophet Mohammad, and what he said shocked me. "Why should I consider Mohammad; he has never been in my kampung to see me, not even once".' (Abdul Rahman 1978: 24–6).

It is evident from various negative and unflattering reports from the second half of the nineteenth century that the Sam Sam community in Malaya was not well-regarded by officials, nor within Malay circles. Two reasons recur as to why the 'Thai-speaking Muslims' were so despised: their habitual laxity concerning Islam, and their association with criminal activity – 'dacoity', cattle-stealing, and kidnapping. Because of these, they were socially discriminated against by the ruling class, the British authorities who, on the whole, type-cast them as 'thievish' and 'knavish' by nature. There appears to be no lack of evidence that Sam Sam were held to be more or less synonymous with lawlessness and crime (Cheah 1988: 124–25, 1985: 34–51). It is not surprising therefore that the British authorities blamed the Sam Sam for the existence of an extraordinary degree of lawlessness and civil instability on the Kedah-Siam, Kedah-Province Wellesley frontiers. In the early part of this century, these areas were well-populated by the Sam Sam; they were also notorious for robbery and cattle-stealing. Maxwell, the first British Adviser to Kedah, wrote in 1910 blaming the high crime rate in the border areas on the 'mixed-blood Malays' and the Sam Sam: 'they seem to be without the moral sense which regards a human life as being different from that of an animal' (Maxwell 1911: 34).

There was some truth in the accusation that Thai-speaking Muslims had a disproportionate share of criminal activities during the first few decades of the twentieth century. During the 'golden age' of gang robbery and other lawless activities in the Kedah-Satun area – approximately 1900–1920

– the Sam Sam provided at least two of the four fiercest and most notorious gang leaders – Awang Poh and Salleh Eh Tui (Cheah 1985: 34–51, 1988: ch.2). Both were ranked by society as *panglima penyamum*, captain-robbers. Some people in Padang Terap still recall the audacity and terror associated with these captain-robbers. Tunku Abdul Rahman reminisced about his childhood fear of Salleh Tui (Abdul Rahman 1978: 23–5). From the official point of view, the Sam Sam represented a criminal class which deprived society of law and order.

Part of the reason why the Sam Sam were stereotyped as a crime-prone community arises from the fact that they represented the lowest social stratum in Kedah, Perlis, and Satun. In Kedah and Perlis in particular, they were mostly involved in the agrarian sector of the economy, namely as paid-planters. They constituted a social class which had to bear almost unlimited demands on its services during the pre-colonial period, and later as main targets of the various taxes – land tax, land rent, unpaid services, etc. – imposed by British and Thai administrations. When faced with the problems of poor land, occasional disasters such as drought, poor harvests, or other natural disasters, these peasants were left with only one recourse for their survival – namely theft (Cheah 1988: 44). Padang Terap, Kubang Pasu, Kota Setar, Kuala Muda, Satun, and Perlis were the heart of paid-farming. Not surprisingly, under such socio-economic hardships, this would become a region of gang-robbery and theft. The Kedah districts bordering Siam seem to have been more prone to crime, especially from 1900 onwards, apparently as an effect of the administrative reform carried out by Bangkok, which caused the breakdown of the traditional patron-client linkage in rural localities. Many bandits, accustomed to operate in collusion with, and enjoying immunity from local chiefs – who, in turn, exercised some control over lawlessness within their own territory – found themselves without their traditional protection (Graham 1924 vol.3: 325–26). Consequently, crime increased and, as Cheah Boon Kheng observes, even spilled over from the Thai side of the border to Perlis, Kedah and Kelantan. As early as 1898, Kubang Pasu had acquired a reputation as a hideout for dangerous bandits from far and near (Cheah 1988: 21–25). Many of the non-salaried *penghulu*/headmen became involved in crime to augment their income. They were thus ineffective in reducing and solving crime in their territory. Both Graham in Kelantan and the British Adviser of Kedah agreed that the *penghulu* were of little value in government efforts to make law and order prevail in frontier areas (Graham 1924; *Kedah Annual Report for A.H. 1933 [19 November 1914–8 November 1915]* 1915). Eventually, as Cheah Boon Kheng puts it, the Kedah government had to resort to the strategy of using a thief to catch a thief by appointing powerful bandit chiefs to head the bandit-infested villages and parishes. Not until the 1930s did this strategy begin to bear fruit, and the problem of bandits and dacoits was brought under some control.

With this kind of socio-economic background, it is understandable why both the rural Malays, Thai, and Thai-speaking Muslims were so involved in crimes of dacoity and theft. This had little to do with their immoral nature, but much to do with the socio-economic conditions in which they were forced to eke out their livelihood. They were victims of socio-economic and political forces beyond their control, which in turn made them susceptible to the crime and lawlessness described by the authorities. Nevertheless, by the second decade of this century, the Sam Sam had effectively been portrayed as a community of lawless people who were 'habitually predatory', and who possessed the 'instinct of dacoits'. Thai-speaking Muslims had become the target of official prejudice in both Kedah and Perlis. Little was done to improve the socio-economic conditions of these under-privileged people. Until 1957, when Malaya obtained independence, the Sam Sam remained in a socio-economic backwater, befitting their unofficial second-class citizen status (Frost 1912). Their counterparts in southern Thailand suffered a similar fate.

Comparative Analysis

The assimilation of the Sam Sam in contemporary Malaysia is being achieved not primarily because the Malaysian authorities employ any particular socio-political programme, though there are general social pressures towards assimilation, but rather because the Sam Sam themselves prove willing participants in processes of assimilation. Why should this be so?

The elders observe that new generations of the Thai-speaking Muslim community of Kedah possess no pride in, nor strong attachment to their socio-cultural heritage – a quality which evidently urges their Malaysian Thai-speaking Buddhist contemporaries to strive to preserve the very aspects the younger generation of Sam Sam has discarded. They behave as though they were ashamed of being Thai-speaking Muslims. It is not certain whether this impatience and shame is the result of socio-cultural pressure from the Malay-speaking Muslim peers, or a desire to wipe the slate clean and begin anew, or something of both. It is clear, however, that the accelerated assimilation of the Sam Sam into the Malay socio-cultural mainstream is not the result of any action by federal or state administration. It is the outcome of an explicit refusal on the part of new generations of Sam Sam to uphold the language tradition of their forefathers. In other words, it is the Malaysian Sam Sam themselves who are destroying – at least inside Malaysia – forms of Sam Sam society and culture which for centuries have made them a unique community in the Malay peninsula.

The experience of the Thai-speaking Muslims in the northwestern Malaysian states is in marked contrast to that of their Sam Sam brothers and sisters in the Thai socio-cultural environment. While the Sam Sam in

Malaysia have found no difficulty in adjusting to the cultural mainstream on account of sharing the religion of the majority Malays, the Sam Sam of southern Thailand live under a basically Thai Buddhist administration. However, they form a majority in Satun province and a sizeable minority in the province of Songkhla. By sheer numbers alone, they are a regional socio-cultural force to be reckoned with. Nonetheless, Islam is not the official religion of Thailand, a staunchly Buddhist country. Muslims constitute about 4 per cent of the total population of Thailand. In the South they are a majority in Pattani, Yala, Narathiwat, and Satun. Moreover, the Muslims in the South are not an immigrant community, but indigenous to the area.

These two facts enable the Malay Muslims of Pattani, Yala, and Narathiwat to demand and receive certain socio-cultural and religious privileges not accorded to other minority ethnic groups in Thailand. Satun, where Thai-speaking Muslims form an approximate 83 per cent majority, has played a passive role in the efforts of Thai Muslims against the central government (McVey 1989: 33, 35–6; Omar Farouk 1988: 12). There is a marked difference in attitude between Thai-speaking Muslims of Satun and Songkhla, and Malay-speaking Muslims of the three provinces which were formerly parts of the Pattani kingdom. Despite this, or perhaps because of a desire to generalize about Muslims in the South and their recalcitrant attitude towards Bangkok, scholars have tended to ignore or gloss over this difference, and concentrate on the Thai Malay Muslims of Pattani, Yala, and Narathiwat. (Arong 1989: 19; Astri Shurke 1973; McVey 1989; Forbes 1989).[10]

Thai-speaking Muslims in southern Thailand thus live in a more advantageous socio-cultural and demographic setting than their Malaysian counterparts. Though a minority among the population of Thai Buddhists at the national level, the Muslims form a substantial majority in their locality. They are granted certain privileges in accordance with their religious teachings. Because their mother tongue is Thai, the Sam Sam of Satun and Songkhla are able to maintain a more than live-and-let-live relationship with their Thai-speaking Buddhist neighbours – something the Thai-speaking Muslims in Malaysia are unable or unwilling to do. Is language then a key to the process of national integration in Thailand? The Thai establishment and the majority of Thai leaders tend to assume it is (Likhit 1978: 266–71; Khajatphai 1976: ch.8). This can be seen by the government's direct and indirect programmes to promote the Thai language among its Malay Muslim subjects, as well as a serious campaign to persuade the Muslim community that Malay is not the religious language of Islam as they have long believed. The existence of sizeable Thai-speaking communities of Sam Sam in Satun and Songkhla affords Bangkok some leverage against the argument of local religious leaders that Malay is synonymous with Islam, and that the Thai language and Islam are incompatible and irreconcilable, and that attempts to mix them amounts to treachery against both Islam and their Malay cultural heritage, in short is sinful (Omar Farouk 1988: 12; Suara Siswa n.d.; Gowing 1975: 3–9; Thomas 1966: 89–105).

Although to become a 'hundred per cent Thai' presupposes being of Thai ethnicity, which includes speaking Thai, following the teaching of Buddhism, and upholding certain Thai cultural values, yet this highly constructed concept of Thai-ness is gradually disintegrating in the face of the nation's awareness of the multi-racial, multi-cultural components of its population. Buddhism may remain the national religion, but other religions are respected, and given freedom to propagate and practise their teachings. Bangkok has also taken pains to project its image as protector and patron of all faiths of its subjects, and to portray Thailand as a practitioner of religious plurality.

The relationship between the Thai Buddhist establishment and the Thai Muslim population reflects considerable religious toleration, and correct and cordial ties between them. Bangkok has contributed financially by providing and improving religious institutions and facilities in the 'deep South'. Bangkok aims rather at the integration than the assimilation of its Muslim subjects, most particularly in the South, through the introduction of the Thai language into the everyday life of its Muslim community. In the long run, Bangkok hopes to inculcate a common Thai Muslim identity among the Muslim population throughout the country and, through it, to strengthen the concept of a unified Thai nation based on socio-cultural plurality. To a large extent such a policy goes down well with the Thai-speaking Muslims in southern Thailand. Since 'full assimilation' is not required, the Sam Sam of Satun and Songkhla find that their language is to their socio-cultural advantage as compared with their Malay Muslim brothers in the three other provinces. The Satun Sam Sam play an exemplary role in the national integration process for their Malay co-religionists to follow. The Sam Sam are living proof that the Thai language and other Thai cultural features which have nothing intrinsically to do with Buddhism, are reconcilable with Islam.

Of equal significance, the Thai-speaking Muslims confirm that Muslims can live peacefully and fruitfully under the rule of non-Muslim authority so long as religious toleration and religious plurality are respected. Unlike their Sam Sam brothers and sisters in Malaysia, the Sam Sams of Thailand emerge from their experience of socio-cultural and political socialization not only with their Sam Sam identity intact, but also with their place in the Thai nation strengthened and valued. The Sam Sam of Satun have shown pride in their heritage and a determination to preserve it even in the face of great difficulties.[11]

At the risk of oversimplifying the socio-political and religious differences between the Thai-speaking Muslims in Malaysia and those in Thailand, I suggest that the Thai-speaking Muslims, at least those of Satun and

Plate 13. 'A Yak'

Songkhla, demonstrate that religious pluralism does not in itself necessarily pose an insurmountable obstacle to the process of national integration of a nation-state. Satun in particular is one of the most impoverished and isolated areas in Thailand. Like some of the Sam Sam in Malaysia, Thai-speaking Muslims of Satun are still socially and economically marginal. However, and in this they are similar to the Malaysian Sam Sam, these conditions have not affected their positive attitude towards the establishment. It seems that language, race, and religion need not always be negative factors in the integration of a multi-racial nation. But while the response of Sam Sam in Satun to the programme of political integration and socialization leads to the strengthening of their distinct socio-cultural and religious identity as a sub-ethnic community, that of the Malaysian

Sam Sam leads to a weakening of their socio-cultural heritage and its gradual disappearance.

Notes

1 The Sam Sam of Kedah prefer and often become experts in Thai-oriented culture such as *wayang kulit Siam*, and *manora*. (See Nakazawa 1991: 52–80; Rahmah 1979: 34–63).

2 Some examples of the *bahasa Sam-Sam* are given by Crawfurd (1987: 29), for example: *Saya na pai naik keh bun gunung* (I want to ascend the mountain) of which, according to Crawfurd, the words *na pai, bun gunung* are Siamese. Actually, the Siamese words are *pai* and *keh bun*, while *saya, na, naik* and *gunung* are Malay.

3 Banks (1983) later modified his view, stating that the Sam Sam 'were Thai-speaking peasants from South Thailand' who moved to the northern part of Kedah in the eighteenth and nineteenth centuries. They were called Sam Sam pejoratively by their Malay-speaking neighbours. Again, no historical or socio-economic evidence is offered to validate this claim. Certainly there was a continuing flow of Muslim and Buddhist labour migration to and fro within the Siamese-Malay frontier zone. The *Phongsawadan Muang Songkhala* (The Chronicle of Songkhla; 1967: 217–19) records the migration of southern Thai to the interior of the Malay peninsula because of floods and scarcity of food. Such migrations were unlikely to have first occurred at the time proposed by Banks, if only because the factors which encouraged migration in the eighteenth and nineteenth centuries must have existed long before that.

4 Banks disagrees with Newbold considering it improbable that the Sam Sam were Malays who changed language rather than Siamese who changed religion (Banks, 1988).

5 Skeat differentiates between Sam Sam and 'Malayising' Siamese who were called Ma'alap (converts or proselytes) and became Muslim because they married a Malay wife. Neither 'Malayising' Siamese nor Sam Sam were particular about what they ate.

6 According to Annandale, *bahasa Sam Sam* is a dialect of Siamese which is liberally 'interlarded' with Malay words or phrases. From my own observation, *bahasa Sam Sam* in Kedah in 1992 was not much different from Annandale's description of the language in Trang in 1903.

7 In my own fieldwork (May-June 1992) mainly in the districts of Kubang Pasu, Kota Setar, and Padang Terap, I did not come across a community of Archaimbault's 'Sam Sam Siam'. There are Thai-speaking Buddhist communities which include ethnic Thai, Chinese and Thai-Chinese, the members of which identify themselves as Thai or Chinese, but not Sam Sam. It seems that dividing the Sam Sam by religion, as Archaimbault did, no longer reflects the true picture of the Thai-speaking community in Kedah.

8
Province	Thai-speakers (%)	non-Buddhist Thai-speakers	Muslims	Buddhists
Trang	99.6	13.4	12.1	86.2
Phattalung	99.0	4.7	4.9	94.3
Satun	98.0	81.3	82.9	16.7
Songkhla	96.0	19.1	18.6	77.9
Pattani	37.0	15.0	77.8	22.0
Yala	42.0	13.5	61.1	28.5
Narathiwat	33.0	12.0	78.2	21.0

Thailand Population Census 1960 Changwat Series, Bangkok, 1960

9 Cheah Boon Kheng argues that the Sam Sam's ancestors might have migrated *to* Satun, Perlis, and Kedah in the 1830s, or arrived in northern Kedah several centuries earlier (Cheah, 1988: 14–15). It seems contrary to the historical evidence available that the Sam Sam should have migrate *to* instead of *from* Satun. In any case, by the 1830s they were well-established throughout the northern and eastern parts of Kedah.

10 A welcome exception is Angela Burr's study of a village in Songkhla, where Thai-speaking Buddhists and Thai-speaking Muslims live together in apparent harmony. Of 299 households, 203 are Muslim and 96 Thai Buddhist (Burr, 1972: 183–215). See also Golomb's study of a Thai village in Kelantan which is also successful in forging cordial ties with Kelantan Malays through various socio-cultural interactions while keeping its Thai Buddhist identity (Golomb, 1978: ch.6).

11 The Thai Sam Sam had a hard time during the Phibun administration's policy of forced assimilation. They did not succumb to force and intimidation, and strongly adhered to their socio-cultural identity.

References

Abdul Rahman, Tunku (1978), *Viewpoints*, Kuala Lumpur: Heinemann.

Annandale, Nelson, Robinson, Hervert (1903 Part 1), (1904 Part 2), *Fasciculi Malayenses, Anthropological and Zoological Results of an Expedition to Perak and Siamese Malay States, 1901–1902*, London: The University Press of Liverpool.

Archaimbault, C. (1957), 'A preliminary investigation of the Sam Sam of Kedah and Perlis', *Journal of the Malayan Branch of the Royal Asiatic Society*, (30)1, 75–92.

Arong Suthasasna (1989), 'Thai society and the Muslim minority', in A. D. W. Forbes (ed.), *Politics of the Malay-speaking South*, vol.2, Bihar: Centre for South East Asian Studies.

Astri Suhrke (1973), 'The Thai Muslim border provinces: some national security aspects', in R. Ho and E. C. Chapman (eds.), *Studies of Contemporary Thailand*, Canberra: Research School of Pacific Studies, ANU, Canberra.

Banks, D. J. (1977), 'Thai-Malay power relations and the distribution of Thai-speaking Muslims, in Gordon P. Means (ed.), *Development and Undevelopment in Southeast Asia*, Ottawa: Secretariat, Canadian Society for Asian Studies, Canadian Council for Southeast Asian Studies.

—— (1980), 'Politics and ethnicity on the Thai-Malay frontier: the historical role of the Thai-speaking Muslims of Kedah', *Khabar Seberang Sulating Maphilindo*, 7, July, 98–113.

—— (1983), *Malay Kinship*, Philadelphia: Institute for the Study of Human Issues.

Burney, Henry (1910–14), *The Burney Papers*, Bangkok, Vajirañana National Library. 5 vols.

Burr, A. (1972), 'Religious institutional diversity – social structural and conceptual unity: Islam and Buddhism in southern Thai coastal fishing village', *Journal of the Siam Society*, vol.60, pt.2, July, 183–215.

Cheah Boon Kheng (1981), 'Social banditry and rural crime in north Kedah 1909–1929', *Journal of the Malaysian Branch of the Royal Asiatic Society*, (54)2, 98–130.

Crawfurd, J. (1987), *Journal of an Embassy to the Courts of Siam and Cochin China*, Singapore: Oxford University Press.

Damrong Rajanubhab, Prince (1962), *Phra Ratcha Phongsawadan Krung Rattanakosin*, The Royal Chronicle of Bangkok Reign 2, Bangkok: Khlang-Witthaya, 2502.

Enloe, C. H. (1970), *Multi-ethnic Politics: the case of Malaysia*, Research Monograph Series, Center of South and Southeast Asia Studies, University of California, Berkeley.

Forbes, A. D. W. (1989), 'Thailand's Muslim minorities: assimilation, secession or co-existence', in A. D. W. Forbes (ed.), *Politics of the Malay-speaking South*, vol.2, Bihar: Centre for South East Asian Studies.

—— (ed.) (1988), *The Muslims of Thailand*, vol.1, *Historical and Cultural Studies*, Bihar: Centre for South East Asian Studies.

—— (1989), *The Muslims of Thailand*, vol.2, *Politics of the Malay-speaking South*, Bihar: Centre for South East Asian Studies.

Frost, M. (1912), *The Annual Report of the Adviser of the Kedah Government for the Year 1329 A.H. (2 January–21 December 1911)*, Kuala Lumpur: FMS Government Printing Office.

Golomb, L. (1978), *Brokers of Morality: Thai ethnic adaptation in a plural Malaysian setting*, Honolulu: Asian Studies Program, University of Hawaii, University of Hawaii Press.

Gowing, P. G. (1975), *Moros and Khaek: the position of Muslim minorities in the Philippines and Thailand*, in Banthon Ondam, (transl.), Bangkok: Kamon Kheemthong Foundation, 2518.

Graham, W. A. (1924), *Siam*, London: Alexander Moring, 2 vols.

Kuroda, Keiko (1992), 'The Samsams of Kubang Pasu – the historical relations between Kedah and Siam viewed from a "kampung"', in K. Miyazaki (ed.), *Local Societies in Malaysia*, Tokyo: Institute for the Study of Languages and Cultures of Asia and Africa, Tokyo University of Foreign Studies, 89–109.

Khajatphai Burutphat (1976), *Thai Muslims*, Bangkok: Phrae-phitthaya, 2519.

Kobkua Suwannathat-Pian (1988), *Thai-Malay Relations, Traditional Intra-regional Relations from the Seventeenth to Early Twentieth Centuries*, Singapore: Oxford University Press.

Likhit Dhiravegin, and Friends (1978), *Minority Ethnic Groups in Thailand*, Bangkok: Phrae-phitthaya, 2521.

Logan, J. R. (1885), 'Plan for a volunteer police in the Muda District, Province Wellesley, submitted to the Government by the Late J. R. Logan in 1867', *Journal of the Malaysian Branch of the Royal Asiatic Society*, December 1885, 173–202.

Maxwell, W. G. (1911), *The Annual Report of the Adviser to the Kedah Government for the Year 1327 A.H. (23 January 1909–12 January 1910)*, Kuala Lumpur: FMS Government Printing Office.

McVey, R. (1989), 'Identity and rebellion among southern Thai Muslims', in A. D. W. Forbes (ed.) *Politics of the Malay-speaking South*, vol.2.

Miyazaki, K., (ed.) (1992), *Local Societies in Malaysia*, Tokyo: Institute for the Study of Languages and Cultures of Asia and Africa, Tokyo University of Foreign Studies.

Mohd. Yusoff Ismail (1980), *The Siamese of Aril: a study of an ethnic minority village*, Bangi: Monograph no.3, Faculty of Social Sciences and Humanities, Universiti Kebangsaan Malaysia.

Nakazawa, Masaki (1992), 'Kg. Tas: a rural Siamese village in the state of Kedah', in K. Miyazaki (ed.), *Local Societies in Malaysia*, Tokyo: Institute for the Study of Languages and Cultures of Asia and Africa, Tokyo University of Foreign Studies.

Newbold, T. J. (1971), *British Settlements in the Straits of Malacca*, vol.2, Kuala Lumpur: Oxford University Press.

Omar Farouk (1988), 'The Muslims of Thailand – a survey', in A. D. W. Forbes (ed.), *The Muslims of Thailand*, vol.1, *Historical and Cultural Studies*, Bihar: Centre for South East Asian Studies.

Rahmah Bujang (1972), 'Kedah performing art', in Asmah Haji Omar (ed.), *San Somdet: correspondence between Prince Narit and Prince Damrong Rajanubhab*, vol.17, Bangkok: Kurusapha, 2515.

Scott, J. C. (1985), *Weapons of the Weak, Everyday Forms of Peasant Resistance*, New Haven and London: Yale University Press.

Skeat, W. W. (1953), 'The Cambridge University Expedition to the north-eastern Malay states and to Upper Perak 1899–1900', *Journal of the Malayan Branch of the Royal Asiatic Society*, (26)4, December, 1–114.

Strobel (1908), FO/371/521, London: Public Record Office.

Suara Siswasa (n.d.), *Pattani Liberation Movement* .

Tibbets, G. R. (1957), 'Early Muslim traders in South-east Asia', *Journal of the Malayan Branch of the Royal Asiatic Society*, vol.xxv, pt.1.

Winzeler, Robert L. (1985) *Ethnic relations in Kelantan: a study of the Chinese and Thai as ethnic minorities in a Malay state*. Singapore: Oxford University Press.

Chapter Eight

Emergence and Transformation of Peripheral Ethnicity: Sam Sam on the Thai-Malaysian Border

Ryoko Nishii

Introduction

The peoples who have been called 'Sam Sam' are Thai-speaking Muslims. They inhabit the western coast of the Malay Peninsula on either side of the Thai-Malaysian border. This is a frontier area between the Thai and Malay worlds. In the former the people chiefly practise Buddhism and speak Thai; in the latter the people chiefly practise Islam and speak Malay. The salient cultural characteristics of Sam Sam ethnicity are found in their peculiar combination of religion and language, the main factors demarcating ethnic boundaries. They practise Islam, yet use the Thai language, which has resulted in an alienation of Sam Sam ethnicity from the main Thai and Malay ethnicities.

The main purpose of this chapter is to illustrate the process of emergence and transformation of peripheral ethnicity through an examination of ways in which the Thai-speaking Muslims known as Sam Sam have been and continue to be regarded as inferior, and of their situation as a peripheral ethnicity. It also enables us to elucidate the relationship between Thai and Malay people at the grass-roots level, which is rarely mentioned in official records.[1] The approach adopted here is to set views from the outside, ascertained by analyzing records concerning the Sam Sam from the early nineteenth century, against views from the inside, derived from the historical memories of the Sam Sam regarding a local hero – To Nai Sim. He was the last focus of independent local power on the periphery between the Thai and Malay worlds.

Thai-speaking Muslims in Thailand have not been much concerned either culturally or politically with their own historical background. This is in contrast with Malay-speaking Thai Muslims who have become an influential minority because of their number and political power, which was focused by their separatist movements in the 1960s and 1970s. Compared with the suspect allegiance of the Malay-speaking Muslims on the eastern coast of southern Thailand, Thai-speaking Muslims are officially regarded as a good example of a Thai national group that follows a non-Buddhist faith. In Malaysia Thai-speaking Muslims have not been given much attention. There are few official records about the Sam Sam. The first book about the Sam Sam was published in 1988 (Cheah 1988).

Historical Background

The boundary between Siam and Kedah (which was culturally Malay, but tributary to Siam) was ambiguous until the beginning of the twentieth century. The border was an area beyond the periphery of direct control by the core power centres to the North and South. A distinct and effective boundary between British Malaya and Siam was drawn across the map for the first time following the Anglo-Siamese agreement of 1909.

Before this, from the nineteenth to the early twentieth century the area suffered from social unrest caused by several wars. The greatest disturbance came with the Siamese invasion of Kedah in 1821, which caused the large scale immigration of ethnic Malays into the southern part of Kedah. The population of the British Province Wellesley increased from 5,457 to 16,479 between 1820 and 1824 (Low 1836: 124–28). It also resulted in the re-settlement of Thai-speaking Muslims (Sam Sam) in the formerly Malay-peopled area of northern Kedah near the border of Siam (Newbold, 1971 [1839] vol. 1: 419–20). Banks' explanation for this was that the existence of Thai-speaking Muslims flattered Thai government pretensions of ruling a multi-religious empire (Banks 1980: 108).

The border area was a lawless land largely outside the control of the rulers and whatever forces they had to police it. Kubang Pasu, in the North of Kedah, which is inhabited by many Thai-speaking Muslims even to this day, showed an extraordinarily high crime rate. The Sam Sam were reported to be by nature 'thievish' or 'knavish'. The area's natural topography and thick jungle meant that was impractical to pursue lawbreakers. Nonetheless, large numbers of Sam Sam were convicted of cattle theft and burglary (Cheah 1988: 13–18).

The View from the Outside

Records and Studies of the Sam Sam

There are two kinds of accounts of the Sam Sam. One kind is that given in the writing of British travellers and colonial officers during the nineteenth and early twentieth centuries. Their main purpose was to record the customs, habits and character of the inhabitants of British colonial possessions. Academic research in ethnology and history was not undertaken until the latter half of the twentieth century.[2]

John Crawfurd provided the earliest colonial report of the Sam Sam whom he encountered in 1821, describing them as follows: 'By Samsams, are meant people of the Siamese race, who have adopted the Mohammedan religion, and who speak a language which is a mixed jargon of the languages of the two people' (Crawfurd 1828: 29). Logan expressed similar ideas about forty years later stating that Sam Sam were descendants of the rude inland Siamese of Kedah who, some generations earlier, had been converted to 'Mahomedanism' (Logan 1885: 200). In 1839, Newbold offered the contrary opinion that they were actually a race of Malays who had adopted the religion and language of the Siamese (Newbold vol. 1 1839: 420). Skeat visited the northern states of Malaya in 1899 and 1900, and recorded information about the Sam Sam. He described the Sam Sam as Malays who had turned Siamese in everything but their religion, and suggested that they were *ma'lap* (he claimed this was the Arabic term), converts or proselytes (Skeat 1953: 133). In 1901 and 1902 Annandale and Robinson went on an expedition to southern Thailand and northern Malaysia. They saw the Sam Sam as Thai-speaking Muslims and noted how 'Mahommedanism sits lightly upon the Samsams', offering as evidence the Sam Sam practice of 'tree-burial' and the fact that it was not uncommon for a youth to become a Buddhist ascetic – presumably to undertake ordination – if any misfortune befell himself or his family, without renouncing his former religion (Annandale and Robinson 1903 Part 1: 59). Elsewhere it has been reported that Prince Damrong quoted the opinion of officials in Satun province to the effect that Sam Sam (*bangsa sam sam*) were not Malays but a distinct race (Kobkua 1991: 3). It must be pointed out that all these views of the Sam Sam are derived from Malay ideas.

The first ethnographic study of the Sam Sam appeared in 1956 and emphasized the mixed characteristics of the Sam Sam. It distinguished two types; the Sam Sam Siam who are Buddhist, and the Sam Sam Melayu or Sam Sam Masok Islam who are Muslim, both of them using a Thai dialect different from the Thai spoken in Bangkok (Archaimbault 1957). Banks has conducted historical research to explain the origins of the Sam Sam, finding that Thai speakers in the Kedah area sought the protection of the Kedah Sultan, because of the policies and activities of Ligor (Nakhonsithamarat), and thus converted to Islam (Banks 1980: 107).

Characteristics of the Sam Sam Viewed from the Outside

The characteristics of Sam Sam in these records and studies can be analyzed using three terms: race, language, and religion.

Race

It can be deduced from the records by colonial officers and travellers from the nineteenth century and the beginning of the twentieth century, that the Sam Sam were treated as a single race apart and independent from the Thai and Malays. Describing the component population groups inhabiting Kedah, Crawfurd and Newbold included the Sam Sam as one category, and the Malay and Siamese peoples as other categories. Annandale and Robinson enumerated the distinctive physical characteristics of the Sam Sam, such as skin and hair colour. Prince Damrong wrote to Prince Narit that the Sam Sam were a distinct race. In studies since the mid-twentieth century, the emphasis has moved from the Sam Sam as a racial category to the Sam Sam as a unique cultural group with mixed cultural features.

The racial *origin* of Sam Sam has frequently been discussed. The two main camps are those who consider that they were Thai who became Sam Sam by religious conversion (Crawfurd, Prince Damrong, Banks, Kobkua) and those who consider they were Muslim Malays who adopted the Thai language (Newbold, Skeat). This kind of discussion is inconclusive due to lack of data. What is clear is that Sam Sam have participated in a mixed existence with Thai and Malay in their history.

Language

These reports all state that the Sam Sam speak a kind of Thai dialect. But they differ concerning the relative importance of Malay: Crawfurd, and Annandale and Robinson refer to an intermixture of Thai and Malay words; Logan holds them to be bilingual, equally using Thai and Malay; and exclusive use of Thai is reported by Skeat, Abdul Rahman, and Archaimbault.

Religion

The records are nearly unanimous (excepting only Newbold and Archaimbault) in observing that the Sam Sam are Muslims. Furthermore, they agree that the religious practices of the Sam Sam are not strictly Islamic. Skeat recorded the following details from a story about a Sam Sam family told by a local Raja in Perlis: 'when one of Eman's brothers died, Eman and Ikut stole the body and burnt it according to the Siamese (Buddhist) ritual'.[3] 'The members of this family were suspected of attending the Buddhist wat, secretly, though this delinquency had not been proved' (Skeat 1953: 138–39). Annandale and Robinson quoted rumours about Sam Sam tendencies toward tree-burial and Buddhist asceticism notwithstanding that they were Muslims.

There are some villages of Sam Sam Siam, defined as Buddhist Sam Sam by Archaimbault, Naka Siam, Padang Pusing, Titi Akar, and Kalai in Kedah, that are at present inhabited by Buddhists. Although their mother tongue is Thai, most of them can also speak Malay. Considering that they are Thai-speaking Buddhists, it would seem more consistent to refer to them as a Thai minority in Malaysia, rather than as Sam Sam Siam. But the latter is the usage reported by Archaimbault.

The characteristics of the Sam Sam which we can derive from analyzing these three aspects coincide with definitions given in Malay dictionaries: 'Sam Sam – Siamese-speaking Muslims' (Collins Gem 1986 [1964]); or 'A name given to a mixed half-Siamese race inhabiting the northern parts of the Peninsula' (Macmillan 1988 [1976]). On the other hand it is interesting that we cannot find any entries in Thai dictionaries under 'Sam Sam' referring to Thai-speaking Muslims.[4] We can therefore say that the term Sam Sam only exists in the Malay language.

Emergence of Peripheral Ethnicity

References to the Sam Sam as bandits and criminals can be found in records dating back to the nineteenth century. Logan wrote in a report to British Government in Penang, 'many of them are more stupid and ignorant even than the Malays in the same condition of life, and many are knavish, thievish, and addicted to gambling and opium-smoking' (Logan 1885: 200). Though this is taken from a British officer's view of the Sam Sam, there are other descriptions of Sam Sam groups which indicate perceptions of the inferiority of Sam Sam ethnicity, a valuation in the main deriving from cultural factors, above all religious and linguistic.

In 1899–1900 Skeat wrote, 'The Samsam generally gave up attendance at the Mosque, as well as the 'Hours of Prayer', and even ate 'unclean' things, such as turtles (*kura-kura*)'[5] (Skeat 1953: 133). In 1902 Annandale and Robinson, referring to the practices of Thai-speaking Muslims noted that the term 'Samsam' was offensive to villagers who said that it denoted mixed racial origins. Banks also mentioned stereotypes of Thai speakers as crude, rural dwellers residing in unhealthy housing conditions. Tunku Abdul Rahman cited a story of how a place where Sam Sam lived acquired its name and reputation, 'the people there never practised religion, and in fact ate anything that came their way, including pork' (Abdul Rahman 1978: 26). In my research in 1991, statements of the same kind were made by Thai-speaking Muslims themselves, 'it is said that Thai are filthy because they eat everything, including lizards and frogs, the Sam Sam are the same'. These negative images of the Sam Sam were also much in evidence; commonly heard were statements such as: 'Sam Sam speak Thai even though they are Muslims', 'their religious practices are like Buddhists', 'they eat anything like Buddhists', 'they are filthy'. When Malays speak of Thai-speaking Muslims as Sam Sam the connotation is pejorative.

These reiterated associations, emphasising the mismatch of religion and language, have constructed the Sam Sam as a peripheral ethnicity. The discursive moments in creating this peripheral ethnicity were probably as follows. First, the proper association of religion and language is defined and the equation of Islam and Malay language is justified. When Islam is seen to occur with Thai language it is judged to be an impure mixing of Islam and Thai culture i.e. Buddhism, a prohibited infidel mingling of Buddhistic factors into Islam. In short, the Thai language and the Muslims who speak it are degraded and eliminated from the Malay world in the name of Islam.

Present Conditions

At present the Sam Sam living in the border area are divided politically into Thais to the North, and Malays to the South. The Sam Sam in each country have proceeded in different directions through their different experiences.

In the first Thai constitution in 1932, *satsana* which had hitherto been virtually tantamount to Buddhism underwent a semantic change to include all religions. The royal protection of the King of Thailand, traditionally considered to be the protector or upholder of Buddhism, was then extended to all the religions in the land, including Islam (Ishii 1977: 347–53). This policy was intended to extend the traditional prescription that Thai are Buddhists, to create a plurality of Thai nationals, Buddhists and non-Buddhists, including Muslims. Furthermore, in 1945 'The Royal Decree on the protection of Islam' was legislated to place Islam under state control. Since the 1960s *pondok*, the traditional institutions of Islamic education, have been obliged to register as private schools and to conduct lessons in the Thai language. The purpose of this policy was to include the population of Malay-speaking Muslims into the Thai nation both institutionally and culturally.

These Thai-izing policies by the Thai government stimulated different reactions from Malay-speaking Muslims on the East coast (Patani, Yala, and Narathiwat), and Thai-speaking Muslims on the West coast (Satun) in southern Thailand. On the eastern coast numerous Muslim separatist movements have come into being since the late 1960s. On the other hand, the Thai-speaking Muslims on the West coast have been integrated into the Thai nation without much difficulty and have adjusted themselves to the newly created category of Thai Muslims.[6] These are the present Sam Sam in Thailand. But they do not perceive themselves as Sam Sam.

In Satun there were only 13 villages of Malay-speaking Muslims among the 241 villages I looked at in 1991. The Malay words that had been formerly mixed into grammatically Thai sentences in daily conversations had diminished almost to the point of disappearance.[7] Thai-speaking Muslims in Satun speak the southern dialect of Thai in daily life, but are now also able to speak and write the standard Thai language.

In Malaysia, the province of Kedah, previously a tributary state of Siam, fell under the control of British Malaya in 1909, and then the Federation of Malaya when it became independent in 1957. Since then the government has consistently implemented its policy of promoting the Malay language. In Article 152 of the Federal Constitution, it is prescribed that 'the national language shall be the Malay language'. As a result of the 'Malay First', or 'Bumiputera' Policy, which has emphasized the Malay language as the national language and given privileges to Malays since 1971, the long-standing conception that Malays are Muslims who speak Malay has become a prescription and effectively penetrated daily life. In this situation the Sam Sam have tried to become complete Malays by adopting the Malay language as the mother tongue for their new generations at the expense of their Thai language.

Sam Sam villages in Malaysia are concentrated around Perlis and northern Kedah (Kubang Pasu, Padang Terap). During research in 1991, I found 31 villages in Kubang Pasu and 16 villages in Perlis, but have no information for Padang Terap. Most of the Sam Sam villages have two names, one in Thai and one in Malay. In many cases the Malay name is a translation of the previous Thai name. The existence of the Sam Sam villages, that is Thai-speaking Muslim villages, is little known to Malay-speaking Muslims, even in Kedah. Among the Sam Sam villages, however, there is both detailed and general knowledge about which of the Muslim villages are Thai-speaking. The fact that Sam Sam villages are so closed to the outside and that the inside information network is so effective is an indication of the extent to which the existence of the Sam Sam has been concealed from the Malay-speaking Muslims, to an extent they had probably also formerly hidden themselves. This is exemplified by the fact that in Kampong T (with 53 households and 247 persons) inter-marriage among Thai-speaking Muslims before the 1960s accounted for more than 80 per cent of all marriages, and while the rate fell in the 1980s still accounts for about 50 per cent.

Recently Sam Sam villages have changed rapidly. In Kampong T, although 78.2 per cent of villagers who are over 31 years old can speak Thai, only 4.8 per cent of villagers who are younger than 30 years old are able to speak Thai. The mother tongue for the under-30s is already Malay and not Thai. The emergence of generations who cannot speak Thai is the result of family education policy; parents speak only Malay to their children lest they pass on a Thai accent (*takut pelat Siam*).

Thai-speaking Muslims themselves feel that speaking Thai is old-fashioned (*kuno*) and shameful (*malu*) for Muslims. They say the ability to speak Thai does not make for progress in anything (*tak ada kemajuan*) in Malaysia. They may speak a southern Thai dialect in daily life, but they cannot understand standard Thai broadcast from Thailand. On the other hand, for the majority of native Thai speakers who are not Sam Sam, other languages cannot replace the comfort and familiarity of the Thai language. These people generally define Sam Sam in the following way; 'Muslim, but speak Thai', 'our Thai is not standard, but only a southern dialect without writing'. Sam Sam on the Malaysian side have a paradoxical feeling for the Thai language, they cannot stop speaking it, but it has only a negative value for them.

The Sam Sam straddling the border between Thailand and Malaysia have today been turned toward two poles of aspiration. The former have become, relatively unproblematically, Thai nationals who speak Thai, but have faith in Islam. The latter aim to become complete Malays who speak Malay and have faith in Islam. Comparing these two groups of Thai-speaking Muslims, memories of the Sam Sam are cherished more profoundly among the Sam Sam in Malaysia who are surrounded by Malay-speaking Muslims. They have found themselves occupying a peripheral status in the Malay world because of their language. The Sam Sam in Thailand who are surrounded by Thai-Buddhists do not even find the word 'Sam Sam' itself useful and have dropped it from their lexicon. The Sam Sam as a social category continue to exist only in the Malay world, a state of affairs confirmed by the fact that the term Sam Sam can be found only in Malay dictionaries.

In the next section, I discuss historical accounts of a memorable Sam Sam hero as related to me by Sam Sam informants resident in Malaysia. I consider the dynamics of local power in a peripheral situation, an indefinite boundary between larger national polities.

The View from the Inside

Stories concerning To Nai Sim, the Sam Sam ruler of Kubang Pasu from the middle of nineteenth to the beginning of the twentieth century, as told by the Sam Sam themselves, represent the Sam Sam view from the inside.[8] Even today the name of the village where he used to live, Kampong T, is mentioned together with his name. At present the fourth generation of people descended from To Nai Sim and his era are living in the village. He is said to have been born in about 1840 and to have died sometime between 1927 and 1929. His active life largely corresponded with the time of Sultan Abdul Hamid who reigned from 1882 to 1942.

The name of To Nai Sim can be found in three books published in Malaysia. The first record is in *Salasilah atau Tarekh Kerajaan Kedah* [Genealogy of Kedah Kingdom] by Wan Yahaya (1911). He wrote that

Kubang Pasu was made a District in 1898 and continued: 'Kubang Pasu had no peace, being occupied with so many rascals before that, as there was a boss named Nai Sin or Penghulu Mahamad Hashim who was fond of intercourse with rascals.[9] In 1907 he had already been expelled from Negeri by the Government of Kedah' (Wan Yahaya 1911: 19). After this short account there was no further mention of To Nai Sim until the late 1980s. *The Peasant Robbers of Kedah 1900–1929* mentions that 'an official Kedah report for 1906–8 recalled that cattle stealing "was in the past becoming the chief industry of North Kedah under the guidance of a penghulu, or headman, named Nai Sim, who has since departed for Mecca, and his male relatives who are now in gaol"' (Cheah 1988: 21–22). Another book, from 1990, has the following: 'In Kubang Pasu, Penghulu made the people's existence difficult because of his preference for the company of scoundrels. For this reason Raja Muda Tunku Abdul Aziz applied to Tunku Yaakop (who acted for the Sultan) to build up a police station in Changlon. Penghulu, that is Nai Sim (Muhammad Hashim), had already been expelled from the state (negeri)' (Mohammad 1990: 58–59). In these three books, To Nai Sim is portrayed as a reprehensible leader of bandits, an exemplar of the Sam Sam who were notorious as cattle thieves and robbers.

The intensity and content of recollections of To Nai Sim differ in proportion to the degree of his local influence, which diminished as it extended from the central village where he lived, and the villages which had a direct relationship with him. We can divide the area of Kubang Pasu into three categories:

1 Kampong T, the home village of To Nai Sim, and neighbouring Kampong K, where many descendants of To Nai Sim still live today – both villages contain Thai-speaking Muslims.
2 Neighbouring villages which were under the direct authority of To Nai Sim, a sphere of influence which included villages of both Thai- and Malay-speaking Muslims.
3 Villages on the periphery of Kubang Pasu where the influence of To Nai Sim was less substantial, an area including villages of both Thai- and Malay-speaking Muslims.

In this section, I will first analyze some aspects of To Nai Sim as a ruler, and then go on to consider To Nai Sim as a Sam Sam, a Thai-speaking Muslim.

To Nai Sim as a Ruler

It is commonly said that To Nai Sim was a ruler or raja of Kubang Pasu. Most versions hold that he was appointed by the Sultan of Kedah, and some that he was appointed by a Siamese ruler. Kubang Pasu is adjacent to the

Thai border on the road along which tribute from Kedah was conveyed to Siam by elephants. It is of particular note that most of the Sam Sam villages in Kubang Pasu are situated along this road. The most distinctive image of To Nai Sim as a ruler is a fearful one, because of his power. His powers were diverse: as a judge, as a man of wealth person, and as a possessor of magical power.

The Realities of To Nai Sim's Rule

The degree of To Nai Sim's rule lessened step by step within a certain area of influence, diminishing with increasing distance from his home village, Kampong T, to the edge of Kubang Pasu. In the peripheral villages his authority was limited in practice to his absolute role in sentencing criminals as he saw fit, as there was no enforceable code of law at that time. His fearful image as a ruler, possessing the power to kill people at will, is derived from his role as judge. Villages in categories A and B above relate similar stories, with varying amount of concrete detail. They say that To Nai Sim could only fine or sentence Malay criminals to imprisonment; death sentences had to be approved by the Sultan of Kedah. On the other hand, Thai who were taken from Thailand were often executed by To Nai Sim; even today people are scared of the Lubok Den (hole of Siam)[10] at Kampong K, where the corpses of Thai who were killed by To Nai Sim were disposed of, believing that the vicinity is haunted by their ghosts.

One of the best-recalled features of his rule, which was often brought up in the villages of category B was corvée (*kerah*) labour for the opening of forests, construction of roads, and cultivation of fields. This work was never mentioned in category C villages. Mobilizing labour was the role of the village headmen who were known as the men (*tangan*) of To Nai Sim. These village headmen were also entrusted with the care of To Nai Sim's cattle. In these villages, informants say that elephants belonging to To Nai Sim trampled over crops at night while they were loose, but no one dared protest. The area demarcated by the villages subject to corvée coincides with the area containing villages giving accounts of these straying elephants.

Only in the core villages of category A do the villagers have any recollection of To Nai Sim acting as an intermediary between Siam and Kedah in the sending of *Bunga Mas dan Perak*, the symbol of the tributary relationship between Kedah and Siam. To Nai Sim is said to have used his elephants to convey tribute from Kedah to Nakhonsithamarat[11] in southern Thailand, every three years, along the road which passed through Kubang Pasu.[12] This is possibly an exaggeration; because he was merely a provincial penghulu it is perhaps more reasonable to regard To Nai Sim as a bodyguard who accompanied the envoys of high rank and whose mission it was to convey the tribute.

To Nai Sim as a Wealthy Man and Trader

Kampong T was full of elephants belonging to To Nai Sim. As well as being used as pack and work animals in daily life, elephants were a high status means of transport, and a source and symbol of power. The main trade goods with Siam were slaves and elephants. In those days about 40 people, including To Nai Sim's family and slaves from Siam, lived in his big wooden house. He sold slaves from Siam to the Chinese in Alor Star (capital of Kedah) and to the Sultan of Kedah. It is likely that the trading of stolen cattle and buffalo was an important part of To Nai Sim's business. We can see him as a Sam Sam trader and bandit who moved freely across the border between Siam and Kedah.

Adjectives which were often used to characterize To Nai Sim are *takut* (fearful) and *kaya* (wealthy). The connection of these ideas is found in the phrase of a villager from category B: 'Whoever is powerful can become wealthy (*siapa kuat, orang itu boleh kaya*)'.

Magical Power of To Nai Sim

To Nai Sim's magical power was famous throughout Kubang Pasu. As the following remark illustrates, a man of power was believed to prove his possession of magical powers through the wielding of power: 'it is certain that To Nai Sim had a magical power (*ilmu batin*) because everyone was scared of him'. In short, every man with power has magical power.

To Nai Sim is said to have established his rule and maintained public peace in the lawless border-land beyond official control with a quality of magical power similar to that possessed by robbers and bandits generally but to a much greater degree. One of the descendants of To Nai Sim, living in Kampong K, category A, described this as follows:

> 'There was no peace in this state [Negeri] in those days. Many bandits, robbers and rascals plundered around. They were skilled, strong, and had magical power (*ilmu batin*). Most of them came from Siam. To Nai Sim could foresee that robbers would break into his village on any day. To Nai Sim himself was destined to be a ruler with magical power. In those days a ruler had to rule with strong power because weak power would let rascals infest the area at will.'

It is said that most bandits and robbers in the border area came from Siam. The magical power these Thai bandits possessed is said to have been more powerful than that of the Malays. In Kampong T there have been stories about a method of execution adopted only for Thais, by fastening the body to a bamboo float and then drowning them in the stream beside the village for five minutes. The reason given for this special method of execution for Thai was that 'Thai are brave and invulnerable; although we shoot them, bullets can not enter their body'. This invulnerability was also possessed by To Nai Sim; his invulnerability is represented as a body which 'bullets cannot enter and blade cannot scar'. In a story told in Kampong T, he is represented as an embodiment of Thai magical power. We can find here the inversion of the negative interpretation of Sam Sam characteristics: the admixture of Thai culture, rejected by Malay Islamic purists, is re-evaluated and seen as a source of power.

The Relationship with the Sultan of Kedah

To Nai Sim had once been expelled from Kubang Pasu by the Sultan of Kedah. There are several stories as to the reason for this expulsion: killing an impolite Indian money lender, being charged with the crime of his son's cattle stealing, and so on. Another explanation, that his power grew strong enough to rival that of the Sultan of Kedah, helps to confirm the recognition that To Nai Sim maintained his own power (*kuasa sendiri*) in Kubang Pasu independently of the Sultan, who lived in Alor Star and whose effective power was confined to the city.

This expulsion did, however, mark the end of To Nai Sim's actual rule, even though the Sultan had little positive power to intervene in the exile's former sphere of influence. This must have taken place around the beginning of the twentieth century. A Malay-speaking Muslim aged 96, whose grandfather had been killed by To Nai Sim explained the expulsion thus: 'people wised up and found a means to escape from the oppression of To Nai Sim's rule, and forced the Sultan to expel him'. In any case, provincial power centres based on individual prowess were generally declining at this time in the periphery. Even the ambiguity of the periphery itself came to an end at about this time. In 1909 Kedah had come under the control of the British through the Anglo-Siamese agreement. To Nai Sim is said to have been expelled to either Penang or India. After a while To Nai Sim was released from exile and allowed to return to Kampong T; but he could never again regain his power.

It is said that in exchange for his release from exile To Nai Sim donated a vast amount of land South of Kubang Pasu to Tunku Sulung, the eldest son of the Sultan. Another version of his release illustrates the relationship between the Sultan and men of power in the provinces:

'The Sultan wanted to kill the boss of Kulim (in southern Kedah), a Chinese, because he was too powerful. But no one succeeded in doing this, so the Sultan called back To Nai Sim to carry out the mission. To Nai Sim adopted sophisticated tactics, rejecting the use of rough methods against a rough person. He sent a fine palanquin from the Sultan and deceived him into believing that the Sultan wanted to be on good terms with him. He invited him to the Sultan's palace. As soon as the palanquin entered the forest, To Nai Sim killed the Chinese boss.'

For this distinguished service, the Sultan permitted him to go back again to Kubang Pasu. The kind of strategy adopted by the Sultan is described in *The Peasant Robbers of Kedah 1900–1929* as '"using a thief to catch a thief" by replacing the criminal headmen with powerful bandit chiefs who were prepared to take an oath to wipe out crime in their areas' (Cheah 1988: 25).

In this way the Sultan tried to establish his rule in the peripheries beyond his control by utilizing a patron-client relationship with provincial bosses. Because his rule had no secure base in the provinces, he had to try to use whatever means he could to create a balance of forces in the mosaic of little powers that surrounded him.

To Nai Sim as a Thai Speaker

The different categories of village have different views about To Nai Sim's mother tongue. In villages of category A his descendants say that To Nai Sim spoke Thai, and because of his ability with the language he could act as an intermediary between Siam and Kedah. They add that ability in the Thai language was evaluated positively in those days: 'In those days Siam was advanced. To Nai Sim had probably studied at a *tokong Siam* (Thai Buddhist temple). When Siam invaded here (Kubang Pasu), local people evacuated the area and Siam made To Nai Sim a ruler here because he could speak Thai'. They explained the distribution of the Sam Sam villages along the road on which tribute was sent from Kedah to Siam by elephants as follows: 'the reason for the concentration of Sam Sam villages along this road is that the ability of the Sam Sam to speak Thai was perceived as convenient for the King of Siam'.

Villagers in category B tend to differ according to own mother tongue. Thai-speaking villages agreed that To Nai Sim spoke Thai. In Malay-speaking villages when asked, they say first of all that To Nai Sim spoke Malay; some that he could speak only Malay, others that he was bilingual in Malay and Thai. To sum up, in villages in category B, To Nai Sim, the ruler of Kubang Pasu, is generally taken to have shared the villagers' mother tongue. In villages in category C recollections of To Nai Sim are so limited that they cannot comment on cultural characteristics such as his language.

To Nai Sim as a Muslim

The perception that To Nai Sim was a Muslim is common to all categories of village, but evaluations on his religious practices are varied. In category

A, villagers insist that To Nai Sim was strict in his religious practice. They point out that he went to Mecca as a pilgrim, taking his time and travelling for three months by boat, consequently becoming a 'Hajji' and attaining high religious prestige in the Islamic world. They say that he practised strict religious observances in daily life. Here we can assume that this high evaluation of religious practice by To Nai Sim is an attempt to oppose the negative evaluation of the religious activities of the Sam Sam by Malays.

In category B, evaluations follow different courses, that do not coincide with linguistic divisions. Some villagers argue that To Nai Sim strictly observed religious practices because it was said to be the source of his magical powers. Others stress that he could not have been a pious Muslim because his actions, such as killing so many people, showed his indifference to religion. These evaluations correspond to different aspects of To Nai Sim as a ruler; the former to the ruler who possessed magical power, and the latter to the ruler who oppressed people. Villages in category C have not provided sufficient data to allow us to evaluate their opinion of the religious activities of To Nai Sim.

The Relationship with Thai People

There used to be many Thai in Kampong T. Some of them married Muslims and converted to Islam.[13] In neighbouring villages it is said that inter-religious marriages had often taken place. In most cases it was Thai women who had married Muslim men, thus converting to their husbands' religion. To Nai Sim himself married three Thai women who converted to Islam and one of his other two wives was a Thai-speaking Muslim and the other a Malay-speaking Muslim.

One of the Thai wives of To Nai Sim was named Ya Sin. She died in 1948, so many older villagers still had vivid memories of her. Her name Sin came from her place of origin, Siam. A descendant of To Nai Sim related a version of a story about Ya Sin as follows:

'She was a daughter of a poor Siamese peasant. At about the age of ten, she was taken by her father to be sold as a slave. When they came to Kubang Pasu, her father asked To Nai Sim to take her somewhere to sell. But on seeing the little girl, To Nai Sim felt pity and asked her father to leave her here. This little girl was very diligent and had a good nature. She converted to Islam and was renamed Tijah. She was not very beautiful, but her kindness and gentle behaviour charmed To Nai Sim and they were married. To Nai Sim loved her more than his other wives. He took only Tijah with him on his pilgrimage to Mecca. Tijah's father, it is believed, was perhaps skilled in love magic. Before To Nai Sim took her, her father had called Tijah and spoke some words while breathing on her.'

There was frequent cross-border traffic between Siam and Kedah. Numerous Thai came across the border, especially as slaves or labourers, as is illustrated by the stories of Ya Sin and accounts of To Nai Sim as a trader.

Many Malays believe that the Thai people are skilled in the use of love magic, as shown in above story of Ya Sin, and even more clearly in another version of the same story: 'Ya Sin was a slave who was taken from Siam by To Nai Sim. To Nai tried to sell her several times but did not succeed. At last To Nai married her. This is because Ya Sin used love magic, so he could not sell her to anybody; she made To Nai love her'.

While inter-marriage with Thai was formerly frequent, this is no longer the case today. Indeed at present we rarely find inter-religious marriages. This gap between past and present is reflected in the behaviour of many villagers, who stress that their ancestors were not Thai, while telling us that there used to be many inter-religious marriages within the village. It appears that acknowledging past connections with the Thai is evaded in contemporary Malaysia, where the Sam Sam strive to be complete Malays who speak Malay and have faith in Islam.

Local Power in the Periphery

Several aspects of To Nai Sim as a leader, even a ruler, point to one basic feature: he was a man whose personal power made others fear him. Having the power to put people to death and the power to obtain surpassing wealth are regarded as the consequence of possessing magical powers. Conversely, being feared can give a person power and wealth. If this type of primordial wielder of power is able to instil fear he can diversify this power into other kinds of social, economic, and broader political influence. The stories of To Nai Sim indicate that indigenous power centres which grew up in the periphery were able to maintain their own areas of jurisdiction, into which bigger power centres, such as Kedah, were unable to intervene.

We have need to consider further the local belief that every man of power has magical power (*ilmu batin*). Wolters has pointed out that the leadership of 'men of prowess' depended on their being attributed with an abnormal amount of personal and innate 'soul stuff'. In his model of the traditional states of South East Asia, the mandala represented a particular and often unstable political situation in a vaguely definable geographical area without fixed boundaries. In each mandala one king, identified with divine and 'universal' authority, claimed personal hegemony over the other rulers in his mandala, who in theory were his obedient allies and vassals (Wolters 1982: 16–17). The boundaries of these states would expand or shrink according to the individual spiritual quality of the king. What kind of quality is this? Endicott has pointed out similarities between the shaman and the king in Malaya. Among other similarities he reports that both have been credited with the possession of familiars and with supernatural ability to injure, to heal, and to control the weather (Endicott 1991 [1970]: 22).

There are, however, basic differences between the ideology surrounding the kings of states at the centre of big power centres and the ideas mobilized around local powers such as To Nai Sim. In the former, the king's spiritual quality is a more metaphysical idea, buttressed with the ideology of Buddhist kingship and decorated with Indianized conceptions of divine kingship. The smaller the power base the more the individual's quality of leadership is likely to be concretely expressed and more physically envisioned in the form of magical powers and invulnerability. Onghokham has examined the importance of *kebal* (invulnerability) as legitimizing the authority of peasant leaders (Onghokham, 1984; 336). Turton has proposed that, analytically, three types of popular leaders are apt to be considered invulnerable: '(a) informal *ad hoc* pioneer leaders, who are historically often founders of local communities, (b) "outlaws" (robbers and bandits), and (c) religious virtuosi, especially millenarian type leaders'. These leaders tend to come to the fore 'either when state powers are absent or relatively weak . . . or when state powers are being asserted, and meet with opposition' (Turton 1991: 170–71). To Nai Sim corresponds with two of these categories: he was a local power who grew up in an interstice between large power centres, managing to maintain his own domain in which larger states were unable to intervene; he was also infamous as a leader of bandits and cattle thieves.

Turton has also noted 'the widespread co-existence of ideas of invulnerability with those of invisibility'. These ideas correspond to 'the behaviour of "underground" leaders and organizations'. He has argued that 'if "intimidation" and "surveillance" are major and related means of the exercise of power . . . then popular ideas of "invulnerability" and "invisibility" are among their opposites, in thought certainly, but also occasionally in political practice' (Turton 1991: 176). I would like to concur from my own research that invulnerability and invisibility are two of the means by which local leaders endeavour to cope with power of established states impinging from the outside. To Nai Sim was also said to have possessed both of these qualities: invulnerability and invisibility.

To Nai Sim has several dimensions; viewed from inside he can be seen as a protector, but from the outside he was no more than a bandit. This type of image coincides with that of the *nakleng*, as Johnston refers to local leaders who were opposed to the central authority in central Thailand until the beginning of the twentieth century (Johnston, 1980: 95–96), and with that of the social bandits described by Hobsbawm: 'they are peasant outlaws whom the lord and state regard as criminals, but who remain within peasant society, and are considered by their people as heroes, as champions, avengers, fighters for justice, perhaps even leaders of liberation, and in any case as men to be admired, helped and supported' (Hobsbawm, 1972: 17). There is an empirical difference between this kind of social bandit and To Nai Sim: Hobsbawm regards social banditry as a special type of peasant protest and rebellion within a state boundary. To Nai Sim established his rule in a peripheral area beyond the reach of state power. Historical recollections of To Nai Sim illustrate the workings of local power on the periphery in shared Thai and Malay cultural idioms of popular leadership.

Emergence and Transformation of Peripheral Ethnicity

From the foregoing consideration of the ethnicity of the Sam Sam, we can see that different criteria are employed in drawing ethnic boundaries among Thai, Sam Sam, and Malay. Thai who are Thai-speaking Buddhist make only two religious category distinctions, *khaek* and *thai*. *Khaek* signifies a Muslim regardless of Malay or Sam Sam ethnicity, and *thai* means Thai. Sam Sam also call both themselves and Malays by the same term, *khaek* (in Thai) or *Melayu* (in Malay). They have not made any distinctions between Thai-speakers and Malay-speakers among Muslims. For them the term Sam Sam denotes a dialect, 'Thai language with a sprinkling of Malay words', as used in phrases such as 'to speak Sam Sam' (*cakap Sam Sam*). For Thai-speaking Muslims there is no ethnic group called Sam Sam. It is the Malays who draw boundaries between Thai-speaking Muslims and Malay-speaking Muslims by calling the former Sam Sam and the latter *Melayu*. So the ethnic category Sam Sam can be regarded as a representation in a Malay ideology that connects religion and language in an attempt to defend the Malay world from invasion by Thai elements, thus alienating Thai-speaking Muslims in the Malay world.

Historical memories of To Nai Sim's ability to speak the Thai language and assessments of his religious practices differed according to the degree of former proximity to him. People who had the closest relationship with To Nai Sim, for example his direct descendants in category A villages, lay stress on the facts that he spoke Thai and was a pious Muslim. Descendants of those ruled by To Nai Sim are less concerned with language, and are sometimes not even sure which language he spoke. This indicates that the language spoken by To Nai Sim was not an important symbolic characteristic of a leader or ruler at that time.

It is probable that To Nai Sim freely used both the Thai and Malay languages. Only in the last 30 years have the Sam Sam begun to adopt the Malay language as their mother tongue, even though they have long been discriminated against by Malays, as is evidenced by records dating back to the nineteenth century. This suggests a former situation where the boundaries of religion and language were more vague and relaxed in the ambiguous periphery, and lacked the strident connotations of the

Plate 14. 'The Rachasee: king of beasts'

contemporary Malay world. Malay discourse concerning Sam Sam had been limited to gossipy, direct personal judgements and discriminatory behaviour that had little obvious direct impact on their behaviour or beliefs. When the nation-state of Malaysia officially legislated the traditional prescription that Malays were Muslims who spoke Malay, old forms of ideological discrimination began to have practical consequences. This has encouraged the Sam Sam rapidly to abandon the Thai language in daily life. The context has changed; old ambiguities are less tolerated and less useful, as there is little play in the borders of modern states. As if to emphasize lines drawn on the map, the boundaries of religion and language have also hardened and become more differentiated. In their present context, some Sam Sam recall their ancestor's cultural characteristics – as a Thai-speaking Muslim – as being superior characteristics from the past. Through their memories they can salvage a paradoxical identity at odds with their pragmatic response to the cultural pressure that surrounds them.

197

Notes

1 Field research was conducted at Satun in Thailand from October to December 1991, at Kubang Pasu in northern Kedah, Malaysia from August to September 1991, and during September 1992.

2 For recent works on Sam Sam, see Cheah (1988), Mohammad Isa (1990), and Kobkua (1991).

3 The corpse of a Muslim must be buried in the ground; the corpse of a Thai Buddhist is normally cremated.

4 In the 'Dictionary of Southern Thai Dialect' the entry for *sam sam* gives only (i) to suppose, guess; (ii) to use mixed. It does not designate a group or category of people.

5 Tortoise or turtle meat is considered impure by Muslims; Buddhists do eat it.

6 Chaiwat, in a paper analyzing violent events in the four southern provinces of Thailand between 1976 and 1981, lists the location of 21 events which received most attention from the Press as follows: Yala – 10; Narathiwat – 4; Pattani – 2; Bangkok – 5. Excepting the capital, which more readily receives attention, all events occurred on the eastern coast of southern Thailand, none occurred in Satun (Chaiwat, 1987: 10–12).

7 At the village in Satun where I conducted research from July 1987 to October 1988, Thai-speaking Muslims could not speak Malay although their kinship terms were Malay.

8 *To Nai* is a term of respect for a boss in this area. As *To* is Malay and *Nai* is Thai, this is a hybrid term peculiar to the Sam Sam.

9 Penghulu is head of a Mukim, the administrative unit above a Kampong (village).

10 *Den* means 'eminent' in standard Thai but here it means 'those who have been ordained as monks' and is often used to denote Thai men in general.

11 Tribute was sent from Nakhonsithamarat to Bangkok by boat.

12 There are many places named after elephants along this tributary road; for example, Changlun, north of Kubang Pasu, means 'elephant fell', said to be named after the fact that an elephant conveying tribute had fallen into the river at this place.

13 Sam Sam call the conversion to Islam *masuk Islam* (enter Islam), but do not refer to it as *masuk Melayu* (become Malay) as Malay-speaking Muslims in Pattani do.

References

Abdul Rahman, Tunku (1978), *Viewpoints*, Kuala Lumpur: Heinemann.

Annandale, Nelson, Robinson, Hervert (1903 Part 1), (1904 Part 2), *Fasciculi Malayenses, Anthropological and Zoological Results of an Expedition to Perak and Siamese Malay States, 1901–1902*, London: The University Press of Liverpool.

Archaimbault, C. (1957) [1956 BEFEO], 'A preliminary Investigation of the Sam Sam of Kedah and Perlis', B.A.V. Peacock (transl.), *Journal of Malayan Branch of the Royal Asiatic Society*, 30(1): 75–92.

Ayabe, Tsuneo (1982), 'Minzoku to Gengo' (Ethnicity and Language), *Motto Shiritai Tai*, Tokyo: Kobundo: 79–92.

Banks, David J. (1980), 'Politics and Ethnicity on the Thai-Malay Frontier: The Historical Role of the Thai-speaking Muslims of Kedah', *Kabar Seberang Sulating Maphilindo*, 7: 98–113.

Chaiwat Satha-anand (1987), *Islam and Violence: a Case Study of Violence in the Four Southern Provinces, Thailand, 1976–1981,* USF Monographs in Religion and Public Policy.

Cheah Boon Kheng (1988), *The Peasant Robbers of Kedah 1900–1929,* Singapore: Oxford University Press.

Crawfurd, John (1987) [1828], *Journal of an Embassy to the Courts of Siam and Cochin China,* Singapore: Oxford University Press.

Dato' Wan Ibrahim Wan Soloh (1990) [1970], 'Kedah, Setul and Perlis Seventy Years Ago: Skeat's Reminiscences of visits', *Alor Setar 250 Tahun,* Kerajaan Negeri Kedah Darulaman, 95–102.

Endicott, K. M. (1991) [1970], *An Analysis of Malay Magic,* Singapore: Oxford University Press.

Hobsbawm, E. J. (1972), *Bandits,* London: Penguin Books.

Ishii, Yoneo (1977), 'Taikoku niokeru "Isuramu Yogo" nitsuiteno Oboegaki' (A Note on the 'Protection' of Islam in Thailand), *Southeast Asian Studies,* 15(3), Kyoto: 347–61.

Johnston, David B. (1980), 'Bandit, Nakleng, and Peasant in Rural Thai Society', *Contributions to Asian Studies,* Vol.15: 90–101.

Kobkua Suwannathat-Pian (1988), *Thai-Malay Relations: Traditional Intra-regional Relations from the Seventeenth to the Early Twentieth Centuries,* Singapore: Oxford University Press.

—— (1991), *The Sam-Sam: an Intricate Aspect of Historical and Cultural Assimilation,* unpublished mimeograph.

Kuroda, Keiko (1989), '"SamSam" to Yobareta Hitobito: Tai-Mareishia Kokkyouchitai no Thai-Speaking Muslim' (The people called 'Sam Sam': Thai-speaking Muslims in the border area of Thai-Malaysia), *Mareishia Shakaironshuu,* Vol. 2, Tokyo: ILCAA, Tokyo University of Foreign Studies: 41–76.

—— (1991), 'Taraankou no Hakai: Rama 1 seiki (1785–1808) Siam niokeru Malay Hantou Hokubu Nishi Kaigan Kouekikougun no Yakuwari' (The Destruction of Muang Thalaang – the Role of Siamese Ports as Entrepots on the North-Western Coast of Malay Peninsula in the Reign of Rama 1 (1785–1808)), *Nanpo-Bunka,* Vol. 18: 56–81.

—— (1992), 'The Samsams of Kubang Pasu – the Historical Relations between Kedah and Siam Viewed from a "Kampung"', in K. Miyazaki (ed.), *Local Societies in Malaysia,* Vol.1, Institute for the Study of Languages and Cultures of Asia and Africa Tokyo University of Foreign Studies, 89–109.

Leach, Edmund R. (1960), 'The Frontiers of "Burma"', *Comparative Studies in Society and History,* 3: 49–68.

Logan, J. R. (1885), 'Plan for a Volunteer Police in the Muda District, Province Wellesley, Submitted to Government by the late J. R. Logan in 1867', *Journal of the Malay Branch of the Royal Asiatic society,* 16: 173–202.

Low, James (1836), *A dissertation on the soil and agriculture of the British Settlement of Penang on Prince of Wales Island in the Straits of Malacca including Province Wellesley. . . .* Singapore, (321pp.); [reprinted 1971 as The British Settlement of Penang, James Jackson ed., Singapore, Oxford University Press].

Moerman, Michael, (1992), 'Ariadne's Thread and Indra's Net: Reflections on Ethnography, Ethnicity, Identity, Culture, and Interaction', Paper presented at the Symposium on Identité, Ethnicité: Culturalisme ou Interactionisme, Paris (October).

Mohammad Isa Othman (1990), *Politik tradisional Kedah 1681–1942,* Kuala Lumpur: Dewan Bahasa dan Pustaka Kementerian Pendidikan Malaysia.

Newbold, T. J. (1971) [1839], *British Settlements in the Straits of Malacca,* 2 vols., Kuala Lumpur: Oxford University Press.

Nishii, Ryoko (1989), 'Minami Tai no Gyoson niokeru Musurimu to Bukkyouto no Tsuukon' (Intermarriage between Muslims and Buddhists in the Fishing Villages of Southern Thailand), *Kikan-Jinrui Gaku,* 20(4), Kyoto: 51–111.

—— (1991), 'Minami Tai no Sonraku Seiji nimirareru Musurimu-Bukkyouto Kankei; Samsam teki Musurimu Shakai niokeru Shuukyou to Seiji' (The Relationship between Muslims and Buddhists in a Southern Thai Village; Religion and Politics in Sam Sam Muslim Society), *Southeast Asian Studies,* 29(1), Kyoto: 64–102.

Onghokham (1984), 'The Jago in Colonial Java, Ambivalent Champion of the People', *Senri Ethnological Studies,* 13, Osaka: National Museum of Ethnology: 327–43.

Skeat, W. W. (1953), 'The Cambridge University Expedition to the North-Eastern Malay States, and to Upper Perak, 1899–1900', *Journal of the Malayan Branch of the Royal Asiatic Society,* Vol.26, pt.4: 9–147.

Tambiah, S. J. (1976), *World Conqueror and World Renouncer, a Study of Buddhism and Polity in Thailand against a Historical Background,* Cambridge University Press.

—— (1992), *Buddhism Betrayed? Religion, Politics, and Violence in Sri Lanka,* University of Chicago Press.

Turton, Andrew (1991), 'Invulnerability and Local Knowledge', *Thai Constructions of Knowledge,* School of Oriental and African Studies, University of London: 155–82.

Wan Yahaya Wan Mohd Taib (1911), *Salasilah atau Tawarikh Kerajaan Kedah,* Alor Star.

Wijeyewardene, Gehan (1990), 'Thailand and the Tai: Versions of Ethnic Identity', in Gehan Wijeyewardene (ed.), *Ethnic Groups across National Boundaries in Mainland Southeast Asia,* Singapore: Institute of Southeast Asian Studies, 48–73.

Wolters, O. W. (1982), *History, Culture, and Region in Southeast Asian Perspectives,* Singapore: Institute of Southeast Asian Studies.

Part IV

LAOS: A POLY-ETHNIC STATE

Introduction

These four studies of Laos allow us to consider the case of a largely 'Tai' state, outside contemporary Thailand and, like the Lanna states (that are the subject of the next section), also outside the heartlands of the ancient Siamese state of Ayutthaya. Mayoury's account emphasises the complex historical contexts of changing social identities: Siamese overrule (1827–1893), French colonial rule (1893–1954), partial independence and United States domination (1954–75) and subsequent attempts by a socialist regime (1975-continuing) whose slogans are to encourage 'a multi-national Lao people' to become a 'single Lao nation', a paradoxical attempt that no previous rulers seem to have deemed even necessary let alone possible.

Keyes quotes a French historian of the colonial period to the effect that 'Laos is a manifestation of geography that corresponds to no ethnographic reality'. This clearly reflects in part a rationale for colonial intervention and rule. There are arguably some corroborative facts: first, the eventual 'Laos français' was an assemblage of political units that had hitherto had no single relationship, being variously subject to the sovereignty of neighbouring Vietnam, China or Siam; secondly, the majority 'Lao' population was always a considerably smaller majority than say Burmans in Burma, Vietnamese in Vietnam, or Thai in Thailand; and thirdly, Laos contains no ethnic groups 'whose entire population lives within the borders of Laos' (Kossikov). However, as we have seen in so many other Tai polities, the social relations did indeed constitute a historically patterned 'ethnographic reality' – if not yet a strongly ethnicised one – with the Tai(Lao)-Kha relation at the core.

Grant Evans examines this relation in detail from contemporary field research in a small village in Houa Phan province in northern Laos. To the outside officials this is a uniformly Black Tai village, but the insiders are mutually defined as Tai and Sing Moon (Xing Mul). The latter speak a

Mon-Khmer language heavily influenced by Tai and Lao; this is their chief distinguishing feature but they generally lack 'cultural confidence', and in this and other respects (e.g. scapegoating) they bear interesting comparison with the case of the Sam Sam discussed earlier. But Evans does not find evidence for rapid or complete 'Tai-ization'. He first contrasts the situation with that in northern Burma analysed by Leach in his highly influential ethnographic 'classic' *Political systems of Highland Burma* (1954) in which 'Kachin' and 'Shan' (Kha and Tai social categories respectively) interact, giving rise to 'oscillation' betwen the two systems and an intermediary one, over longish historical periods. This is contrasted with the situation in so-to-say 'Highland Indochina' where Georges Condominas argues that a historical process of irreversible and often forcible 'Tai-ization' of non-Tai peoples has taken place. Evans agrees that prior to the arrival of Tai social relations in the area, there were probably no 'chieftainships', nor any supra-village political systems, nor any ranked lineages among the non-Tai, in contrast with the Kachin (or Jingphaw) cultural area. But he argues the case for Tai-zation (a) being a much slower process, (b) not affecting all non-Tai people equally, partly due to certain 'cultural limits' and partly to do with 'class' differences, (c) a greater degree of voluntary Tai-ization, especially by upwardly mobile non-Tai (in this respect more similar to the Kachin). Evans also puts forward the more general arguments that neither Tai nor non-Tai groups are uniform across the region, that there are many levels and elements to 'Tai-ization', and that viable multiple identities are probably the norm. Like Tanabe later in this volume, Evans shows clearly that despite continuous processes of conversion, the distinct categories of social identity remain intact.

Mayoury and Kossikov bring contrasting approaches to bear on a macro-level review of the ethnic or nationalities policies of the revolutionary post-1975 government of Laos. Kossikov problematises various classifications that have been used to distinguish the many different peoples in Laos, especially the language based criteria favoured by Soviet and Russian academicians – which produces about 60 distinct 'ethnoses' or ethnic groups – and the more ideological 'trinomial' classification in which the entire population (excepting certain 'non-indigenous' peoples such as Chinese, Vietnamese and European) are divided into the 'Lao' of valleys, foothills or mountain tops respectively. Kossikov uses the term 'Laotian' for the inclusive non-ethnic category of citizen of Laos – this has resonances with the use of 'British' and the need to avoid the term 'English' for the citizens of the United Kingdom (which is still 'England' in many other languages) not that all citizens like this term either! The tripartite classification was a patent attempt to create 'meta-ethnic entities' (though below the level of the state) somewhat in accordance with Stalinist conceptions of 'nationalities', based – selectively and inconsistently as Kosskov shows – on a combination of largely material and social evolutionary characteristics including: ethnogenesis, common geographical living conditions, similar economic and cultural patterns, and levels of social development. Kossikov emphasises the artificiality of these categories, the coercive nature of attempts to make them into social realities, and the degree of resistance to state policies based on them, manifested in continuing armed rebellion and the large scale voluntary movement of some 10% of the population out of the country.

Mayoury accords considerable weight to the specifc historical effects of French colonial rule in selectively creating, reinforcing, disregarding and generally exploiting ethnic relations and hierarchies. Her title and the reference to 'the hegemonic rule of one tribal group' nonetheless ironically implicate the dominant Lao as part of the problem. Mayoury documents the large scale involvement of non-Tai groups in the anti-colonial and liberation struggles in Laos and the efforts and achievements of the state since 1975 in the fields of economy, education and health, and in diminishing prejudice and discrimination. Yet 'Despite such progress, obstacles and many unmet needs still exist' and the challenges are 'overwhelming'. Above all the failure to address adequately the social status and conditions of women, generally and not only among minorities, is a standing condemnation. But Mayoury's final assessment is that what has been achieved towards the 'unification of all ethnic groups under one national umbrella' is a net gain and more impressive than any pre-revolutionary regime had brought about.

Keyes' opening chapter in this section treats the historical relation between the Thai of Thailand or Siam and the Lao generally at the highest level of state, nicely complementing Evans' micro-study of Lao-Tai-non-Tai relations. First, a masterly overview of Thai political discourse on the Lao reveals a dialectic of closeness and disparagement that parallels the Tai-Kha relation with its assumption of common origin – 'one family that has become separated', though these are the words of a Lao nationalist Prince Phetsarath – on the one hand and on the other hand presuppositions of inferiority of the Lao and their need for a civilizing influence from the Thai, and Prince Damrong's deliberate policy of distancing the Lao within Thai national borders – the 'docile other' in Thongchai's terms – from those of Laos, referring to them as 'northeastern Thai' (*thai isan*).

Keyes subtly interprets a state visit by Princess Maha Chakri Sirindhorn to Laos in 1990 and concludes that this marked 'a water-shed in Thai-Lao relations' and 'a major break with the colonial view of Laos', this time a reference to a Siamese 'colonial' predatory and discriminatory gaze upon the Lao. The visit is set in the context of changing historical discourses in which the categories Lao and Thai are constructed and involved in power relations. Taking up a dominant theme in this volume, Keyes stresses the importance of ritual or symbolic practices in relations not only between Tai and non-Tai but here between Thai and Lao. In particular he highlights the national transformations of the *that luang* monument and related ritual – the principal palladium of the nation, supposedly containing of a relic of the Buddha, destroyed by the Siamese in 1827 – and the *basi sukhuan* which is a popular ceremony to call and secure the 'vital essence' or soul of a person, that has become 'the Lao national rite'. In various forms this ceremony is found throughout the Tai cultural area, and is much used in encounters between Tai and non-Tai. The participation of the Thai Princess in such rituals is judged to be among the key markers of cultural respect and even deference that signify at least the possibility of a transformed relationship.

Each of the studies in this section deals with historically situated practices both in the more distant and the more recent past. They all end with challenging, and almost prophetic statements as to the shape of things to come. Mayoury as we have seen, represents an extreme of cautious hopefulness, while Kossikov claims more gloomily that: 'As the disparity in living standards and the renewed estrangement betweeen Lao and ethnic minorities continues to increase, the menace of aggravating the latent contradictions betwen ethnic groups becomes more evident. Escalation of these contradictions threatens the unity and territorial integrity of Laos'. As for external relations, Keyes is careful to say that what he terms a hopeful new 'counter-narrative' of Thai-Lao relations has not yet supplanted the older, still dominant one. Evans concludes with a reminder that political assumptions or fantasies about the nature of cultural and ethnic identity and identification – that are 'currently wreaking havoc around the globe' – are based on flawed and no longer tenable essentialising and positivistic assumptions – long supported by mainstream philosophy and social science – about the boundedness and primordiality of 'culture(s)'. Awareness 'that people participate differentially in different [and multiple] identities and different cultures' (Evans) is an important pre-requisite for a more reflexive, tolerant, mutually respectful approach. This may not be new, but this volume has above all tried to situate these relations in changing and transforming power-laden historical contexts in a cultural and political region, circumscribed here as that of Tai states and *müang*, which offers an outstanding region for comparative analysis and an expanded definition of T(h)ai/Lao studies.

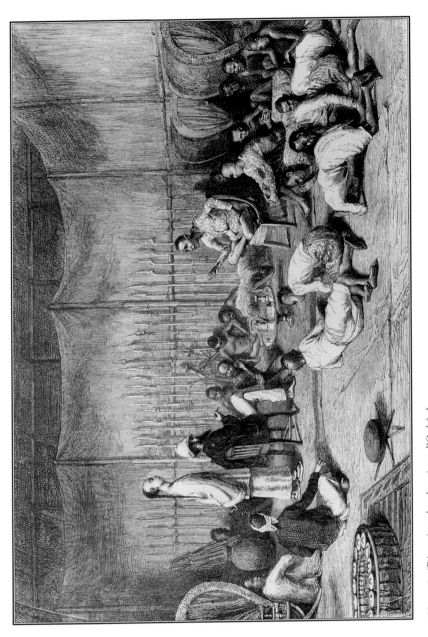

Plate 15. 'Réception chez le prince d'Oubôn'

A Princess in a People's Republic: A New Phase in the Construction of the Lao Nation

Charles F. Keyes

Introduction

In March 1990 HRH Princess Maha Chakri Sirindhorn, daughter of the King of Thailand, made a state visit to the Lao People's Democratic Republic. Her visit, and the account she wrote of her visit, represents, I will argue in this chapter[1], a major break with the colonial view of Laos and the Lao that has dominated Siamese thought since at least the early part of the nineteenth century. In that view, the Lao have been seen as needful of the civilizing influences the Siamese can provide; Lao should, moreover, be rightfully under Siamese domination. It follows from the Siamese perspective that any claim by the Lao to belonging to a separate nation living in a state independent of Thailand can be only a spurious claim.

In a set of highly symbolic actions during her week's visit to Laos, and in her own account of these acts in her book, *Boeng bo than boeng bo mot* (Too little time; can't see everything) (Princess Sirindhorn 1990), Princess Sirindhorn gave unprecedented Siamese legitimation for a separate Lao national identity. Prime ministers, foreign ministers, and commander-in-chiefs of the army or military might represent the Thai state, but Princess Sirindhorn who had, with the backing of her father, King Bhumipol, assumed since the late 1970s many of the ceremonial functions involving the Thai monarchy and had subsequently achieved great popularity in Thailand, travelled to Laos as the embodiment of the Thai nation. Her actions in Laos, therefore, carried a deeper cultural meaning for both Thai and Lao than the political ones expressed in the actions of other emissaries from Thailand.

In the late twentieth century we have become acutely aware that national cultures are not the 'natural' historical legacies of 'primordial' communities who have gained or who seek self-determination. If this were the case, one would expect those living in Thailand who share the same cultural heritage as the Lao of Laos to seek separation from Thailand and

Plate 16. 'The city of Luang Prabang'

incorporation into Laos. And one might also expect that the half of the population of Laos who are not ethnic Lao would be seeking realization of their national aspirations outside of the framework of the Lao state. Neither is happening. Nationalism is not simply ethnicity writ large. How then are nations 'imagined' (Anderson 1991) and national cultures 'invented' (Hobsbawm and Ranger 1983)? I maintain that the process depends on situating memories of power contested within the framework of narratives by those who hold compelling authority (see, in this connection, Bhabha 1990)[2]. It is with this approach in mind that I will examine the story of the visit of Princess Sirindhorn to Laos in 1990. The significance of her narrative can be understood, however, only by first considering other narratives about Lao and Laos that preceded it.

Lao as Uncivilized and Rebellious Colonial Subjects

Lao national culture has its beginnings in the nineteenth century with the colonial expansion of the Siamese state and the construction of the Lao as the colonized subjects of this state. During the Ayutthayan period, the Tai principalities lying to the North in those areas known as Lanna Thai and Lan Xang[3] were viewed by the Siamese court as sometime feudal subordinates of the Burmese whose cultural and linguistic links to the Siamese made them open to joining them in an alliance against the Burmese. After Siam recovered from the Burmese destruction of Ayutthaya in 1767, King Taksin and Rama I sought to ensure that the Lao states were more securely linked to Siam in order to make them a buffer against future Burmese attacks (see Wyatt 1984: 155). Toward this end, General Chakri, the future Rama I, led an attack on Vientiane in 1778 to remove a ruler who had allied himself with the Burmese (Wyatt 1963). In other words, the Siamese court in the late eighteenth and early-nineteenth century sought to persuade the Lao to shift their feudal loyalties from Burma to Siam.

The Lao in the late eighteenth century, as a consequence of upheavals caused by Burmese expansionism, were divided into a number of small states and principalities, the most important of which were the successor states of Lan Xang: Luang Prabang in the North, Vientiane in the centre, and Champasak in the South. A resurgent Siam was able to extend overlordship over all three of these states. The small principality of Xieng Khouang and the even smaller principalities of the Black and Red Tai in the northeast were more tenuously linked to Bangkok both because of their great distance from the Siamese capital and because they were subject to influences from Vietnam.

In the early nineteenth century, Vientiane emerged as the strongest of the Lao states. With support from the Siamese court, King Anou, who had come to the throne in 1804, placed his own son on the throne of

Champasak. Vientiane also at this time had control over Xieng Khouang and the Black Tai areas of Houa Phan. Luang Prabang, however, remained independent of Vientiane.

Siamese feudalism began to give way to colonialism in the reign of King Rama III (1824–1851). A war fought between Siam and the Lao kingdom of Vientiane in 1826–28 was the major event leading to this change. In 1825 King Anou, who had been on the throne of Vientiane for 20 years, went to Bangkok to participate in the funeral of Rama II. While there he had felt humiliated by his treatment by the new Siamese king, Rama III (Vella 1957: 81). He must also have learned during this time of the British conquest of lower Burma in 1824, as he was subsequently persuaded (perhaps on the basis of faulty intelligence) that the British also posed a threat to Bangkok. After he returned to Vientiane, he began preparations for a war with Siam whose purpose would be the wresting from Siamese control territories inhabited by Lao living on the right bank of the Mekong in what is today northeastern Thailand. In short, King Anou began to entertain the ambition of making a re-emergent Lan Xang a major power (Mayoury Ngaosyvathn and Pheuiphanh Ngaosyvathn 1989).

Although initially successful – Anou's troops advanced as far as Saraburi at the foot of the hills leading to the Khorat Plateau – his challenge to Siamese rule in the end proved disastrous. In 1827 Siamese forces began a counter-attack and by mid-April had not only pushed back the Lao troops but had taken Vientiane city as well. Rama III ordered the complete destruction of the city and the incorporation of all the subjects of Vientiane into domains that, although retaining some feudal characteristics (they had, for example, their own hereditary lords), were firmly integrated into Siam. Vientiane was razed to the ground, with even the important Buddhist shrine of That Luang being destroyed. All inhabitants of the city were resettled elsewhere.

In 1828 King Anou, his closest associates, and his family were captured and were sent to Bangkok. Anou and thirteen other prisoners were placed in iron cages where they could be insulted and spat upon by ordinary people (Vella 1957: 86). This treatment of Anou and his associates symbolized the Siamese view that the Lao were less than human. This view also finds expression in the Siamese accounts of the Anou revolt (see, for example, those contained in *Cotmaihet ruang prap khabot wiangchan* (Documents Concerning the Suppression of the Vientiane Revolt) 1926). These accounts lie, I believe, at the root of a Siamese colonial discourse about Laos and the Lao.

Lao historians of today see the events of 1826–28 in a very different light. The officially-sponsored history of modern Laos published in 1989 (Thongsa Sayavongkhamdy et al. 1989) devotes three chapters to the 'resistance' against Siamese 'aggression' that culminates in King Anou's failed attempt to recover the Lao nation. The Lao historians, Mayoury and

Pheuiphanh Ngaosyvathn (1988a, 1988b, 1989), have also sought in writings in Lao, Thai, and English to counter the Siamese view of Anou as a rebel and to demonstrate that he was truly a Lao national hero. The Lao counter-narrative to the Siamese interpretation of the story of King Anou is part of the effort of Lao to assert a claim that the Lao are not subjects of the Siamese but have a 'nation' that is worthy of respect by the Siamese. That claim has been difficult to sustain given the long history of colonial subjugation experienced by the Lao.

From the time of the destruction of Vientiane until 1893 when the French began to create a French Laos as part of Indo-China, Siamese authorities set out to bring most Lao under the domination of the Siamese state. This was done primarily by resettling a large proportion of the population who had lived in the former domains of Vientiane on the left bank of the Mekong to newly created domains on the right bank where they would be more accessible by Siamese officials.[4] By the end of the nineteenth century approximately nine times as many Lao were living on the Khorat Plateau as were living across the Mekong.

The treaties of 1893 and 1907 that France forced the Siamese court to sign gave French Indo-China control not only of all Lao territories on the left bank of the Mekong, but also territories on the right bank that historically had been under Luang Prabang and Champasak. These concessions were seen by the Siamese as resulting in the loss of territory that the Siamese court had come to consider rightfully belonged under its rule. To ensure that no further losses took place, the Siamese court instituted reforms that eliminated forever any semblance of local autonomy of the Lao domains in northeastern Siam. By the early part of the twentieth century, Prince Damrong, who as Minister of the Interior had been the architect of the reforms that centralized authority throughout the kingdom, sought to expunge the use of the term Lao to refer to peoples living in northeastern and northern Siam (Damrong 1971 [1935]: 318–320).

The assimilationist policy of the Siamese state met with resistance by the Lao living on the Khorat Plateau in the early part of the twentieth century. But the putative magical powers of the leaders of 'holy man' rebellion in 1901–02 proved to be no match for the Gatling guns and other modern weapons used by Siamese forces (Tej Bunnag 1967; Ishii 1975; Keyes 1977). Coercion alone did not, however, succeed in making the Lao of the region think of themselves as members of a Siamese nation. As I have argued elsewhere (Keyes 1966a, 1966b, 1967, 1977, 1991, in press), the acceptance of an identity as an ethno-regional minority – called *Isan* – within the Thai nation was primarily a product of the co-optation of monks from the region into a Thai state-sponsored Sangha and the institution of compulsory education throughout much of the region. Through attendance at government schools, increasing numbers of people in northeastern Thailand (as well as elsewhere in the country) gained competence in the Thai national language and became familiar with Thai national symbols and Thai national history. By the 1930s, the historical experience of Lao in northeastern Thailand had diverged significantly from that of the Lao living on the right bank of the Mekong who were under French rule.

French Laos and the Development of Lao Nationalism

'Laos' – the 's' was added by the French for reasons that are obscure – was a creation of the French. Le Boulanger, who wrote the first narrative history of colonial Laos, *Histoire du Laos Français*, begins his work by stating that 'Le Laos est une expression géographique qui ne correspond à aucune réalité ethnographique' ('Laos is a manifestation of geography that corresponds to no ethnographic reality') (Le Boulanger 1931: 9). In Laos, the French combined the Kingdom of Luang Prabang, the territories on the left bank of the Mekong that had formerly been part of the Kingdom of Vientiane, the principalities of Champasak and Xieng Khouang, and the even smaller domains of Houa Phan and Muang Sing. Laos included not only ethnic Lao but also such other Tai-speaking peoples as the Lue, Black Tai, and Red Tai. At least a third of the population was made up of Austroasiatic-speaking peoples living in village-based societies in the uplands. And there were significant numbers of Tibeto-Burman-speaking groups (notably the Akha, called Kaw in Lao) and Hmong and Mien (Yao) belonging to the Miao-Yao language family.

The French *mission civilisatrice* in Laos was quite weak; very few in Laos received any formal education during French rule and there was little direct challenge to pre-colonial cultural practices. Nonetheless, French rule represented a fundamental break from the pre-modern political world that most in Laos had known (see Gunn 1988, 1990a). The experiences of living under the French and the Vietnamese officials who filled most positions in the colonial bureaucracy were fraught with tensions that few colonial officials recognized. There were numerous localized rebellions, often by upland or highland peoples, that typically assumed millenarian forms (Gunn 1990a). Memories of these rebellions would later be woven into the revolutionary history of Laos (see Thongsa Sayavongkhamdy et al. 1989).

The French also promoted in their own colonial narrative a view of Siamese relations with the Lao as being illegitimate. The French colonial narrative about Laos has its roots in the work of Auguste Pavie and his associates on the local histories, legends, myths, folklore, and literature of the diverse peoples living in what was to become French Laos (Pavie 1898–1919). It was given full form in Le Boulanger's *Histoire du Laos Français*, published in 1931. Le Boulanger first considers the prehistoric roots of the kingdom of Lan Xang and then draws on Lao chronicles to trace the history of Lan Xang and its successor states of Vientiane, Luang Prabang, and Bassac (Champasak) from the mid-fourteenth to the early nineteenth centuries. The nineteenth century, in his account, is one characterized by Siamese expansion; then in the early twentieth century French intervention leads to the creation of 'Le Laos français'.

Although concluding with the Lao as belonging to French Indo-China, Le Boulanger's history became, nonetheless, the basis of a counter-narrative that has served to promote Lao nationalism.[5] It is noteworthy that Le Boulanger expresses particular gratitude 'pour l'inestimable documentation et la véritable collaboration' to Prince Phetsarath, a man who would in the 1940s become the foremost proponent of Lao nationalism.

A distinctive Lao nationalism began to take shape during World War II in opposition not only to French colonialism but also to a new form of Thai imperialism. In the late 1930s a faction of the Thai élite which had come to power following the creation of a constitutional monarchy in 1932 drew inspiration from the fascist projects of Germany and Japan to promote a new type of Thai nationalism. The goal of this faction, headed by Phibun Songkhram and whose chief ideologue was Luang Wichit Watthakan, was to make Siam a major power in Asia. Luang Wichit found in the Austrian *Anchluss* with Germany a model for a Thai project to unite all peoples who were related in culture and language to the Thai (that is, the Lao and other Tai-speaking peoples) and all those who had once been under Siamese rule (most notably the Khmer) (Stowe 1991:102). Luang Wichit promoted Phibun's 'pan-Thai policy' through such plays as *Maha Thewi* (The Great Queen) and *Chaoying Saenwi* (Princess of Hsenwi) that made people in Thailand aware of the historical connections between different Tai-speaking peoples (Jiraporn Witayasakpan 1992: 197). Phibun was able to begin implementing this policy when he became Prime Minister, with the backing of the military, in 1938.

The proclamation on 24 June 1939 that changed the name of the country from Siam to Thailand signalled the intention of the Phibun government to re-define the place of the country within the region. The outbreak of war in Europe later in the same year gave Phibun the opportunity to translate this intention into action. The German conquest of France and the creation of the Vichy regime significantly weakened French colonial control over Indo-China. The colonial authorities, who were loyal to Vichy, could not call on the resources of the metropolitan power to deal with problems in their domains. In early 1941 the Thai began a small-scale war with French forces near both the Cambodian and Lao borders. Although the battles were not very conclusive, Japanese intervention in the subsequent negotiations between representatives of French Indo-China and Thailand led to Thailand re-claiming an area of northwestern Cambodia and lands on the right bank of the Mekong in

French Laos that had been ceded to France in the treaty of 1907. Thailand was also later to take advantage of the Japanese victory over British forces in Burma to take control of Kengtung, one of the most important of the Shan states of Burma.

If the pan-Thai policy of Phibun had been continued, it is probable that all of Laos would have been incorporated into an expanded Thailand. The alliance between Thailand and Japan, on which pursuit of this policy depended, began, however, to falter long before Japan was defeated. The alliance was undermined by the Free Thai Movement, headed within Thailand by Phibun's chief rival, Pridi Phanomyong.

Pridi, who during World War II served as Regent for the absent King Ananda, found strong support for the Free Thai movement from a new group of political leaders in northeastern Thailand.[6] These leaders had their roots in the Lao cultural traditions of the region. Their kinship, both symbolic and real, with leaders on the other side of the Mekong led the Free Thai movement to foster the development of the Lao Issara or Free Lao movement. Because both the Free Thai and Free Lao had the immediate common objective of helping the allies to defeat the Japanese, the nationalist goals of the Lao from northeastern Thailand and the Lao from Laos were not clearly distinguishable. Indeed, ambiguity about these goals remained after the War when Thai governments led by Pridi or his close associates promoted the idea of a South East Asian Union that would include Thailand and the former Indo-Chinese countries (see Keyes 1967: 31 for further discussion of this idea). In this environment, Lao political leaders from both sides of the Mekong were rather equivocal about the distinction between Lao and Thai nationalism.

John Coast, writing of the immediate post World War II period, observed that Lao politicians from northeastern Thailand sought greater local autonomy, but not independence from Thailand (Coast 1953: 50). Prince Phetsarath, the leader of the Lao Issara, was appreciative of Thai support for his movement and although he maintained that 'we Lao must carry our own responsibilities' (that is, become independent) saw Thai and Lao as closely related: 'Thai-Lao culture from ancient times shows that by blood and marriage we are one family that has become separated' ('3349' 1978: 23).

A clear division between the aspirations of Lao living in northeastern Thailand and those living in Laos began, however, with the return of the French as rulers of Indo-China in 1945 and then of Phibun as Prime Minister of Thailand in 1947. The Phibun government moved against the leaders from northeastern Thailand, murdering the most well-known and arresting others. Some fled to Laos where they were eventually to reject their Thai identity and to work for Lao nationalist causes. While Phibun could not resurrect his pan-Thai policy, his government sought to ensure that no government hostile to Thailand emerged when France granted Laos independence (Thak Chaloemtiarana 1979: 242).

213

Thailand formally recognized Lao independence in 1954, but Laos was not considered by those in power in Thailand throughout the 1950s, 1960s, and 1970s to be a truly independent nation. Between 1954 and 1975, successive Thai governments supported rightwing elements in Laos closely linked to Thailand and sought to use economic means, primarily through control of trade to land-locked Laos, to exercise dominance over the country. Thai soldiers were also employed in the American 'secret war' in Laos. Although never openly formulated as official policy, the implicit assumption behind the Thai stance toward Laos for the period between 1954 and 1975 was that ultimately Laos would be absorbed into a Thai world if not a Thai state. Thai assumptions about Laos had to be reconsidered, however, when the Pathet Lao headed by the Communist Party known as the Lao People's Revolutionary Party took power in 1975.

The Lao People's Democratic Republic and Thai-Lao Relations

After the founding of the Lao People's Democratic Republic and the abolition of the Luang Prabang monarchy in December 1975, Thailand became very hostile towards Laos. Thailand offered first asylum to the tens of thousands of Lao who were opposed to the new regime and fled the country. Thailand also supported Lao insurrections, particularly those organized by the Hmong, and impeded the shipping of goods from the Port of Bangkok to Vientiane. There were also border skirmishes, culminating in the Ban Rom Klao war of 1987–88 (see, in this connection, 'Mitrasamphan' n.d. [1988]; Pheuiphanh Ngaosyvathn 1985; Sarasin Viraphol 1985, Yothong Thapthiomai 1988).

This war, that appears to have begun over a logging dispute (Stuart-Fox 1989: 83–4), was intense and costly, although brief. 'Thailand's military expenditure stood at around 2 billion baht (US$80 million) and its casualties numbered 103 dead and 802 wounded. According to Thai sources, Laos had suffered 340 killed and 257 wounded' (Stuart-Fox 1989: 84). Thai were shocked that Lao could not only hold out against the attack of Thai forces, but succeeded in inflicting heavy casualties and shooting down two Thai fighter aircraft. The war proved the Lao could more than hold their own in their efforts to protect what they considered their national interests. The changing political climate of the late 1980s – the adoption of a 'new economic mechanism' in Laos and Vietnam that allowed the re-introduction of capitalism, and the decline of the Vietnamese threat to Thailand – coupled with the outcome of the Ban Rom Klao war, stimulated a re-appraisal in Thailand of its relations with Laos.

In early 1988, following secret negotiations in Vientiane between former Thai Prime Minister Kriangsak Chomanan, representing Prime

Minister Prem Tinsulanond, and Kaysone Phoumihane, Secretary-General of the Lao People's Revolutionary Party, General Chaovalit Yongchaiyuth, the Commander of the Thai army, travelled to Vientiane to arrange a ceasefire in the Ban Rom Klao war with his counterpart, General Sisawat Keobounphan, the Lao Chief-of-Staff (Stuart-Fox 1989: 84). Thai interest in improved relations with Laos picked up even more when Chatichai Choonhavan became Prime Minister following elections in July 1988.

> 'Prime Minister Chatichai stated that his government intended to turn Laos into 'Thailand's friend'. The government launched a number of initiatives leading up to Chatichai's visit to Laos at the end of November, including the opening of border crossings, a reduction in the number of goods prohibited from export to Laos, and a proposal to set up a joint border commission.' (Nikisch 1989: 171).

The next year saw a series of visits, including a summit meeting between Chatichai and Kaysone, and exchanges between General Chaovalit and General Sisavat, all of which led to pledges of new types of co-operation between the two countries (Gunn 1990b: 85). It was in this context that a visit by Princess Sirindhorn was first proposed.

Visit of Princess Sirindhorn to Laos

Princess Sirindhorn is the leading princess of the House of Chakri and second in line to the Thai throne. In addition Princess Sirindhorn is an accomplished scholar trained in Thai and South East Asian archaeology and cultural history. Her master's thesis at Silapakorn (Fine Arts) University, *Thotsabarami nai Phutthasatsana Therawat* (The Ten Virtues in Theravada Buddhism) (Princess Sirindhorn 1982), is a study of the virtues which according to the Theravada Buddhist tradition should be manifest in the righteous monarch. Her books on travels to various countries are drawn directly from her own obviously very detailed notes and have sold well not only because their royal imprimatur makes them ideal coffee table books in the homes of Thai élite, but also because they are informative and well written. Proceeds from sales of her books go to a charitable foundation.

The potential political significance of the Princess's visit to Laos made the proposal for her trip quite controversial. In 1989 when the Princess's visit was first suggested publicly, most certainly on the initiative of the Chatichai government, former Prime Minister Kukrit Pramote was outraged. His strong disapproval stemmed in part from his contention that having just fought a bitter border war, it would be inappropriate for her to go. He also spoke from the perspective of one who still retained the Thai colonial view of Laos. Although Kukrit had retired from active politics, he still commanded considerable respect and had, as a member of royalty, some influence on the royal family. His opposition led to plans for the visit being put on hold for a time. But the trip was postponed, not cancelled, and even as opposition was publicly expressed it is probable that negotiations for the trip continued since it would have taken much preparation before she could actually go.

Although Princess Sirindhorn's visit was not intended to produce any agreement between Laos and Thailand, it was, nonetheless, politically highly significant.[7] The politics of the trip and of her account are symbolic, entailing deep meanings rather than ones relating to the on-going concerns – such as trade, border disputes, refugees, and so on – of the current leaders of the two countries. The symbolic meanings of her trip are manifest not in communiqués or treaties, but in the very acts – visits to carefully chosen monuments and sites, participation in rituals and ceremonies, and meeting (or not meeting) selected individuals – that made up her trip.

Princess Sirindhorn travelled to Laos on Thursday, 16 March 1990, and remained in Laos until the following Thursday. Her first two days were spent in Vientiane and on the third she travelled to the Nam Ngum hydroelectric project North of Vientiane. On her fourth day she flew to Luang Prabang where she spent two days. From Luang Prabang she flew, via Vientiane, to southern Laos where she visited Wat Phou in Champasak province and ended the day in Saravane Province. The following day she flew to Savannakhet and then back to Vientiane. She may have requested to visit the Plain of Jars in Xieng Khouang province and perhaps Sam Neua in Houa Phan province, but was not able to do so. Phoumi Vongvichit, the Acting President of Laos and her official host, told her that it was not possible to make trips to these provinces because there was too much haze caused by upland people burning fields for planes or helicopters to fly to them safely (Princess Sirindhorn 1990: 12–13). Even without going to these provinces, the Princess visited more areas of Laos, however, than any other Thai who had been to the country since 1975.

It would be fascinating to have some account of the negotiations that led up to her trip, but there is nothing in the public record to show how her itinerary was put together by representatives of the Thai and Lao government and by the Princess herself. One can only draw some deductions about these negotiations from reading between the lines in the Princess's book itself.

Constructing a New Thai View of Laos

The Lao government must have realized the value of having the Princess cast a royal gaze on those sites and monuments that collectively symbolize the Lao national cultural heritage (*moladok haeng sat Lao*) order to further its recently adopted policy of promoting tourism. At the same time the

Princess, as a student of South East Asian cultural history, could use visits to these places as a means to pursue her own scholarly interests.

In Vientiane the Princess visited the four most important religious monuments of the city: That Luang, the Haw Pha Kèo National Museum, Wat Sisaket, and Wat Ongtu. That Luang, the shrine located on the edge of the city believed to contain an actual relic of the Buddha, is, without question, the most well-known monument in Laos. Princess Sirindhorn notes that she first encountered the image of the shrine on a Lao postage stamp she had seen when she was ten years old and adds that it is somewhat ironical that the image still appears on Lao stamps (Princess Sirindhorn 1990: 21). Haw Pha Kèo was formerly the shrine of the Emerald Buddha (*phra kaeo morakhot* as it is called in Thai), today the national palladium of Thailand. Since the French period it has been a museum, primarily for the Buddhist antiquities of the country. Wat Sisaket and Wat Ongtu are two of the oldest wats in Vientiane, the former having first been built in the sixteenth century, although little of the original structure remains, and the second dating from the early-nineteenth century. Wat Sisaket is also a museum, but Wat Ongtu is still very much a functioning wat.

In opening her discussion of That Luang, she says that she has chosen to use Lao rather than Thai spelling for names of places and people in Laos (Princess Sirindhorn 1990: 16). Thus, instead of the Thai spelling that retains the orthographic form, *dhatu,* from Sanskrit even though it is pronounced *that,* she uses the Lao phonetic spelling. Although she is not consistent throughout the book, her effort to use Lao rather than Thai spellings of words shows, I suggest, a respect for the Lao as having a separate language from Thai. She also gives many Lao words and then in parentheses gives the Thai equivalent (e.g. Lao *khua* for Thai *saphan,* 'bridge'; Lao *makmai* for Thai *phonlamai,* 'fruit'). And the very title of her book, *Boeng bo than boeng bo mot* (Too little time, can't see everything), is a Lao phrase both in its vocabulary and its structure.[8]

In her notes on That Luang and Haw Pha Kèo, there is a conspicuous absence of any mention of Siamese destruction of these monuments in 1827–28. She describes their original construction in the sixteenth century and then mentions their reconstruction under the French. Princess Sirindhorn, who is extremely well-versed in Siamese history, could not be ignorant of how Siamese forces had razed the city of Vientiane, destroyed That Luang and Wat Pha Kèo, and carried off the Emerald Buddha to Bangkok. By avoiding any mention of these acts, she does not have to choose between the contradictory interpretations of them by Thai (as punishment for the rebellion led by King Anou) and Lao (as Siamese aggression) in their respective histories.

Her trips outside Vientiane were even more focused on cultural sites. In Luang Prabang, she visited the famous wats of Xieng Thong, Sène Soukhalam, and Visoun, climbed the Pousi hill in the centre of the city, and went to the royal palace that is now a national museum. The ancient monument at Wat Phou was her primary destination in the South, but she also visited the Liphi waterfall that the Lao government has tried to make more accessible to Thai tourists by improving the road to the border where it could be linked to a good road to Ubon in northeastern Thailand. And in Savannakhet she went to Wat Sayaphoum.

In both Vientiane and in Luang Prabang the Princess was the honoured guest at that most typical of Lao rituals, the *basi sukhuan* (*baci soukhouan*). This ritual is performed to 'call' (*su*) the 'vital essence' (*khuan*) and secure this essence to the person for whom it is performed. Traditionally, the rite was performed for a person about to embark on a major change in life (when marrying, moving into a new house, or embarking on a long journey, for example) or for someone who is ill, that is, at times when the essence might be frightened and leave the body. The ritual has evolved into what has been deemed the Lao national rite (Mayoury Ngaosyvathn 1990). It is now performed at state functions to honour a distinguished guest, and it is also often performed for tourist groups, especially for groups who go to Luang Prabang.[9]

The Princess's account of her participation in the *basi sukhuan* ritual and her descriptions of the monuments and shrines she visited, together with the well-produced photographs (many of which she herself took) that accompany her text as well as the images of her trip projected on TV, have, without question, spurred new interest among Thai in the cultural heritage of Laos.[10]

Princess Sirindhorn was more than a very special tourist in Laos. The Lao and Thai governments were well aware that many of her acts would be televised and that audiences in both countries (since Thai TV is watched to a far greater extent in Laos than is Lao TV) would interpret Lao–Thai relations with reference to what they saw. The first public act she undertook after she had arrived in Laos signalled a radical break with the strongly negative stance toward a Laos headed by a revolutionary Communist party that had been dominant in Thailand since the Lao People's Democratic Republic was created in 1975. After being received by Phoumi Vongvichit, the Acting President of the country, she went in a motorcade to the Monument of the Unknown Revolutionary Soldier (*anusaowali naklop nilanam*) in Vientiane and laid a wreath on the monument (Princess Sirindhorn 1990: 8–9). Built in the form of a Buddhist reliquary shrine (*that*), but topped with the red star representing both the party and the revolution, this monument is the prototype for similar, albeit smaller, ones found in every province throughout the country. Collectively, they represent all the lives that were sacrificed in order to create a revolutionary Laos.

Official Lao historiography emphasizes that the revolutionary struggle was against French and then American imperialists, but it was also against

Lao who were supported not only by French and Americans but also by several Thai governments and even against Thai troops who were sent to Laos. Although the Princess's account simply records the act of placing the wreath on the monument, it had a profound meaning in that it signalled the acceptance by Thai of the Lao revolution. One would like to know something of the discussions between representatives of the Lao and Thai sides involved in preparing for her visit that culminated in an agreement that this act would be her first one.

This act was immediately followed by a 'lecture' (*banyai*) by Phoumi Vongvichit at the President's residence (Princess Sirindhorn 1990: 11–13). Phoumi made only passing reference to revolutionary struggles and devoted his talk primarily to detailing the economic and educational accomplishments of Laos since 1975. He also talked about the problems of Laos being a very underdeveloped country. Princess Sirindhorn recorded this speech in her book almost verbatim and without any commentary. In other words, she includes in her account an indigenous voice speaking for the Lao revolution and, thus, provides a royal imprimatur for Thai acceptance of this revolution on its own terms.

The Princess did not, it is worth noting, visit the revolutionary museum where she would have seen an extended exposition, created with the help of Soviet and Vietnamese advisors, of photographs and objects relating to the revolution. This would probably have been the only place where she would have had to engage directly the Party-created narrative of Lao history.

On her second day in Laos, she visited a model primary school (Nahaidieo Primary School), the main secondary school of Vientiane, Dong Dok College, currently a teacher's college but planned to become a full university in the future, and the polytechnic college built with aid from the former USSR. She described these visits in some detail, again without comment. The speech of Phoumi she recorded had, however, underscored the importance of education as both the means of ensuring the success of the Lao revolution and a major product of the revolution (cf. in this regard Chagnon and Rumpf 1982).

The visits she paid to hydro-electric projects at Nam Ngum near Vientiane and Tat Set in Saravane province in the South both underscored the importance of Laos as the source of electricity used in Thailand. On her visit to the Ngam Ngum dam, the Princess released 99 *pla boek* fry brought from Thailand. *Pla boek* is a large scale-less catfish whose primary habitat is the Mekong River. In recent years, this fish, that once figured prominently in both the diets and folklore of Lao and Thai on both sides of the Mekong, has become very rare. The Thai Department of Fisheries has used modern technical means unavailable to the Lao to raise *pla boek* and restock it not only in the Mekong but in reservoirs on tributaries of the Mekong as well. The 99 *pla boek* fry released by the Princess in the Nam Ngum reservoir signalled symbolically (and the number 99 is an especially auspicious number for Lao as well as Thai Buddhists) that the Thai had technical aid to offer the Lao.

Although Princess's Sirindhorn's visit served to legitimate for a Thai audience the existence of a separate Lao nation shaped to a significant extent by the revolution led by the Lao People's Revolutionary Party, some of her actions also raised in an oblique way the question of the place of the Luang Prabang monarchy in the Lao national heritage.

When the French created a colonial Laos, the King of Luang Prabang was made first de facto and then in 1941 de jure King of all Laos. The Luang Prabang monarchy never achieved the popularity or the status of the Bangkok monarchy. While King Sisavang Vong (1905–1959) remained a strong ally of the French until nearly the end of his reign, senior princes of the line of the *uparat*, the second most prestigious royal line, had by World War II become leaders of a Lao nationalist movement. Prince Phetsarath, the *uparat* in the 1930s and 1940s and the chief patron of the Lao Issara, openly broke with King Sisavang Vong over the return of the French after World War II. His half brother, Prince Souvanna Phoumma, would become the major proponent of Lao neutralism and would serve as Prime Minister for much of the period from the early 1960s until 1975. Another half-brother, Prince Souphanavong, became the head of the Pathet Lao and after the take-over of the government by the Lao People's Revolutionary Party became the President of the Lao P.D.R. until his retirement in 1990. After King Savang Vatthana, the son of Sisavang Vong, ascended the throne in 1959, he became linked with right-wing political elements opposed both to the neutralists and communists.

On 2 December 1975, King Savang Vatthana was persuaded to abdicate and the Lao People's Democratic Republic was founded. About thirty of the King's relatives left the country, but the King, the Queen, and the Crown Prince, Savang Vong, were sent to a re-education camp in northern Laos. The King, Queen, and Crown Prince are presumed to have died in the camp, although the official story is that since being sent there has been no word about them.[11]

After the founding of the Lao P. D. R., Vongphetch Saikeryajongtua, a Hmong from Xieng Khouang who was one of the highest ranking members of the Party from a minority group, was appointed as Chairman of the Luang Prabang Administrative Committee, that is Governor of the province. He sought to de-emphasize the royal and Buddhist traditions for which Luang Prabang was best known. The transfer of legitimacy from the Kingdom of Laos to the Lao P.D.R. was signified in 1977 by the placing in the grounds of the palace in Luang Prabang a large statue of King Sisavang Vong granting a constitution (a similar statue was also unveiled in Vientiane). The palace itself became an historic relic and was made into a museum, although it had very few visitors until the late 1980s when tourists once again began to be allowed to visit Luang Prabang in significant numbers.

On 19 March 1990 Princess Sirindhorn was taken to visit the palace/museum. In her account, she notes that the palace had been the residence of King Savang Vatthana until 1975 when it was converted into a museum (Princess Sirindhorn 1990: 158). She nowhere records that she asked or was given any answers about what had happened to the King, the Queen, and the Crown Prince. She placed a wreath at the statue of King Sisavang Vong granting the constitution (Princess Sirindhorn 1990: 165), but this act had, at best, an ambiguous meaning given the history of the statue that the Princess herself records.

Of far greater significance, however, were her two meetings with Princess Maneelai, the wife of the Crown Prince. The first came at a *basi sukhuan* ceremony organized for Princess Sirindhorn on 18 March. In her book she notes that one of the people who had come to honour her by tying strings around her wrist was Princess Maneelai. They had a conversation during which Princess Maneelai recalls having met the King of Thailand when her father was ambassador to Thailand. But, Princess Sirindhorn notes, this was a long time ago, before she was born. Although Princess Sirindhorn does not record it, I learned from a Lao who travelled with the entourage that she asked one of her group to arrange another meeting with Princess Maneelai. This took place at Wat Nong Sikhunmuang on the following afternoon. Princess Sirindhorn went to this wat and records that she met the abbot of the wat and Princess Maneelai who was the head of this wat's congregation (Princess Sirindhorn 1990: 165). A picture of the two at Wat Sikhunmuang appears in the book (Princess Sirindhorn 1990: 166). What the Princess does not record, but what I learned from an informant, was that when Princess Sirindhorn approached Princess Maneelai she saluted her by putting her hands together and bowing so that her head was lower than that of Princess Maneelai's. This indicated that Princess Sirindhorn acknowledged that Princess Maneelai was of high status.

I was told by a number of Lao who I interviewed about the visit of Princess Sirindhorn that the respect she showed Princess Maneelai helped to bring the Lao royal family back to popular attention in a positive way. I found evidence of this in February 1993 when I had an opportunity to visit Luang Prabang again. I stayed at a new charming small hotel, La Villa Princesse, located on land belonging to Princess Maneelai and operated by her daughter and son-in-law.

Conclusion

In this paper I have only begun to analyze the significance of Princess Sirindhorn's trip to Laos in 1990. I have argued that her trip and the account she wrote of it have created a highly visible and authoritative counter-narrative to the dominant colonizing view of Lao and Laos that has for so long held sway among Thai. However, I do not maintain that this counter-narrative has supplanted the older one. A minor incident in early 1993 shows how tenuous the cultural relationships between Lao and Thai are.

A young Thai pop-singer, Uthen Phromminh, known by his nickname Teh, is reported to have said in a TV interview on 21 January 1993, that he could never marry a Lao girl because they are ugly and stupid. Since Thai TV programming is now watched far more than is Lao TV in Laos, Teh's statement caused an immediate furore in Laos with his many fans. Despite the fact that the statement was made by a teenager and despite Lao official disapproval of pop-music, the Lao Foreign Ministry felt compelled to take official note of the incident.[12]

Such sensitivities notwithstanding, and recognizing that Lao political leaders remain wary of Thai intentions – and at the risk of over-interpretation – I still maintain that the visit of Princess Sirindhorn Maha Chakri to Laos in 1990 represents a significant water-shed in Thai-Lao relations. I conclude by quoting part of an editorial that appeared in *The Nation*, an English-language newspaper published in Bangkok, shortly after the Princess's visit:

> 'Now that the Princess, who defied considerable impediments to ensure a successful visit to Laos, has given her blessings, it's now up to concerned authorities in the two countries to keep the spirit alive.' (*The Nation*, 26 March 1990).

Notes

1 A version of this chapter was first presented at the Association for Asian Studies annual meeting, Los Angeles, March 1993; it was then revised for presentation at the Fifth International Conference on Thai Studies, London, July 1993. At the London conference, HRH Princess Sirindhorn very graciously engaged me in conversation about my paper. I am deeply admiring of her patronage of scholarship about the culture and history of Thailand and its neighbours even when such scholarship offers diverse perspectives. I am grateful to Andrew Turton for inviting me to present this paper at the session of the conference on 'Minorities within Tai/Thai Political Systems: Historical and Theoretical Perspectives' and to Mayoury Ngaosyvathn for her insightful response to the paper at the session.

2 This chapter is part of a larger project concerned with the relationship between ethnic identity and national culture as manifest among Tai-speaking peoples in South East Asia (see Keyes 1992, 1993, 1994).

3 I follow conventions, first devised by French scholars, in transliterating Lao names and words. I do so in part in order to signal that there are differences between Thai and Lao languages and written discourses.

4 On Thai views of this resettlement, see Mom Amorawong Wicit (M.R.W. Pathom Khanecon (1963 [1915]) and Toem Wiphakphacanakit ('Toem Singhatsathit') (1956 and 1970). Also see Koizumi (1992) and Snit Smuckarn and Breazeale (1988).

5 I recognize I am ignoring other French narratives which tended to orientalize and eroticize the Lao. Jean Ajalbert ('de l'Académie Goncourt')'s *Sao Van Di* (1922), a popular romance, was one of the first of such narratives. My concern here is with the development of a discourse about the Lao nation rather than with French colonial discourse about Laos and the Lao.

6 I have discussed some of these leaders in my *Isan* monograph (see Keyes 1967: 27–33). I now realize that more research is needed on those who became teachers as well as politicians in the 1930s to understand fully the evolution of both Lao nationalism and Isan ethno-regionalism.

7 I first became aware of the significance of Princess Sirindhorn's visit to Laos when I was in Vientiane in October 1990 to lay the groundwork for research I was to carry out in Laos in 1991. One evening I watched on video in the home of Lao friends a Thai-made documentary of the Princess's visit. Since my research project involved inquiry into how Lao national culture had been shaped and promoted since the creation of the Lao People's Democratic Republic in 1975, I was fascinated to see that Princess Sirindhorn's journey had been organized around visits to monuments and places considered to belong to the Lao national heritage. My interest was further piqued when the Princess's book was published in late 1990. I used the book, which I gave to several people in Laos in 1991, as an opening for asking Lao who had been involved in her visit about the significance of the trip.

8 I learned in Laos that Princess Sirindhorn heard this phrase from Thongsa Sayavongkhamdy, a Lao archaeologist who shortly before her visit had become the Director of the Lao Department of Museums and Archaeology in the Ministry of Information and Culture. The title of her book is echoed, whether consciously or not I do not know, by that of another recent book by a Thai visitor to Laos *Boeng Lao: Lao mai mi arai tae mi arai* (Looking at Laos: the Lao have nothing, but have something) (Maitri Limpichat 1989).

9 In February 1993 I was with a tour group in Luang Prabang and participated in a *basi sukhuan* rite which immediately followed one performed for another group. The rituals for tourists are much attenuated compared to traditional performances. The person (or persons) whose essence is to be called sits with legs folded in front of sweet-smelling flower blossoms arranged in a tiered structure (the *basi* proper) on a silver or bronze footed-tray. On the tray or nearby are foods and liquor which are also enticements to the essence. A ritual specialist – often an ex-monk, but never an active monk – uses ancient formulae which call upon deities of the Hindu pantheon to assist in making the event auspicious and then calls the essence itself with pleasant words. When the ritual specialist finishes chanting, he and guests approach the *basi*, remove from it cotton threads, and tie these round the wrists of the recipient(s) to secure the essence.

10 Such is evident, for example, in a recent book, *Cak Luang Prabang thung Wiangcan* (From Luang Prabang to Vientiane) by M.L. Sarasawat Suksawat, an art historian at Chiang Mai University (1992). Mom Luang Sarasawat was a member of a group organized by Chiang Mai University library which visited Laos in late October and early November 1990.

11 In 1991 when I first visited the royal palace/museum in Luang Prabang, I was told by a guide that nothing was known about the royal family since they had been sent to the camp. The same guide repeated the same story when asked by members of a

tour group which I was accompanying in early 1993. The national guide from Vientiane, however, said that he thought the King and Queen were dead. Stuart-Fox and Kooyman (1992: 125, 167) in their *Historical Dictionary of Laos* record that King Savang Vatthana 'is reported to have died of natural causes (in Vieng Say) in or about 1979' and Prince Savang Vong 'is believed to have died of malaria, though this has never been officially confirmed'.

12 Teh denies ever making the statement. It seems that another pop-singer may have been the source of the comment even though it was ascribed to Teh.

References

Ajalbert, Jean (1922), *Sao Van Di*, Paris: Les Editions G. Crès.

Amorawong Wicit, Mom (M.R.W. Pathom Khanecon), comp. 1963 [1915], 'Phongsawadan huamuang monthon Isan' (Chronicle of the domains of Isan circle), in *Prachum phonsawadan phak thi 4 lae prawat thongthi cangwat Mahasarakham* (Collected Chronicles Part 4 and History of Mahasarakham), Mahasarakham, Published on the Occasion of the Royal Cremation of Phra Sarakhammuni, 1963, (First published in Bangkok on the occasion of the cremation of Phraya Sisamruat, 2458 [1915].)

Anderson, Benedict (1991), *Imagined Communities: Reflections on the Origin and Spread of Nationalism*, revised edition, London and New York: Verso.

Bhabha, Homi K., ed. (1990), *Nation and Narration*, London and New York: Routledge.

Chagnon, Jacqui, and Roger Rumpf (1982), 'Education: the Prerequisite to Change in Laos', in Martin Stuart-Fox (ed.), *Contemporary Laos: Studies in the Politics and Society of the Lao People's Democratic Republic*, New York: St. Martin's Press, 163–80.

Coast, John (1953), *Some Aspects of Siamese Politics*, New York: Institute of Pacific Relations.

Cotmaihet ruang prap khabot wiangchan (Documents conerning the suppression of the Vientiane Revolt) (1926), distributed on the occasion of a Royal Kathin offering presented by Prince Nakon Sawan Woraphinit at Wat Ratchapradit, Wat Thepsirintharawat, Wat Makut Kasatriyaram, 2469.

Damrong Rajanubhab, Prince (1971) [1935], Nithan boran khadi (Historical anecdotes). Bangkok: Phrae Phithaya.

Gunn, Geoffrey (1988), *Political Struggles in Laos (1930–1954)*, Bangkok: Editions Duang Kamol.

—— (1990a), *Rebellion in Laos: Peasants and Politics in a Colonial Backwater*, Boulder, Colorado: Westview.

—— (1990b), 'Laos in 1989: Quiet Revolution in the Marketplace', *Asian Survey*, 30.1:81–7.

Hobsbawm, Eric, and Terence Ranger, (eds.) (1983), *The Invention of Tradition*, Cambridge: Cambridge University Press.

Ishii, Yoneo (1975), 'A Note on Buddhistic Millenarian Revolts in Northeastern Siam', *Journal of Southeast Asian Studies*, 6.2:121–6.

Jiraporn Witayasakpan (1992), 'Nationalism and the Transformation of Aesthetic Concepts: Theatre in Thailand during the Phibun Period', Ph.D. thesis, Cornell University.

Jit Phumisak (1976), *Khwampenma khong kham sayam thai lao lae khom lae laksana thangkansangkhom khong chüchat* [Etymology of the terms Siam, Thai, Lao and Khom, and the social characteristics of ethnonyms], Bangkok: Social Sciences Association of Thailand.

Keyes, Charles F. (1966a), 'Peasant and Nation: a Thai-Lao Village in a Thai State', Ph.D. dissertation, Cornell University.

—— (1966b), 'Ethnic Identity and Loyalty of Villagers in Northeastern Thailand', *Asian Survey*, 6.7:362–9.

—— (1967), *Isan: Regionalism in Northeastern Thailand*, Ithaca, N.Y.: Cornell University Southeast Asia Program (Data Paper No. 65).

—— (1977), 'Millennialism, Theravada Buddhism, and Thai Society', *Journal of Asian Studies*, 36.2:283–302.

—— (1991), 'The Proposed World of the School: Thai Villagers Entry into a Bureaucratic State System', in Charles F. Keyes (ed.), *Reshaping Local Worlds: Rural Education and Cultural Change in Southeast Asia*, New Haven: Yale University Southeast Asian Studies, 87–138.

—— (1992), 'Who Are the Lue Revisited? Ethnic Identity in Laos, Thailand, and China', Cambridge, Massachussetts: Massachussetts Institute of Technology, The Center for International Studies, Working Paper.

—— (1993), 'Who Are the Tai? Reflections on the Invention of Local, Ethnic and National Identities', Paper prepared for 'Seminar on the State of Knowledge and Directions of Research on Tai Culture', sponsored by the Office of the National Culture Commission, Bangkok, Thailand, September 10–13.

—— (1994), 'The Nation-State and the Politics of Indigenous Minorities: Reflections on Ethnic Insurgency in Burma', Paper prepared for conference on 'Tribal Minorities and the State', organized by the Henry Frank Guggenheim Foundation, Istanbul, February.

—— (1995), 'Hegemony and Resistance in Northeastern Thailand', in Volker Grabovsky (ed.), *Regions and National Integration in Thailand 1892–1992*, Wiesbaden: Harrassowitz, 154–182.

Koizumi, Junko (1992), 'The Commutation of *Suai* from Northeast Siam in the Middle of the Nineteenth Century', *Journal of Southeast Asian Studies*, 23.2: 276–307.

Le Boulanger, Paul (1931), *Histoire du Laos Français*, Paris: Plon, (reprinted, Farnborough, England: Gregg International, 1969.)

Maitri Limpichat (1989), *Boeng Lao: Lao mai mi arai tae mi arai* (Looking at Laos: the Lao have nothing, but have something), Bangkok: S.Ph. Ton, 2532.

Mayoury Ngaosyvathn (1990), 'Individual Soul, National Identity: the *Baci-Sou Khuan* of the Lao', *Sojourn*, 5.2:283–307.

Mayoury Ngaosyvathn and Pheuiphanh Ngaosyvathn (1988), *Cao Anu, 1767–1829: Pasason Lao lae asiakane (luang kao, panha mai)* (Cao Anu, 1767–1829: The Lao People and Southeast Asia (Old story, new meaning)), Vientiane: Samnakphim camnai S. P. P. Lao.

—— (1988), 'Cao Anu: ruang kao panha mai' (Cao Anu: old story, new meaning), *Sinlapawatthanatham*, Art and Culture, Bangkok, 9.11:58–74, 2531.

—— (1989), 'Lao Historiography and Historians: Case Study of the War Between Bangkok and the Lao in 1827', *Journal of Southeast Asian Studies*, 20.1:55–69.

'Mitrasamphan' (n.d.) [1988], *Phinong Thai-Lao? saphap khwampenma khong khwamsamphan Thai-Lao* (Are Thai and Lao Siblings: Evolving Character of Thai-Lao Relations), Bangkok: S.Ph. Natrisat.

The Nation, Bangkok.

Nikisch, Larry A. (1989), 'Thailand in 1988: the Economic Surge', *Asian Survey*, 29.2:165–73.

Pavie, Auguste (1898–1919), *Mission Pavie en Indochine, 1879–1895*, 11 vols, Paris: Leroux.

—— (1942), *A la conquête des coeurs: Le Pays des millions d'éléphants*, Paris: Presses Universitaires de France.

Pheuiphanh Ngaosyvathn (1985), 'Thai-Lao Relations: a Lao View', *Asian Survey,* 12:1242–59.

Sarasin Viraphol (1985), 'Reflections on Thai-Lao Relations', *Asian Survey,* 12:1260–76.

Sarasawat Suksawat, M. L. (1992), *Cak Luang Prabang thung Wiangcan* (From Luang Prabang to Vientiane), Bangkok: S.Ph. Muang Boran, 2535.

Sirindhorn, HRH Princess (Somdet Phra Thepratanaratchasuda Sayamboromratch-akumari) 1982. *Thotsabarami nai phutthasatsana therawat* (The ten virtues in Theravada Buddhism), Bangkok: Mahamakutratchawithayalai, 2525.

—— (1990), *Boeng bo than boeng bo mot* (Too little time, can't see everything), Bangkok: Munnitthi Somdet Phrathep Rattanaratchasuda, 2533.

Snit Smuckarn and Kennon Breazeale (1988), *A Culture in Search of Survival: the Phuan of Thailand and Laos*, New Haven: Yale University Southeast Asia Studies, Monograph Series 31.

Stowe, Judith A. (1991), *Siam Becomes Thailand: a Story of Intrigue*, Honolulu: University of Hawaii Press.

Stuart-Fox, Martin (1989), 'Laos in 1988: in Pursuit of New Directions', *Asian Survey,* 29.1:81–8.

Stuart-Fox, Martin and Mary Kooyman (1992), *Historical Dictionary of Laos*. Metuchen, N. J.: The Scarecrow Press, Asian Historical Dictionaries, no. 6.

Tej Bunnag (1967), 'Khabot phu mi bun phak Isan R.S. 121' (Millenarian revolt in northeastern Thailand, 1902), *Sangkhomsat parithat* (Social Science Review), 5.1:78–86.

Thak Chaloemtiarana (1979), *Thailand: The Politics of Despotic Paternalism*, Bangkok: Social Science Association of Thailand and Thai Khadi Institute, Thammasat University.

Thongsa Sayavongkhamdy, Bounkong Thongsavat, Dèng Phonsavan, Sounet Phothi-san, Singthong Singthapangna, Viengvijit Sutthidet, (comp.) (1989), *Pawatsat Lao, lem III: 1893 thung pacuban* (History of Laos, Vol. 3: 1893 to the Present), Vientiane: Kasuang suksa lae kila, sathaban khonkhua withañasat sangkhom (Ministry of Education and Sports, Social Science Research Institute).

'3349' (1978), *Iron Man of Laos: Prince Phetsarath Ratanvongsa*, John B. Murdoch (transl.) David K. Wyatt (ed.), Ithaca, N.Y.: Cornell University, Southeast Asia Program, Data Paper No. 110.

Toem Wiphakphacanakit ('Toem Singhatsathit') (1956), *Fang khwa Maenam Khong* (Right Bank of the Mekhong), 2 vols., Bangkok: Samnakphim Khlang Witthaya.

—— (1970), *Prawatsat Isan* (History of Isan), Bangkok: Samnakphim samakhom sangkhomsat haeng prathet thai (Social Science Association of Thailand Press).

Vella, Walter F. (1957), *Siam under Rama III, 1824–1851*, Locust Valley, N.Y.: J. J. Augustin, Association for Asian Studies Monographs, IV.

Wyatt, David K. (1963), 'Siam and Laos 1767–1827', *Journal of Southeast Asian History,* 4.2:13–32.

—— (1984), *Thailand. A Short History,* New Haven: Yale University Press.

Yothong Thapthiomai (1988), *3,000 lan bat thi Ban Rom Klao: buang lang khwam khat yaeng rawang Thai-Lao* (Three billion baht at Ban Rom Klao: background to the Thai-Lao conflict), Bangkok: Klet Thai, 2531.

Chapter Ten

Nationalities Policy in Modern Laos

Igor Kossikov

A Poly-ethnic Population

The aim of this chapter is to analyse the present national (ethnic) policy of the Lao government and its influence on the ethnic situation in the country.

The territory of Laos, the Lao People's Democratic Republic (LPDR), covers 236,800 square kilometres. Its population was officially estimated in the middle of 1989 at 4,053 million persons (*khomun sathiti tonto*, 1990: 14). Hence its average population density was about 17 per square kilometre. In 1989, the population of the LPDR consisted of 1986 million male (49 per cent) and 2067 million female persons (51 per cent) (ibid.). The level of infant mortality was relatively high – about 118 (down to 106 in 1992 (Denisovitch 1993b: 26)) per 1,000 infants under one year. In spite of the lowering of the general mortality rate from 24 to 16.6 per 1,000 among children under five in recent years, at 156 per 1,000 it is still one of the highest in Asian countries (though lower than Cambodia). Average life-expectancy is 50 years. Despite all these unfavourable demographic indicators, the population of the LPDR is growing at an average of about 2 per cent a year. The population is distributed extremely unevenly. A considerable portion of the population is concentrated in the valleys of the Mekong and its tributaries along the Thai border. The rest of the territory is sparsely populated, especially in the mountainous northern provinces of the country. Vast areas in eastern Laos became depopulated as a result of the Indo-China wars.

Laos is a poly-ethnic state with a complex and as yet poorly studied ethnic composition. One of the major features of the ethnic composition of Laos is the absence of any ethnic groups whose entire population lives within the borders of Laos. There is not a single ethnic group in Laos whose population does not extend to neighbouring Indochinese countries. According to different estimates, Laos is populated by some 30 to 70

Plate 17. 'Convoi de sauvages esclaves'

various ethnic groups [the author's original term 'ethnos' (plural 'ethnoses') has been changed throughout to 'ethnic group', despite a certain advantage in the less familiar term Ed.]. From our own investigation, Egorunin and I estimate the number of the ethnic groups residing in Laos to be about 60 (Kossikov and Egorunin 1991: 30–31).

The recent population census (1985) failed to determine the number of ethnic groups in Laos. Data on the ethnic composition of the country's population have not as yet been made public. According to the information collected by the authors, official Lao investigators received 820 different names in response to questions about ethnic affiliation. The great majority of these responses were not designations of what are conventionally regarded as ethnic entities (i.e. 'ethnonyms'). Persons being questioned tended to identify their ethnic affiliation with the name of their tribe [e.g. local ethnic sub-group, clan etc. Ed.], their kin, the name of their settlement or place of residence, or some other name. Even if we ignore the appropriateness of the questions, we can see that the majority of respondents gave their ethnic affiliation by referring to local entities, which in many cases did not coincide with established ethnic entities. This indicates a weak ethnic consciousness of a considerable part of the population of Laos. The data collected during the census contrasts with the official policy of rapid consolidation of all the inhabitants of Laos into a single indivisible state entity. More than 800 registered entities have been 'united', conceptually and even constitutionally, first into 210, and then into 47 entities. Despite a different methodology, this latter figure is close to the estimated number of 60 ethnic groups referred to above (Kossikov and Egorunin 1991). In spite of the semi-secret character of these facts, they are well known to the majority of researchers on Laos. There is also one significant but little-known fact which eloquently characterizes the complexity of ethnic processes in modern Laos: about 30 per cent of the registered residents of the capital Vientiane refused to reply, or found difficulty in identifying their ethnic affiliation (nationality).

According to the classification of linguistic groups adopted in Russian (formerly Soviet) ethnology, the population of Laos can be classified in three main linguistic groups (Paratai, Austroasiatic, and Sino-Tibetan) embracing seven linguistic sub-sections.The Paratai linguistic family is represented by the Tai group; the Austroasiatic by the northern (Palaung-Wa), the southeastern (Mon-Khmer), the Viet-Muong, and the Miao-Yao groups; the Sino-Tibetan by the central and Chinese groups.

1. The majority of the population of Laos belongs to the Tai group of the <u>Paratai linguistic family</u>. The most numerous, and the politically and economically most developed ethnic group within that language group is Lao. According to the 1985 census, the number of Lao is 1.8 million (50.3 per cent of the country's population). Other Tai entities of Laos

are: Lue (102,700), Yuan (33,000), Phuon (58,000), Tai (Phuthai, 440,000), comprising Tai Dam, Tai Deng, Tai Khao, Phuthai, and others, Yang, Sek, Thai Phak, Thai Khoen, and Shan. Among Tai-speaking groups of Laos there are also immigrants from Thailand, including Tai (Siamese) and Lao from the northeast of Thailand, Lao Isan or Khon Isan.

2. The Austroasiatic linguistic family in Laos includes about forty different peoples belonging to four ethno-linguistic groups:

   (a) *The Palaung-Wa group* comprises Khmu (390,000), Lamet (14,000), Thin (14,000), Xingmul, Bit (Khbit).

   (b) *The Mon-Khmer group* in Laos is represented by twenty small peoples residing both in the North and the South of the country. The problem of classifying the Mon-Khmer ethnic groups of Laos is far from resolved due to insufficient information. Sometimes researchers divide them into a few conditional sub-groups. According to the scheme suggested by Vietnamese researcher Ngo Duc Thinh (Malyje narody Indokitaja 1983: 99), there are the northern sub-group, including Samtau, Doi, and Phong (Samtau and Doi are considered by some researchers to be related to the Palaung-Wa), the Katu-Bru sub-group, including Katang, Mangcong, Suai, Katu (Khatu, Ktu), Chaly, Taoi, Pako, Negh, Talieng, and some others, and the Laven-Brao sub-group (Laven, Lave (Brao), Alak, Niaheun (Yaheng, Niahenh), Cheng (Chenh), Oy, Sapuan). In this scheme, representatives of the Sedang people in Laos belong to the Bahnar-Mnong sub-group. The Mon-Khmer group of Laos also includes Khmer or Cambodians, compactly residing in the southern provinces of Laos. The smallest Mon-Khmer ethnic group in Laos is the Yumbri who number 24 persons.

   (c) For a long time no researchers mentioned the existence of *Viet-Muong-speaking groups* on the territory of Laos (except Vietnamese residents in the towns). Investigations of isolated groups in inaccessible regions along both sides of the Vietnamese-Lao border conducted by Vietnamese ethnologists, revealed the existence of several small ethnic entities. According to the Vietnamese researchers, they belong to the Viet-Muong linguistic group. So the Viet-Muong population of Laos includes the Tum (Vietnamese designation Tho) divided into Poong, Danlai, Maka, and Lyha groups; Muongs (at least 2,000); Nguon (1,000) an ethnic sub-division of Viet (Vietnamese); and a very small number of Kri (Vietnamese designation Chut). There is a sizeable ethnic Vietnamese population in Lao towns (according to Lao statisticians about 18,000; we estimate the actual number to be much higher).

   (d) *The Miao-Yao group* in Laos includes Hmong (Miao, Meo, 231,000), and Mien (Yao, 18,000).

3. The Sino-Tibetan linguistic family is represented in Laos by members of two linguistic groups, Central (previously Tibeto-Burman) and Chinese (Sinitic).

    (a) *The Central group* includes Akha (Ko, 58,500), Phunoi (23,000), and Lahu (designated in Laos by two names Musoe and Kui). There are also representatives of Sila, Lolo, and Hani.

    (b) *The Chinese (Sinitic) group* includes Chinese-speaking Ho (Haw) or highland Chinese (6,400) and ethnic Chinese (6,800) in towns. Amongst the latter are Cantonese, Yunnanese, Hainanese, Swatow, and Hakka.

The 'Trinomial Classification'

The official classification of ethnic groups living in Laos adopted by the LPDR government ignores ethnolinguistic principles, but utilizes, selectively and inconsistently, several distinct factors such as ethnogenesis. According to the official conception, the main criteria for the formation of ethnic entities were common geographical living conditions, similar economic and cultural patterns, levels of social development, and so on. Such an approach resulted in a so-called trinominal conception of the ethnic composition of the country's population. According to this conception, the population of Laos divides into three big 'national groups' that are sometimes called 'nations', 'nationalities', even 'ethno-zone entities' (Ngo Duc Thinh 1980; though this latter term appeared only in a few publications in Russian). These are: Lao Lum (lowland or valley Lao), Lao Thoeng (Lao of the foothills or mountain slopes) and Lao Sung (highland Lao). This conception was elaborated in the mid-1940s as an ideological basis for the policy of integration of all ethnic groups residing in Laos into a single ethnic entity, or nation (the designation for this entity in Russian ethnology is 'meta-ethnic entity'). The founders of this conception were the leaders of the first Lao independence movement Lao Itsala (Lao Issara or Free Lao). It is striking that in this trinominal classification the initial name 'Lao' is common to all three groups. Such ethnonymic unification had a distinct political orientation. It expressed the subjective desire of the originators to emphasize the unification of different ethnic groups in a single state formation. It was also intended to inculcate the idea of unity into the consciousness of the various ethnic groups.

One of the basic ideas of this classification consisted in a rather arbitrary amalgamation of all the Tai-speaking groups of the country into a single entity of Lao Lum. It could be argued that all Tai-speaking peoples are linked by common lineage. Furthermore, they are close to each other linguistically, culturally, in morals, and in manners. But according to other criteria of the trinominal classification, such as common geographical living conditions, and similar economic patterns and so on, such an amalgamation would be inaccurate. A certain tension between Lao and numerically smaller Tai-speaking peoples should also be mentioned. This tension was provoked principally by the dependence of these Tai-speaking groups on the Lao in a hierarchical ethnic system which was formed long ago. Many researchers have noted the scornful attitude of Lao to ethnically closely related, smaller groups of people, perceived to be more archaic. They have recorded that the latter considered themselves to be discriminated against, notwithstanding that some of their kinsmen held government posts.

It seems that amalgamation of all Tai-speaking peoples within the Lao Lum group had two main goals. First, it was directed at rapid consolidation of all these peoples into a single ethnic entity, which would facilitate their absorption by the more numerous Lao. The second goal was to conceal the true number of population considering themselves Lao and thus substantiate ethnic Lao political domination in the state that carries its name. It is no secret that Lao constitute only about a half of the inhabitants of Laos. Amalgamation of groups of the Paratai linguistic family into a single entity in fact possessing ethnic markers of only one Tai-speaking group, namely the Lao, created the illusion of an ethnic majority in Laos. This very illusion justified the consolidation of state power in the hands of Lao. Under such conditions, members of Mon-Khmer, Miao-Yao, and other linguistic groups of Laos become ethnic minorities, with the political, legal, and social consequences that are implied by minority status. Practical implementation of the trinominal classification thus restricted the question to the recognition of the rights of ethnic minorities by the state, while the problem of ensuring real equality for all peoples of Laos was ignored.

This complete ignorance of the ethnic features of non-Tai ethnic groups was further manifested by the arbitrary amalgamation of peoples of the Miao-Yao group of the Austroasiatic linguistic family and Chinese and Central (Tibeto-Burman) groups of the Sino-Tibetan linguistic family into the Lao Sung group, and the peoples of Mon-Khmer, Palaung-Wa, and Viet-Muong groups of the Austroasiatic family into the Lao Thoeng group. In all fairness it should be mentioned that Tai-speaking groups themselves gained some advantages from being included in the Lao Lum group.

In due course the Lao by and large succeeded in establishing their domination of the Lao state, although initially their claims to supremacy were often disputed by representatives of other ethnic groups. After French withdrawal from Indo-China, the disintegration of Laos into small states headed by ethnic and regional chiefs, was imminently possible. Nevertheless, the Lao authorities eventually managed to inculcate the basic ideas of the trinominal classification into the minds of many of the people of Laos, along with a sense of belonging to one of its national groups. This notion applies mainly to the town-dwellers and especially to the ethnic Lao themselves. The trinominal conception excludes so-called non-indigenous (alien) residents of Laos: Chinese, Vietnamese (Viets), and migrants from Thailand.

Nationalities Policy in Practice after 1975

The accession to power of the People's Revolutionary Party of Laos (the PRPL) and the creation of the LPDR in 1975, were implicitly apprehended as a success of left-oriented, marxist-leninist forces. The Moscow October (1976) Plenum of the CPSU Central Committee actually proclaimed Laos to be a member of 'the fraternal family of socialist states'. However, in reality, the PRPL-LPDR leadership, which was dominated by the Lao in 1975 (a considerable number originating from the traditional Lao élite), consisted of adherents of a policy of building a Lao nation-state. In many respects their aims resembled those of the first Lao national movement Lao Itsala, which had proclaimed the independence of Laos in October 1945. Socialist rhetoric played an important, but superficial role for the new regime. It fulfilled a double task: on the one hand it assured assistance from states with a socialist ideology, while on the other, marxism-leninism, although obscure not only to the majority of the people of Laos but also to an overwhelming majority of the ruling party members and even to many of the PRPL cadres, performed the role of a coherent belief system uniting the heterogeneous population of the country. The bureaucratic system of state government under the guidance of a ruling party, enabled the PRPL-LPDR leadership to create a powerful centralized state, controlling the entire territory of Lao, all the spheres of Lao society, and all its ethnic groups. Socialist slogans, propagation of revolutionary asceticism, flat condemnation of Western values, patriotism, and the popularization of the idea of an 'indivisible, independent and prosperous Laos' became important components of official PRPL-LPDR ideology. Another significant aspect was 'the development of fine national traditions', which meant following the customs and rites of folk Buddhism as widely practised. As national policy, the PRPL-LPDR leadership declared such postulates as 'friendship of peoples', 'multinational Lao people', etc. But at the same time they proceeded to reinforce the conception of 'Lao national entity', 'a single Lao nation'.

Under the socialist slogans, the national policy of the PRPL-LPDR leadership was an attempt to accomplish rapid cultural and ethnic assimilation of the whole non-Lao population of the country, that is, to realize an objective that none of the previous rulers of Laos could realize. In the towns this objective was implemented by means of nationalization of property aimed at appropriating the property of so-called 'alien residents' (Chinese, Vietnamese, Europeans, and others). In the countryside this was achieved by means of collectivization. Undoubtedly these two large-scale actions were also aimed at taking control of that part of the population of the ethnically Lao proper which had been living in the former Royal Government zone. Nationalization, collectivization, and indeed the whole process of establishing the PRPL regime, were accompanied by acts of force by the authorities, suppression of opponents of PRPL rule, and numerous conflicts and clashes of an ethnic or class nature.

The policy of the LPDR authorities provoked resistance amongst different strata of Lao society, including a number of smaller ethnic groups. But the new government considered the Hmong, a people noted for their yearning for independence, to be their main antagonists. Long before the official abolition of the monarchy, Lao communists (then the Patriotic Front of Laos, PFL) began to establish control over Hmong districts, formerly under the control of the anti-communist leader of the Hmong in Laos, General Vang Pao. The People's Liberation Army of Laos (PLAL) units were stationed in Hmong settlements. According to a Lao researcher of Hmong origin, Yang Dao, in May 1975 the PFL-controlled information agency Khaosan Pathet Lao (KPL) reported the necessity of the total eradication of the Meo minority (Downing and Olney 1982: 13). After the shooting of participants in a peaceful march of 40,000 Hmong in Vientiane by PFL soldiers on 29 May 1975, thousands of Hmong fled from Laos to Thailand, hundreds of them perishing on the way. At the end of 1975, Hmong extended organized resistance to the new authorities of Laos. When, during a skirmish with PLAL men, some Hmong civilians were killed, the Hmong rose in rebellion in the vicinity of the Phu Bia mountain range. Rebellion then spread throughout the countryside populated by Hmong to the South of the Plain of Jars.

Soon after, some members of the Khmu also rebelled. At the end of the 1970s and the beginning of the 1980s, a real war was waged in Laos between the LPDR government, assisted by 17,000 members of a Vietnamese expeditionary force, and an insurgent movement of Hmong, Khmu, and some others. Unable rapidly to suppress the uprising, Lao and Vietnamese troops unleashed large-scale terror against the civilian population, using heavy artillery and aircraft, often dropping napalm, and even using chemical weapons. This caused considerable protest throughout the world. By dint of such measures, the LPDR authorities managed to suppress the activities of the Hmong insurgent movement by the middle of the 1980s. The Hmong, who had suffered more than other ethnic groups of Laos in the second Indo-China war, were once again subject to heavy losses. According to a statement by Vang Pao (possibly exaggerated), during the period 1975–78 alone, 50,000 Hmong died as a result of chemical weapons used against them, and another 45,000 died from starvation and various diseases, or were shot down in attempts to flee to Thailand (Stuart-Fox 1982: 214).

Tragic events at the end of the 1970s and the beginning of the 1980s led about one-third of the Hmong, some 100,000 (Downing and Olney, 1982: 18) of the original 293,000 (Stuart-Fox, 1982: 199), to flee the country. From the end of 1980, Hmong who had supported the Lao left-wing in the civil war, or had initially collaborated with the LPDR authorities, began to appear amongst the mass of refugees fleeing from Laos. The mass flight of Hmong from Laos compelled foreign countries – first of all the United States – to receive several tens of thousands of Hmong refugees together with hundreds of thousands of other Indochinese refugees. In 1985 alone the US government allowed 138,000 refugees from Laos to resettle in the USA (*Countries of the World* 1989: 783). The campaign of resettling Hmong in the West led to the formation of a considerable Hmong diaspora, which began to influence Hmong people remaining in Laos. At the beginning of the 1980s, 40,000–50,000 Hmong resettled in the USA, some 6,000–8,000 in France, 1,000 in French Guiana, and over 2,000 in Canada and Australia. Some Hmong were resettled in other countries, for example, the People's Republic of China. Subsequently the number of Hmong leaving Laos continued to increase.

As Hmong resistance to the LPDR authorities was the most active, it became widely known. At the same time, all the information about the real situation in the country was, as a rule, painstakingly concealed by the PRPL-LPDR leadership. Nevertheless, there have been other reports about conflicts between smaller ethnic groups and the new authorities. In 1982–83 the Akha people in the North-East of the country were in a state of ferment. Considerable unrest was to be observed after PRPL seizure of power in areas populated by Lue, and so on.

Communities of so-called non-indigenous residents, concentrated for the most part in the towns and virtually controlling the economic system of Laos, were another obstacle to the establishment of PRPL control. Thus the campaign 'for the re-organization of the private sector of the national economy' was directed at the suppression of these ethnic groups. The property of many 'persons of alien nationalities' was nationalized, and repressive measures of various kinds were taken against them. The Chinese community of Laos in particular suffered. According to unofficial information, some of its leaders (for example, the head of the Chinese Association of Vientiane, Tang Kim Chia) were sent to special 're-education' camps in remote districts of Laos, intended for the opponents of the PRPL-LPDR regime. Persecution of the so-called 'non-indigenous population' of Laos forced them to leave the country in great numbers. At the beginning of the 1980s, the number of Chinese was reduced from 40,000 to about 10,000, Vietnamese from 40,000 to 15,000, and the Europeans abandoned Laos completely. Even at the end of the 1980s, the once populous and boisterous Chinese quarter of Vientiane appeared to be practically deserted.

Not only the non-Lao population of Laos, but also almost all inhabitants of the country were subjected to terror and suppression by the PRPL–LPDR regime. Dread of the oppressive tyranny of the new authorities, deterioration of the economic situation, and a number of other reasons provoked a mass flight of people of all ethnic origins from their country. From April 1975 until May 1983, about 350,000 people, almost one-tenth of the population, left Laos. Among them were reported to be 143,000 representatives of smaller ethnic groups (Brown and Zasloff 1985: 189; Zasloff and Brown 1982: 221–22).

Although Buddhism was at first suppressed, it was eventually adopted as the 'state religion', under the firm control of the Party and the government. Although LPDR officials called themselves atheists, they began to promote Buddhism throughout the country. Little by little, leaders of the Party and the state began to participate in official religious ceremonies as had the monarchs of previous times. At the same time, all other worship was declared to be 'superstition and prejudice', stigmatized as reactionary, and persecuted. Those who practised such worship were subject to various penalties.

Finally, the consolidation of the whole population into a single meta-ethnic state was accelerated by the ubiquitous dissemination of the Lao language. As far back as 1956, the Lao language had been declared the official language of the former kingdom by the Royal Government of Laos. LPDR authorities also proclaimed Lao to be the state language, the language of intercourse among all the nationalities of the country. Promises 'to assist some nationalities in the perfection of their scripts' contained in the PFL Twelve-Point Programme (1968) had not, as yet, been realized. In one of the rare official documents on national policy, Kaysone Phomvihan's comments on the Resolution of the Politburo of the PRPL Central Committee noted that the method of making scripts for smaller ethnic groups should take into consideration both general and particular interests. It was stressed that activities in this field should not lead to the isolation of peoples (Kaysone Phomvihan 1982: 65–66). Setting up national schools using the languages of smaller ethnic groups was not even mentioned. PRPL leaders insisted that there was a number of objective obstacles to the development of indigenous languages, namely, 'the absence of the necessary material base', 'small population size of ethnic groups', 'shortage of competent personnel' etc. The activities of the PRPL–LPDR leadership after 1975 contrasted distinctly with PFL policies during the war, when representatives of smaller ethnic groups could learn their own languages. There were attempts to create original scripts for some indigenous languages. For example, a Hmong script was created based on the Lao alphabet.

Shortage of financial means, and perhaps reluctance to procure them, may explain the fact that other PFL promises to assist smaller ethnic groups actively in economic development, in education, and in improving welfare standards, remained unrealized. Lao customs and traditional culture became compulsory for everyone. Representatives of central and local authorities and senior Party cadres, the majority of whom were ethnic Lao, actively began to promote Lao customs throughout the country. Regardless of official slogans concerning the preservation of other ethnic traditions and culture, they were, in fact, considered 'retrograde and reactionary'. Those who adhered to them were persecuted. Every expression of ethnic originality was regarded as 'counter-revolutionary activity', and those who disagreed with compulsory 'Lao-ization' were subject to repressive measures.

Continuing 'Meta-ethnic' Nationalities Policies

The sharp deterioration of the socio-economic situation in the country, and the ensuing drop in the standard of living even in comparison with the war period, provoked the mass flight abroad which we have documented. The negative effect of suppression compelled the PRPL-LPDR leadership to correct its political course at the beginning of the 1980s. It virtually abandoned collectivization, and generally alleviated its policy towards the people. Following mass migration of the opponents of the regime, and punitive actions of government army and Vietnamese troops, the rebel movement in Laos also abated in the mid-1980s. This played an important role in changing PRPL-LPDR policy. The crisis and subsequent total breakdown of the world socialist system, and the dramatic disintegration of the Soviet Union, caused a sharp reduction and then the complete suspension of all kinds of aid to the PRPL-LPDR regime from recent allies. This forced the leadership to change the basic orientations of its policies. Though nominally the PRPL still upholds the principles of marxism-leninism, its leaders officially admitted that building socialism without passing through a capitalist stage of development had not as yet been fully accomplished. They declared that the building of socialism should be preceded by a 'quite long' transitional period. An active policy of economic liberalization was initiated, as the PRPL recognized the necessary co-existence of all sectors of the national economy. They have declared economic activities of various kinds to be completely free. The LPDR took steps towards the normalization of relations with China, Thailand, and various Western countries in order to attract foreign investment and aid to Laos.

At the same time, the political course of rapid, forced consolidation of a meta-ethnic entity within the Lao state remained unchanged. Indeed, propaganda concerning the unity of a 'multi-national Laotian people', 'a single Lao nation' intensified. At present, some Lao theorists propose to abandon the trinominal conception that had already fulfilled its purpose, and to substitute it with the conception of the Lao nation (in this intended sense I shall from now on use the term 'Laotian', reserving 'Lao' for 'ethnic Lao'). Lao culture and customs are inculcated as obligatory as before. For eighteen years the policy of active exclusion of representatives of non-Lao ethnicities from political and economic spheres of Laotian society has ensured that the Lao have acquired virtually unlimited access to power. Even in areas with small Lao populations, they hold leading government posts with few exceptions. At the national level, they enjoy complete control. At the beginning of the 1990s, only two persons of non-Lao origin were members of the Politburo of the PRPL Central Committee. Two representatives of smaller ethnic groups [the author's original 'minor ethnoses' has been rendered 'smaller ethnic group's for the most part, but from here on 'ethnic minority' will be used Ed.] participated in the work of the LPDR government (the Minister for Internal Affairs and the President of the State Bank). It should be mentioned that some representatives of ethnic minorities do work in the central bodies of the Party and the state. At the same time, assimilation within the ethnic Lao majority and renunciation of ethnic origin were indispensable conditions for obtaining access to central power in Laos. Children of the numerically small ethnic minorities residing in larger towns, as a rule already consider themselves to be 'Lao' ('Laotian' in the usage employed here) that is to say members of the entity that the LPDR authorities are trying to create. These young people avoid contacts with their 'uncivilized' kinsmen, fearing to be ousted from prestigious Lao society. Similarly, the ethnic Lao themselves often continue to feel distrust and estrangement in relation to ethnic minorities. One can also ascertain that the policy of creating a national consciousness among the population, of fostering a sense of affiliation to a single state, has yielded positive results. Thus, amongst inhabitants of the towns of the Mekong basin areas, a group with developed national–ethnic consciousness, aware of its affiliation to the state of Laos, seems to have been formed. Awareness of affiliation to the Laotian state manifests itself in the deliberate separation of themselves from the Lao population of Thailand.

After eighteen years of PRPL rule, Laos remains an extremely poor country with an annual income of about US$70 per capita. The low level of socio-economic development is recognized by the LPDR authorities. Documents of the Fifth Congress of the Party (March 1991) indicated such recognition. Further, the limited resources of the LPDR have been unevenly distributed. They have been concentrated mainly in Vientiane and, to a lesser extent, in provincial centres of the Mekong basic area. Despite promising slogans, the PRPL-LPDR regime has done little towards achieving the raising of living standards for the majority of Lao peasants and of members of ethnic minorities, some of whom actively supported the PFL during the civil war. Promises given to the Front, the external face of the PRPL, have thus remained unfulfilled. It is small wonder that the ethnic minorities feel themselves to have been deceived. Besides that, many measures taken by the LPDR authorities (such as the policy of preservation of forests, poorly thought-out attempts to force ethnic minorities to adopt a settled economy in foothills etc.) provoked opposition from a number of peoples of northern Laos. In particular, the Hmong considered these actions to be directed at bringing them under the strict control of the PRPL-LPDR regime. Hmong demands for partial autonomy, shared by many Hmong members of the PRPL, were rejected by the current Laotian leadership.

In 1987, the Hmong insurgent movement recommenced, and for many of these people resistance has become a way of life. Hmong rebel detachments were joined by members of other ethnic groups. Their activities intensified at the end of 1989 and the beginning of 1990, when a fierce struggle developed between rebels of various ethnic origin and government troops. Assassinations of Hmong, including those who were loyal to the PRPL-LPDR regime, and the extermination of whole villages, had been frequent occurrences throughout the PRPL-LPDR. Cruelty towards Hmong, and the failure to supply them with minimum requirements, had alienated many Hmong, even those who had previously supported the government.

In 1990–91 the LPDR government officially announced its desire to settle ethnic conflict by peaceful means. A notion of 'national concord' (reconciliation) appeared in its lexicon. The government announced an amnesty for rebels, allowed ethnic minorities to observe traditions that differ from the compulsory Lao traditions, and to practise their own forms of worship. Nothing is known for the present about the practical results of these actions. On the other hand, it is clear that even if the LPDR government possesses the will to do something positive, it has not the financial means to assist the population. And there is some evidence that raises doubts even about the intentions. The present-day development of commodity relations in Laos only aggravates the disparity in living standards between the populations of the Mekong river valleys and other inhabitants of the country. Ill-concealed contempt and arrogance towards ethnic minorities is observable amongst the increasingly rich Lao officials and townspeople, even though such treatment is censured by the PRPL-LPDR regime. As the disparity in living standards and the renewed estrangement between Lao and ethnic minorities continue to increase, the menace of aggravating the latent contradictions between ethnic groups becomes more evident. Escalation of these contradictions threatens the unity and territorial integrity of Laos.

In spite of extremely limited information from Laos, an increase in ethnic consciousness amongst the larger ethnic groups is already evident, especially amongst the Hmong. They persistently try to maintain their traditions, culture, and mother tongue. As the PRPL-LPDR regime not only ignores the issue promoting the study of native languages and the development of a Hmong script, but also impedes these activities, the Hmong pursue this study on their own. According to the author's information, about half of Laotian Hmong can read and write Hmong script, while no more than a third can read and write Lao. Among Hmong women aged between 18 and 50, competence in Lao script scarcely reaches 10 per cent. Scattered throughout the world, many Hmong actively endeavour to maintain contacts with their kinsmen in Laos and to promote the preservation and development of Hmong culture and language.

There is also evidence of the growth of ethnic consciousness among the Khmu, Lue, and some other Laotian peoples. The consolidation of all Tai-speaking groups of Laos into a single entity now seems far from inevitable, although until recently the idea was popular amongst a number of researchers. Thus, even the Phuon people, attributed to the Lao ethnic group by official Laotian statistics, preserve a consciousness of affiliation to an original entity distinct from the dominant Lao ethnicity.

As regards the process of intra-ethnic consolidation, one can suppose that such phenomena exist amongst the above-mentioned Lue and other Tai as well. Here again, a serious lack of information about actual ethnic processes in present-day Laos should be noted. Little can be said, therefore, about the ethnic situation of the Mon-Khmer peoples of Laos, especially the numerous groups in southern Laos such as the Suai. Residing mainly in the river valleys, they were considerably influenced by the Lao and Phuthai. According to Laotian researchers, the younger generation of Suai prefer to speak Lao and hardly use their native language now; consequently many have forgotten it. A similar process is occurring amongst the Katang, another quite large Mon-Khmer-speaking group.

One of the results of current economic liberalization is the gradual return to Laos of persons of Chinese origin. By the end of the 1980s, many of them had re-possessed enterprises, stores, and other property which they had lost. These measures favour the revival of the Laotian economy. In such favour circumstances, the enterprising Chinese community of Laos will undoubtedly try not only to restore their former financial–economic positions, but considerably strengthen them as well.

Another significant aspect of the contemporary ethnic situation in Laos is the uncontrolled mass migration from Vietnam, about which the LPDR authorities are, at present, keeping carefully silent. Population increase, overpopulation of many regions, shortage of land suitable for agriculture, extremely low standards of living of the majority of Vietnamese, and other reasons, compel them to migrate within and outside their fatherland. At the beginning of the 1980s, persecution of representatives of the so-called 'alien population' by LPDR authorities decreased, and the process of Vietnamese migration to Laos recommenced. At first the new migrants were mostly Vietnamese women married to Laotian citizens who had been staying temporarily in Vietnam. (At the beginning of the 1980s, the number of Laotian students in different forms of education amounted to more than 7,000.) The number of these women was considerable relative to the poplation of Laos. Later taking advantage of a lessening of LPDR authorities' control over the population, and the common Laos-Vietnam border, a stream of immigrants from Vietnam poured into Laos. They were of various ages, and both male and female. The new immigrants settled mainly in towns.

According to unofficial information, immigration from Vietnam, principally of Viets, is increasing and amounts to at least 10,000 per annum on average. Thus figures for Vietnamese residents in Laos recorded in the population census (about 18,000) do not correspond to the facts. In the town of Savannakhet, every year about 10,000 immigrants from Vietnam are discovered and deported back to their fatherland. Presumably, Vietnamese immigrants of Viet and/or other ethnic origin can be found not only in Laotian towns, but in the countryside as well. The process of uncontrolled immigration from Vietnam – and its present rate of growth is unlikely to fall in the near future – will lead to considerable changes in the ethnic and demographic situation in Laos. This may provoke conflicts between Viets and other groups of the country's population and/or the Laotian authorities. There is a real possibility of large-scale settlement of Laotian territory by immigrants from Vietnam. Such a situation could lead to a formal or virtual annexation of parts of Laotian territory by Vietnam, in order to 'release' Vietnamese residents from the control of Laotian authorities. All these perspectives are fraught with serious consequences for the region and cast doubt on the viability of Laos as an independent state. Beyond all question, the problem of immigrants from Vietnam should be approached with full respect for their human rights.

The increase of Vietnamese residents in Laotian towns will undoubtedly cause concern to the Thai authorities. They have expressed concern about the possible peopling of Laos by Viets, and the consequent inclusion of its territory in some form into the political structure of Vietnam. Thailand itself has its own interests in Laos. Thai economic penetration of neighbouring economically-developed areas of the Mekong river valleys has recently increased. Some researchers suggest that this could lead to the inclusion of these areas in the economic structure of Thailand. Such a possibility also threatens the unity of the Laotian state, and this threat is fully recognized by the PRPL-LPDR leaders.

The ethnic processes developing in Laotian society at present are closely interwoven with socio-economic processes. These processes may aggravate social, demographic, political, and ethnic problems. Ethnic contradictions could possibly worsen in the near future, with the possible involvement of foreign states in internal conflicts in Laos. The problem arises once again of the viability and the right of the Laotian state to exist within its contemporary borders. The tragic experience of ethnic conflicts in other regions of the world demands the avoidance of similar outbreaks here. The responsibility of all political interests, and of all ethnic groups in Laos, is considerably increased. There is no secret that the possibilities of solving these problems by Laos alone are limited, but neither is foreign aid sufficient. Laotians, Lao and others, are famous for their tolerance, deliberateness, common sense, and inclination to compromise. Compromise and reconciliation between the different ethnic and social groups of Laos are essential in the present situation. This situation demands decisive actions on the part of the Laotian leadership, as the very existence of the state is at stake.

References

Abulchatin, Marat (1991), 'Sozdana Kompanija razvitija gornych rajonov Laosa' (Company for the development of Lao highland regions is established), *Kompas (BPI)* 225, 21.11:27–9.

Asia Yearbook (1987), Hong Kong.

Bromley, Yu. V (ed.), (1988), *Narodny mira (istoriko-etnografisheskij spravochnik)* (Peoples of the World (Historical-Ethnographic Handbook, Moscow: Sovetskaja Enciklopedija.))

Brown, MacAlister and Joesph Zasloff (1985), *Apprentice Revolutionaries: the communist movement in Laos, 1930–1985*, Stanford: Stanford University, Hoover Institution Press.

Bruk, S. I. (1986), *Naselenie mira. Etnodemografiicheskij spravochnik* (Population of the World, Ethno-demographic Handbook), Moscow: Nauka.

Countries of the World (1989), vol.1, Detroit.

Denisovitch, Alexander (1993a), 'Laos: itogi, zadatchi i perspektivy razvitija strany' (The development of Laos: results, tasks and prospects), *Kompas (BPI)* 45, 10.03:11–15.

—— (1993b), 'Orazvitii obrazovanija i zdravoochranenija v Laose' (The development of education and public health systems in Laos), *Kompas: (BPI)*, 113, 07.07:23–9.

Downing, Bruce T. and Douglas P. Olney (eds.), (1982), *The Hmong in the West*, University of Minnesota: Centre for Urban and Regional Affairs, Southeast Asian Refugee Studies Project.

Egorunin, O. V. (1992), 'Nacional'naja politika rukovodstva NRPL-LNDR na sovremennom etape' (Current Nationalities policy of the PRPL-LPDR leaders), in *Vtoraja Dal'nevostochnaja konferencija molodych istorikov. Tezisy dokladov* (Papers of the Second Far East Conference of Young Historians), Vladivostok: Russian Academy of Science, Far East Branch, Institute of History, Archaeology and Ethnography, 117–20.

Galkin, Alexander and Viktor Pritula (1988), 'Laos na puti reform' (Laos on the road to reform), *Za rubezhom* 49 (1482), 2–8 December: 12–13.

Gerasimov, Vyatcheslav, Khutphaythun Sinlavong and Pyotr Tsvetov (1993), 'Iz odnogo bambuka ne postroit' dom' (One bamboo pole cannot build a house), *Pravda*, 28 July.

Hiebert, Murray (1987), 'Showing some imagination', *Far Eastern Economic Review* (hereafter as *FEER*), vol.138, 53, 31 December: 44–6.

Khamsao Kaysong (1989), 'Phau le sy hiek khong phau', *Vannasin* 108, February: 26–8.

Khutphaythun Sinlavong (1993), *Politika Nacional'nogo soglasija i social'nyj mechanizm jego osuschestvlenija (social'nyj analiz na materialakh Laosa)* (National Concord Policy and Social Mechanism of its Realization (Social Analysis of Lao Data)), Moscow: Russian Academy of Government.

Kossikov, I. G. and O. V. Egorunin (1992), 'Sovremennaja etnitcheskaja situacija v Laose' (Contemporary ethnic situation in Laos), *Etnografitcheskoje obozrenije* 1: 27–39.

Le Cu Nam (1990), 'Doi net ve cu dan va su phan bo cac dan toc hien may o Cong hoa dan chu nhan dan Lao', *Dan toc hoc* 1 (65):54–61.

Malyje Narody Indokitaja (National Minorities of Indochina) (1983), Moscow: Nauka.

Morev, L. N. (1989), 'Laos. Novyje gorizonty' (Laos: new horizons), *Asia i Afrika segodn'a* 12 (390):16–19.

Ngo Duc Thinh (1979), 'Etnitcheskij sostav i sovremennoje rasselenije narodov Vostotchnogo Indokitaja' (Ethnic structure and contemporary disposition of peoples of eastern Indochina), Sovetskaja Etnografija 2:72–8.

—— (1980), 'Etnozonal'nyje obschnosti sovremennogo naselenija Laosa' (Ethno-zone entities of the contemporary population of Laos), *Rasy i narody* 10; 142–57.

Nguyen Quoc Loc (ed.), (1984), *Cac dan toc it nguai o Binh Tri Thien, Hue: Nha xuat ban Thuan Hoa.*

Paisai Sricharatchanya (1987), 'Fighting a phantom army' *FEER*, vol.138, 47, 19 November: 30.

—— (1988), 'Body smugglers', *FEER*, vol.139, 6, 11 February: 26.

Phoumi Vongvichit (1990), 'Ot teorii k praktike' (From theory to practice), *Pravda*, 26 February.

Privesentsev, Mikhail (1991), 'V s'jezd Narodno-Revol'ucionnoj partii Laosa' (Fifth Congress of the People's Revolutionary Party of Laos), *Kompas (BPI)* 72, 12.4:19–22.

Slovesnaja, N. G. (1985), 'National'nyj vopros v Tailande' (The national problem in Thailand), Moscow: Nauka.

Stuart-Fox, Martin (ed.), (1982), *Contemporary Laos*, New York: St. Martins Press.

—— (1991), 'Laos at the crossroads', *Indochina Issues*, a publication of the Indochina Project, 92, March: 1–8.

Tim hieu lich su van hoa nuac Lao (1978), 'Ha noi: Nha xuat ban khoa hoc xa hoi', tap I.

Tim hieu lich su van hoa nuac Lao (1981), 'Ha noi: Nha xuat ban khoa hoc xa hoi', tap II.

Tyurin, V.A. (ed.), (1980), *Laos. Sravochnik* (Laos, A Handbook), Moscow: Nauka.

Velicoredchanin, Oleg (1991), 'S socializmom potoropilis' (Too early to introduce socialism), *Ekho Planety* 20, 11–17 May: 22–2.

Wilkinson, Julia (1988), 'Letter from Ban Vinai' *FEER*, vol.139, 12, 24 March:134.

Zasloff, Joseph J. (ed.) (1973), *The Pathet Lao: leadership and organization*, Lexington, Mass.: D.C. Heath.

Zasloff, Joseph J. and MacAlister Brown (1982), 'Laos: coping with confinement', *Southeast Asian Affairs*, Institute of Southeast Asian Studies: Heinemann Asia, 211–28

Official Documents and Statistics

Basic Statistics about the Socio-economic Development in the Lao People's Democratic Republic for 15 years (1975–90) (1990), Vientiane: Ministry of Economy, Planning and Finance.

Kaysone Phomvihan (1982), Som khanjai Munnsya heng khwam samakhi lavang phau tang tang nai Vongkhanan'at heng sat lao thi pen ekephap, det diew pokpak haksa pathet sat vai hai mankhong le kosang sangkhomn'in'om hai samlet phon (Kaysone Phomvihan's report on the nationalities policy in Laos), Vientiane (in Laotian).

Kong pasum n'ai phu then thua pathet khang thi II khong neo lao sang sat (9–11 cann'a 1987), Vientiane, 1988.

Khomun sathiti tonto dan kanphathana setthakit sangkhom khong SPP Lao (Basic data about the social and economic development of the Lao People's Democratic Republic, 1988 (1989), Vientiane: Ministry of Economy, Planning and Finance, Statistics Division.

Khomun sathiti tonto dan kanphathana setthakit sangkhom khong SPP Lao (Basic data about the social and economic development of the Lao People's Democratic Republic) 1989 (1900), Vientiane: Ministry of Economy, Planning and Finance, Statistics Centre.

IV s'jezd Narodno-revol'utsionnoj partii Laosa (Fourth Congress of the People's Revolutionary Party of Laos), Moscow, 1987.

Chapter Eleven

Tribal Politics in Laos

Mayoury Ngaosyvathn

The Hegemonic Rule of One Tribal Group

Tribal minorities have been a driving force for change in the social fabric and politics of Laos, particularly during the Lao revolutionary war when they fulfilled a 'vital function' in sustaining the Pathet Lao movement.

Laos is a landlocked country of 236,800 square kilometres, of which 4 per cent is cultivated, 4 per cent grassland, 47 per cent thick forests, and 17 per cent open savannah and woodland. With a density of about 17 inhabitants per square kilometre and endowed with rich agricultural, forestry, mineral, and power resources, Laos possesses great economic potential. Laos is also one of the world's least developed countries and is among the ten poorest nations. In 1988, an estimate of the Lao GNP per capita was US$142 (Economist Intelligence Unit 1988–89: 30).

In 1827 Laos lost its independence to Siam, and in 1893 became a French colony. During the French period, Laos was seriously neglected, and did not benefit from even the most minimal development efforts which most colonial powers deemed necessary to invest in their colonial possessions (Rochet 1946). After the end of the French administration in 1954, the American era began. Like Vietnam and Cambodia, Laos was engulfed in protracted revolutionary war. The ensuing twenty-year conflict destroyed the Lao economy and disrupted its peaceful society. In 1975, the change in the regional balance of power affected Laos too. The Lao King abdicated, and a communist regime superseded the Kingdom of Laos. The country was ruled by the Lao People's Revolutionary Party (LPRP), an offshoot of the Indochinese Communist Party created by Ho Chi Minh.

According to government statistics in 1988, the population of Laos totalled 3,940,000 (1,930,600 males and 2,009,400 females) comprising 47[1] ethnic groups (*History of the LPRP* 1989: 2) living in some 11,512 self-contained and self-sufficient villages across the country. Those 47 ethnic groups can be said to belong to three major cultural groups. There were the

Plate 18. The ancestors Pu Nyoeu and Nya Nyoeu learn to make the salutation to show respect (*wai*) before the dance during the New Year festival at Wat S'ieng T'ông, Luang Prabang [1952].

lowlander Lao Lum, Lao living in the valley, mostly on the Mekong plains, together with 'Hill Tai' constituting 64.4 per cent of the country's population. There were the uplanders, or Lao Theung (formerly known by the pejorative term Kha or 'slaves')[2] forming 29.2 per cent of the population. They lived on the mountain slopes. Finally, there were Lao Sung or highlanders, Lao of the mountain-tops. The majority of Lao Sung are Lao Hmong, formerly known by the derogatory term 'Miao' or 'Mèo',[3] and the Mien or Yao. Lao Sung made up 6.4 per cent of the population. These patterns of ethnic settlement, centred on geographical topography, are described by Whitaker et al. (1979).

The greater majority of Lao Lum are concentrated in the plains of the Mekong valley and its tributaries. With the exception of the 'Hill Tai' they are Theravada Buddhists who also practise a mixture of Brahmanism and animism. Nowadays Brahmanism, animism, Buddhism, and socialism co-exist (Khamtan Thepbuali 1976a, 1976b; Sulak Sivarak 1981; Stuart-Fox 1983; Reid 1988; Kamm 1990; Mayoury Ngaosyvathn 1989, 1990). The hinterland is sparsely populated and most of the North bordering Burma and China consists of rugged mountains. The jungle trails make commercial and other social exchange difficult in these areas, and inter-provincial communication is inadequate. Many roads are usable only in the dry season. This situation has discouraged trade with the main cities, and has enforced self-sufficiency. This makes it virtually impossible for the lowland people to assimilate ethnic minorities, and hinders a sense of national identity and unity (Helm 1989).

Pax Franca's Divide and Rule

The original inhabitants of the land of Laos were the Lao Theung. They received ceremonial recognition during the annual rites in Luang Prabang until 1975 [see Tanabe in this volume Ed.]. The Lao Theung also served as state officials during the first unified Lao kingdom under Fa Ngum (AD 1353–94), but later the Lao Theung (Gay 1989a: 9) and the Lao too were enslaved by Siam. In particular, females of minorities were considered of great value economically and as an ostentatious sign of wealth, for example, a female slave cost a quarter more than a male slave (Taupin 1888: 87).

For many decades, the Lao Theung suffered injustices perpetrated by the powerful foreign master and the local privileged class. They also had to endure other age-old grievances, aggravated by the French with their disregard for existing patterns of tribal rule. The Lao Theung were divided into 29 tribes,[4] and belonged to two main language groups (Mon-Khmer and Malayo-Polynesian).[5] After the abolition of slavery in 1893, the social status of the Lao Theung did not change.

The French did not set up separate administrative mechanisms to alleviate tribal clashes. In fact, the French established a multi-racial administrative system to divide and rule through Tai and Lao Lum intermediaries (Burchett 1959; McCoy 1970; Gunn 1990; Evans 1990). Alfred McCoy (1970: 80) has called the system a 'brutal ethnic hierarchy'. By penetrating highland areas where even the Lao lowlanders had failed to gain access, or had suffered setbacks, the French often by-passed traditional tribal ruling élites by appointing village chiefs or district officers. For example, a Lamet village chief had to report to a Tai Lue tax collector, who in turn was in turn responsible to a Lao lowlander canton chief, subordinate in turn to a Vietnamese functionary under the French officials in charge of the province (McCoy 1970; Whitaker et al. 1979). The same policy was employed by the French administration for the Tho minority in northern Vietnam (Wekkin 1982).

When the French decided to remedy their fiscal disasters, they began to exploit the local population as they had done in other Indochinese countries, such as imposing increasingly heavy burdens. Every ethnic Lao male between the ages of 18 and 60 had to contribute corvée labour for at least 100 days per annum (Thongsa Xayavongkhamdy et al. 1989: 26). The first corvée, commonly called *kan luang* (public work), was a liability established at sixteen days for Lao Lum and Lao Sung, and twenty days for Lao Theung (ibid.). Those who did not want to be incarcerated, could hire someone for 50 to 100 kip to do this corvée (ibid.). This imposition could be redeemed in cash for a payment known as *kha thay kan* (redemption). The average redeemable fee for the Lao Lum was 4.30 kip per day, and 2.40 kip for the Lao Sung. Lao Theung had to pay 7 kip for their redemption (ibid.). All had to provide extra unremunerated labour for the privileged colonial and local officials for up to 20–30 extra days. This extra duty was commonly called *lam* (bondage) in Upper Laos, and *hua* (head) or *van* (day) in Central and Lower Laos, including the Lao Lum areas (Deydier 1954; Phoumi Vongvichit 1968; Doré 1987: 313; Gay 1987; Gunn 1990: 49; Khamphan Thipmountaly 1990). This could include travelling time of another two to four months (Thongsa Xayavongkhamdy et al. 1989: 27).

After the *kan luang*, another category of corvée imposed by the French on every male between the ages of eighteen and sixty was *kan cang* (paid work). This was demanded on an average of three occasions each year: sixteen days for Lao Lum and Lao Sung, and twenty days for Lao Theung. Lao Lum and Lao Sung worked sixteen days and received 0.40 kip per day from this work, while Lao Theung worked for twenty days and earned 0.20 kip per day or half the amount (ibid.: 26).

There was also the *phasi kha hua* (head tax) levied on ethnic Lao males between the ages of eighteen and sixty. This tax was different for each ethnic group. For instance, according to the local archives, in the early nineteenth century the Hmong in Xieng Khuang had to pay a head tax in cash to which was added an extra tax of one kilogramme of opium per head (*History of the LPRP* 1989: 8).[6] In the mid-nineteenth century, the Lao Lum and the Lao Sung paid the same average head tax of 9.60 kip, surprisingly the Lao Theung were taxed at 4.80 (Thongsa Xayavong-khamdy et al. 1989: 28–30).

Lao females of ethnic groups were not exempt from the French taxes. Every female had to pay a head tax in cash on the size of their breasts (*History of the LPRP* 1989: 8)

'In some provinces, there was a tax on women's breasts. It varied according to their fullness and pregnant women avoided markets squares, pagodas, and other meeting places during the later stages of their pregnancy to avoid the tax-assessor's eyes. (Such an enormity was almost but not quite matched by the Japanese feudalists in Korea who imposed a levy on women's hair and enforced the annual contribution in kind).' (Burchett 1959: 205).

It is not surprising that tax-collectors could assess the size of women's breasts, because even in 1959 Nhouy Abhay noted that women did not wear upper garments.

Collection of taxes involved excesses of corruption by exploitative local mandarins who took a proportion of the proceeds for personal profit (McCoy 1970). This situation led to hatred of the Lao lowlanders by the Lao Theung (Wekkin 1974). This feeling is even common among the Hill Tai groups – Tai Dam, Tai Daeng, Tai Neua, Tai Lue, and Phu Tai – towards their ethnic kin the Lao lowlanders, who are closely related by language and cultural heritage though separated by Hill Tai animistic beliefs. The Hill Tai were regarded by the lowland Lao lords and local authorities with much the same disdain and arrogance as they regarded the Lao Theung.

The establishment in 1893 of the French administration in Laos and its economic consequences, created discontent among ethnic minorities, particularly the Lao Sung. For the first time, in 1896, there was open resistance, leading to an armed clash in Xieng Khuang (Yang Dao 1975; Lee 1982). The Hmong revolts were followed later by others, particularly millenarian movements, such as those of the *phu mi bun*,[7] which took place in 1901–02 on both sides of the Mekong river and in southern Laos (Khemmarath). The fervour of the *phu mi bun* movements soon spread to the Lao Theung in Saravane, joined by others on the Bolovens Plateau. In the North, there were revolts of the Tai Lue in Meuang Sing, Phongsali, Sam Neua, and Luang Nam Tha. One revolt occurred in Vientiane in 1920 (Thongsa Xayavongkhamdy et al. 1989; *History of the LPRP* 1989). The cause of these revolts was principally the heavy taxes imposed throughout the colonial epoch (Fletcher and Gunn 1981; McCoy 1970; Thee 1973; Stuart-Fox 1986; Gunn 1990; Evans 1990) the culmination of nearly a century of foreign exploitation, by both Siamese and French, of ethnic rivalries (Hiebert 1982; Gunn 1990).

In attempting to balance their domestic budget, the French became more and more interested in opium in Indo-China, from which they received considerable revenue (Gunn 1990). Beginning in 1901, the French promoted the establishment of 1,512 opium refineries and 3,098 opium dens in Saigon alone for the consumption of opium among the peoples of Indo-China (Thongsa Xayavongkhamdy et al. 1989: 33). When the Chinese opium supply was cut, the French became interested in the

Lao poppy crop, prompting bloody rivalry between mountain clans vying for the lucrative trade, despite the fact that they were inter-related by marriage.

Some of these ethnic cleavages continue today. The tribal split that has had the most long-standing consequences was that among the Hmong. Under the French, and continuing under the Americans, some Hmong were recruited as colonial and neo-colonial troops because of their energy and organizational strength. Others rallied to support the communists in their anti-colonial struggle (Hafner 1965). Yet neither Lao Sung nor Lao Theung were ever soldiers under the Tai lords (Proschan 1989). Of the three broad groups, the Lao Theung and the Hill Tai formed the majority of the Pathet Lao armed forces (Wekkin 1982; Sisouk Na Champassak 1961; Stuart-Fox 1987; Zasloff 1973). The *kong Patcay* (Patcay's, or Pai Cai's battalion), named after the Hmong leader of an uprising against the French in 1918, was established in September 1947 during the national liberation struggle (Thongsa Xayavongkhamdy et al. 1989).

'Royal' Ignorance of the Ethnic Clash

Under the Royal Lao Government, in spite of the proclamation that all inhabitants were equally Lao citizens, not all ethnic groups were treated equally. Lao Sung and particularly Lao Theung continued to be 'second-class citizens'. This had wide-ranging social and economic consequences. For example, Joel M. Halpern noted that: 'The Lao government had no explicit policy with regard to her minority groups. Government officials, in effect, still practise discrimination, as, for example, in the allocation of funds for schools and other projects' (Halpern 1960: 65–66). Moreover, the Lao Theung were virtually unrepresented in the Royal Lao hierarchy (Whitaker et al. 1979; Fletcher and Gunn 1981). Few Hmong held public offices higher than that of village chief, though some at least were in the Royal Government services.

As a result of the 1954 Geneva Agreements, the Pathet Lao independence fighters were forced to withdraw to the provinces of Sam Neua (now Huaphanh) and Phongsali in northern Laos. The ethnic composition of these two provinces was largely minority tribes who constituted the bulk of their troop strength. Recognizing the tactical and strategic importance of the hill tribes, the Pathet Lao gained much tribal support by consciously incorporating minority issues, capitalizing on past alienations, and promising social and political equality with the Lao lowlanders. Political policy on minority issues was presented first at the National Congress of the Nèo Lao Itsala[8] on 13 August 1950 (Wekkin 1982; *History of the LPRP* 1989; Brown and Zasloff 1986). Several Lao Theung leaders on the Bolovens Plateau in southern Laos (Sithon

Kommadam) and Lao Sung leaders (Faydang Lobliayao and Nhiavu Lobliayao) were given high positions in the Pathet Lao movement as Vice-Chairmen of the Central Committee of the Neo Lao Itsala as early as 1950. Both Faydang Lobliayao and the late Sithon Kommadam were elected Vice-Presidents of the Supreme People's Assembly in 1975. In contrast to the conception of nations built on the premise of 'one people, one language, one nation' – as in neighbouring Siam/Thailand for example – the Pathet Lao developed a Hmong script. Even in the literature of the Pathet Lao, the Lao from all ethnic groups, such as Lao Theung and Lao Sung were portrayed as safeguarding the country, as in the story of *May, la jeune Lao Sung* [May, the Lao Sung Girl].[9] The Pathet Lao also sent members of the Hmong and other tribal groups to school within the areas under the Pathet Lao control, as well as overseas, for tertiary education. By contrast, in 1974–75, in the Royal Lao Government areas, where 60 per cent of the general population was illiterate, 99 per cent of the Hmong could not read or write (Yang Dao 1974: 39), and there was only one Hmong with a doctorate degree from France (Lee 1982: 204).

The Royal Lao Government, with US strategic support, promised the Hmong faction an autonomous zone or 'Hmong Free State' in exchange for Hmong active participation in the 'Secret War' (Wekkin 1982: 188; Barney 1967: 274).[10] This strategy of the United States of America, 'was seen as a familiar tactic of dividing so as to conquer' (Proschan 1989: 219).[11] While severe dislocation affected the whole Lao population during the decades of war, the Hmong was the ethnic group most affected by the fighting (Whitaker et al. 1979; Lee 1982). Many Lao Theung groups underwent a similar ordeal (Proschan 1989).

A Poly-ethnic State

In a country already so strongly divided along ethnic lines, the new government looked forward to a unified Lao state in which all ethnic groups and both sexes would have equal opportunities to participate. This was reconfirmed by the new Constitution (Stuart-Fox 1991a). The population of Laos, whatever their ethnicity, were to have their opportunity to achieve political and social positions from district to national levels. In the minority-dominated provinces of Xieng Khuang, Huaphanh, and Luang Prabang, provincial, district, and canton committees now have an ethnically proportionate mixed leadership (Chagnon and Rumpf 1980, 1982, 1983; Gunn 1982; Stuart-Fox 1987). Or, as in Sekong in the South or Phongsali in the North, minority cadres control the provincial administration (Stuart-Fox 1991a). The administrative provincial committee of Luang Prabang has three members from each of the three major ethnic groupings and the chairperson changes every two years in rotation.

At the national level, ethnic minorities share positions of authority. Khamtay Siphandone, who is a Lao Theung and a member of the Politburo, was one of five Vice-Chairmen of the Council of Government named in 1982. He was recently promoted to Prime Minister and President of the LPRP. A Hill Tai (but Lao Lum), Sisavath Kèobounphanh, was a member of the Politburo till 1989, and a member of the Party Central Committee Secretariat and Secretary of the Party Committee of Vientiane Municipality. Formerly Minister of the Interior, he recently headed negotiations with the Thai General Chaovalit Yongchaiyuth to bring an end to the bloody frontier war in 1988, and is presently Minister of Agriculture, Forestry, and Co-operatives. Another Hill Tai, Sisomphone Lovanxay, was a member of the Politburo and one of the Vice-Presidents of the Supreme People's Assembly,[12] as well as the President of the powerful Commission of the Organization of the LPRP, in charge of all cadre policy. He was elected by the Fifth National Congress of the LPRP to membership of the Advisory Committee. In 1992, he was appointed one of the Vice-Chairmen of the Council of Ministers (Economist Intelligence Unit 1992). In 1993, another Hill Tai, Bouasy Lovanxay, was appointed one of the Vice-Chairmen of the Economy, Planning, and Finance Committee of the National Assembly. A Hill Tai, Maysouk Saisomphèng, was Minister of Industry and Handicrafts in 1985, and was then appointed ministerial head of the Prime Minister's office. He is presently President of the Lao Front for National Construction. At the Fifth National Congress of the LPRP, he was elected a Party Central Committee member.

Among the Lao Sung, Yao Phonevantha, a Hmong, was appointed Minister of Finance in 1985. Nhiavu Lobliayao has been appointed Chairman of the State Nationalities Committee. Axang Laoli was endorsed by the National Assembly in February 1993 as Minister of the Interior. Similarly, in 1993 another Lao Sung, Vongphet Xaikeuyachongtoua, was appointed as one of the Vice-Presidents, a member of the Parliamentary Standing Committee, and Chairman of the Ethnic Affairs Committee. In 1993, Chaleune Yiapaoheu was also appointed a member of the Parliamentary Standing Committee, and Chairman of the Secretariat of the Parliamentary Standing Committee. The Party's Central Committee, since its Second National Congress held in February 1972, has included the Lao Theung Boualang, the Lao Sung Nhiavu Lobliayao, and the Hill Tai Inpong Khaignavong, former Vice-Minister and chief of the LRPR section of the Ministry of Foreign Affairs, now chief of Khammuane province, southern Laos. The Fifth National Congress of the LPRP elected members of ethnic minority groups to the Party's Central Committee, such as Axang Laoli, Vongphet Saykeuyachongtoua, Yao Phonevantha, Inpong Khaignavong, Inkong Mahavong, and Mrs Pany Yathotou. Chaleune Yiapaoheu was elected one of seven secretariat members of the Lao People's Revolutionary Youth Union at its National First Congress in 1983.

In the LPRP hierarchy, minority cadres have been gradually promoted (Stuart-Fox 1986). Many Lao Theung in the South-East and Lao Sung in the North, the hill tribe minorities (Tai Lue, Tai Neua, Yuan) in North and North-East Laos have been members of the Party. It was estimated that before 1975 Lao Lum made up only 36 per cent of Party membership, whereas Lao Theung accounted for 60 per cent and Lao Sung 4 per cent (Chou Norindr 1982: 41). The Third National Congress of the LPRP in 1982 elected 55 Central Committee members of whom 79 per cent represented Lao Lum, 15 per cent Lao Theung and 6 per cent Lao Sung. Even at the same National Congress of the LPRP, among 228 people from all strata and different regions who attended, 64 were Lao Theung, and 19 Lao Sung (*History of the LPRP* 1989: 145); *Documents of the Third National Congress of the LPRP* 1982: 203). However, at the Fourth National Congress of the LPRP, there was no mention of the percentage of Party membership or their attendance. It is not surprising that the Lao Theung or Lao Sung had earlier been promoted in the Party because it was in these two provinces in northern Laos (Phongsali and Huaphanh) that resistance fighters have settled. The majority of the inhabitants of these two provinces, together with those of the Bolovens Plateau in southern Laos, were thus selected to join the Party, or were recruited into the army. As Wekkin (1982: 185) states, 'at all times a majority of the armed forces were Lao Theung and Hill Tai'.

Ethnic groups are represented in key positions in the mass organizations, such as the Federation of Lao Women's Unions, the Lao People's Revolutionary Youth Union, the Lao Federation of Trade Unions, the Lao Committee to Defend World Peace, and the Lao Front for National Construction.

Since 1975, the central government has organized the supply of basic commodities, such as salt, tools, and clothing, to ethnic minorities in remote areas despite the extreme difficulty of transportation. On the other hand, the policy of restricting shifting cultivation on the mountain slopes and promoting wet-rice agriculture in the valleys has gradually intensified. The Lao PDR government aimed from the start to achieve 'the three revolutions' (in 'relations of production', 'ideological and cultural relations', and 'the scientific and technological revolution'). It insisted on the need to promote education for both sexes of its minorities, and in particular to intensify the formation of women cadres. By raising the educational level of ethnic minorities, it was hoped to integrate them into the national community. The system of educational incentives means that after five years in primary school, children of all ethnic groups could receive an allowance from the government to attend lower secondary school (three years), or upper secondary school (three years), and later the Technical School, the Teacher's Training College, the National Polytechnical School, and the Medical School. There is a lack of data on the enrolment of minority students. However, Chagnon and Rumpf reported that the number of tribal students attending, for instance, Vientiane's secondary schools and the medical university had increased (1982: 177). Since 1975, a great number of ethnic minority students have been sent for study or training overseas, both in Eastern and Western Europe. After completing their studies, they were appointed to various ministries, state enterprises, and local administrations. For instance, in Xieng Khuang province, in northern Laos, several young Vientiane teachers volunteered to work up-country (ibid.). At the same time a genuine attempt has been made to avoid problems in appointing people to work in remote areas, such as posting Lao Sung cadres to Lao Theung or Lao Lum areas, and vice-versa; or supplying inappropriate goods, for instance, sending toothpaste and brushes to the Lao Theung who have never used them (*Khaosan Pathet Lao* 1976).

The priority given by the Lao government to universal education is described as one of the 'most useful policies contributing to solving Lao's complex ethnic-unity problem' (Chagnon and Rumpf 1982: 177). After more than a decade, many efforts have been made to extend educational provision. From 1975 to 1986 nation-wide, 71 first-level technical schools, 136 second-level technical schools, 70 technical training centres, and 20 schools for Lao minorities' youth were built (*Seuksa Mai* 1986: 18).

Health care has been another priority field where the Lao government has attempted to assist minorities. This has been done on a nation-wide basis by promoting, at the village level in minority areas, a network of health stations and dispensaries, increasing the ratio of medical facilities. The government is aiming to ameliorate maternal and child health, and reduce infant and child mortality through improved sanitation and access to clean drinking water for 25 per cent of minorities in the remote areas (*Report for the Second Round Table of the Least Developing Countries of Asia and the Pacific* 1986). Nation-wide, only 19 per cent of the whole population has access to tap water (Lao PDR *1988 Report*). Mobile health teams sent to remote areas are teaching methods of basic hygiene and elementary health care. At present, the country's medical network has served the Lao population from 1976 to 1990 through eight centrally managed hospitals, sixteen provincial hospitals, one municipal hospital, and 115 district hospitals, with 937 dispensaries (State Statistical Centre 1990: 134). These facilities are attended by a total of 1,173 physician doctors, 2,731 physician-assistant doctors, and 5,874 primary-level medical practitioners. By 1988, the ratio of doctors and assistants was 2.3 doctors and 8.3 assistant physicians respectively per 10,000 inhabitants (Lao PDR 1989).

Although the Lao Theung and the Lao Sung were considered 'second-class citizens' in the past, such attitudes are now fading away. No more do stories make fun of *Meo*, nor is this pejorative name heard; neither is the term *Kha* used in the Lao PDR (Stuart-Fox 1987: 332). The state Constitution has also ruled that 'all acts of creating division and discrimination among ethnic groups are prohibited' (Stuart-Fox 1991a:

173, 1991b: 306). Surprisingly however the 1989 Criminal Code did not contain provisions concerning discrimination against minorities, and the term 'multi-ethnic population' was not used.

Overall, all ethnic groups today have greater access to education and health care than ever before. Their self-image and expectations are gradually changing. Despite such progress, obstacles and many unmet needs still exist. For instance, in the educational field there are 1.5 million people scattered in 250,000 mountain villages demanding teachers who can teach in local languages (Hirashima 1989: 23). Girls from poor families, peasant families, and ethnic minorities have difficulty in attending school (Stuart-Fox 1986; Pfister 1989; Lao PDR 1989). They also tend to abandon school studies before completion. This is due not only to lack of family financial support, but also to parental attitudes which may give preference to educating sons and taking daughters out of school to do household work at home (Khao San Pathet Lao 1977; Manivone Viravong 1987; Batson 1988; Pfister 1989).

Generally, girls and young women from ethnic groups face more special problems because of the remoteness of their villages and their inability to speak Lao (Batson 1988). Female minorities attending school are fewer at higher levels. For instance, in 1988–89 at primary school level, Lao Theung made up 39 per cent, Lao Sung 25 per cent, and Lao Lum, 44 per cent. At lower secondary school level, Lao Theung made up 31 per cent, the Lao Sung average was 14 per cent, and Lao Lum comprised 41 per cent. At the upper secondary school level, Lao Theung made up 27 per cent, with Lao Sung 10 per cent, and Lao Lum 40 per cent (*Report of the Ministry of Education* 1990).

After many years of the new regime, serious problems remain, particularly in areas where ethnic minorities live. In addition to those already mentioned there is the lack of state finance and school books, low salaries for the teachers, and many schools were abandoned (Ruiming 1983; Pfister 1989; Evans 1989; Stuart-Fox 1991a). The Asian Development Bank estimated that 35 per cent of primary school teachers and 14 per cent of lower school teachers were untrained (Queensland Education Consortium 1990). The country still has no university. In some remote areas, due to the high costs of transportation, children who have finished primary school in their village cannot attend the secondary school in another district. In the early 1980s, some students of ethnic minorities, after finishing high school in Vientiane or overseas, were not interested in returning to teach or work in their own village, despite the efforts of the central government to extend official services to the local administration and providing facilities.

In the field of public health, many hospitals and dispensaries have been built and the number of doctors has increased. However, many problems persist. Laos continues to be a country with a low nutritional standard. Life expectancy is short, as low as 46 years for women (Economist Intelligence

Unit 1988–89). Infant mortality rate is over 200 per 1,000 (Ljunggren 1992), while the crude birth rate is over 46 per 1,000 (Lao PDR 1989; Pfister 1989). The World Bank (1990: 20) estimated in 1988 that 45 per cent of females were of reproductive age (see also Pfister 1989: 18), with a fertility rate of over six children per woman. Parallel to high fertility, Laos also had a high mortality rate. In 1987 the United Nations Development Programme reported that one child in five died before reaching the age of five years (Lao PDR *1988 Report*) [reduced by 1992 to 16.6 per 1,000, see Kossikov this volume, Ed.]. Lao children of ethnic minorities are threatened by many dangerous diseases. For instance, in remote areas of Vientiane province, the rate of contracting malaria is 90 per cent (Wilson 1987). At the same time, many clinics have been closed for lack of finance (Stuart-Fox 1991a).

Laos is still one of the world's ten least-developed countries, and the majority of all ethnic groups continue to suffer from this impoverished situation. Transportation and communication in the areas where most ethnic minority groups live are very poor, and practical only in the dry season. Although main cities have adequate supplies of electricity, 85–90 per cent of the population lives in rural areas with little or no electricity. Laos exports much of its electricity to Thailand.

Conclusion

The challenges outlined here are overwhelming. A major concern of the government's social programme is the protection of the interests of all ethnic groups. Even during the war years, the Lao revolutionary leaders were mindful of their promises and made efforts to pursue that policy. Hence, despite harsh conditions during the war and the lack of financial and material resources, the government helped build a rudimentary social infrastructure in the liberated areas where basic literacy, elementary education, and health care services were made available. Since 1975, primary schools and health care facilities have been set up to reach minority areas. Teaching-training schools, medical and agricultural colleges have been set up in the provincial towns of minority areas. At the same time, with intensive social mobilization through the Party's mass organizations, the rights of women and ethnic minorities have gradually been promoted. Despite criticism of superstitions, cultural and religious beliefs of minorities have been recognized. Minority dances, music, folk arts, and crafts have been encouraged (Stuart-Fox 1987). Oral stories about the ancestors or the customs of ethnic groups have been recalled, and the radio broadcasts programmes in some minority languages (Rakow 1992).

Not only in terms of the Party line towards all ethnic groups, and in particular the Lao Theung and Lao Sung but also in practice their political situation and status are much better than that of women in the population as a whole. For instance, in 1993, only men were appointed in the Parliamentary Committee of the Lao People's National Assembly, including its five committees and secretariat. Among the seven Parliamentary Standing Committee members two are Hmong, but there are no women. Generally speaking, cultural barriers to gender equality continue to plague Lao women of all ethnic groups. At the Fourth National Congress of the LPRP held in 1986, four women from all ethnic groups were elected as full members and one as an alternate member of the Party's Central Committee. Not until the Fifth National Congress of the LPRP in March 1991 were two more women elected as full members, and two as alternate members. There are no women in the Politburo. Government functionaries and technicians include men from ethnic minority groups. Directors and heads of factories and work units are almost entirely male (Ireson et al. 1989; Ireson 1992). There are few women from any ethnic group heading ministerial departments, or in the provincial leadership. After more than one decade of the Lao PDR, the former Lao Prime Minister's speech at the Fourth National Party Congress in 1986 recognized that 'currently, the number of women cadres, of ethnic minority cadres, in different levels and services is still low' (*Documents of the Fourth National Congress of the LPRP* 1986: 208).

Government policy alone cannot promote equal rights between men and women, or between people from different ethnic groups, as long as notions of the superiority of lowland Lao and males, and the inferiority of Lao Theung, Lao Sung, and women, remain deep-rooted. Even though the Constitution of 1990 promulgated equal rights for all, this will not occur quickly. Moreover, 'decadent' culture imported from outside, in particular Thai culture, now threatens the cultures of all ethnic groups in Laos more than at any other time since 1975. Lao girls between ten and fifteen have been lured into slave-labour factories in Bangkok by 'job-placement agencies'. Most of them were smuggled into Thailand through Ubon Ratchathani, Khemmarat, or Mukdaharn provinces (*Bangkok Post* 1989). Reports published by the Australian *Sunday Mail* (see also Paul and Walden 1992) on 23 February 1992, indicate that there are 800,000 prostitutes under sixteen in Thailand, and that over 90 per cent of child prostitutes in Thailand are from southern China, Burma, Laos, and the minority groups of northern and northeast Thailand.

To combine forty-seven ethnic groups into one 'new' Lao identity and nation is going to be hard to achieve. Not all ethnic groups can speak the Lao Lum language, which is still the only official language, and only a few Lao Lum can speak Lao Theung or Lao Sung languages. However it is fair to say that government policy on the unification of all ethnic groups under one national umbrella is gradually obtaining positive effects, which however limited, are all the more notable when compared to those of the previous royal government.

Notes

1 From 1975, the Lao PDR government officially recognized 68 ethnic minority groups. This number was confirmed in September 1988 by an interview with a Khmu cadre (Maha Vangkham Souryadej) from the National Committee of Social Sciences. However, in 1987, *Vientiane Mai*, a daily newspaper published a list of 53 ethnic groups. In 1989, the *History of the LPRP* gave a figure of 47, and the same number was mentioned on 15 May 1990 by the President of the National Committee of Social Sciences, Sisana Sisane. Responding to my question concerning what had happened to the others, he said that some of the ethnic groups were tiny and had been merged.

2 It was a 'term and condition perpetuated by the French colonialists', as Turton (1977: 280) points out.

3 Hmong means 'free man' and is the name which the tribespeople call themselves. The name 'Miao', which means 'barbarian', was the pejorative name given them by the Chinese (Vang-Tou-Fu 1979: 93). It was introduced to Indo-China at the end of the nineteenth century, and became 'Mèo' when pronounced by the French administrators (Yang Dao 1975: 6).

4 This was published in *Vientiane Mai* in 1987. The same journal also reported that the Lao Sung numbered thirteen ethnic groups and the Lao Lum constituted eleven ethnic groups.

5 Six main groups of languages are recognized in Laos: Tai-Lao, Mon-Khmer, Tibeto-Burman, Hmong-Yao, Viet Muong, and Hô (*History of the LPRP*, 1989).

6 Burchett (1959: 217) gives a figure of two kilogrammes, regardless of whether the person grew or smoked it.

7 For accounts and analysis of millenarian movements in Laos and Siam, see Burchett 1959; Halpern 1966; Tej Bunnag 1967; Murdoch 1974; Sanyan Dongdeng 1974; Ishii 1975; Keyes 1977; Moppert 1978; Turton and Tanabe 1984; Gay 1987, 1989a; Phoumi Vongvichit 1968: 40; Gunn 1985, 1990.

8 *Nèo Lao Itsala* (Free Lao Front) was founded on 13 August 1950 in Sam Neua. Its name was changed on 6 January 1956 to *Nèo Lao Hak Xat* (Lao Patriotic Front), and then to *Nèo Lao Sang Xat* (Lao Front for National Construction) on 20 February 1979.

9 Written in 1973 by Kèo Mani. There are also examples of literature written by French authors in the colonial period which show how Lao Lum despised men from ethnic minorities as 'dirty', and portrayed women of ethnic minorities as sexual exhibitionists (Ajalbert 1905; Gay 1989b: 9).

10 Led by Vangpao who now lives in exile in the United States.

11 Pathet Lao policy contrasted in this respect with the policy followed by the former Union of the Soviet Republics and Vietnam (See Kunstadter 1967: 25).

12 The Supreme People's Assembly has been renamed the National Assembly by the new Constitution.

References

Ajalbert, J., (1905), *Sao Van Di* (Lady Van Di), Paris: Charpentier.

Asian Development Bank, (1989), Education Sector Study, Advisory Technical Assistance Project, Lao PDR, Manila, (September).

Bangkok Post, 9 November 1989.

Barney, G. L., (1967), 'The Mèo of Xieng Khouang Province, Laos', in Peter Kunstadter (ed.), *Southeast Asian Tribes, Minorities and Nations*, New Jersey: Princeton University Press, 271–94.

Batson, Wendy A. (1988), 'Women in Development in Lao PDR', Paper presented at the Round Table on Women in Development, held in Vientiane, LAO PDR, July.

Brown, MacAlister and J. J. Zasloff, (1986), *Apprentice Revolutionaries: the communist movement in Laos, 1930–1985*, Stanford: Hoover Institution Press.

Burchett, W. G. (1959), *Mekong Upstream. A visit to Laos and Cambodia*, Seven SEAS Books.

Chagnon, Jacquie and R. Rumpf (1980), 'Dignity, national identity and unity', *Southeast Asia Chronicle*, no. 73, Washington.

—— (1982), 'Education: the prerequisite to change in Laos', in Martin Stuart-Fox (ed.), *Contemporary Laos. Studies in the politics and society of the Lao People's Democratic Republic*, London: University of Queensland Press, 163–80.

—— (1983), 'Decades of division for the Lao Hmong', *Southeast Asia Chronicle*, no.91, October, 10–15.

Chou Norindr, (1982), 'Political institutions of the Lao People's Democratic Republic', in Martin Stuart-Fox (ed.), *Contemporary Laos. Studies in the politics and society of the Lao People's Democratic Republic*, London: University of Queensland Press, 39–41.

Deydier, H. (1954), *Lokapala: génies, totems et sorciers du nord Laos*, Paris: Plon.

Documents of the Third National Congress of the Lao People's Revolutionary Party, 1982, Vientiane: Hong Phim Haeng Xat.

Documents of the Fourth National Congress of the Lao People's Revolutionary Party, 1986, Vientiane: Hong Phim Haeng Xat, 1987.

Doré Amphay, P. S. (1987), *Aux Sources de la Civilisation Lao (Contribution ethno-historique à la connaissance de la culture Louang-Phrabanaise*, Mémoire pour le Doctorat d'Etat ès-Lettres et Sciences Humaines, France.

Economist Intelligence Unit (1992), *Country Profile, Indochina: Vietnam, Laos, Cambodia*, London.

Evans, Grant (1989), 'Aid, loans prop Laos's trade efforts', the *Asian Wall Street Journal*, 17–18 February, 22.

—— (1990), *Lao Peasants under Socialism*, London: Yale University Press.

Fletcher, D., and G. Gunn (1981), *Revolution in Laos: the fourth generation of people's war?*, Southeast Asian monograph Series, no.8.

Gay, Bernard (1981), 'Les Mouvements Millénaristes du Centre et du Sud Laos et du Nord Est du Siam, 1895–1910', thèse, Centre d'Histoire et Civilisations de la Péninsule Indochinoise, Documents et Travaux sur la Péninsule Indochinoise, Paris.

—— (1989a), 'La perception des mouvements millénaristes du sud et du centre du Lao (fin du XIXème), C.N.R.S.-U.R.A. 1075, Paris, unpublished paper.

—— (1989b), 'Les relations entre hommes et femmes au Cambodge et au Laos vues par la littérature coloniale de fiction', C.N.R.S.-U.R.A. 1075, Paris, unpublished paper.

Gunn, Geoffrey C. (1982), 'Theravadins and commissars: the state and national identity in Laos', in Martin Stuart-Fox (ed.), *Contemporary Laos. Studies in the politics and society of the Lao People's Democratic Republic*, London: University of Queensland Press, 76–100.

—— (1985), 'A scandal in colonial Laos: the death of Bac My and the wounding of Kommadam revisited', *Journal of the Siam Society*, January–July, 42–60.

—— (1990) *Rebellion in Laos. Peasants and politics in a colonial backwater*, USA: Westview Press.

Hafner, James A. (1965), 'The Pathet Lao and change in traditional economies of the Meo and Kha, 1958–61', in *Papers of the Michigan Academy of Science, Arts and Letters*, vol.L, 431–6.

Halpern, Joel M. (1960), 'Laos and her tribal problems', *Michigan Alumnus Quarterly Review*, vol.67, no.10, December, 59–67.

—— (1966), *Tribal People of Laos*, Cambridge, Mass.: Harvard University Press.

Helm, Glenn E. (1988), 'The Lao PDR: a study in national security', master's thesis, Texas University at Tempe, December.

Hiebert, Murray (1982,) 'The Lao dilemma: division or dependence', *Indo China Issues*, Washington, no.27, August.

Hirashima, S. (1989), 'Perspective of the economic development of the ESCAP least developed countries: Bhutan, Lao PDR and Maldives', *Economic and Social Commission for Asia and the Pacific*, Bangkok, 10 October.

History of the Lao People's Revolutionary Party (Pavat Phak Pasason Pativat Lao, 1989, Vientiane: Committee of Social Sciences, mimeo.

Ireson, C. J., Boun Nyang Boutsady, Minavanh Kennavong Douang, Deuane Bounyavong, Bouaphet Khotnhotha, Arun Saydarath, (1989), 'The role of women in forestry in the Lao People's Republic', unpublished research.

Ireson, C. J. (1992), 'Women of opportunity: differing responses of rural Lao, Khmu and Hmong women to economic liberalization in the Lao PDR', Paper delivered at the symposium on 'Laos: Cultural Crossroads of Asia', the Southeast Asian Studies Summer Institute, University of Washington, Seattle, 24–26 July.

Ishii, Yoneo (1975), 'A note on Buddhistic millenarian revolts in northeastern Siam', *Journal of Southeast Asian Studies* (Singapore), vol.VI, no.2, September, 122–6.

Kamm, Henry (1990), 'In Laos, communism and Buddhism co-exist', *The Straits Times*, Singapore, 25 January.

Keo Mani (1973), 'May, la jeune Lao Sung' (The Lao Sung girl named May), in Neo Lao Hak Xat (ed.). *Les Fils du Mekong*, Laos: Neo Lao Hak Xat, 35–8.

Keyes, Charles (1977), 'Millennialism, Theravada Buddhism and Thai society', *Journal of the Siam Society*, (65)2, February, 283–304.

Kham Pheng Thipmountaly (1990), 'A Few Features of the Communal Rice Field System of the Thai minority in Huaphan Province of PDR Lao', unpublished paper.

Khamtan Thepbuali (1976a), *Kan meuang kab satsana phut* (Politics and Buddhism), Laos: Neo Lao Hak Xat.

—— (1976b), *Satsana phut kab kan pativat* (Buddhism and Revolution), Laos: Neo Lao Hak Xat.

Khaosan Pathet Lao, News Bulletin of Laos, 23 June 1976.

News Bulletin of Laos, 1 June 1977.

Kunstadter, Peter (ed.) (1967), *South Asian Tribes, Minorities and Nations*, Princeton: Princeton University Press.

Lao PDR (1989), *1988 Report*, United Nations Development Programme (UNDP), July.

Lao PDR (1989), *Report on the Economic and Social Situation, Development Strategy, and Assistance Needs of Lao PDR/External Assistance Priorities and project Profiles*, prepared for the Round Table Meeting, Geneva, Lao PDR, April.

Lee, Gary Y. (1982), 'Minority policies and the Hmong', in Martin Stuart-Fox (ed.), *Contemporary Laos. Studies in the politics and society of the Lao People's Democratic Republic*, London: University of Queensland Press, 199–219.

Ljunggren, Borje (1992), 'Market Economics under Communist Regime: reform in Vietnam, Laos and Cambodia', Ph.D dissertation, Southern Illinois University.

Manivone Viravong (1987), 'Role of Lao women in rural development', Paper resented at the seminar on the 'Role of Women in Socio-Economic Development with Special Reference to Rural Development', Tashkent, former Union of the Soviet Republics, 17–27 September.

Mayoury Ngaosyvathn (1989), 'Trend of research on women in Cambodia, Laos and Vietnam', a country paper delivered at the Expert Group Meeting Sub-regional Workshop on 'Research Methodologies, Perspectives and Directives for Policy in Women/Gender Studies in Southeast Asia', organized by the KANITA Research Programme, School of Social Sciences, University Sains Malaysia and UNESCO, Population and Human Settlement Division, Penang, 12–15 December.

—— 1990, 'On the edge of the Pagoda: Lao women in Buddhism', Working Paper Series Thai Studies Project Women in Development Consortium in Thailand. An Institutional Linkage Programme, York University, Toronto, Paper no.5.

McCoy, Alfred, 1970, 'French colonialism in Laos, 1–1945', in Nina S. Adams and Alfred W. McCoy (eds.), *Laos. War and revolution*, New York: Harper Colophon Books.

Moppert, F. (1978), 'Mouvements de Résistance au Pouvoir Colonial Français de la Minorité Protoindochinoise du Plateau des Bolovens dans le Sud Laos: 1901–1902', thèse de Doctorat de IIIème Cycle, Université de Paris VII.

Murdoch, John B. (1974), 'The 1901–1902 holy man's rebellion', *Journal of the Siam Society*, vol.62(I), January, 47–65.

Nhouy Abhay (1959), 'Le nouvel an Lao', April, Vientiane, n.p.

Paul, Eddy and Sara Walden (1992), 'Deadly business: sex and terror in the land of smiles', *The Australian Magazine* (Queensland), 19–20 September, 10–18.

Paxaxon (The People) Vientiane, 2 March 1989.

Pfister, Linda (1989), 'Traditional Lao Birth Practices and their Implications for improving Maternal and Child Health Services', Ph.D thesis, Madison: University of Wisconsin.

Phoumi Vongvichit (1968), 'Le Laos et la Lutte Victorieuse du Peuple Lao contre le Nèo-colonialisme Américain', Laos: Nèo Lao Hak Xat.

Proschan, Frank (1989), 'Kmhmu Verbal Art in America: the poetics of Kmhmu verse', Ph.D dissertation, University of Texas at Austin.

Queensland Education Consortium (Australia) (1990), 'Technical Proposal. Education project Lao People's Democratic Republic'.

Rakow, Meg Regina (1992), *Laos and Laotians*, Centre for Southeast Asian Studies, School of Hawaiian, Asian and Pacific Affairs, University of Hawaii.

Reid, Anthony (1988), 'Report on a week in Laos, August 1988', *Thai Yunnan Project Newsletter*, Canberra: Australian National University, no.3, December, 6–7.

Report for the Second Round Table of the Least Developing Countries of Asia and the Pacific, 1986, Geneva.

Report of the Ministry of Education: results of the seminar in Education, vol.II, 1990, Vientiane: Lao PDR, mimeo.

Rochet, Charles (1946), *Pays Lao. Le Laos dans la tourmente, 1930–1945*, Paris: Jean Vigneau.

Ruiming, W. (1983), 'Brain drain, economic reforms make marketplace vending more profitable than teaching school', *Southeast Asia Chronicle*, no.91, October, 6–9.

Sanyan Dongdeng (1974), 'Recalls based on history of the revolts of Father Kaduad', re-edited by Khamphanh Praisithided, mimeo.

Seuksa Mai (New Bulletin of Education, Ministry of Education of Lao PDR), no.72, October 1986.

Sisouk Na Champassak (1961), *Storm over Laos*, New York: Praeger.

State Statistical Centre (1990), *Basic Data about the Social and Economic Development of the Lao People's Democratic Republic*, Ministry of Economy, Planning and Finance, Vientiane: Lat Visahakit Camnai Seuksa.

Stuart-Fox, Martin (1983), 'Marxism and Therevada Buddhism: the legitimation of political authority in Laos', *Pacific Affairs*, vol.56, 428–54.

—— (1986), *Laos. Politics, Economics and Society*, London: Frances Pinter.

—— (1987), 'Minority policy in the Lao People's Democratic Republic', Paper presented at the Third International Conference on Thai Studies, Australian National University, Canberra, 3–6 July, Conference Proceedings, vol.II, compiled by Ann Buller, 331–8.

—— (1991a), 'Laos 1991: on the defensive', in *Southeast Asian Affairs 1992*, 163–80.

—— (1991b), 'The Constitution of the Lao People's Democratic Republic', *Review of Socialist Law*, The Netherlands, no.4, 299–317.

Sulak Sivarak (1981), *A Buddhist Vision for Renewing Society*, Bangkok: Thai Watana Panich.

The Sunday Mail (Australia), 23 February 1992.

Taupin, M. J. (1888), *Rapport à Mr. Le Gouverneur Général (Résultats de sa Mission au Laos)*, Saigon: Bulletin de la Société d'Etudes Indochinoises.

Tej Bunnag (1967), 'Kabot phu mi bun phaak Isan R.S. 121' *Sangkhomsat Parithat*, (The 1901–1902 'holy men' rebellions in northeast Thailand', *Social Science Review*, (5)1, 78–86.

Thee, Marek (1973), *Notes of a Witness: Laos and the Indochinese War*, New York: Vantage.

Thongsa Xayavongkhamdy, Bounkong Thongsavath, Dèng Phomsavanh, Sounet Phothisane, Singthong Sinthapangna, Viengvichit Southidet, 1989, *History of Laos 1893 up to Present Day (Pavatsat Lao 1893 Therng Pa Cuban)*, Vientiane: Ministry of education and Sports, Vol.III.

Turton, Andrew (1977) 'Laos: a peasant people's struggle for national liberation', *Race and Class*, vol.XVIII, no.3, 279–92.

Turton, Andrew and Shigeharu Tanabe (eds.) (1984) *History and Peasant Consciousness in South East Asia*, Osaka, National Museum of Ethnology.

Vang Tou-Fu (1979), 'The Hmong of Laos, in John K. Whitmore (ed.), *An Introduction to Indochinese History, Culture, Language and Life,* Ann Arbor: Centre for South and Southeast Asian Studies, University of Michigan.

Vientiane Mai (Vientiane News), 5 March 1987.

Wekkin, Gary D. (1974), 'Tribal politics in Indochina: the role of high-land tribes in the internationalization of internal wars', in Mark W. Zacher and Stephen Milne (eds.), *Conflict and Stability in Southeast Asia*, New York: Anchor Books, 121–47.

—— (1982), 'The rewards of revolution: Pathet Lao policy towards the hill tribes since 1975', in Martin Stuart-Fox (ed.), *Contemporary Lao. Studies in the politics and society of the Lao People's Democratic Republic*, London: University of Queensland Press, 181–98.

Whitaker, D. P., Helen A. Barth, Sylvan M. Berman, Judith M. Heimann, John E. MacDonald, Kenneth W. Martindale, Rinn-Sup Shinn, *Laos. A country study*, Washington, D.C.: Foreign Area Studies Handbook.

Wilson, T. Hunter (1987), 'The work of peace: changes in Laos under the Lao People's Democratic Republic', *Indochina Newsletter*, 48, November-December, 3–6, 12.

World Bank (1990), *Lao PDR. Issues in Public Economics*, New York, 10, August.

Yang Dao (1974), 'L'éducation chez les Hmong du Laos', in Martin and Doré (eds.), *Sangkhom Khady Sane*, Vientiane: Park Pasak, June.

—— (1975), *Les Hmong du Laos Face au Développement*, Vientiane: Siaosavath.

Zasloff, J. J (1973), *The Pathet Lao*, Lexington, Mass.: D.C. Health.

Chapter Twelve

Tai-Ization: Ethnic Change in Northern Indo-China

Grant Evans

Introduction

Field studies carried out in mainland South East Asia are among the most sophisticated investigations of ethnicity and ethnic transformation anywhere, and this is due in no small measure to the influence of Edmund Leach's *Political Systems of Highland Burma: a Study of Kachin Social Structure* (1970 [1954]). Because of wars, revolutions, and military rule at one time or another in the states of the region, most subsequent research has been conducted in northern Thailand; little fieldwork has been carried out in Burma, southern China, Laos, or northern Vietnam. One of the purposes of this chapter is to spread the empirical field of the debate to the northern Indo-China highlands.

It was Leach's rejection of essentialist ideas of ethnicity and his argument concerning ethnic transformations that most caught the imagination of anthropologists in the field. Leach saw the question of ethnicity as central to his book. The 'main theme of my book had best be understood [as] What is the difference between Kachin and Shan?' (Leach 1970: 107). The Shan, a Tai group organized into small states and practising Theravada Buddhism, was the key group by which the Kachin defined themselves, and into which many Kachin were assimilated, becoming 'Tai-ized'. Most striking was his argument that the ethnicity of the Kachin was pliable and not primordial. He argued that as their political system oscillated between a hierarchical ideal based on a Shan model, and an egalitarian one (*gumlao*) – with a Kachin-hierarchical model (*gumsa*) intermediate – so they tended to shift from Kachin to Shan and back to Kachin identity. The issue of ethnicity was side-tracked in subsequent debates which concentrated on Leach's structuralist account of this oscillation (Donahue 1984; Friedman 1979, 1986; Leach 1983a, 1983b; Nugent 1982, 1983). Friedman is preoccupied with the dynamics of systemic evolution and the role of ecological constraints on the system. He says that the process by which

Plate 19. '. . . les aborigènes par l'offrande d'une jarre d'alcool, renouvellent le contrat ancien . . .'

Kachin become Shan 'is not a process in any meaningful way. It is a case of changed identity, a borrowing of cultural traits' (Friedman 1979: 251). Nugent claims that region–wide political and economic change explained the oscillations between *gumsa*/hierarchical and *gumlao*/egalitarian forms of social organization. Friedman (1986) later stressed the importance of the opium economy, and regional political and economic change. Placing micro changes in a macro context has been an important shift in anthropological writing since Leach's book, and since Eric Wolf's *Europe and the People Without History* (1982) few anthropologists ignore the wider political, social, or economic context of even the apparently most isolated peoples.

This chapter places the process of ethnic change among a group called Black Tai and a non-Tai group, the Sing Moon, in a relatively remote part of Laos into a broader context. It discusses three issues: first, the concept of 'Tai-ization' of non-Tai ethnic groups in the highlands; second, systemic elements that either restrict or facilitate ethnic transformation; and finally, the impact of the modern state on the process of ethnic change.[1]

Tai-ization

Since the late nineteenth century the process of Tai-ization of subordinate ethnic groups has been commented on by French colonial officials during their travels in the Indo-China highlands. Leach's work, however, is perhaps the first major anthropological study of the process. More recently Georges Condominas, in his *Essay on the Evolution of Thai Political Systems* (1990 [1976]), argues that 'Tai-ization' of non-Tai peoples in northern Indo-China was a key element in the expansion of Tai peoples into South East Asia from southern China. The absorption of non-Tai peoples is thought to explain the assumed rapidity of Tai expansion and to be a basic element of the overall social structure: 'where they succeeded in consolidating their power, the Tai were able to strengthen their position through a thorough policy of "Tai-ization" of the subjugated population. . . Elsewhere, especially in the Shan states and other Tay principalities, the bulk of the population remained composed of non-Tay. . .' (1990: 45). The process of 'Tai-ization' in northern Indo-China is distinct, Condominas argues, from what Leach observed in his study of the Kachin of Burma. 'Oscillation' is absent in Indo-China where 'we see the apparently irreversible expansion of Tai-ization of the non-Tay groups. . .' (1990: 70). Leach rejects ideas of 'fabulous large scale military conquest': 'Shan culture . . . is an indigenous growth resulting from the economic interaction of small-scale military colonies with an indigenous hill-population over a long period . . . large sections of the peoples we now know as Shans are descendants of hilltribesmen who have in the recent past been assimilated into the more sophisticated ways of Buddhist-Shan culture' (Leach 1970: 39). But both authors agree on the end result − 'Tai-ization'.

Condominas's study limits itself to 'intermediate social spaces', 'to Thai political systems, which have not yet reached the dimensions of a state; it concerns the *müöng* which remained in the mountains and valleys of northern Indo-China' (1990: 78). The geographical confinement of the *müöng* [sc. *müang*. Ed.] to upland valleys ensured that centralized states did not emerge, only confederations, e.g. the *Sip Song Chau Tai* (Twelve Tai Principalities[2]) in northern Vietnam and Laos. Thai states emerged only in the 'open spaces such as the middle Mekong' (1990: 84). The Tai in the upland valleys of Indo-China have been referred to as 'tribal' Tai, presumably because they have not formed separate states. The key groups are White Tai, Black Tai, and Red Tai who overlap into Laos, and the Tay (Tho) and Nung who overlap into China from Vietnam. In Vietnam these groups number over 2 million people. In Laos there are almost half a million Phu Tai (i.e. all Tai groups except the Lao – a problematic catch-all category) and in Houa Phan province, where research for this chapter was conducted, they number 76,000 persons.[3]

Crucial to the process of becoming Shan is 'the adoption of Buddhism', argues Leach (1970: 30). However, he notes that 'In Indo-China there is a group known as the "Black Tai" who are not Buddhist, but I am concerned here only with the Shans of the Kachin Hills Area'. The Tai-ization that Condominas investigates, however, does not entail conversion to Buddhism but refers primarily to the adoption of Tai culture and ritual by non-Tai groups. Thus Tai-ization is not a uniform process across the region, something which draws our attention to the fact that Tai groups themselves are not uniform, and suggests that there are different levels and elements to Tai-ization.

Systemic Elements of Ethnicity

In *Political Systems* and his essay 'The Frontiers of "Burma"'(1960) Leach asserts that there is a fundamental, systemic contrast between valley people and hill people across the region. 'Culturally there is far more in common between the Lakher in Assam and the Lamet in Laos than there is between either group and their nearest Valley neighbours.' He goes on: 'Yet the pattern of political relations which I have previously described might have led us to expect something different. After all, Hill People and Valley People are racially the same and languages are very easily changed, so what is it that keeps the two groups apart?' (Leach 1960: 65). 'Valley culture', he argues, 'has an Indian style', which includes Buddhism, while 'Hill culture has a Chinese style' (ibid.: 66). In the former marriage does not establish alliances between kin-groups, and there is almost caste-like endogamy which makes 'marriage with the barbarians' (ibid.) difficult. Among the latter 'high valuation is placed on extended kinship relations' and one's position in a lineage is crucial for one's position in society'. Furthermore, 'the "animism" of the Hill People is fundamentally a cult of dead ancestors which has many Confucianist parallels' (ibid.: 65). He concludes: 'This contrast of ideologies about the nature of authority illuminates, even if it does not explain why 2,000 years of Indian rule has not eliminated the radical separation between Hill and Valley society' (ibid.: 67).

Yet, across the region, historically we find conversion of Hill People into Valley People, even if the categories remain. One of the virtues of *Political Systems* is that it tries to isolate the systemic barriers to ethnic conversion among the Kachin. The organization of the latter into a system of ranked lineages (absent from Tai society) had, he argues, important implications for social exchanges, especially marriage exchanges where wife-givers rank higher than wife-takers in a context of generalised exchange. Among the Shan, on the other hand, those who receive – tribute, wives, etc. – are superior to those who give. Thus, a 'situation in which a Kachin chief gives a woman to the Shan chief in whose territory he resides would be directly contradictory – it would imply to the Kachin that the Kachin was overlord, and to the Shan that the Shan was overlord. Such a marriage could therefore only occur where Kachin and Shan respect one another's status as independent monarchs of equal status' (Leach 1970: 219). The situation for commoners, however, is radically different. He writes of the assimilation of Kachins into the Shan system at a commoner level:

'In thus settling in a Shan valley the Kachin cuts himself off altogether from his own kinsfolk. He adopts the nats ['spirits' Ed.] of his Shan wife – that is to say he becomes a Buddhist – and from the Kachin point of view he becomes a Shan (*sam tai*); but he enters the Shan system at the bottom of the scale as a person of the lowest caste, he is virtually a slave. The Shan terms which are used to denote Kachins in the mass . . . all have the prefix Kha meaning 'serf' or 'slave'. Within the Kachin Hills Area nearly all low class Shans are probably either of slave or commoner Kachin origin.

The reverse kind of assimilation from commoner Shan to commoner Kachin is unlikely, since life in the hills offers no attractions to the plainsman . . .

We must therefore distinguish clearly between the assimilation of Kachin to Shan at aristocratic and at commoner level. Aristocratic Kachins can 'become Shan' in the sense that they can become sophisticated and establish a *mayu-dama* marriage relationship with an aristocratic Shan lineage, but they do not thereby surrender their status as Kachin chiefs. On the contrary, their chiefly status as Kachins is enhanced; it is the culmination of *gumsa* ideals that the Kachin *duwa* should be treated as a *saopha* by his Shan counterpart. Commoner Kachin on the other hand can only become Shan by ceasing to be Kachins. At a commoner level the Kachin and Shan systems, though linked economically, are totally separated by barriers of kinship and religion.' (ibid.: 222).

This 'class' dimension in the hills of Burma is an important contrast with the situation in upland Indo-China. Other important contrasts are, first, and perhaps most importantly, that among Indo-China uplanders potentially subject to the Tai (so leaving to one side Hmong and Yao) lineage forms of organization are uncommon. Leach's assumption of a commonality across the region is based on his understanding of certain problematic interpretations Izikowitz made concerning Lamet 'clans' (Izikowitz 1951).[4] I return to the question of patronymics later, but let me assert for the moment that clans do not exist. In fact bilateral systems of kinship are more common in the northern Indo-China highlands (Murdoch 1960), though the picture remains confused, especially in relation to claims of matriliny (Olsen 1976), partly because of the continuing influence of nineteenth-century evolutionism on Vietnamese ethnographers (Evans 1985).[5]

Secondly, chieftainships and ranked lineages are rare in northern Indo-China. Claims are made by Vietnamese ethnographers that the autochthonous Mon–Khmer had chieftainships before the coming of the Tai. Outside of folktales and myths, however, there is not much evidence. Proschan (1989) has surveyed the evidence for the existence of a Khmu kingdom, Muang Svaa, in northern Laos, and found it inconclusive. Nor is there evidence for Khmu political organization above the village since the coming of the Tai. The absence of strong chieftainships may be the result of the absence of major trade routes through these highlands.[6] Leach, for example, claims that control of trade 'gave the early Jingphaw power . . . which enabled the *gumsa* to become feudal satellites of the Shan princes rather than their serfs . . . . My suggestion is that Jingphaw culture spread over the Kachin Hills Area at the expense of the culture of the other miscellaneous tribal cultures because the Jingphaw achieved a relatively superior political status *vis-à-vis* their Shan overlords' (1970: 251). In Indo-China the comparable groups were unable to gain control of trade routes and therefore tended to become serfs of the upland Tai. So a distinctive feature of the northern Indochinese Highlands was that the various Mon–Khmer groups never formed political organizations capable of resisting the Tai. This was not true of the Hmong and Yao, both of whom used clan and lineage organizations as a basis for resisting Tai encroachments, and not surprisingly the main millenarian revolts in the northern highlands have been led by Hmong (Gunn 1990; Corlin and Tapp in this volume).

Laos: a Poly-ethnic State

Laos is one of the most ethnically diverse countries in mainland South East Asia. It is a land-locked country which lies between the major states of the region: China on its northern border, Vietnam to the East, Cambodia to the far South, Thailand to the South and West, and Burma in the far North-West. Populations from all of these neighbours overlap into Laos. Unlike these other countries the lowland, ethnic Lao after whom the country is named, do not constitute an overwhelming majority of the population. Of a total population of a little more than 4 million the Lao make up between 1.8 and 1.9 millions, not quite half the population. If, however, an ethno-linguistic classification is used – putting together all speakers of Tai dialects, of which Lao is one – then the Tai-Lao group rises to between 2.3 and 2.4 millions, or just over half the population. In neighbouring countries the dominant ethnic group – Vietnamese, Chinese, Thai, Cambodian, Burmese – make up more than 80 per cent of the population or even more than 90 per cent. The relative balance between ethnic groups in Laos is therefore unusual and one can see the political attractions of particular ways of drawing the ethnic map. These issues are discussed fully in chapters in this volume by Mayoury Ngaosyvathn and Kossikov.

I conducted research in Muang Xieng Kho, Houa Phan province in 1988, 1990, and 1993. When I first arrived in the Muang and told officials that I wanted to study a Black Tai village they sent me to Ban Sot which they assured me was 'thoroughly Black Tai'. The village in 1988 was composed of three hamlets – Ban Sot South, Ban Sot North, and just over the Nam Ma (river), Ban Na Wan. One of my first surprises was to learn that Ban Na Wan was composed of Mon-Khmer Sing Moon (also romanised as Xing Mul, see below) – something passed over, or unperceived, at the level of Muang organization. In 1988 there were 40 houses in Ban Sot South, 29 in Ban Sot North, and 17 in Ban Na Wan. These figures have since fluctuated only slightly as some people have moved within the village or migrated. The population, again in 1988, was Ban Sot South 265 persons (average of 6.6 persons per household), Ban Sot North 166 persons (average of 5.7 persons per household), and Ban Na Wan 77 (average of 4.5 persons per household), and this has risen slightly over the past five or so years. The village of Ban Sot was established in the 1930s by Black Tai settlers from neighbouring Son La Province in Vietnam. The population has been augmented by further migrations from Vietnam, especially after 1954, and by marriage. Ban Sot North was begun in 1974 and Ban Na Wan joined the village after 1973.

Administrative Integration of Ban Na Wan

In the traditional Black Tai system aristocrats were privileged to receive gifts of forest products and labour; the majority group were ordinary Tai who worked their own land, and as 'warriors' had rights in village decision-making; the next group were Tai who had become debt 'slaves' of the major households; then there were non-Tai who had to perform labour on the aristocrats' fields but had no political rights. Sometimes the latter were house 'slaves', *kon heun*, but it would appear that more often they lived in separate villages close-by (Dang Nghiem Van 1971: 182–83, uses the term 'bonded peasants'). The latter were called *xá* or *sa'*, similar to the Lao word *kha* for 'slave' commonly used in the not so distant past as a term for most 'tribal' peoples. The general term *Sa'* is sometimes used by Sing Moon today to describe themselves or other similar groups, such as the Khmu. They have also been called Puok (Phwak), and also sometimes refer to themselves this way. The exact origins of this term are unclear; it is often attributed to the French colonial officials. Sing Moon in fact is a Lao rendering of K'tsing Mul (Xingmul), which is how the people themselves pronounce their name. They are also sometimes referred to as Lao May (new Lao).

Muang Xieng Kho is, apparently, the only place in Laos where these people live. The majority (9,000 persons) are in Vietnam, where they have been studied by Vietnamese ethnographers (Dang Nghiem Van et al. 1972; Dang Nghiem Van et al. 1984), and there are other scattered references (see Schrock 1972). According to the Lao Institute of Ethnography, in 1988 there were 2,164 Sing Moon people in Muang Xieng Kho (probably an underestimation); in 1993 I listed 33 villages in the Muang ranging from 11 to 70 families. One Tasseng (canton, or sub-district), Lao Houng, contained only Sing Moon villages, eleven of them. The most obvious distinguishing feature of this group today is their language which is different from the surrounding Tai, Lao, and Vietnamese, although it has borrowed heavily from them. In the past they were more reliant on swidden agriculture. Their social organization is broadly egalitarian, and the kinship and marriage system reflects a stronger bilateral orientation than the neighbouring Tai.

The Sing Moon in Ban Sot used to live in Ban Houey Wan up in the watershed (*houey* means stream). The same background can be found among other Sing Moon in the area. According to my informants, after 1973 soldiers went into the Sing Moon villages and instructed them to move down to the plains because they were allegedly 'destroying the forest'. This corresponded with the policy of the communists who were soon to come to power in Vientiane and attempt to put this policy into effect throughout the country.[7] Sing Moon who were moved down were administratively integrated into neighbouring Black Tai villages. One intended consequence of this was that they should have access to paddy land. In fact, in Ban Houey Wan the Sing Moon had already cleared paddy terraces which they combined with swidden cultivation, and the move to the valley initially disrupted their use of these upland terraces. When the collectivization programme was launched in Laos in 1979 the Sing Moon, who had been relocated to Ban Na Wan, were relocated yet again, to Ban Sot South. This was in keeping with the intended political role of co-operatives which was to establish even tighter political control over the population (see Evans 1990, Chapter 8). The co-operative in this village lasted until 1985 when it collapsed for reasons I have dealt with elsewhere (Evans 1990). The people in the village talk of the cumbersomeness of trying to do paddy and upland fields collectively here. But even before the collapse of the co-operative in 1983, the Sing Moon had left Ban Sot South and returned over the river to the site of Ban Na Wan.

One could see this attempted integration as state sponsorship of 'Tai-ization', with the Lao-dominated government as the overall agent, and their cousins the Black Tai the immediate beneficiaries. But the picture is more complex. The Black Tai of Ban Sot were not pleased to have Sing Moon integrated into their village, even as a separate hamlet. Among themselves the Black Tai are quite contemptuous of the Sing Moon. When I mentioned Sing Moon in any context Black Tai invariably chuckled and made jokes about their assumed lower level of culture and intelligence. Similar mirth is also reserved for the highland Hmong, but interestingly not for the similar Yao. One Yao man has married into the village, and while he has to deal with occasional patronizing remarks, the villagers have given Yao 'honourary' valley dweller status and deny that they are Lao Soung.

Cultural Diacritica and Ehos

In discussions of cultural differences people invariably mention language, and Black Tai joke about what, to them, is the funny sound of Sing Moon speech. Interestingly, one 'upwardly mobile' Sing Moon, said that the only difference between Black Tai and Sing Moon culture was that Sing Moon could speak not only their own language, but Black Tai as well. I found only one older Black Tai man who could speak reasonable Sing Moon, because in the early 1950s he had worked with the French in Sing Moon villages in Vietnam. The Sing Moon in Ban Na Wan speak their own language at home and in the village, although the language is now heavily influenced by Black Tai and Lao vocabulary. The Black Tai comment on how the Sing Moon use Black Tai (and Lao) songs and dances, and other elements of popular and material culture. It is not as marked as Condominas noted for the Laha, however: 'Ethnographically speaking, evidence which is immediately visible when entering a Laha village is the extent of Tai-ization: clothes, houses, tools, are all the same as those used in a Black Tai village' (1990: 54). Although it is partly true for Ban Na Wan. The women, especially when they dress up, adopt traditional Black Tai costume – if they have one. Only six of the seventeen houses in the village are built in the large and sturdy Black Tai style, but none have the large stocks of timber one finds under better-off Black Tai houses. Other houses are smaller, and less solidly built; the poverty of the village compared with Ban Sot South and North is striking. The Black Tai in Ban

Sot say that the houses in Ban Na Wan are 'not beautiful, and are like huts in the forest'.

But the most strident charge the Black Tai level at the Sing Moon is that they are 'lazy'. They claim they do not like to work paddy land and prefer to scavenge in the forest. This laziness, they said, led to ill-feeling when the Sing Moon had been integrated into Ban Sot South between 1979 and 1983. They claimed the Black Tai would go off to work early in the morning and Sing Moon would stay at home. The ill-feeling caused the Sing Moon to move back over the river. One can guess that problems associated with 'lazy' people in the co-operatives, expressed widely throughout Laos at the time, here found a convenient ethnic scapegoat in the Sing Moon. Furthermore, the Black Tai are contemptuous of Sing Moon because they are prepared to hire out their labour when they are short of money instead of trying to create wealth for themselves. A Tasseng official claimed that this was true of all 'Lao Theung' groups throughout the Muang, and he singled out the Khmu. It was said that if Black Tai marry into a Sing Moon village then they become lazy, but if Sing Moon marry into a Black Tai village then they learn to work hard. The Tasseng official, a politically astute man, was quick to point out, however, that not all Sing Moon were lazy. There were, he said, some households in Ban Na Wan who worked hard, had good houses, and emulated Black Tai ways. The presence of three opium addicts in the Sing Moon village was a further source of disdain, despite the fact that it was one of the Black Tai in Ban Sot who sold them opium.

None of this overt hostility is reciprocated by the Sing Moon as far as I could tell – but then I cannot speak the Sing Moon language either, and perhaps there is a vibrant 'hidden transcript', typical of power-laden situations (Scott 1990), waiting to be discovered. Perhaps one symptom of 'resistance' was that none of the Sing Moon would admit to having worked for Black Tai in Ban Sot in the recent past. They travelled to the next Black Tai villages to seek wage work, building houses, and clearing land for *hai*. The Black Tai in Ban Sot were not concerned about how recently the Sing Moon had worked for them; the simple fact of having done it in the past and the continued sale of their labour to others was enough to establish their lower status. One could interpret the attempt by Sing Moon to seek work in villages other than Ban Sot as a way of asserting, however minimally, their independence from Ban Sot and transpose the unequal relationship onto more distant Tai. The reluctance to work for Ban Sot South may also be part of an ongoing dispute I discuss below.

I would also like to raise the idea of a different 'ethos' between the groups. The idea of an 'ethos' often makes intuitive sense and has been widely used in the social sciences. Few ethnographies, however, have documented the formation of an ethos. Bateson's *Naven* (1958) is probably the most famous exception. Compared with the Sing Moon one is struck by the personal self-confidence and competitiveness of most Black Tai. This feeds into the high value they place on hard work, which gives them the resources to compete for status in the village. This is manifest in ability to give lavish post-harvest parties which require quantities of home-made liquor. Drinking itself is intensely competitive. In both Black Tai and in Sing Moon villages, however, competitive religious expenditure is less than amongst lowland Lao or Thai, where Buddhist practices absorb 'ceremonial funds' and provide a conduit for status competition.

An important element of cultural organization of the White, Black, and Red Tai is the use of patronymics or *sing*. The élite are generally *sing Lo* or *Lo Gam* whose origin myth justifies aristocratic status (Lafont 1955). These patronymics serve ritual purposes and are associated with social status. *Sing Lo*, for example, is associated with the traditional élite, and while this élite no longer exists people are quick to inform others that they are *sing Lo* when the occasion arises because their origin myth asserts that they are intrinsically 'higher'. Although wealth differentials in the village are relatively small to an outsider, they are enough to assert small status differences – and to be both better-off and *sing Lo* helps in status competition. Some better-off members of the village are from commoner *sing*, and claims to aristocratic lineage no longer play a key role in ordering the social structure. By contrast, Sing Moon who also have patronymics do not appear to use them in a competitive way, for the reason, I would suggest, that they are not as culturally deeply rooted among this group; nor do they have any analagous status seeking ritual.

Life in Ban Na Wan is generally more muted and the atmosphere less competitive, and no doubt this is one source of Black Tai charges of laziness. This manifests itself in less intense drinking sessions, and more egalitarian participation in them. This may seem paradoxical given that wealth differentials are clearer in Ban Na Wan than in Ban Sot; namely between the six 'upwardly mobile' households in their large Black Tai style houses, and the other households, some of whom live in tiny bamboo huts. But at parties held in these better-off households even the poorest villagers participate and are not made to wait at the edge of the participating group until invited in, as I have seen in Black Tai households. This culturally less pressing need to compete for status means that people are less anxious about working hard, and less concerned with long-term planning. In this context Black Tai claims of laziness make sense. Only if Sing Moon want to be Black Tai do they have to work as hard as Black Tai. This involves an important shift in world-view or ethos. As Lehman (1979: 247) has remarked:

'In interethnic systems where, by mutual agreement as well as objectively, the parties are of unequal status and have very unequal access to mutually desired economic resources and ecological 'niches', ambivalence seems to be a function of the very fact of ethnic distinctiveness. That is, in many respects, the choice of a subordinate ethnic category is motivated by the perceived advantage of having alternate cultural standards as against competing with apparent promise of failure in the arena of someone else's cultural standards of achievement.'

Some brief mention should be made of two poor Khmu households who are perched precariously at the edge of Ban Sot North. These two households live in the poorest houses of the village, engage in no paddy production, and generally find themselves in a similar situation to the poorer Sing Mool and are treated with similar disdain. They work as blacksmiths and engage in occasional wage labour.

Access to Resources

Paddy rice-land in Black Tai villages today is mostly held in common. The land in the village is periodically redistributed to households, theoretically according to their needs, calculated according to the number of workers they can put in the field and the number of mouths they have to feed. There is some privately held paddy land, and all swidden land is privately held and worked. The traditional system of holding paddy land is described by two Vietnamese writers as follows:

> 'Collective ownership of the land and the ricefields is defined according to the following principle: *the peasant has only the right of occupation and exploitation of the land, but has absolutely no right to private ownership* . . . A peasant who has been exploiting a ricefield for such a long time that he does not even know any longer who used it before him, can still in no way take ownership of it. However, he is sure of one thing: this rice-field is the property of the *müöng* (a communal rice-field) which he or any other member of the community has the right to cultivate if it is allotted to him . . . .' (cited by Condominas 1990: 56).

So we can see that the traditional system is largely still intact in the villages I have studied. The main difference is that village leaders, rather than aristocrats, have the right to allocate land. This is done annually, although this may mean no change for individual families from the year before. Where there are intractable disputes, the Tasseng is brought in, and then the Muang.

Between Ban Sot South and Ban Sot North there is a small valley of collectively owned rice-fields. It is worked in both the wet and the dry season, and the size of the land able to be worked fluctuates a little according to whether there is enough water available, especially in the dry season. The area of land able to be worked in the wet season varies from

11 hectares to 15 hectares, depending on the availability of water, while in the dry season it varies between 5 and 7 hectares. At Ban Na Wan there is around 3 ha, some of which is shared with families from Ban Sot South. During the dry season close to 2 ha of this land can be worked. If we take 1990 as an example, on average each household in Ban Sot South and North worked around 0.12 ha in the wet season and in the dry season 0.09 ha making an average of paddy worked for the year of 0.21 ha. The largest amount worked by any one household in that year was 0.55 ha of paddy and the smallest 0.048 ha. This last household quickly dissolved as it contained a single widowed woman who soon moved to live with relatives, whereas the hoseholds which worked close to half a hectare had between 8–11 members in the household. Fluctuations around the average are largely dictated by the number of workers available in the household. This is also true for Ban Na Wan. There the average worked by households in the wet season was 0.16 ha, and 0.12 ha in the dry season, giving an average for the year of 0.28 ha. The largest amount worked by one household was 0.39 ha and the lowest 0.14 ha. Once again this distribution roughly corresponded with available labour in the households. It is worth observing, in the light of Black Tai comments that Sing Moon are 'lazy' and do not like to work paddy fields, that they tend to cultivate the same amount of paddy land per household as the Black Tai.

Swidden fields (*hai*) are a fundamental part of the upland economic system. In Ban Sot South and North in 1990 they made up 36.8 ha, an average of 0.64 ha per household, and in Ban Na Wan accounted for 10.4 ha, and 0.65 ha per household. Combined paddy and *hai* meant that each household cultivated just under 1 ha of land per year. The largest amount of *hai* cultivated was 1.3 ha, and in general the families able to cultivate close to 1 ha of *hai* were the larger families with more labour. In 1993 the total amount cultivated by Ban Sot South and North had fallen to 30.7 ha, while in Ban Na Wan it had gone up slightly to 12.56 ha. In 1988 Ban Na Wan had cultivated 15.7 ha of *hai*, but in that year only the six 'upwardly mobile' Sing Moon families worked on collective paddy land – one of the early signs of strain over the use of this land. The amount of *hai* worked by people in Ban Sot South and North in that year also seems to have been higher, closer to 50 ha.

I would like to argue that what we are seeing in the vicinity of Ban Sot (and throughout the upland valleys of Laos and Vietnam) is a growing crisis in the upland system in several ways.[8] Population growth (approximately 2.9 per cent) is a key factor. Previously, limited paddy land could be offset by larger amounts of *hai*. However, availability of land for *hai* is now exhausted and intensified use of the land brings lower yields. One consequence of extensive upland cultivation is less water in the streams, and so less water for paddy fields in the dry season. Small scale irrigation dams are beginning to be put in place throughout Houa Phan province and elsewhere by foreign aid organizations, but these will probably only arrest a system on the verge of devolution. Other possibilities have recently emerged to relieve pressure on resources. Until Lao government changes of policy, particularly since 1988, new mouths to feed had to be absorbed by the village economy. Now, however, there are possibilities of branching out into trading. Over 1991–93, with improved relations between China and Laos and Vietnam, Vietnamese traders have arrived from Son-la on bicycles, motorbikes, or on the local bus (truck) carrying Chinese and Vietnamese goods. Some villagers have begun to take advantage of these opportunities. It has led to an increase in manufactured goods in the village. For example, in 1988 there were one or two radios in the village, now there are many, and this has increased villagers' exposure to the outside world. Migration of young people has grown, either to the provincial centres or to Vientiane. Once established, they will provide a basis for further migration. As one old man commented, once they go there is little for them to come back to.

The crisis in the upland system has recently taken a more 'political' form. In early 1991 Ban Na Wan approached the Tasseng to request that they become a separate village. The administration agreed. At the base of this request is a dispute about paddy land. Increased overall pressure on land has led to arguments among Black Tai about distribution of paddy land. Even small shifts in proportions are significant for individual households. In deciding the amount of land three considerations are taken into account; the number of workers in the household, the ratio of non-workers to workers, and the quality of the land. Three qualities of land are used for tax purposes, but not everyone agrees about the quality of their land and its productivity. There is also a fuzziness about when a young person becomes a worker and when an older person becomes a dependant. There is much to argue and grumble about when it comes to access to communal resources. The village leaders who distribute the land are generally from the stronger and better-off families in the village. They look after themselves and their allies: not outrageously, nor in the sense that they act like a class, as with the former Black Tai aristocrats, but as a slowly shifting set of household alliances in the village. This provides a source of complaint for less well-off Black Tai villagers.

These complaints, however, had an ethnic outlet by opposing the accommodation of Sing Moon villagers onto Ban Sot paddy land. This had come to the surface in 1988 when, as indicated above, only the six 'Tai-ized' Sing Moon households cultivated paddy. The Black Tai claimed that the Sing Moon did not want to do paddy that year, preferring to cultivate *hai*. I had the impression that poorer Sing Moon villagers were excluded from the paddy fields that year by the Black Tai in collusion with the 'Tai-ized' households who, it should be remembered, were still part of Ban Sot village at that time. The control of paddy land near Ban Na Wan in mid-1993 was in dispute and it was up to the Tasseng to decide on the matter. The Tasseng had persuaded Ban Sot to 'loan' the land to Ban Na Wan because otherwise they would have had 'nothing to eat'. This appeal to a moral economy is a strong one and provides an interesting counter-force to the ethnic divide. On the other hand, this same moral economy binds the upwardly mobile Sing Moon to poorer villagers insuring solidarity in the dispute with the Black Tai.

Consistent with the continuing claim of Ban Sot is the fact that the village head of Ban Sot, in conjunction with the village head of Ban Na Wan, has decided over recent years who will work the collective plot of paddy fields, and some Ban Sot households have continued to work there. Interestingly, most people in Ban Na Wan and Ban Sot claim not to know who is the original owner of this land. 'No-one knows' is a common response, except from several old men of old-established families in the village who claim to know who cleared the land and established paddy fields. At the bottom of these divergent claims is anxiety about future changes in policy which would allow the privatization of communal land. Acknowledgement of who was here first may give those older households prior claims. The decision will be made by Tasseng officials who are Black Tai, some of whom expressed opinions about the laziness of Sing Moon and their reluctance to cultivate paddy fields. But they are bound by a government policy which still encourages minorities to settle in the valley. If Sing Moon are excluded from the collective paddy fields, there is little incentive for the poorer families, who have no terraced fields, to stay where they are. Thus there is strong pressure from above for the Tasseng to decide in favour of Ban Na Wan's collective control over that land. The decision for the 'Tai-ized' Sing Moon was whether to make a play for the land as a separate village, or to risk trying to operate as full Black Tai in the distribution game. They chose to go as a separate village. In some ways, for them, it does not affect the process of 'Tai-ization'. That is largely dependent on their relative affluence and ability to establish kinship links with Tai, which is helped by more secure access to resources.

Throughout Muang Xieng Kho similar forces have led to the exodus of Sing Moon villages from Black Tai villages into which they had been administratively integrated. Of the thirty-three Sing Moon villages in the Muang ten had been integrated into Black Tai villages. One Tasseng was occupied only by Sing Moon and thus there were no Tai villages close by into which they could have been integrated. The others were either too high up in the mountains and escaped the relocations of the 1970s or were too remote from neighbouring villages. But of the ten integrated at that time, nine have chosen to break away since 1990, the political manifestation of growing conflict over resources in the mountains.

The dilemma for the Government administration bears some comparison with the traditional system in which the village had exclusive rights to allocate land to its members (Condominas 1990: 57). The laws of the *müöng* in the upland areas of northern Indo-China now have to be congruent with the laws and policies of the over-arching states, and these allow the over-riding of the 'supreme' rights of one *ban* in favour of another. Thus throughout the Muang the administration will have to mediate disputes over rights to communal land between Black Tai villages and separating Sing Moon villages in accordance with larger national priorities. The Lao state certainly appears to have established its right to do this as most of the villagers acknowledged the Tasseng's right to decide.

Inter-ethnic Marriage in the Uplands

Rates of inter-marriage in these villages also gives us some idea of the relationship between groups in the highlands. The process of 'Tai-ization' should register itself here. In general, the Black Tai of Ban Sot marry other Black Tai or Tai Wat (a localized group of Black Tai from Muang Wat in Vietnam). Data gathered in 1988 showed that in Ban Sot South three daughters and two sons had married out to Lao, two daughters and one son had gone with White Tai, and one son with Red Tai, while only one daughter had married out to a Khmu who was a soldier. Three Red Tai women had married into the village, and two Sing Moon women. In Ban Sot North two daughters had married out to Lao, two sons with Red Tai, and one daughter had married a Khmu. Marrying in were one Lao woman, two Red Tai women, one Yao man, and one Sing Moon woman. In general in Ban Na Wan Sing Moon marry other Sing Moon. One daughter had married out to a Lao. On the other hand two Lao men had married into the village, and one Black Tai woman. (Since gathering this data in 1988 I know of three more Sing Moon women who have married into Ban Sot South.)

Marriage patterns in a neighbouring Black Tai village and its Sing Moon satellite in 1990 revealed a similar picture. Overwhelmingly, Black Tai marry other Tai related groups, and Sing Moon marry other Sing Moon. While women go from Ban Na Wan to the Black Tai of Ban Sot, no men do. Similarly, only one Ban Sot Black Tai woman had married into Ban Na Wan, no men. Generally, in these villages children are considered to belong to the ethnic group of their fathers, so the mobility of women does little to change group ethnicity. An exception to this was a poor Lao man who had no relatives elsewhere and had married into the village, and now considered himself and his children to be Sing Moon. The other Lao, whose father-in-law is one of the 'upwardly mobile' Sing Moon, considers his children to be Lao. But the better-off members of the Sing Moon village are able to marry-in either Lao or Black Tai women and marry their daughters to Black Tai men. In this way they establish kinship links with

Black Tai, which provides a line of potential assistance and enables them to acquire a Black Tai lifestyle.

But with such relatively low rates of inter-marriage between Tai and non-Tai we need to take a closer look at the arguments concerning 'Tai–ization'.

Tai–ization?

Sing Moon are in practice culturally subordinate to Lao-Tai and especially Black Tai culture. Condominas is right to observe that 'Tai-ization [is] born of the conquered peoples' hope of reaching a better status . . .' (1990: 71). Several Sing Moon were doing their best to acquire Black Tai status, and one had held the important position of Nai Ban (village head) from 1988 until 1991. But in the present, and perhaps also in the past, the process of conversion is voluntary, not coerced as Condominas's stress on military conquest by the Tai in earlier times suggests. Becoming 'Tai' is a way of raising one's social status.

Among the Sing Moon one observes little cultural self-confidence or pride in being Sing Moon.[9] In contrast, the Black Tai are conscious that they possess a 'great tradition'. The Black Tai in Ban Sot were embarrassed when I first arrived with books written in Black Tai which they could not read, and with questions about their history that they could not answer. They felt they should know, and the older men put their heads together to come up with accounts of their origin and so on. The anthropologist's presence caused a minor cultural revival (at one point mocked by a slightly drunken younger man who danced around laughing and singing a ditty: 'I'm a Tai Dam, I'm a Tai Dam'). Knowledge that they have a great tradition and are surrounded by Black Tai material culture gives the Black Tai cultural confidence *vis-à-vis* surrounding groups, especially Sing Moon. When that great tradition was maintained by a Black Tai élite their general cultural confidence must have been stronger. By contrast the Sing Moon appear to possess no great tradition that they know of, and Black Tai material culture is acknowledged to be better than anything they have and they adopt it whenever possible. Consequently they express no confidence in their culture, and they appeared to be embarrassed about discussing Sing Moon culture, having absorbed some shame from the Tai concerning their assumed cultural inferiority. The reconsolidation of Ban Na Wan following its separation from Ban Sot has not caused noticeable re-assertion of Sing Moon identity. The change has led to less daily cultural interaction between the groups, but the long-term aim of at least the better-off households in Ban Na Wan is to emulate their Black Tai neighbours.

In the Indochinese highlands the notion of 'Tai-ization' implies the adoption of Tai material culture, Tai ritual and cosmology, and Tai language. 'Tai-ization', apparently, has been going on for hundreds of years yet we do not know if any small groups have actually disappeared in the process. The latter claim is implied in Condominas's argument. But it is equally plausible to suggest that Tai expansion took place at the slow pace suggested by Leach for the Shan, with the gradual conversion of people from surrounding ethnic groups, and that the expansion of Tai populations occurred primarily because of higher population growth in the more productive valleys. Small groups may have disappeared over a long period, but we need to consider to what extent there are cultural limits to this process and to what extent it is possible for these non-Tai groups to establish viable multiple identities.

I suggested one such limit in an earlier publication on funerals among upland Tai. Despite the extent to which Sing Moon share Black Tai cosmology, they diverge from them in burial practices that encode their prior 'ownership' of the land. While some Sing Moon have aristocratic patronymics (*sing*) they do not follow the funeral practices of these *sing* and cremate their dead. They bury them. This priority is acknowledged in Black Tai ritual: 'the Black Tai each year pay ritual homage to the Lao Theung's prior dominion over the land. Until the coming of the Tai, one villager told me, "the Lao Theung were in charge of the land. . . . If we do not hold a ceremony for the *phii* of the Lao Theung before the harvest then the rice harvest will not be good". Ritually this fundamental fact must be recognised, even in death. So there is cremation for the invaders from *muang fa* [heaven] and burial for the owners of the earth' (Evans 1991: 96).

According to Vietnamese ethnographers there is a parallel Sing Moon ritual in some villages when offerings are made to the village protective spirit, the *sul col*. 'In some places people believe that the *mal te* ceremony must make offerings to the dead *phia tao* and *a-nha* of the Thai people in order to get their spiritual protection' (Dang Nghiem Van et al. 1972: 302). This was not the case in Ban Na Wan whose rituals for the village *sul col* were autonomous from the Black Tai. So ritual practices chart one boundary between Sing Moon and Tai, and because these rituals encode the Sing's Moon prior rights to the land they have good reason *as a group* to maintain them and therefore sustain Sing Moon identity.

Maintenance of Sing Moon language is a partial limit to ethnic interchange, especially in Sing Moon villages where it is used inside and outside the home. But Sing Moon also know Tai, and it has been up to them to cross the linguistic barrier. Their need to do this, in both past and present, has been dictated by power relationships within the highlands. If they wish to raise their social status they need to know the dominant language.

The other main limit on ethnic change is not primarily cultural so much as an outcome of the social structure given that Sing Moon, and similar groups, have the lowest status in the society. Few Tai, for example, wish to marry down and those that do come from the poorer members of the dominant society. In a sense, ethnic endogamy tends to correspond with 'class' endogamy. Only upwardly mobile Sing Moon can pursue more ambitious marriage strategies.

This is linked to the other systemic factor inhibiting ethnic conversion, namely access to resources. We have seen that conflicts over access to resources in the uplands tend to be articulated along ethnic lines. Such conflicts were a dilemma primarily for the upwardly mobile Sing Moon who were divided as to whether to play up their acquired Black Tai identity and throw in their lot with the Black Tai of Ban Sot against the other Sing Moon, or whether to act as members of the Sing Moon village. Initially they tried the former approach but more recently they, and many other Sing Moon villages in the Muang, have chosen to go it alone. A key factor in this decision is extraneous to the immediate environment of the highlands, namely government policy on re-settling people in the valleys. In this context, the upwardly mobile Sing Moon, by appealing beyond the social space dominated by Black Tai, can secure their access to resources and remain the highest status families in the village, rather than attempting to be accepted as poorer members of a Black Tai village.

Their low status is certainly a factor inhibiting Sing Moon 'Tai-ization', but these barriers are not the same as those found in societies with aristocratic, ranked lineages. Although traditional Black Tai society possessed 'aristocratic' patronymics, *sing*, with their separate myths, these patronymics are distributed throughout highland ethnic groups and social strata in a puzzling way. The Sing Moon possess *sing* including aristocratic *sing*. One of the explanations given is that they acquired them from their overlords. If a group of Sing Moon were subject to an aristocrat *sing Lo* then they would acquire his *sing* as a mark of their subjection to that patronymic group. Vietnamese ethnographers have written: 'Long ago Xinh mul [Sing Moon Ed.] people did not have family names, they only had an individual name. When the Thai came to the North-West, for various reasons Xinh mul people adopted Thai family names. For instance, the Vi family in Moc Chau is a Thai aristocratic family. Perhaps the Xinh mul people there . . . because they were under the 'care' and 'protection' of the Thai landlords, had to bear the family name Vi' (Dang Nghiem Van 1972 *et al.*: 280). This strikes me as a plausible explanation, and perhaps the adoption of patronymics by Sing Moon who were not directly subject to the Tai was for reasons of status, in which case it would also constitute an element of 'Tai-ization'. Diffusion of these patronymics through marriage is another way.

One important consequence of this culturally diffuse use of patronymics was that they were not a source of ethnic exclusivity. Unlike the different and incompatible perceptions of rank and status between Shan and Kachin demonstrated by Leach (also Lehman 1989), rank and/or status is perceived and understood in broadly the same way by Sing Moon (and Khmu and others) and the Tai thus allowing Sing Moon incorporation into Tai social structure. Thus while many factors favour 'Tai-ization' of subordinate ethnic groups in the highlands, there are important cultural, social, and political factors which inhibit it and produce something more like dual identity among the Sing Moon. Today, however, the constitution of localised dual identities have been complicated by the expanding influence of the modern state.

Nationalism and Ethnicity

The social space of the upland regions has changed dramatically from the traditional system which occupied the intermediate social spaces that Condominas set out to examine (see Condominas 1980: Introduction). Perhaps when both Black Tai and Sing Moon lived in delimited, intermediate social spaces the obvious source of cultural emulation for the Sing Moon was the dominant Black Tai. But as Condominas is aware these upland confederations were always constituted as elements in larger political entities, either the Chinese state or the Vietnamese state, and the Tai emulated these systems as well. Old photographs of Black Tai aristocrats show that they are dressed as Vietnamese mandarins ('Vietnamization'). They adopted or accepted titles from the Vietnamese state. Black Tai vocabulary is studded with Vietnamese words. The White Tai went further and adopted Vietnamese funeral practices; among the Tho (Tay) the ritual incorporation of the élite was almost complete. The Vietnamese court consolidated its alliance with the Tho (Tay) élite, the Tho Thi, through exchange of daughters in marriage. So matrimonial alliances with indigenous chiefs, which Condominas suggests were an important element in the expansion of the Tai, were a more general strategy pursued by pre-modern élites.

So the social space of the upland Tai élite was always larger than an intermediate localised space. The composition of that space was not only geographically, but also politically determined by relations with lowland states. The Tai élite controlled access to a wider space because the source of their power was control over a delimited intermediate space. In the tributary structure they needed only to be partially 'Vietnamized' in order to retain control of that space. Within that space was a Tai domain in which some peoples became 'Tai-ized' or partially 'Tai-ized'. On the other hand one can also say that the Tai élites at least had dual identities, being more Vietnamese when dealing upwards in the political structure, more Tai when exercising power and influence downwards. This graduated, partial ethnic transformation was possible in tributary state systems which were more tolerant than the modern nationalist state of semi–autonomous, intermediate social and cultural spaces.

It should be noted, however, that throughout the region, ethnicity has been crucially influenced by policies of the colonial state. Leach recognized this: 'The British prevented by force any further trend towards *gumlao* organisation; they encouraged existing *gumlao* headmen to behave as if they were *gumsa* chiefs . . .' (Leach 1970: 258). Thus the British helped prepare the ground for the post-colonial ethnic revolts and separatist nationalist movements which have continued in Burma to this day. The Shan states were recognised as protectorates rather than as colonies, and so 'Partly because of their separate administrative status, the Shan states were never affected by the pre-World War II nationalist movement to the same extent as Burma proper' (Lintner 1984: 405). In Indo-China we can observe something similar. French colonialism supported the upland Tai against Vietnamese encroachments and in 1948 attempted to establish a Tai Federation in the region of the old Sip Song Chau Tai. In contrast to Burma, and because of the historical peculiarities of the development of nationalism and communism, separatist nationalism in Vietnam and Laos failed (Fall 1962; McAlister 1967; Dassé 1976). In further contrast to Burma, none of the other upland groups, except for the Hmong in Laos, became politically mobilized. Thus in northern Indo-China we do not find, in the recent period, strong political movements which can give expression to localized feelings of ethnic identity.[10]

Yet this generalization too needs refinement. To use the terminology introduced by Leach, among the 'Indianized' Tai there was a greater assumption of intrinsic, caste-like differences between rulers and ruled, and therefore toleration of greater differences between the rulers and poly-ethnic commoners. This is not so true of Sinitic state structures where there is a greater attempt to propagate élite culture and values at lower levels of the social structure, a 'culturalist' project which was used to assimilate minorities into the dominant culture. It is of great interest that the Black Tai appear to straddle both systems more than any other group in the region. As indicated above the White Tai, Tho, and others are more clearly Sinified. Among the traditional Black Tai intrinsic, caste-like differences are expressed in the idea that aristocratic patronymics descended directly from heaven, and this is reflected in their use of cremations at funerals (Evans 1991). They also have cultural features derived from a Sinitic universe. The 'Sinicized' Vietnamese state tolerated cultural autonomy among the Tai of the Sip Song Chau Tai largely because of political expediency and the weakness of the traditional state. Thus in the northern Indo-China highlands, we can observe a peculiar twist to Leach's generalizations concerning Indianized 'Valley people' and Sinicized 'Hill people': the Tai 'Valley people' are in fact more Sinicized than the 'Upland people' (Mon-Khmer), and in a culturally refracted way the Tai set out to assimilate surrounding uplanders using a Sinitic strategy of cultural emulation of higher groups by lower ones.

The coming of the modern nation-state to Laos and Vietnam has fundamentally altered relations within the intermediate social spaces. The Lao state has never been strong, but it has now penetrated the local level to an unprecedented degree (Evans 1990: Chapter 8), and I think it is fair to say that these intermediate social spaces have effectively disappeared. The overthrow of the old Tai aristocracy by the communists saw the disappearance of religious rituals associated with the *lak müang* which defined intermediate political spaces, and these rituals devolved to the village (*ban*) level where only *phi ban* and *phi heun* rituals are now observed [cp. the situation in Nan province, Thailand discussed by Ratanaporn this volume, Ed.]. Rituals which define the larger social spaces are now connected to the nation-state, such as National Days etc. Buddhist rituals similar to those in Thailand and Burma are re-emerging in Laos parallel to these state occasions, and increasingly in conjunction with them. Unlike Thailand, but more like Burma, Buddhism covers perhaps only 50 per cent of the Lao population. It is not fully effective as a national ideology or vehicle for 'Lao-ization'. For example, in Muang Xieng Kho, which is dominated by Tai peoples, only the occasional village has a *vat* because upland Tai are generally non-Buddhist Lao who marry into a Black Tai village often drop all Buddhist rituals and *tue phi seu seu* (simply worship spirits), while Black Tai who marry into a Lao cultural universe begin to adopt Buddhism.

In the modern context the direction of ethnic change at both national and local level has become more complex and problematic. In the past Black Tai had a direct economic interest in the incorporation of Sing Moon into their village structures as a source of surplus labour. With the abolition of the traditional system and the implementation of formal equality and citizenship in a nation-state, the Black Tai no longer have a direct economic interest in the Sing Moon, and in some ways the modern state increases the distance between them. The Sing Moon are able to become detached politically, economically and ritually from the Black Tai.[11] Hence Ban Sot's reluctance to incorporate the Sing Moon after 1973. In fact incorporation took place under the direction of the communist state.

The aspiration, or fantasy, of modern nationalism is that within a delimited social space, the nation, people will be culturally of the same type; there is an assumed congruence between nation-state and culture (see Anderson 1983; Gellner 1983; Hobsbawm 1992). The fact that this fantasy often does not correspond with reality is currently wreaking havoc around the globe. Unlike tributary systems modern nationalism is generally intolerant towards semi-autonomous, intermediate social and cultural spaces. The modern state sets out systematically to 'Thai-ize' or 'Vietnamize', for example, their populations in order to make them congruent with the legitimizing assumptions of modern nationalism. Even where modern political systems appear more tolerant there remain tensions and contradictions. Charles Keyes in his discussion of Karen identity in

Thailand claims, 'it is not necessary in Thai society for one to hold an exclusive ethnic identity. One can be *both* Thai and Chinese, Thai and Khmer, Thai and Lao, and so on' (1979: 19). Yet many Thai officials disagree. 'A local district officer in Mae Sariang, for example, . . . asserted that, "to be Thai is to speak only Thai, to be Buddhist." There are even some people who would make such an idea legally binding on the nation' (Keyes 1979: 19). This view, I would argue, is common in Thailand.

Lowland Lao culture is propagated through the education system, the media, government propaganda, government meetings, the high profile given to Buddhist rituals, and so on (Ireson and Ireson 1991). Young Black Tai are becoming Lao in their speech patterns, their dress, and their aspirations to a Lao life-style. When I took photographs, younger women would race to put on their Lao style *sin* rather than traditional Black Tai dress. (Something similar happens in Sing Moon villages.) Wedding dress for women copies lowland Lao style as does the ritual that accompanies it. Older people comment on how the younger people are 'throwing away' (*tim ork*) Black Tai traditions. But even these older Black Tai themselves have made an adaption to Lao culture by using Lao names for themselves, just as Black Tai over the border use Vietnamese names. A striking change in Ban Sot is the building of a house in Laotian style, complete with a roof made of concrete sheeting.

Today not only the élite have access to wider social spaces, but the whole population. As a consequence Black Tai culture no longer has a monopoly over Sing Moon culture and can be by-passed by the latter who adopt elements of lowland Lao culture. A similar process is occurring to both groups in relation to Vietnamese culture just over the border. A young Black Tai from Son La, who in 1991 had married into the household where I stayed, learnt Vietnamese at school and speaks Tai with a Vietnamese accent. Despite limited possibilities of moving out of the uplands, his social and intellectual horizons are wider than a Black Tai universe. Young Tai women marry Vietnamese men as a way of marrying up socially and becoming geographically mobile in order to find a more interesting way of life.

Only within the context of the modern nation state can we talk with Condominas' confidence of the 'irreversibility' of 'Tai-ization' under the guise of what is really more like '*Thai*-ization' and '*Lao*-ization'. Even the latter categories are problematic inasmuch as they are now subject to global cultural influences. Anthropologists are confronted with complex hierarchies of identification, ranging from the most parochial to the global, and in a way that reinforces Leach's original argument against ethnic essentialism. The ethnic groups at the centre of this chapter are still primarily subject to local social and cultural processes. But this is less and less true. Since 1988 I have been struck by the speed at which not only radios have proliferated in the villages and the accompanying thirst for pop

285

music, but also the presence of small video shows in the smallest market towns showing everything from beauty pageants in far off Bangkok to gangster movies from Hong Kong.

Charles Keyes (1992) remarks that the distinctive identity of the Tai Lue may become so attenuated that it persists either by force of habit (i.e. a self-appellation lacking cultural content) or because it is encouraged by a private or state-sponsored tourist industry which promotes outward signs of ethnicity – weaving and costumes etc. Something similar may occur for the Black Tai, but nothing similar is likely to happen for the Sing Moon. They, like other Mon-Khmer groups in the North, do not have a distinctive material culture like the highland Tai, Hmong, Yao, or Akha, which will enable them to become part of tourism's 'revival' of identity. They will not be featured in the ethnic minority park being built on the outskirts of Vientiane for tourists (the latest of many such parks to be built in Asia). When they eventually become disengaged from local conditions which continue to give meaning to being Sing Moon, their identity is unlikely to survive in the modern world, even in an attenuated form.

★ ★ ★

Popular ideas of ethnicity suggest that identity is primordial. Whether we like it or not, anthropological discussions are dogged by this perception. We shadow-box with ethnic essentialism because it is linked to a manageable, bounded concept of culture. Current anthropology has been vigorously deconstructing these comfortable ideologies. The outcome appears to favour a conception of society as a theatre peopled by freewheeling social actors who voluntaristically construct their personal cultural montage, a unique, individual identity.

Old ideas of ethnic essentialism and bounded cultures were wrong, and it is one of Leach's lasting achievements to point anthropologists in new directions. Subsequent research in mainland South East Asia has shown that people participate differentially in different identities and different cultures. Individuals and groups try to make choices as to who they are and how they will act, but they are always constrained socially, culturally, politically, and economically. The difficult task of fieldwork is to assess what relative weight to give to each of these factors in an ever-evolving historical situation.

Notes

1 A version of this paper was given at the Fifth International Conference on Thai Studies, SOAS, London, July 1993. Helpful comments have subsequently been given by F.K. Lehman, Yves Goudineau, Khampheng Thipmuntali, Randy Ireson, and Kelvin Rowley.

2 One sometimes sees this written as Sip Song Chu Tai. *Chu* is an old Black Tai word which, as in Lao, means group but in this context carries the connotation of *müang* or principality. I prefer *Chau*, also commonly used, because it more clearly denotes a political organization.

3 A figure given to me by the Institute of Ethnography in Vientiane in 1988.

4 Lehman (1967: 115) insists on qualifying Leach's generalizations about 'Hill People' in Burma. For other useful critiques of Leach's models, see also Lehman 1963, 1989, 1993.

5 The Central Highlands of Vietnam, whose groups overlap into southern Laos and into north-eastern Cambodia, include groups for which lineage forms of organization are important, including examples of matrilineal organization.

6 More historical research on the early history of the Lao highlands is necessary. The civilization associated with the Plain of Jars in Xieng Khouang province Laos was tied into salt trade routes (Colani 1935: 191–98). Dang Nghiem Van (1975: 8) paints a picture of Dien Bien Phu as a centre for widespread trade in the region: 'For centuries Dien Bien Phu was a transit place for long caravans carrying goods from Burma, Xip Xoong Pa Na and Muong La to Lai Chau, Lao Cai, Son La and Nghia Lo . . .' He is talking about routes created since the coming of the Tai; control of these routes was no doubt a source of power for Tai aristocrats in the region.

7 In 1991 in the province of Attopeu in southern Laos I documented a similar situation among the 'Lavae' as the Lao government calls them – in fact Sedang and Brau – who were forced to move down from the mountains after 1975 (Evans and Boonmataya 1991).

8 In 1994 emergency rice relief had to be given to Muang Xieng Kho as a result of the failure of the 1993 wet season harvest which caused a serious shortfall. (*Kao San Pathet Lao*, 11 June 1994)

9 In this regard we can compare them, for example, with the Karen who 'usually attribute their relatively low position in the hierarchy to the foolishness or the laziness of the Karen . . .' Kunstadter 1979: 153). Yet the Karen appear to have more pride in their 'Karenness' than the Sing Moon.

10 A similar situation for the Sing Moon has been documented in Vietnam. See Dang Nghiem Van et al. (1972).

11 In Central Highlands in the southern half of Vietnam a separatist highland minorities movement came into being as result of the Vietnam War. This is discussed by Hickey (1982), and for the fate of this movement after 1975 see Evans (1992).

References

Anderson, Benedict O'G. (1983), *Imagined Communities: An Essay on Nationalism*, London: Verso.

Bateson, Gregory (1958), *Naven*, 2nd edn., Stanford: Stanford University Press.

Cam Trong (1978), *The Thai People in Northwestern Vietnam*, Hanoi: Social Sciences Publishing House (in Vietnamese).

Colani, Madeleine (1935), *Mégalithes du Haut-Laos,* Tome Second, Paris: Publications de L'Ecole Français d'Extrême Orient, Les Editions d'Art et d'Histoire.

Condominas, Georges (1980), *L'Espace Social à Propos de L'Asie du Sud-Est,* Paris: Flammarion.

—— (1990), *From Lawa to Mon, from Saa' to Thai: Historical and Anthropological Aspects of Southeast Asian Social Spaces*, Occasional Paper of the Department of Anthropology, RSPS, Australian National University, Canberra, [the 'Essay on the evolution of Thai political systems' which is reprinted here first appeared in *Ethnos*, Stockholm, 41, 1976].

Dang Nghiem Van (1971), 'An Outline of the Thai in Vietnam', *Vietnamese Studies*, no.32.

Dang Nghiem Van, Nguyen Truc Binh, Nguyen Van Huy and Thanh Thien (1972), *Ethnic Groups of the Austro-asiatic Family in the North-West of Vietnam*, Publishing House of the Social Sciences, Hanoi (in Vietnamese)

—— (1973), 'The Khmu In Vietnam', *Vietnamese Studies*, no.36.

—— (1975), 'Dien Bien Phu: Some Ethno-Historical Data', *Vietnamese Studies*, no. 43.

—— et al. (1984) *The Ethnic Minorities in Vietnam*, Hanoi: Foreign Languages Publishing House.

Dassé, Martial (1976), *Montagnards Révoltes et Guerres Revolutionnaires en Asie du Sud-Est Continentale*, Bangkok: D.K. Books.

Donahue, John D. (1984), 'Ideology and Economy in Upland Southeast Asia: a Re-appraisal of Political Systems of Highland Burma', *Ethnos*, Vol. 49, nos. 1–2.

Evans, Grant (1985) 'Vietnamese Communist Anthropology', *Canberra Anthropology*, July/August.

—— (1990), *Lao Peasants Under Socialism*, New Haven, Connecticut: Yale University Press.

—— (1991), 'Reform or Revolution in Heaven? Funerals Among Upland Tai', *Australian Journal of Anthropology* (formerly *Mankind*), Vol.2, no.1.

—— (1992), 'Internal Colonialism in the central Highlands of Vietnam', *Sojourn*, (August).

Evans, Grant and Rattana Boonmattaya (1991), *Possibilities for Community Participation in Forest Areas Selected for Conservation in Laos*, Report to the World Wildlife Fund and the World Bank.

Fall, Bernard (1962), 'Problèmes des Etats Poly-ethniques en Indochine', *France-Asie*, Vol. XVIII, N. 172.

Friedman, Jonathan, (1979), *System, Structure and Contradiction in the Evolution of 'Asiatic' Social Formations*, Copenhagen: Nationalmuset.

—— (1986), 'Generalized Exchange, Theocracy and the Opium Trade', *Critique of Anthropology*, Vol. 7, no. 1.

Gellner, Ernest (1983), *Nationalism*, London: Blackwell.

Gunn, Geoffrey C. (1990), *Rebellion in Laos: Peasants and Politics in a Colonial Backwater*, Colorado: Westview Press.

Hickey, Gerald C. (1982), *Sons of the Mountains: Ethnohistory of the Vietnamese Central Highlands, 1954–1976*, New Haven: Yale University Press,.

Hobsbawm, E. J. (1992), *Nations and Nationalism Since 1780: Programme, Myth, Reality*, Second Edition, Cambridge: Cambridge University Press.

Ireson, Carol J. and W. Randall Ireson (1991), 'Ethnicity and Development in Laos', *Asian Survey*, Vol. XXXI, no. 10.

Izikowitz, Karl Gustav (1951), *Lamet: Hill Peasants in French Indochina*, Göteborg, Etnografiska Museet (Etnografiska Studier 17).

—— (1969), 'Neighbours in Laos', in Fredrik Barth (ed.), *Ethnic Groups and Boundaries*, Boston: Little Brown and Company.

Keyes, Charles F (1979), 'Introduction', in Charles F. Keyes (ed.), *Ethnic Adaptation and Identity: The Karen on the Thai Frontier With Burma*, Philadelphia: ISHI.

—— (1992), *Who are the Lue? Revisited: Ethnic Identity in Laos, Thailand, and China*, a Working Paper from The Center for International Studies, Cambridge, Massachusetts: MIT, Cambridge.

Kunstadter, Peter (1979), 'Ethnic Group, Category, and Identity: Karen in Northern Thailand,' in Charles F. Keyes, *Ethnic Adaptation and Identity: The Karen on the Thai Frontier With Burma*, Philadelphia: ISHI.

Lafont, Bernard (1955), 'Notes sur les familles patronymiques Thai noires de Son-la et de Nghia-lo', *Anthropos*, Vol.50.

Laufer, Berthold (1917), 'Totemic Traces Among the Indo-Chinese', *The Journal of American Folk-Lore*, Vol. XXX, no. CXVIII.

Leach, Edmund (1960), 'The Frontiers of "Burma"', *Comparative Studies in Society and History*, Vol. 3.

—— (1970), *Political Systems of Highland Burma: A Study of Kachin Social Structure*, University of London: The Athlone Press (first published in 1954 by G. Bell, London).

—— (1983a), 'Imaginary Kachins', *Man*, Vol. 18, no. 1.

—— (1983b), 'Imaginary Kachins', *Man*, Vol. 18, no. 4.

Le Bar, Frank (1967), 'Observations on the Movement of Khmu into North Thailand', *The Journal of the Siam Society*, Vol. LV, part 1.

Lehman, F. K (1963), *The Structure of Chin Society*, Urbana: University of Illinois Press.

—— (1967), 'Ethnic Categories in Burma and the Theory of Social Systems', in P. Kunstadter (ed) *Southeast Asian Tribes, Minorities, and Nations*, N.J.: Princeton University Press.

—— (1979), 'Who Are the Karen, and If So, Why? Karen Ethnohistory and a Formal Theory of Ethnicity', in Charles F. Keyes, *Ethnic Adaptation and Identity: The Karen on the Thai Frontier With Burma*, Philadelphia: ISHI.

—— (1989), 'Internal Inflationary Pressures in the Prestige Economy of the Feast of merit Complex: The Chin and Kachin Cases from Upper Burma', in Susan D. Russell (ed.), *Ritual, Power and Economy: Upland-Lowland Contrasts in Mainland Southeast Asia*, Northern Illinois University Center for Southeast Asian Studies.

—— (1993), 'Kachin', *Encyclopaedia of World Cultures*, Vol. V.

Lintner, Bertil (1984), 'The Shans and the Shan State of Burma', *Contemporary Southeast Asia*, Vol. 5, no. 4.

McAlister, Jr., John T. (1967), 'Mountain Minorities and the Vietminh: a Key to the Indochina War', in P. Kunstadter (ed.) *Southeast Asian Tribes, Minorities, and Nations*, N.J.: Princeton University Press.

McKinnon, John and Wanat Bhruksasri (eds). (1986), *Highlanders of Thailand*, Singapore: Oxford University Press.

McKinnon, John and Bernard Vienne (1991), *Hill Tribes Today*, Bangkok: White Lotus-Orstom.

Murdoch, George Peter (ed.) (1960), *Social Structure in Southeast Asia*, Chicago: Quadrangle Books.

Nugent, David (1982), 'Closed Systems and Contradiction: The Kachin in and out of History', *Man*, Vol. 17, no. 3.

—— 1984. 'Reply', *Man*, Vol. 18, no. 1.

Olsen, Neil H. (1976), 'Matrilineal Societies in Southeast Asia: Examples from Highland Vietnam', in D. J. Banks (ed.), *Changing Identities in Southeast Asia*, Chicago.

Proschan, Frank (1989), *Kmhmu Verbal Art in America: The Poetics of Kmhmu Verse*, Ph.D, Austin: The University of Texas.

Schrock, Joann L., et al. (1972), *Minority Groups in North Vietnam*, Ethnographic Studies Series, Washington, D.C.: U.S. Government Printing Office.

Scott, James C. (1990), *Domination and the Arts of Resistance: Hidden Transcripts*, New Haven: Yale University Press.

Wijeyewardene, Gehan (ed.) (1990), *Ethnic Groups Across National Boundaries in Southeast Asia*, Singapore: ISEAS.

Wolf, Eric (1982), *Europe and the People Without History*, Berkeley: University of California Press.

Part V

LANNA AND NEIGHBOURS

Introduction

The following three papers challenge what Bowie claims to be a prevailing assumption that Tai states, and especially the Thai state, have been characterised by ethnic and cultural homogeneity. From this generalization we clearly have to exempt the Lao case reviewed above. Here the focus is primarily on the region that is now known loosely as 'northern Thailand' whose regional capital is indisputably Chiang Mai. The Lanna (or Lan Na, or Lannat(h)ai) Kingdom, is currently used to refer to a succession of states centred largely on Chiang Mai from about 1263 AD, with periods of Burmese overrule and from 1775 increasingly under Siamese sovereignty, up to the final extinction of the royal line and residual ruling function in 1939. The extent of this state varied and gave rise to what has been called a 'greater Lan Na cultural zone' which included at times parts of the Shan states, Sipsongpanna, and Müang Nan.

Within these Tai states 'ethnicity' – if we can use the term with any transhistorical valency at all – counted for less than socio-economic status. It is argued there was a kind of 'ethnic egalitarianism' (if only an equality of exploitation as Bowie suggests) within systems of landholding, office-holding, and related laws governing obligation to provide tribute or corvée labour, and the movement of people, goods, and cattle. Social differentiation and hierarchy were marked especially by ritual. Lua' (or Lawa) are a people who were – or rather as Tanabe argues 'a peripheral social category culturally constructed' by Tai as – the autochthonous former occupiers of Tai lands. They were regarded by Tai as 'barbarous, cannibal, uncivilised, and non-Buddhist' but also as 'ritually superior' a quality that was transferred to Tai rulers in key state rituals that conferred added legitimacy to Tai rule.

Ratanaporn also shows the importance of rituals of local and state identities in the principality (now province) of Nan. But here the 'minorities' were themselves Tai, more and less voluntarily resettled (mostly from their original Sipsongpanna and neighbouring Tai states) after wars and other disturbances. They had to conform to and recognize the powers of state level rituals (*phi müang*), but they were able to retain and develop – albeit under licence for there were lingering suspicions as to the loyalty of such migrants – their own local cult (*phi ban*) in which they often memorialised their previous lords or the founders of new settlements. Such practices enable the Tai Lue of one community near Chiang Mai still to claim and in a sense recall links of descent going back 600 years. And this is despite a parallel process of various sorts of Tai and non-Tai taking on a more or less generic Khon Müang political and cultural identity – a process I suggested in my introductory chapter could be termed *müang*-ization. These complex and dialectical processes of demographic movement, cultural pluralism, and plural identity were constantly renewed, leading to 'multi-ethnic' rural villages and districts being the norm, as well as, less surprisingly, the more cosmopolitan cities.

In common with all the studies in this volume, these examine the consequences of modern and contemporary changes as the nation-state, and the national and world economy intervene. One of the earliest effects was the specialization for wage-labour of certain ethnic minorities in 'private sector' elephant management (in which the owners and employers were commoner Tai as well as European timber companies etc.) at a time when the state could still mobilise the labour of all ethnic groups in a non-wage-labour, pre-modern idiom (Bowie).

In the ritual sphere transformations can be discerned that speak eloquently of changing power relations and changes in the social fortunes of ethnic minorities. But ritual changes are by no means uniform or uncontradictory. In Nan the new sovereignty of Bangkok led rapidly to the decline in *müang* level political cults, but village level practices 'survived' albeit within an increasingly Thai (Thailand) national identity (Ratana-porn). In Chiang Mai the Inthakhin or one might say 'pillar of the state' cult – which memorialised and drew strength from the aboriginal Lua' connection – has become increasingly 'Buddhified', with a standing Buddha image on top of the pillar, large numbers of monks chanting and so on. In what we might call the 'ultra-nationalising' period 1911–1939 old practices of making animal sacrifices, spirit possession, music and dancing were deliberately suppressed. Later the rites were re-invented, this time by the Chiang Mai Municipality. Older 'non-Buddhist' rites migrated to a corner of the city walls, while the hybrid revival of the central cult has become more and more commodified as an international tourist attraction. At the same time these urban rites have become less communal. In these de-contextualizations and re-contextualizations, the Lua' – in a way similar to the Karen referred to by Renard earlier in this volume – have become 'detached from their historical and cultural relations with the Khon Müang and other Tai groups' (Tanabe).

Plate 20. Princess Dara Rasmee wearing tribal 'fancy dress'

Chapter Thirteen

Autochthony and the Inthakhin Cult of Chiang Mai

Shigeharu Tanabe

Introduction

In mainland South East Asia, particularly highland Burma, Leach demonstrated a structural differentiation between hill peoples and valley centred Buddhist peoples with regard to their political systems, which are articulated with ecology, kinship, and economy (Leach 1960). Leach suggests that though such structural differentiation has been maintained for centuries, localised 'ethnic' change has occurred when a hill population adopts, as they start to cultivate wet-rice and become Buddhist, the manners, dress, and language of the dominant Shan, a Tai group. In other parts of mainland South East Asia (e.g. northern Thailand, Laos, and southwestern Yunnan) where more powerful Tai states were established, the structural differentiation, withered away and non-Tai populations in the hills have been more fully incorporated into the dominant Tai political systems (cf. Condominas 1990: 70)

In northern Thailand, the Khon Müang established a powerful kingdom during the late thirteenth century, centred in the Chiang Mai basin, and holding sway over the Khon Müang chiefs in other valleys and basins until the beginning of this century, despite the interruption to their overall hegemony during the Burmese occupation in the sixteenth to eighteenth centuries. The political power of the Chiang Mai monarchy was based on control over political spaces called *müang,* which closely correspond to alluvial plains as ecological units where Khon Müang and other Tai groups cultivate wet-rice. The *müang* has had a particular significance for the self-identification of the Khon Müang as belonging to a *müang* domain.

These domains were surrounded by hills and mountainous areas inhabited by a variety of upland groups over whom Chiang Mai monarchs claimed suzerainty. They included Mon-Khmer speaking peoples in the earlier periods, and later Tibeto-Burman and Hmong-Yao speaking groups. The Lua' (Lawa) is one such group which for centuries has inhabited areas peripheral to the Chiang Mai basin and beyond, and maintained political and ritual relations with the state. Yet the so-called Lua' represent not a discrete category, as conventionally defined in historical linguistics or in official statements of nation-states, but a peripheral social category culturally constructed and historically margin-alized during the development of Tai states.

This chapter examines ways in which a dominant political system incorporates minorities in relation to ideological processes of constructing the legitimate authority of a monarchy. It discusses a particular Inthakhin (pillar of Indra), the most prominent symbol of the political dominion of Chiang Mai, and associated ritual. The significance of minorities within traditional Tai political systems is concerned not only with the creation and maintenance of boundaries, but also with the categorization of others in terms of ritual and political relations. I demonstrate that Lua' was constructed as an autochthnous category to legitimize the authority of the Chiang Mai monarchy in ritual terms, and that this ritual relation historically consolidated the subordination of Lua' within a centre-periphery structure. I also consider the impact of the Siamese annexation of the northern principalities early in this century and the way in which local social categories and centre-periphery relations have been transformed. Incorporation into a nation-state has involved a transformation of ritual relations employing the dominant, centralized Buddhist discourse, emanating from Bangkok. Finally, I consider some ways in which the religious and ritual orders have been redefined in the post-war period, including the subordination of the Inthakhin cult under the control of the Chiang Mai Municipal Council.

The Autochthonous Lua' in Khon Müang Representations

Leach's analysis of structural differentiation fails to comprehend the way in which upland minorities are incorporated into states, partly because his model does not take account of ideological processes wielded against minority groups by states and their rulers. This point has been made by Aijmer (1979), who examines the process of bargaining over authority and power between Lao kings and Mon-Khmer hill peoples, and by Tapp (1986, 1990) who draws attention to a ritually recognized relationship of dominance and dependency between Mon-Khmer hill dwellers and Tai princes, and its contemporary transformations.

We need first to look at the arrangement of the political centre of *müang* domains, which are ecologically distinct from the marginal slopes and hills. In the traditional *müang*, such as Chiang Mai, Lamphun, Lampang, Phrae, Chiang Rai, and Nan, we nearly always find a variety of Tai-speaking groups other than the major Tai group who call themselves Khon Müang (also known as Yuan, Lanna). These groups include the lowland wet-rice cultivators of Lue, Ñong, Khoen, Tai Yai (Ngieo), whose mutually intelligible languages are similar to Kham Müang (the language of Khon Müang), but who maintain distinctive local ethnic identities and cultural practices. Past migrations and displacement from other Tai domains as war captives, refugees and so on, under the traditional policy of *kep phak sai sa kep kha sai müang* (putting vegetables into baskets and *kha* ('slaves') into *müang* domains), accounts for most of their presence within the *müang* domains (Kraisri 1965a; Turton 1980). The differentiation of ethnic composition also derives from recent political and economic changes that have led to migration into the nodes of prosperity in northern Thailand.

Historically the Khon Müang polity has thus been the cause of internal differentiation at the cores of the *müang*, drawing in a variety of distinctive Tai identities. At the same time, these Tai groups have identified themselves as 'Khon Müang', or the people of *müang*, distinguishing themselves from Siamese (Thai) and other neighbouring groups. 'Khon Müang' here signifies the more generic identity of people living in *müang* domains historically under the suzerainty of northern Khon Müang principalities. The internal differentiation within the *müang* domains also relates to the traditional economy in terms of the division of labour and commodity production. For instance, lacquerware production, silversmithing, and long-distance trade have been carried out by these Tai groups, as well as other non-Tai groups.

In contrast to the internal differentiation among the mainly Tai groups at the centre, the Khon Müang principalities recognised different categories of other in the periphery, chiefly non-Tai groups, labelled Lua' (Lawa) and Ñang (Karen). Unlike the Tai groups at the centre, the Lua' and the Ñang remain peripheral and never identify themselves as Khon Müang. These categories within the Khon Müang folk taxonomy refer not to linguistically defined Mon-Khmer speaking Lawa and Karennic speaking Karen, but to various social groups of mainly upland cultivators, including Lawa and Karen speaking populations living on the slopes and hills. Ñang have been upland cultivators for centuries, though some communities cultivate wet-rice in marginal valleys. Lua' are also upland cultivators, but there are a number of wet-rice cultivating Lua' communities in the Chiang Mai basin, which have gradually been turning into Khon Müang villages through marriage and adoption of Buddhist culture. Nonetheless, Lua' and the Ñang remain two peripheral social categories, constructed within the traditional Khon Müang system.[1]

In Khon Müang historical discourse Lua' represent the autochthonous people who are believed to have inhabited the region before Khon Müang and other Tai groups arrived. Accounts of aboriginal Lua' appear in Pali texts such as *Jinakalamalipakaranam* (1968) and *Chamdevivongsa* (1967), believed to have been written from the fifteenth to the sixteenth centuries, and in a Khon Müang chronicle *Chronique de La:p'un (Lamphun)* (1930). These texts cite the story of a legendary Lua' king, Khunluang Wilangka who had established sovereignty in the Chiang Mai and Lamphun areas, but was defeated and pushed into the hills by the people of Hariphunchai (Lamphun), which was subsequently taken over by King Mangrai in the thirteenth century. A Khon Müang chronicle, *Tamnan suwanna khamdaeng* (1972)[2] gives an account of an aboriginal Lua' chief, Mamuttaleng (Muttalang), who gave two girls as wives to Suwanna Khamdaeng, the legendary king who established the kingdom of Lanna.

The Lua' and Khunluang Wilangka also frequently appear in Khon Müang ritual sequences and related ritual texts, particularly those associated with wet-rice farming in Chiang Mai, e.g. rain-making, first planting of rice seedlings, and first harvesting (Tanabe 1993). A striking example is the sacrificial propitiation of Pu Sae Ña Sae (Kham Müang for Grandfather Sae and Grandmother Sae), which takes place annually at two sites in the western foothills of Chiang Mai (Kraisri 1967; Wijeyewardene 1986; Rhum 1987; Tanabe 1994). In the myth associated with this ritual, Pu Sae and Ña Sae are regarded as the cannibal demon (*ñak*) ancestor spirits of the autochthonous Lua', who were later converted to Buddhism yet continue to receive annually a buffalo sacrifice sponsored by the Khon Müang rulers.[3] The Lua' are represented not only as autochthonous, but also as fearful cannibal demons, who in the course of the ritual are converted to Buddhism, becoming the civilized recipients of a sacrificial animal.

One aspect of the myth and related ritual of Pu Sae Ña Sae is the motif of conversion to Buddhism, which has been disseminated in the region since the fifteenth century. The encounter with an autochthonous group, represented as uncivilized non-Buddhist cannibals and civilized Buddhists is a common motif in Buddhist literature (cf. Wijeyewadene 1986: 85–86; Notton 1926: 138; Rhum 1987). It is not unreasonable to suggest that Lua' as an autochthonous category came into being during the conquest of indigenous people by the Tai, and was consolidated by Buddhist missionary discourse that regards non-Buddhist aborigines as living in a state of nature close to animality, but as capable of being civilized through Buddhist moral precepts and practices. The sacrificial ritual propitiating Pu Sae Ña Sae thus represents not only the sensual and cannibalistic properties of the autochthonous category, but also its dramatic transformation (Tanabe 1994).

Barbarity and subjugation are not the sole representations of the Lua': they have also been regarded by Khon Müang as holders of rights to propitiate the tutelary spirits of domains, implying Lua' superiority over Khon Müang in ritual terms. In the sacrificial ritual Pu Sae Ña Sae are regarded as ancestors of the Lua' who became the guardian spirits of the lands of Chiang Mai after their death. The villagers who hold the ritual are considered to be descendants of the autochthonous people, though they have been completely assimilated to the Khon Müang over centuries.

The superior status of the Lua' in dealing with tutelary spirits of domains appears in other Khon Müang rituals. One historical instance is concerned with the royal rites of entrance into Chiang Mai city by King Kawila (reigning in Chiang Mai 1781–1813), the first monarch of the Kawila dynasty (1781–1939) that restored the Lanna kingdom in the late eighteenth century. As described in *Tamnan phünmüang chiang mai*, a version of the Chiang Mai chronicles, in 1796 (Lesser Era 1158) King Kawila left Pa Sang, Lamphun and arrived at Chiang Mai, eventually entering the city through Patu Chang Phüak, the northern gate, after 'making a Lua' carrying a basket on his back and leading a dog to enter first [*hü lua cung ma pha caek khao kon*]' (1974: 106). This ritual sequence implies that in order to establish political power Khon Müang rulers had to follow the ritual practices of the aboriginal owners of the land.

Similar ritual sequences associated with enthronement are found in many legendary and historical instances within various Tai political systems. *Tamnan müang yong*, a version of the Müang Yong chronicles, refers to the coronation rites of a Khoen prince of Chiang Tung, one of the Shan States of Burma. The Khoen prince finally ascended the throne (*ho kham*) after a series of monetary negotiations with Mang Kham and his family (presumably Lawa or Wa) who had previously held the throne (1984: 67).[4]

Royal rituals in Luang Prabang illustrate the ritual superiority of autochthonous people *vis à vis* the Lao, the politically dominant Tai group, as shown by Archaimbault (1964, 1973). Lao kings at Luang Prabang had strong ritual ties with the Kasak, a Mon–Khmer speaking group regarded as autochthonous neighbours living in the mountains to the South-East and believed to be descendants of the elder brother of the first Lao king. The Kasak, led by their chief Phia Kasak, played a special role in rites of ascension to the throne (*raxa phisek*).[5] Phia Kasak shot arrows against the façade of the palace and the Kasak fled when the king threw a rice ball at them, shouting 'May the aborigines living in the mountains perish before I do!' (Archaimbault 1964: 65–66). Blessing the king for longevity is a feature reserved for this autochthonous people. My interviews with Kasak informants at Kiu Tia Luang in 1991 revealed that before liberation in 1975 they had long practised triennial sacrifices of black and white cows at the village and sent tribute of *makman makñun* (literally, a white gourd of strength and longevity) to reinforce the powers of the king's body and soul (cf. Doré 1980: 47–72).

Autochthonous peoples within Tai traditional political systems are thus ambivalently and contra-distinctively represented, as barbarous, cannibal, uncivilized, and non-Buddhist on the one hand, and on the other hand as original land-holders, and therefore ritually superior to the Tai conquerors, particularly in relation to the tutelary spirits of domains. This categorization of conquered and marginalized aboriginal groups has a further political significance, for example people categorised as Lua' are continuously subject to the dominant Khon Müang system, but at the same time, the conceptual construct of an autochthnous and peripheral category came to be associated with the legitimation of the monarchy. In order to elucidate the processes involved in the construction of this autochthonous category, I examine the case of the Inthakhin pillar in Chiang Mai.

The Political Significance of Inthakhin and *lak müang*

Inthakhin is a Kham Müang word derived from Sanskrit/Pali *indra-kila* (*inda-khila*), denoting Indra's pillar, a pillar demarcating a border, or a pillar in front of the city gate.[6] The present Inthakhin pillar is about one metre above the ground level and located in a small pavilion (Wihan Inthakhin) in the compound of Wat Cedi Luang, slightly South of the centre of Chiang Mai walled city. It was moved to its present site from the geographical centre of Chiang Mai at Wat Sadü Müang (currently the site of construction of Chiang Mai Municipality's Tilokkarat Hall) during the reign of King Kawila in 1800 (Sanguan 1969). In the anthropomorphic topography of the Khon Müang, *sadü müang*, or the navel of the *müang* domain signifies the centre, hence the original site of the Inthakhin pillar is frequently identified with that of the former monastery. Apart from this usage, the word 'Inthakhin' has rarely been used among Tai groups, exceptional instances are found in Chiang Mai and Lamphun.[7]

Khon Müang chronicles relate that the Inthakhin pillar was originally installed at the centre of the legendary Lua' city Nopphaburi (Navapura), presumably located in the central area of the present city. Major chronicles with lengthy references to the legend of the Inthakhin pillar include those texts generally called *Tamnan suwanna khamdaeng*[8] and *Tamnan mahathera fa bot*.[9] Some of these texts have been scrutinised by Wijeyewardene (1986: 81–87) and subsequently by Premchit and Doré (1992: 207–214) particularly in relation to the Inthakhin pillar. I shall consequently give only an outline of the installation of Inthakhin relevant to our discussion, based on *Tamnan suwanna khamdaeng*.

Established by the nine Lua' clans, Nopphaburi was prosperous, provided with mines of gold, silver, and gems. Under threat from enemies, the inhabitants (Lua' and Tai) asked a hermit (*rishi*) for help. In response the God Indra sent two Kumphan to install the Inthakhin pillar at the centre of the city to protect it. Later the people neglected to worship the pillar, and the two Kumphan, guardians of the pillar, took it back to the Tavatimsa heaven. When the hermit prophesied impending disaster, the people again asked him for help. He requested Indra to return the pillar, but this time Indra ordered him to make a replica according to his detailed instruction; pairs of cast figures including the 101 races of man and of all the animals were to be put together in metal vases (*ang khang*) and buried in a hole, over which the replica of the pillar made of earth and bricks was to be set up. The people, both Lua' and Tai, thereafter observed the precepts and propitiated the pillar and the two Kumphan statues (*Tamnan suwanna khamdaeng* 1972: 148–160).

The story of the lost original Inthakhin pillar and its subsequent reconstruction implies that impiety results in the loss of the pillar, as argued by Wijeyewardene (1986: 87). The decline of piety and consequent disaster is a recurrent theme that recurs in more historical guise in the Khon Müang chronicles. For example, in the late fifteenth century the relocation of the two Kumphan to a new site in front of Cedi Luang (present Wat Cedi Luang) by the order of King Tilokkarat, the twelfth monarch of the Mangrai dynasty (1259 to mid-sixteenth century), caused the death of the officials in charge (*Chronique de Mahathera Fa Bot* 1926: 53; *Tamnan mahathera pha bot* 1977: 15).

A narrative of the destruction of another material symbol of the domain, *mai sri müang* (the sacred tree of the *müang*) or *mai süa müang* (the tutelary tree of the *müang*) located at the North-East corner of the city-wall, one of the most auspicious and sacred places in Khon Müang geomancy, is also relevant. *Tamnan phün müang chiang mai* (1974: 61–63) refers to the tragic incident that led to the fall of Chiang Mai to the Burmese and the death of King Tilokkarat: a Burmese monk, later called Thera Phukam conspired to induce the King to cut down *mai nikhrot* (banyan tree) the tutelary tree of Chiang Mai, and to modify the city plan, constructing a palace and a new gate at the sacred North-East corner. This story does not so much emphasize disasters deriving from the decline of piety, as punishment for violations of customary practice and the underlying symbolic structure determined by Khon Müang geomancy. Davis has made a similar point concerning the Khon Müang notion of *khüt*, an evil act defying categorically defined distinctions that causes ill omens (Davis 1984: 284–88).

These stories indicate that the Inthakhin pillar and related practices have a political significance in the Khon Müang system. I shall now consider how powerful symbols and practices at the centre relate to inter-group relations, particularly between Khon Müang and Lua'.

The pillar, putting aside its Sanskrit/Pali name, is actually native to the autochthonous Lua' in the Chiang Mai area. For instance, a village pillar called *dong sakang* is found among the Lua' in Chiang Mai and Mae Hongson, while the Wa in Yunnan also have their pillar, known as *khao sikang* (Cholthira 1990: 222; Premchit and Doré 1992: 204–7).[10] Possibly analogous are the wooden posts to which Kachin and others tie sacrificial animals in rites practised in highland Burma (Leach 1954: 118). My interest here, however, is the transformation that the Inthakhin underwent as it was absorbed into the Khon Müang system of representations rather than its cultural distribution.

In Khon Müang folk knowledge, the Inthakhin pillar has been identified as *süa ban süa müang* or simply *süa müang* (the tutelary spirit of the *müang* domain) of Chiang Mai.[11] It has to be periodically propitiated by the ruling princes. *Süa müang* is a representation of tutelary powers encompassing the entire domain, its destiny, its protection from unexpected calamities and enemies, and the welfare of all humans, animals and crops there; it is an overarching power embracing the universe of the domain (Tanabe 1988; Condominas 1990: 36). This omnipotence of the *süa müang* is a feature of the Inthakhin pillar *per se*, as implied by the range of images of humans and animals held to be in vases buried under the pillar. Such powers, which transcend human experiences and day-to-day social relations, can be differentiated from Khon Müang representations of kin groups (*phi pu ña*, or ancestor spirits) and of village communities (*phi ban*, or village spirits). The idea of this overarching 'imagined society', whether attributable to Hindu cultural traits, or to traditions indigenous to Tai groups, is now conspicuously associated with the Khon Müang state, and the legitimation of its monarchy (cf. Turton 1972; Tanabe 1991).

The notion of *süa müang* has an apparent connection with a more generic symbol called *lak müang*, or the foundation pillar of the domain, commonly found in other Tai political domains. We should therefore examine the ethnographic arguments concerning *lak müang* and its political and ritual significance. *Lak müang*, a material symbol, usually a wooden post, relates to the tutelary spirit of the domain, and represents, among other things, political power and its legitimate authority.

Maspéro recognized dichotomous symbols among Tai Khao and Tai Dam on the West bank of the Red River, northern Vietnam: *fi (phi) müng*, the tutelary spirit of the domain which resides at a tree in a grove at the entrance to the chief's village, and is propitiated by the chief and inhabitants before cultivation starts; and the *lak süa* or *lak müang*, is a tutelary spirit associated with the chief and his family. The *lak süa* will be replaced when a new dynasty assumes political power (Maspéro 1929: 238–39, 1950: 172).[12] Maspéro proposes a symbolic opposition between *fi müang* and *lak süa*.[13] This dichotomous distinction between two similar symbols is apparent in many Tai groups, though my own observations in northern Thailand and northern Laos reveal that in some locations the two are merged. Maspéro suggests that *lak müang* is not a permanent symbol of the political domain, but rather attached to a power-holder or his dynasty. To set up a pillar therefore signifies personal prestige; new leaders have to erect a new pillar to affirm their political power. The wooden pillar, perishable and removable, is appropriate to the transitory nature of local power.

A set of other notions such as *phi müang*, *süa müang*, and *cen müang* signify tutelary spirits or deities and a related object, and *mai süa* or *mai ming* denoting the sacred tree. Whatever their origin or earlier meanings, these symbols became differentiated and came to include hierarchical aspects. Condominas says that the *lak müang* is a fixed and immovable monument integrally associated with the tutelary spirits of the *müang* domain in Khon Müang and Lao principalities and kingdoms, as opposed to other Tai systems (Condominas 1990: 59). This would indicate a difference between the central symbols of Buddhist Tai states and those of pre-state Tai political formations.

In Luang Prabang the highest tutelary spirits (*thewada luang*) identified as Pu Ñoe Ña Ñoe, a legendary aboriginal couple, became the focus of propitiation rites (Archaimbault 1964). The *lak man* (Cao Mae Lak Man, or The Mother of the Foundation Pillar) in Luang Prabang is actually of minor importance, propitiated only with pigs and chickens at Ho Pa (the spirit house in the forest) by a community outside the city to the South. It was destroyed after liberation in 1975, but a spirit-medium in the town has continued worship, albeit with no material symbol. At Tseng Hung (Cheng Rung), the capital of the Lue kingdom of Sipsongpanna, one of the highest tutelary spirits, regarded as autochthonous, known as Alawaka Yak, later converted to Buddhism and referred to as Alawaka Soda, was before liberation in 1950 the focus of a royal propitiation ritual (Hasegawa 1993). On the other hand, the pillar called *tsai moeng* (literally, the heart of the *müang*) was long ago transformed into That Tsai Moeng, a Buddhist pagoda, which is worshipped in an entirely Buddhist fashion in a grandiose merit-making ritual (*tan that*) in December (Tanabe 1990).

These cases show a clear break from the non-Buddhist and pre-state Tai systems. The symbolic opposition between tutelary spirits (*phi müang, thewada luang*) and foundation pillar (*lak man, tsai moeng*) has been maintained, while the power overarching the domain and the pioneer ruler's personal symbol have become fused, as Buddhist rulers came to claim superior status in terms of a Buddhist logic, identifying themselves as *dhamma-raja* (the king of dharma), rather than in terms of lineage. In many Buddhist principalities, the tutelary spirits of the domain, strongly associated with the autochthonous people, became dominant; and the *lak müang* type pillar became a minor symbol or was transformed into a Buddhist monument. The process was accompanied by Buddhistic transformations of legendary texts concerning autochthony, as in the cases of Pu Ñoe Ña Ñoe, Alawaka Yak, and Pu Sae Ña Sae The Inthakhin pillar in Chiang Mai is no exception, although it differs from *lak müang* found among Tai groups, in its permanent nature, being made of bricks, and in having a non-Tai name derived from Sanskrit/Pali. This is related to the historical development of the Buddhist sangha in the kingdom from the fifteenth century. Yet, despite its textual Buddhification the Inthakhin pillar has, interestingly, long retained associations with spirit rituals familiar in Tai systems.

This poses the question of how the *lak müang* and other symbols pertinent to dominant power relations are connected with political power and its legitimate authority. A consideration of ritual processes connected with the *lak müang* cult may help to answer this question. The cult almost invariably features animal sacrifice and spirit-possession. Many ethnographic instances suggest that it has political significance associated with the reproduction of the authority of power-holders such as village chiefs and princes (*cao müang*). Elsewhere I have argued that the reproduction of authority in spirit cults is derived from the very process of ritual acts such as sacrifice and spirit-possession (Tanabe 1991, 1994). In the *lak müang* and tutelary spirit cults the ritual is primarily concerned with the transformation of spiritual power into rewarding tutelary power. The spirits invoked, which are viewed as arbitrarily and thus ambivalently powerful at the outset, are ultimately tamed through violent acts such as the killing, cooking, and eating of sacrificial animals. The power of the spirits becomes benevolent and protects the existing social order. The bodies of mediums possessed by the spirits come to represent a tutelary power, and to have divinatory and oracular powers. The tutelary spirits come to recognize the social order and so to legitimate the authority of the sponsor of the rites, usually village chiefs and princes in traditional Tai polities.

Large scale ritual processes naturally involve the exercise of social influence and mobilize multiplex and wide-ranging social relations, including notably, the recurrent appearance of autochthonous groups. Cults which propitiate tutelary spirits governing *müang* domains may require the specialist participation of non-Tai, mainly Mon-Khmer groups. Archaimbault notes that a Mon-Khmer tribesman was hired to slay the buffalo and conduct the sacrifice at a village spirit house near Wat Phu, Campasak in southern Laos (1959: 159). In a Lue community near Vieng Phouka, northern Laos, a Lamet, again a Mon-Khmer group, takes the role of buffalo sacrificer in the annual cult to propitiate *phi muong* and other spirits (Izikowitz 1962: 76). Among the Tai Nüa of Hua Phan province, northern Laos, where I stayed in 1991, the propitiation of *phi müang* had been held in many localities under colonial administration until the 1950s. Ten buffaloes and two cows were sacrificed in the fourth month (around March) at seven different locations including *lak man* (*lak müang*). In the *phi müang* cult rites at Müang Et, at the two most important groves (Dong Süa and Dong Kham) a cow was ritually killed using a hammer by an autochthonous Phwak (sometimes called Tai Phwak by the Tai Nüa), a Mon-Khmer group. In the case of the *phi müang* cult at Xiang Kho, the last of which was held in 1952, twelve buffaloes were killed at different places, including *lak man*, and a cow sacrifice was assigned to a Tai Daeng (Red Tai) village within the domain. In this case the Tai Daeng are regarded as autochthonous (and non-Buddhist) *vis-à-vis* the Lao, having been resident before Xiang Kho was established.

These instances reveal that while a Tai chief claims to be the sacrificer as sponsor, and is eventually recognized as ruler, particular aboriginal groups, often Mon-Khmer, take the role of sacrificer in the ritual. One might say that this role is part of a process of reconciliation in which ability to access tutelary spirits is used by the Tai ruler to justify his claim to ownership of conquered territory. Though superior autochthonous status may be maintained rhetorically, the people are in effect incorporated into the Tai ritual system in which they play the – in strict Buddhist terms impure – role of slayers of large animals in a process which confirms their subordination. This ritual incorporation of autochthony does not occur in every *lak müang* cult or *phi müang* rite. Most notably, no historical source is available to prove Lua' participation in rites associated with the Inthakhin pillar of Chiang Mai, despite their legendary connection.

Categorized as autochthonous and distinguished from other upland groups, the Lua' were involved in more direct political and economic relations that recognized their status as a dependent, peripheral population. Namely, they were perpetually involved in the tributary system that constituted a crucial part of the traditional economy of Chiang Mai. The Chiang Mai rulers developed a system of appropriation that included conscription of corvée labour and collection of tribute from the lowland peasantry, mainly Khon Müang and other Tai. Lua' communities, more peripheral to the *müang* domain were subject to the system in varying degrees. Communities near the centre, strongly assimilated into Khon Müang society in cultural terms, were subject to corvée conscription like other Tai groups, and those in remote areas were categorised as *phrai suai* and had to send tribute (Renard 1988: 29–30). The tributary system and incorporation into the Khon Müang polity became more apparent and systematized from the early nineteenth century, when records indicate that some villages, for example Bo Luang in Hot district, sent iron, but that tributary items from Lua' communities were mostly agricultural and forest products such as herbal medicine, cotton, rice, salt, chilly, kenaf, pumpkin, and orchid (Sratsawadi 1991: 102–103). Lua' chiefs (*saming*) who met the tributary obligations were granted a title by the Chiang Mai princes and received an inscribed silver plate called *tra lap ngoen* (Kraisri 1965b: 233–240). From mid-nineteenth century records found in Lua' communities in Hang Dong and Hot districts of Chiang Mai, the silver plates seem to have been issued to fix the rate of tribute in monetary terms and as a guarantee of exemption from corvée (Khritsana 1988; Sratsawadi 1991).

The tributary system thus brought about a consolidation of political relations within the Lua' communities, because the political authority of *saming* was recognized and legitimated with the silver plate granted by the Chiang Mai princes. As objects of power these silver plates were the focus of a kind of fetishism which can still be observed in some Lua' communities. Khritsana reports that the Lua' chief (*cao hit*) at Bo Luang keeps the plate buried under his house in a pottery jar. Nobody besides himself can look at it because it is protected by a spirit; others who see it may die. When the chief opens the jar to see it, he must make a sacrificial offering of a large pig and two bottles of wine (1988: 22). For centuries Lua' communities in northern Thailand have been structurally included as peripheral groups within the economic system of the Khon Müang principalities. Their relations with the centre were recognized and consolidated through their symbolic representation in rituals. We can see that the ritually constructed centre-periphery relationship would not encourage, within the traditional Khon Müang political system, any social and economic development of groups considered autochthonous. The impact of the nation-state was to transform such relationships.

The Inthakhin Cult and its Transformation

Contemporary rites associated with the Inthakhin pillar have seemingly little to do with the autochthnous Lua' and their relations within the former political system. Some ritual sequences, however, reveal that changes and transformations have occurred in the ritual during its history. In order to elucidate the nature of these, I first give a brief ethnographic account of the Inthakhin cult as observed from 1986 through 1992.[14]

The propitiation of the Inthakhin pillar and associated rituals are held for seven days from late in the eighth month of the Khon Müang lunar calendar through to early in the ninth month, usually middle or late May. This period corresponds to the beginning of the rainy season and marks the commencement of various spirit cult rituals, such as village spirits. The preparation of pillar rituals is currently the official responsibility of the Chiang Mai Municipal Council with assistance from many groups, including Wat Cedi Luang and its lay committee, and spirit-mediums from a group associated with the ritual since the 1940s. The latter have been assigned responsibility for preparing the major offerings. In addition, at least from early this century, *ahak pu acan* (the guardian, venerable teacher), a Brahmanic office attached to the Chiang Mai court, has been in charge of the ritual as a whole.

Major ritual objects are located within the compound of Wat Cedi Luang. In the Inthakhin Hall a statue of standing Buddha (Phra Un Müang) is on the pillar facing to the North. Around the pillar are placed eleven lacquer ware trays, each containing *suai mak* (areca nuts), *suai dok* (flowers), strings of sliced areca nuts, bunches of cowrie-shell money, white cloth, red cloth, gold and silver candles, bananas, a coconut, a bottle of rice spirit. Beside these trays is placed a small basket of unhusked and milled rice grains. To the East there is a large lacquer ware tray (*khan kao* the main tray) containing, in addition to those offerings, a loop and a hook for controlling an elephant, and a large basket of unhusked and milled rice is placed to one side. A bunch of coconuts, a stem of bananas, a tray of flowers, and a big jar containing lustral water (*nam som poi*) are arranged to the North.

These offerings represent fertility and prosperity, but include equipment for controlling elephants, symbolizing regal sovereignty. According to the account written by Phinit Sukhakan (1954), a venerable teacher in charge of the ritual earlier this century, the Inthakhin ritual was formerly more explicitly associated with the security of the *müang*. Ritual appurtenances included weapons and military equipment such as swords, lances, a hundred rifles, eight cannons (in front of the four gates of the hall), a gong, and a drum.[15] Supplicants, ranging from high-ranking *cao müang* to common people, would bring clothes, mirrors, and gold and silver ornaments to place around the pillar in the hope of ensuring the prosperity and welfare of the entire domain. Items placed there by the *cao müang* were brought back after three days, while those of commoners remained for four. These practices have disappeared in the contemporary ritual.

Outside the Inthakhin hall, at the North-East and South-West corners, there are statues of the four guardians; *ratchasi* (lion), *chang* (elephant), *süa* (tiger), and *risi* (hermit). It is surrounded by a *ratchawat*, a ritual fence made of split bamboo with thirty-two shelves for placing flowers. There are two Kumphan statues, one to the North, the other to the South, to which offerings of a boiled pig's head and its four legs, a boiled chicken, and a bottle of rice spirit are made on the morning of the first day. Two rows of thirty-two wooden trays are arranged in front of the Inthakhin hall for *khan sai dok*, the offering of flowers. Women are prohibited from stepping into the hall, and they, together with men, make offerings to the pillar outside, putting flowers at all these thirty-two trays. Located beside these trays is the rain-making image of Buddha called Phacao Fon Saen Ha (the Buddha of One Hundred-thousand Showers) upon which people pour water. Inside the main hall (vihara) of the monastery, in addition to the main Buddha images there are two smaller Buddha statues, one for ritual bathing and one to which gold leaf is affixed, and twelve bowls are arranged in front of them for placing money. Singers and flute players perform traditional music (*so müang*) in a hut on stilts constructed to the South of the Inthakhin hall. Musical performance was restored during the late-1980s after a suspension of more than forty years.

After the main offerings have been made on the first day, the twelve trays of offerings and the rain-making Buddha image are taken in procession from Wat Cedi Luang to downtown Chiang Mai. Teams of dancers, musical bands, and palace guards organized by the Municipal Council accompany the procession. Bearers carry large baskets on poles to receive donations of food and other offerings from people in the town. When the procession returns in the late afternoon, the Chiang Mai city governor lights candles at the Northern gate of the pavilion to declare the beginning of the Inthakhin celebration. Subsequently nine monks sitting around the

Inthakhin pillar begin chanting sutras in Kham Müang language.[16] It should be noted that the fifteen sutras chanted include two relevant to rain-making rituals.[17] The nine monks hold a white cotton string believed to transfer sacred power from the Buddha image on the Inthakhin pillar. The string is stretched over sacred objects including the Kumphan statues, the Yang tree to the South of the pavilion, two pagodas, and jars containing lustral water. For seven days the monks chant around the pillar every evening, and people from in and outside the city continuously join the celebration, putting flowers in the trays and pouring water on Phracao Fon Saen Ha. The celebration is followed by ceremonial almsgiving to 108 monks who chant sutras in the main hall on the following morning.

The Inthakhin cult consists of two differentiated sequences: chanting of Buddhist sutras for propitiation of the pillar, in the hope of prosperity and fertility within the domain, allied with non-Buddhist sacrificial offerings made to two Kumphan. This differentiation in the ritual sequences is suggested in the original myth of the pillar, but is also a reinterpretation of autochthony within a Buddhist discourse. We saw earlier how sacrificial and related practices intrinsic to *lak müang* cults tended to disappear and in some cases the pillar become transformed into a Buddhist monument. Since the Inthakhin cult has historically been regarded as one of the royal cults of the Chiang Mai court, the reason for the decline of sacrifice should be sought in political changes. The integration of Chiang Mai society into the centralized Siamese administration early this century gave rise to pressures to adapt the rites of the cult to be in line with the dominant Buddhist discourse of the centralised Sangha. Wat Cedi Luang was restored from a cluster of small monk's dwellings to a large monastery in 1928 by Thammayut monks, a reformist sect previously inactive in Khon Müang society. They had a mandate to do so originating from King Rama IV, with further support from Cao Kaeo Nawarat (nominally reigning 1911–1939), the last Prince of Chiang Mai, who had effectively lost sovereignty to the Bangkok government. Although no confirmation from historical sources is available, the Inthakhin cult was likely to have begun to lay more emphasis on Buddhist practices.

Despite these Buddhist influences the Inthakhin cult seems to have continued with sacrifice and related practices in the subsequent years. Sanguan gives an account of a big feast and spirit-possession in the Inthakhin cult before World War II:

'During the period under the sovereignty of princes of Chiang Mai, men with big baskets collected donations of vegetables, fish and other foods from the people, shops and markets in the town. Everybody was willing to donate them. The vegetables, fish and food collected in this way were cooked as offerings to the deities and tutelary spirits (*phi süa ban süa müang*). In addition to this food collected from the people, there was meat derived from sacrificed animals such as pigs, cows, buffaloes, chickens and so forth. In addition to this there were occurrences of spirit-possession by tutelary spirits (*phi ban phi müang*) in order to inquire after the fortune of the *müang* domain; whether any disaster would occur; or if the weather and harvests would be good or not. The spirit-mediums would give a forecast. If the destiny of the *müang* domain was not to be good, a magical ritual (*phithi thang saiyasat kae khai*) would take place to blow away and reduce the possible disaster. This ritual is called "the ritual of stretching the destiny of the *müang* (*süp chata müang*)" or so-called "the ritual of merit-making for the *müang* (*phithi tham bun müang*)".' (Sanguan 1969: 26–27, my translation).'

In the late 1980s several informants aged over seventy remembered sacrificial offerings, though exactly when was not specified. These practices may have overtly been taking place around the Inthakhin pillar, most likely before the restoration of Wat Cedi Luang in the late 1920s. Despite some ambiguity in Sanguan's account, we may assume that sacrifice and spirit-possession at the pillar continued at the community level in the area of present Wat Cedi Luang at least until the monastery was restored in 1928.

Some informants have suggested that the sacrificial rites then practised were confined to the communities around the site, and that even Cao Kaeo Nawarat ignored the worship of the pillar towards the end of his life in 1939. A ninety year-old informant (1986) said that the cult practising spirit-possession during the pre-war period was severely suppressed by government officials. Thus the Inthakhin cult immediately before the war seems to have had little to do with the disappearing monarchy of Chiang Mai and was even seen as a subversive practice. After a decline in observance during and after the war, the Inthakhin cult was adopted by the Chiang Mai Municipal Council. Sacrifice, spirit-possession, and related practices were totally eliminated because the administration was concerned to discourage sensual, bloody rituals, at least in the city centre – although offerings of a boiled pig's head to the Kumphan statues were allowed to remain. The cult emphasized the monks' chanting and merit-making practices, as seen today. The Inthakhin cult was redefined as a display of municipal authority within the modern nation-state. A similar shift is discernible in the case of the *lak müang* of Lampang. This transformation initiated by the municipality corresponds to popular Buddhist concerns in the post-war period. In about 1950 a spirit-medium active in the Inthakhin cult since before the war, together with people living near the pillar, asked Khuba Khao Pi to construct a pavilion to replace the ruined one. Khuba Khao Pi – a revered disciple of Khuba Siwichai the leader of the Buddhist revival movement in northern Thailand early this century – has long been highly regarded for his restoration of Buddhist monuments.[18] Mobilizing his followers and lay devotees he finished the project in 1953 when the

Phra Un Müang, Khuba Kao Pi's most respected Buddha image, was placed on the top of the pillar.

The Inthakhin Cult and the Ritual Order Redefined

The development of state-defined Buddhism, as exemplified by the promulgation of the Sangha Act, 1962 brought about an accelerated transformation not only in the formal organisation of the sangha and its practices, but also in popular practices as a whole, considerably eroding Khon Müang traditions. Buddhist discourse and practice became increasingly dominant over various forms of spirit cult, which had hitherto been relatively autonomous, even independent of Buddhist practice. Monastery-centred Buddhist merit-making rituals are becoming increasingly grandiose and spectacular, while spirit cults decline, particularly those associated with the worship of matrilineal ancestor spirits and village tutelary spirits cults. Yet, on the other hand, in the city and adjacent rural areas the number of professional spirit-mediums has been increasing since the 1960s. Most of these mediums are deeply imbued with Buddhist moral concerns, even if the spirit-possession they practice is antithetical to Buddhist doctrine (Irvine 1984; Wijeyewardene 1986; Tanabe 1994).

These Buddhist oriented spirit-mediums, almost exclusively female, when possessed by tutelary spirits pursue a variety of non-discursive practices for their clients, including healing, divination, fortune-telling, love magic, predicting the winning lottery numbers, and so on. None of these practices necessarily represent any discrete disciplinary traditions of Khon Müang society, but they are rather an innovative assemblage of fragmented elements of knowledge and practice derived from Buddhism, spirit-possession, male magic, and other sources. The new spirit-mediums, facing a diminishing role in communal rites, have developed a theatre of non-discursive practice and services, in response to the social insecurity and uncertainty widely experienced by lower and middle strata of the city and rural populations (Tanabe 1994). The proliferation of these non-discursive practices in Khon Müang society, is also significant for the Inthakhin cult.

Almost simultaneously with the death of the last prince of Chiang Mai, Cao Kaeo Nawarat, in 1939, a telling incident happened to a male spirit-medium ('Medium B') who was active in the cult as it was practised among the nearby communities. Medium B (1905–1973), who had long been a cook at the court of the prince was at this time possessed by a tutelary spirit called Cao Lak Müang (literally: The Lord of the Pillar of Müang Chiang Mai) on Doi Suthep, the most auspicious mountain associated with legendary foundation of the ancient state of Chiang Mai. Cao Lak Müang is synonymous with the Inthakhin pillar itself, so the medium was in effect in confrontation with the city authority by setting up an alternative cult centred on the symbol of the pillar, mobilizing local, particularist sentiments unconnected with the central government. During the war – early 1940s – Medium B was thereafter possessed by this powerful spirit in the communally maintained Inthakhin cult held at the pillar, and at other private healing sessions. During this time he was accused of having criticized the ban on the cult ordered by local government officials who were by then already under the control of the Bangkok administration.

After the war, however, the Municipal Council of Chiang Mai decided to restore the cult and bestowed on Medium B the task of arranging the preparation of the main offerings to the pillar in the officially renewed rites described above. Medium B performed this role, with assistance from his disciples and followers until his death in 1973. As a devoted Buddhist, he was firmly opposed to animal sacrifice, although boiled pigs' heads were allowed to be offered to the Kumphan statues, and he did not allow possession sessions during the official Inthakhin celebration. However, at the same time he had already established a cult based on the worship of his familiar spirit, Cao Lak Müang at Ceng Sri Phum, the most auspicious north-east corner of the city wall. He claimed that the Inthakhin pillar was a material symbol of the tutelary spirit of Chiang Mai, Cao Lak Müang, who should be propitiated at the spirit house located at Ceng Sri Phum. Thereafter a propitiation ritual has been held annually at the spirit house seven days after the official Inthakhin ceremony (on the 11th day of the waxing moon of the 9th lunar month; in late May or early June). In this ritual a large number of spirit-mediums dance in honour of the tutelary spirit, with offerings of twelve trays, exactly same as in the Inthakhin ritual.

The symbolic opposition between the central pillar and the north-east corner of the city plan, often manifest in Khon Müang political space, is again discernible. Yet we should bear in mind that there is little differentiation between the two cults at the symbolic level, differences relate more to complicated articulations in the process of redefining the religious order in Chiang Mai.

Buddhist domination has redefined the religious and ritual order in Khon Müang society, leading to the growing popularisation of Buddhist moral concerns. Even spirit-mediums express themselves in a Buddhist idiom. In response to this the Inthakhin cult was split into two cults. The municipality restored the main cult at the pillar as a display of government authority through emphasis on its Buddhist authenticity; while spirit-mediums, though strongly inclined toward Buddhist morality, developed a new cult involving the divinatory and healing practices referred to earlier. This innovation should be viewed not as a creation out of nothing, but rather as an assemblage of fragmented elements that lacked any rigorous Buddhist coherence. The redefined, officially dominated religious order presents a putative unity of Buddhist religiosity and ritual practices, which contributes to legitimation of the centralised power of the nation-state.

The autochthonous representations hitherto embodied in the cult and elsewhere have been withering away. Centre-periphery relations, maintained by the tributary system, were already dissolved during the reign of Cao Kaeo Nawarat. As one of its imperatives for the modernization process in the development of the nation-state, in 1959, the Bangkok government began to realign the peripheral peoples of Thailand in a more direct categorization *vis-à-vis* the state. The Ministry of the Interior determined a revised categorization of upland peoples: the Lua' were classified together with other upland groups under the generic term 'hill tribes' (*chao khao*) which was viewed as a strategic category in the effort to maintain the boundaries of the nation-state against 'communist' threats (Tapp 1990: 155–58). The peripheral economy was drawn into a relationship subordinate to the development of the industrialized core around Bangkok. The Lua' were thus uniformly included in a new state-defined strategic category, and detached from their historical and cultural relations with the Khon Müang and other Tai groups.

With the decreasing threat of 'communist' insurgency and the emergence of a new political environment in northern Thailand and beyond since the 1980s, 'hill tribes' are being involved in a new phase of economic relations. The growth of tourism in the peripheral areas and increasing domestic and foreign demand for the pre-industrial artefacts of the hill peoples have caused an uneven and distorted development among them leading to a kind of underdevelopment (Tapp 1990: 167). The nation-state of Thailand is ever more intimately involved in world capitalist relations, and its economic policies are determined by these global concerns. Development policies are now not only thrust onto the upland groups but also affect Khon Müang society. This is the backdrop against which the Inthakhin rites are held in the Chiang Mai city area. The official Inthakhin cult has taken a new form, not only as a display of the authority of the municipality and provincial government, but as a grand celebratory spectacle. It is becoming a tourist attraction and source of profit as a major religious festival, helping to make Chiang Mai a focus of domestic and international tourism. Its large procession, a confusing agglomeration of arbitrarily selected cultural elements from Khon Müang, Siamese, and other sources, contrasts with the sincere and elegant merit-making conduct of townspeople and inhabitants of the urban hinterland. The rites are becoming an object of consumption, with no necessary connection with their previous symbolic discourse. In other words the motivation of the annual Inthakhin ritual is shifting from the significance it once had within the Khon Müang polity towards being an object of curiosity that domestic and international tourist consumers have to spend money to witness.

Plate 21. 'Phya In or Indra'

Conclusions

I have tried to illustrate the relationship between minorities and dominant Tai systems as a process of ideological incorporation of the former into Tai state formations that have been developing since the thirteenth century AD. Structural differentiation between hill groups and valley states has been maintained in certain areas and in certain periods in mainland South East

Asia. With respect to the Tai Buddhist kingdoms and principalities and their peripheries, however, the differentiation has resulted in complex and varied relationships of dominance and dependency in relation to economic resources (cf. Nugent 1982). One of these relationships is the incorporation of hill peoples into valley-centred Tai states through ritual performances that expressed the political and economic subjugation of the former.

In the Khon Müang political system, the state constructed a category of particular groups of people in the periphery as autochthonous, namely Lua', distinguished from the major inhabitants at the centre and even from other neighbouring hill groups. Lua' were represented ambivalently as both barbarously cannibal and ritually superior, by virtue of prior occupation of the land. In Chiang Mai representations of the Lua' as autochthonous were most evidently attached to the Inthakhin pillar, a kind of *lak müang* pillar common to most Tai political domains. The pillar was associated with a ritual process featuring sacrifice and spirit-possession, through which recognition was given to the legitimate power and authority of the ritual sponsor, the ruling prince. These rites and the mythical background of the Inthakhin pillar were subject to Buddhist influences over many centuries, a common occurrence in Tai Buddhist kingdoms. The monarchy's loss of hegemony and ensuing administration from Bangkok brought about an emphatic change in the Inthakhin cult. Buddhist rituals were increasingly emphasized in official redefinitions of the cult, and sacrifice, spirit-possession, and related practices, which had formerly remained at the communal level, were totally eliminated. The previously important category of autochthony no longer had political and ritual significance in the newly emerging nation-state.

Notes

1 The Ñang, Karennic language speaking groups, had particular roles within the Khon Müang system, including their long-term slave trade with the Khon Müang princes (Turton 1980: 257, 277; see also Keyes (1979: 46–54).

2 *Tamnan suwanna khamdaeng rü tamnan sao inthakhin* 1972, *Chronique de Suvanna Khamdëng* 1926. Wijeyewardene has translated the earlier part of this chronicle, based on the earlier version with notes from the later (Wijeyewardene 1986: 228–36)

3 In some versions of the myth Pu Sae Ña Sae are not referred to as cannibal *ñak*, but as Lawa who have the vicious habit of eating cows and buffaloes.

4 In this coronation rite Mang Kham intends to sell the throne for a higher price to the Khün prince, but settles for 100,000 *bia* (cowrie shell currency) thereby relinquishing all rights (*Tamnan müang yong* 1984: 67). *The Jentgung State Chronicle* (1981: 230) describes a similar ritual: 'When the golden palace had been built, the Lvas living in Bangüng and Bangham were brought down [from their hills] to sit and eat their food on the gem-studded throne in the palace. While they were eating, the Lvas were driven out and the Braya took their place'. Sao Saimöng Mangrai notes that this coronation rite was last performed in 1897 when Prince Kônkaeu Intraeng was consecrated (*ibid.*: 284, Note 45).

5 According to Maha Sila Viravong, Phia Kasak was one of the major government offices appointed by Fa Ngum after he became king in the mid-fourteenth century (Sila Viravong 1957: 55).

6 In Chiang Mai the word 'Inthakhin' is used not only for the pillar at the geographical centre, but also for the city-gate pillars, as found on the inscriptions on them (Prasert na Nagara 1986).

7 In northern Thailand there are at least two columns called 'Inthakhin'; one was found in a ruined monastery in Inthakhin sub-district, Mae Taeng district of Chiang Mai, though it was later stolen; another was found in the compound of Wat Inthakhin at Pa Sang, Lamphun, where the stone pillar is believed to have been restored by King Kawila in the late eighteenth century. In Laos *lak man*, one of the *lak müang* of Luang Prabang, is referred to as 'Inthakhin' in the Thai version of *Phongsawadan lan chang* (1963: 135).

8 A version of this was translated into French by Camille Notton (*Chronique de Suvanna Khamdëng* 1926: 1–33); another version was transliterated into Thai (Siamese) by Sanguan Chothisukharat (*Tamnan suwanna khamdaeng* 1972: 117–60).

9 Notton translated this into French (*Chronique du Mahathera Fa Bot* 1926: 35–80). A similar chronicle is known as *Tamnan mahathera pha bot chabap wat münsan* (1977) transliterated into Thai by Sawat Khamekpasit. Part was transliterated into Thai by Thiw Wichaikhatthakha, a version called *Tamnan mahathera fa bot* (1986), formerly held by Sanguan Chothisukharat.

10 According to my interviews with Lawa informants in Mae La Noi district, Mae Hongson province in 1990, a new *dong sakang* is erected near the old ones when a new village head is appointed. On this occasion sacrifices of a buffalo, a cow, and chickens are held around the pillar to propitiate the village tutelary spirit (*phi sapai ta yuang*).

11 *Cen ban cen müang*, *cen müang* or *cao cen müang* also signify tutelary spirits and deities of the domain.

12 Lafont criticises Maspéro and claims that when the Tai Khao had independent principalities *lak müang* symbolized the spirit of the domain, and only when the dynasty changed would it be replaced by the new rulers. He notes that *cao müang* appointed by the French colonial administration seem to have lost their personal relationship with the spirit of the domain, but that newly appointed *cao müang* removed the old pillar replacing it with a new one (Lafont quoted in LeBar et al. 1964: 225; see also Placzek 1990).

13 In a Tai Dam (Black Tai) village, Xiang Kho district, Houa Phan province in northern Laos, the village spirits (*phi xoen*) represent the ancestors of the lineage called Luang, the pioneer settlers of the village. The *cao süa* (head of the lineage) propitiated the *phi xoen* in rites held at the village pillar (*lak ban*). Among Tai Daeng (Red Tai) in Müang Xoi, Viang Xai district of the same province, the village spirits are classified into two groups, *phi xoen* (ancestor spirits of *cao müang*'s lineage) and *cao din* (lord of the land) and reside in separate spirit houses; there was also a *lak man* (village pillar) until the 1950s. The *Cao müang* as a whole was regarded as the sponsor (*cao süa*) and held, together with the ritual officiant (*cao cam*), the sacrificial ritual propitiating these spirits with buffalo. The differentiation between *phi xoen* and *cao din* is also seen among Tai Daeng in the Xiang Kho area.

14 The contemporary ritual sequences are described by Wijeyewardene (1986: 78–82), Mani (1986: 133–35) and Premchit and Doré (1992: 215–22).

15 I saw lances and swords placed in the hall in 1986, but they had disappeared from the ritual a few years later.

16 Twenty-eight monks chanted in former days according to older informants and Phinit Sukhakan (1954).

17 The rain-making sutras recited are *Sam phuttha (Khatha phya khang khok)* and *Puna parang (Khatha phaya pla chon)*. These are also recited in rain-making rituals at village level.
18 On the Buddhist revival movement led by Khuba Siwichai and Khuba Kao Pi, see Tanabe (1986; 1992a).

References

Aijmer, Göran (1979), 'Reconciling Power with Authority: an Aspect of Statecraft in Traditional Laos', *Man* (N.S.), 14: 734–749.

Archaimbault, Charles (1959), 'The Sacrifice of the Buffalo at Vat Ph'u', in René de Berval (ed.), *Kingdom of Laos*, Saigon: France-Asie, 156–61.

—— (1964), 'Religious Structures in Laos', *Journal of the Siam Society*, 52: 57–74.

—— (1973), *Structures Réligieuses Lao (Rites et Mythes)*, Vientiane: Editions Vithagna.

Cholthira Sattayawatthana (1990), 'Cai ban cai müang lae cai khon (The Heart of Village, the Heart of Müang, and the Heart of the Person)', in B. J. Terwiel, Antony Diller and Cholthira Sattayawatthana, *Khonthai (doem) mai dai yu thi ni* (The Original Thai Didn't Live Here), Bangkok: Samnakphim Müang Boran, 186–230.

Chronique de Mahathera Fa Bot (1926), in Camille Notton (trans.), *Annales du Siam*, Premiere partie, Paris: Imprimeries Charles-Lavauzelle, 38–80.

Condominas, Georges (1990), *From Lawa to Mon, from Saa' to Thai: Historical and Anthropological Aspects of Southeast Asian Social Spaces*, Canberra: Department of Anthropology, Research School of Pacific Studies, The Australian National University.

Davis, Richard (1984), *Muang Metaphysics: A Study of Northern Thai Myth and Ritual*, Bangkok: Pandora.

Doré, Amphay (1980), 'Les Joutes Mythiques entre l'Aîné Kassak et le Puîné Lao: Contribution à l'Étude de la Fondation du Lane Xang', *Péninsule* 1: 47–72.

Hasegawa, Kiyoshi (1993), 'Unnan-sho Tai Kei Minzoku niokeru Bukkyo to Seirei Saishi (Buddhism and Spirit Cults among the Tai Nationality in Yunnan)', in Shigeharu Tanabe (ed.), *Jissen Shukyo no Jinruigaku: Jozabu Bukkyo no Sekai* (Anthropology of Practical Religion: the World of Theravada Buddhism), Kyoto: Kyoto University Press, 221–56.

Irvine, Walter (1984), 'Decline of Village Spirit Cults and Growth of Urban Spirit Mediumship', *Mankind*, 14 (4): 315–24.

Izikowitz, K.G. (1962), 'Notes about the Tai', *Bulletin of the Museum of Far Eastern Antiquities*, 34: 73–91.

Keyes, Charles F. (1979), 'The Karen in Thai History and the History of the Karen in Thailand', in Charles F. Keyes (ed.), *Ethnic Adaptation and Identity: the Karen on the Thai Frontier with Burma*, Philadelphia: Institute for the Study of Human Issues, 25–61.

Kraisri Nimmanhaeminda (1965a), 'Put Vegetables into Baskets, and People into towns', in Lucien M. Hanks, Jane R. Hanks and Lauriston Sharp (eds.), *Ethnographic Notes on Northern Thailand*, Ithaca, N.Y.: Cornell University, Southeast Asia Program, Data Paper No. 58, 6–9.

—— (1965b), 'An Inscribed Silver Plate Grant to the Lawa of Boh Luang', in *Felicitation Volumes of Southeast Asian Studies Presented to Prince Dhaninivat on his Eightieth Birthday*, Vol. 2. Bangkok: The Siam Society, 233–40.

Kritsana Caroenwong (1988), 'Kan samruat chumchon lua nai ha amphoe (A survey of Lua communities in five districts)', in *Ekkasan sammana thang wichakan rüang lwa nai lanna* (Proceedings of the Seminar on the Lwa in Lanna), Chiang Mai: Witthayalaikhru Chiang Mai, 15–24.

Leach, Edmund R. (1954), *Political systems of Highland Burma*, London: London School of Economics and Political Science.

—— (1960), 'The Frontiers of "Burma"', *Comparative Studies in Society and History*, 3(1): 49–68.

LeBar, Frank M., Gerald C. Hickey and John K. Musgrave (eds.) (1964), *Ethnic Groups of Mainland Southeast Asia*, New Haven: HRAF Press.

Mani Phayomyong (1986), *Prapheni sipsong düan lannathai* (The Twelve-month Traditions in Lannathai), Chiang Mai: So Sapkanphim.

Maspéro, Henri (1929), 'Mœurs et Coutumes des Populations Sauvages', in Georges Maspéro (ed.), *Un Empire Colonial Français: L'Indochine*, Paris: G. Van Oest, Vol. 1, 233–55.

—— (1950), *Les religions Chinoises*, Mélanges Posthumes, Vol. 1, Paris: Publications du Musée Guimet.

Moerman, Michael (1965), 'Ethnic Identification in a Complex Civilization: Who are the Lue?', *American Anthropologist* , 67: 1215–30.

Nugent, David (1982), 'Closed Systems and Contradiction: the Kachin in and out of History', *Man* (N.S.), 17: 508–27.

Penth, Hans (1989), 'On the History of Chiang Rai', *Journal of the Siam Society*, 77(1): 11–32.

Phinit Sukhakan, Thao (1992), 'Khrüang phli kam bucha inthakhin (The Offerings to Inthakhin)', *Warasan thetsaban* (Journal of the Chiang Mai Municipality), 17 (166): 6–7.

'Phongsawadan lan chang (The Chronicle of Lan Xang)' (1963), in Krom Sinlapakon (ed.), *Prachum phongsawadan* (Collected Chronicles), Vol. 2 Bangkok: Khurusapha, 134–84.

Placzek, James A. (1990), 'Phi miang: Black Thai Symbols of State and Leadership', in *Proceedings of the International Conference of Thai Studies, Kunming*, Vol. 3, 48–68.

Prasert na Nagara (1986), 'Carük pratu tha phae cangwat chiang mai (The Inscription at Tha Phae Gate of Chiang Mai)', in *Kamphaeng müang chiang mai* (The City-wall of Chiang Mai), Chiang Mai, Anuson nuang nai phithi poet lae chalong pratu tha phae, 79–83.

Premchit, Sommai and Amphay Doré (1992), *The Lan Na Twelve-month Traditions*, Chiang Mai: So Sap Kan Pim.

Renard, Ronald D. (1988), 'Identifying the Lua: an Informal Essay on Who the Lua are and are not', in *Ekkasan sammana thang wichakan rüang lwa nai lanna* (Proceedings of the seminar on the Lwa in Lanna), Chiang Mai: Witthayalaikhru Chiang Mai, 25–32.

Rhum, Michael (1987), 'The Cosmology of Power in Lanna', *Journal of the Siam Society*, 75: 91–107.

Sanguan Chottisukharat (1969), *Prapheni thai phak nüa* (Customs in Northern Thailand), Bangkok: Odeon Store.

Sila Viravong, Maha (1957), *Phongsavadan lao* (History of Laos), Vientiane: Kasvang Süksa.

Sratsawadi Ongsakun (1991), 'Lakthan prawattisat lanna cak ekkasan khamphi bailan lae phap nangsa (The Lanna Historical Materials from Palm Leaf and *Nangsa* Texts)', Chiang Mai (mimeographed).

'Tamnan mahathera pha bot chabap wat münsan' (The Chronicle of Mahathera Pha Bot, the Wat Münsan Version) (1977), Sawat Khamekpasit (trans.) (mimeographed).

'Tamnan mahathera fa bot (The Chronicle of Mahathera Fa Bot)' (1986), Thiw Wichaikhatthakha (trans.), in *Kamphaeng müang chiang mai* (The City-wall of Chiang Mai), Chiang Mai, Anuson nuang nai phithi poet lae chalong pratu tha phae, 42–4.

Tamnan müang yong (Müang Yong Chronicle) (1984), Thawi Sawangpanyangkun (trans.), Chiang Mai: Sap Kanphim.

Tamnan phünmüang chiangmai (The Local Chronicle of Chiang Mai) (1971), Thon Tonman (trans.), Bangkok: Khana Kammakan Catphim Eksan Thang Prawattisat Samnak Nayok Rattamontri.

'Tamnan suwanna khamdaeng rü tamnan sao inthakhin' (Chronicle of Suwanna Khamdaeng or Chronicle of the Inthakhin pillar) (1972), in Sanguan Chottisukharat (ed.), *Prachum tamnan lanna thai* (Collected Chronicles of Lanna Thai), Bangkok: Odeon Store, 117–60.

Tanabe, Shigeharu (1986), *Nung lüang nung dam* (Wearing the Yellow Robe and Wearing Black Garb: The Story of a Peasant Leader in Northern Thailand), Bangkok: Sang San.

—— (1988), 'Spirits and Ideological Discourse: the Tai Lü Guardian Cults in Yunnan', *Sojourn*, 3 (1): 1–25.

—— (1990), 'Sipsong Panna no Butto Girei to Kugi' (Pagoda Ritual and Sacrifice in Sipsong Panna, Yunnan), in Shigeharu Tanabe (ed.), *Jozabu Bukkyo Ken ni okeru Shukyo to Shakai* (Religion and Society in Theravada Buddhist Cultures), Osaka: National Museum of Ethnology (mimeographed).

—— (1991), 'Spirits, Power, and the Discourse of Female Gender: Phi Meng Cult in Northern Thailand', in Manas Chitakasem and Andrew Turton (eds.), *Thai Constructions of Knowledge*, London: School of Oriental and African Studies, 183–212.

—— (1992a), 'Notes on *Ton Bun*, Millennialism and Revivalism in Lanna', Paper presented at the conference on Buddhism in Lanna, Chiang Mai Teacher's College, May 1992.

—— (1992b), 'Reconstruction of Spirit Cults: Professional Spirit-mediumship of Northern Thailand', Paper presented at the symposium on Religious Renewals in Asia, National Museum of Ethnology, November 1992.

—— (1993), 'Inadama no Yukue: Kita Tai no Inasaku Girei' (The Rice Soul's Whereabouts: Agricultural Rites in Northern Thailand), in Komei Sasaki (ed.), *Noko no Gijutsu to Bunka* (Agricultural Technology and Culture), Tokyo: Shogakukan (forthcoming).

—— (1994), 'Sacrifice and the Transformation of Ritual: the Pu Sae Ña Sae Spirit Cult of Northern Thailand', in Katsumi Tamura and Ananda Rajah (eds.), *Spirit Cults and Popular Knowledge in Southeast Asia,* Singapore: Institute of Southeast Asia (forthcoming).

Tapp, Nicholas (1986), 'Buddhism and the Hmong: a Case Study in Social Adjustment', *Journal of Developing Societies*, 2: 68–88.

—— (1989), *Sovereignty and Rebellion: the White Hmong of Northern Thailand*, Singapore: Oxford University Press.

—— (1990), 'Squatters or Refugees: Development and the Hmong', in Gehan Wijeyewardene (ed.), *Ethnic Groups Across National Boundaries in Mainland Southeast Asia*, Singapore: Institute of Southeast Asian Studies, 149–72.

Terwiel, B. J. (1978), 'The Origin and Meaning of the Thai "City Pillar"', *Journal of the Siam Society*, 66(1): 159–71.

'The Jengtung State Chronicle' (1981), in Saimong Mangrai (trans.). *The Padaeng Chronicle and the Jengtung State Chronicle Translated*, Michigan papers on South and Southeast Asia, Ann Arbor: University of Michigan, Center for South and Southeast Asian Studies, 197–291.

Tho Kluaimai na Ayutthaya (1982), *Lak müang krung rattanakosin* (Lak Müang Pillars in Rattanakosin Dynasty), Bangkok: Samnak Lekhathikan Nayok Ratthamontri.

Turton, Andrew (1972), 'Matrilineal Descent Groups and Spirit Cults of the Thai Yuan in Northern Thailand', *Journal of the Siam Society*, 60 (2): 217–56.

—— (1980), 'Thai Institutions of Slavery', in James L. Watson (ed.), *Asian and African Systems of Slavery*, Oxford: Basil Blackwell, 251–92.

Wijeyewardene, Gehan (1986), *Place and Emotion in Northern Thai Ritual Behaviour*, Bangkok: Pandora.

Chapter Fourteen

Tai Lue of Sipsongpanna and Müang Nan in the Nineteenth-Century

Ratanaporn Sethakul

Introduction

The Xishuangbanna Dai Nationality Autonomous Prefecture, as the Chinese term it, is situated in the southwestern part of Yunnan province in the People's Republic of China. It is known among the Thai people as Sipsongpanna, the land of the Tai Lue. Historically, Sipsongpanna had a long relationship with Lanna, the ancient kingdom of the northern part of Thailand. King Mangrai, who founded Chiang Mai as the capital of the Lanna kingdom in 1296, was a grandson of King Rung Kaen Chai of Jinghong (Cheng Hung) capital city of Sipsongpanna (Prime Minister's Office 1971: 8).

Intermarriage between the people of Lanna and Sipsongpanna kept them very close. During the early period of the Mangrai dynasty (1296–1558), the states co-operated in fighting the Chinese who invaded southward into Sipsongpanna (Sai Sam Tip 1976: 88–106). Later, when Lanna grew more powerful during the reign of King Tilok (1442–87), several cities and towns of Sipsongpanna were included in the Lanna territory (ibid.: 58). Long-distance trade was continuously carried on between the two peoples. Besides seasonal transactions, there was also the movement of a considerable number of Lue people who migrated to settle down permanently in Lanna. For example, a distinctive Lue community is still located in Amphur Doi Saket whose inhabitants claim that their Lue ancestors moved here 600 years ago (Ratanaporn 1984: 13). The Lue people got along well with the Tai Yuan of Lanna since they shared many cultural traits including language, religion, and ways of living. There was a considerable degree of similarity in basic material culture, namely costume, cooking, weaving technology and style, basketry and pottery. Their common agricultural system was wet-rice cultivation, so they preferred the same ecological environment of lowland river-valleys where the supply of water was abundant. Thus we can say that since they were rice-planting

Plate 22. 'Khattha Kumara . . . in royal costume with a man'

peoples, their ways of life were similar. Sipsongpanna and Lanna retained a close relationship as *ban phi müang nong* (literally, village of elder sibling, town of younger sibling), meaning states with a very close relationship, until the nineteenth century.

The Lue in Nan

In the nineteenth century Nan was a Tai Yuan state located on the West bank of the Nan river and bordering Laos to the North and East, Phrae and Uttaradit to the South, and Phayao to the West. It was founded in the middle of the thirteenth century and annexed by the Lanna kingdom in the reign of King Tilok (Collection of Chronicles Part 10: 421–22). After Chiang Mai fell under Burmese power in 1558, Nan automatically became a tributary state of Burma.

The long period of Burmese over-rule witnessed repeated efforts by the people of Nan to cast off the Burmese yoke. In 1703 the Burmese sent a big force to suppress a Nan uprising. It was a period of disaster for Nan. People fled from the city to the forests and other remote areas. A large number of people who could not flee were carried off to Burma. Moreover, important Buddha images, sacred pagodas, temples, and other buildings were burned down. A year later, Lao and Vietnamese forces plundered Nan, and again dispersed people from the city. Many people were taken away, while others fled into the mountains where some hid in caves (Collection of Chronicles Part 10: 437–38).

The Burmese king realized that there was no way to rule Nan without the co-operation of the local leaders. He then appointed a prominent local leader to rule Nan together with a Burmese governor. Later on, local leaders were appointed to rule by themselves under Burmese suzerainty. Although peace and order ensued, it did not last long. Burmese rule was still so strict and exploitative that it caused strong resentment among the Lanna people. Some states initiated uprisings which were followed by harsh Burmese suppression. Wars broke out between Nan and the Burmese and with other Lanna states. These wars further decreased Nan's population. Besides the large number that died in the fighting and disorder, thousands more were taken away to Ava, Chiang Saen, Luang Prabang, Vientiane, and Ayuthaya. The Nan Chronicle states that in 1783:

'Our Müang Nan was left devastated
There were no rulers to govern.
The *phrai* or *thai* in the villages
And towns had fled to hide
In the streams and ridges.' (Collection of Chronicles Part 10: 457).

In the late eighteenth century, Lampang took the lead, with help from Chiang Mai and Lamphun, in throwing off Burmese rule (Prachakitkor-achak 1972: 439–43). Starting in 1775, the process took almost thirty years before the Burmese were driven out of their last stronghold in Chiang Saen, on the Mekong river. In this effort, the northern states received considerable support from Bangkok. Following the successful eviction of the Burmese, the northern states were able to enter a period of restoration during which they found it necessary to rebuild their population base.

Former residents of Lanna tried to return to their villages. At the same time, the northern states waged several wars with neighbouring states in order to accumulate people, who were seen as the basis of a state's strength.

Old temples, palaces, irrigation systems, and houses were rebuilt, and new facilities were constructed.

Nan was a latecomer to this process of restoration in the northern states. After the ruler of Nan, Chao Luang Attaworaphunyo, had placed Nan under Bangkok's suzerainty in 1788, he started the policy of *kep phak sai sa kep kha sai müang* (gather vegetables in baskets, gather people in towns; see Kraisri 1965) [*kha* is a categorical term for non-Tai, upland peoples, or 'slaves', see especially Renard and Turton in this volume Ed.]. As this process unfolded, some people came willingly while others came only after being captured in battle, or following military campaigns. Those that came to settle in Nan included members of many different ethnic groups. About 600 Yong families – a Tai group related to the Lue, from Müang Yong, which in the late twentieth century is in the Shan State of Burma, about 100 kilometres North of the Thai border-town of Mae Sai – came willingly to be subjects of Nan in 1790 because of the lack of internal tranquillity in their homeland. A year later, the Chao Luang (prince) of Chiang Khong and his followers, comprising 500 families, took refuge in Nan (Collection of Chronicles Part 10: 464–65). In 1805, the prince of Nan sent an army which was able to defeat Sipsongpanna. Many of the ruling family and various officials were sent to Bangkok along with tribute offerings (ibid.: 473). In 1812, the Nan chief sent an army to take away 6,000 people from Müang La, Müang Phong, Chiang Khaeng, and Müang Luang Phuka (ibid.: 480). During invasions of Cheng Tung ordered by King Mongkut between 1850 and 1855, Nan was responsible for sending troops to assist attacks on Sipsongpanna. Although the main force did not succeed in defeating the capital city of Sipsongpanna, Chiang Rung, the Nan forces did meet with some success. After capturing a number of prisoners of war, including Lue Chao from Sipsongpanna, these captured officials and some of their followers were sent to Bangkok. At the same time, over a thousand were taken to settle territory that Nan had formerly controlled but subsequently lost in battles with Burma. By sending them there, the ruler of Nan hoped to reclaim these areas, including Chiang Muan and Chiang Kham. In 1856, Nan again took away a number of people from Chiang Khaeng (Müang Sing) (ibid.: 502). Because of these successes, and due to its location and accessibility, Nan came to represent Bangkok in its dealings with Sipsongpanna.

Although it is not specifically mentioned in the chronicles, ethnic minorities such as the Htin and other Mon-Khmer-speaking peoples, as well as Tibeto-Burman speakers such as the Akha, came to live in Nan. Together with other minorities, they continue to live in Nan and sometimes have oral traditions telling of their arrival from Sipsongpanna. Among the Tibeto-Burman peoples were the so-called 'Kaw', which seems to refer to the Akha (who are called 'Kaw' or 'I-Kaw' in Tai dialects [see Alting von Geusau in this volume Ed.]). While some of their descendants have settled into the area around Nan city, there is still a community of speakers in Ban Sakoen on the old route to Chiang Kham. Here the people say they were resettled by the ruler of Nan to mine bat guano for the Chao Muang which he used to make gunpowder.

Lue and other people often came seeking refuge in Nan during times of political turmoil or famine. Some of the people who moved to Nan at that time were assimilated into Nan ways of life and are no longer recognizable as Lue today, such as many living in Nan city. However, in rural areas to the North of Nan, such as Ban Nong Bua in Tambon Pa Khan, Amphur Tha Wang Pha, the 'Lue-ness' of the villages is still obvious. In addition to a short paragraph in the Nan Chronicle saying that the Chao of Sipsongpanna sent a mission asking to buy six elephants from Nan (Collection of Chronicles Part 10: 486), the *pap sa* (mulberry paper notes) of Pho Ui (grandfather) Chanta, written in 1814, describe in detail the political conflict among the Chao of Sipsongpanna which drove two Lue Chao and their subjects from Muang La to settle in Nan (Chanta ms 1814). After establishing themselves in the villages of Ban Pa Khan, Ban Nong Bua, Ban Don Mun, and Ban Ton Hang in Nan, they continued to pay homage to Chao Luang Müang La, (the spirit of a former chief or royal prince of Müang La) whom they consider their tutelary deity to the present day.

These four villages are located to the North of Nan city. In this area four districts (Thung Chang, Chiang Klang, Pua, and Tha Wang Pha) and one sub-district (Santisuk) alone currently contain about fifty Lue villages (Somchet 1992). These Lue came from several *müang* of Sipsongpanna, such as Müang Len, Müang Phuan, Müang Chiang Rung, and Müang La. Several villages also recalled that their ancestors moved from Müang Yong.

The existence of numerous Lue communities in Nan has convinced some scholars that the Nan social system and culture were influenced by the Lue, and in some cases actually comprised assimilated Lue people (Chana 1984: 44–52). There is no need to argue whether the Lue culturally dominated the Tai Yuan or the latter dominated the former. It is, however, interesting that both cultures share many elements of a pre-existing common Tai culture with each other as well as with other Tai groups. Thus, when they lived together in a state, there were no serious conflicts between the rulers of Nan and the Lue people. Besides sharing cultural traits, the scarcity of manpower in the late eighteenth to the nineteenth century also forced the ruling class to compromise with the ethnic groups under their control. As long as the latter recognized the former's power and fulfilled its obligations, they were left alone freely to observe their own culture (Ratanaporn 1991: 49–51). The case of Lue in Nan points to similarities between the Lue system of control of people and that of the Tai Yuan. The Lue kept their social and cultural identities while fitting in well with the Tai Yuan system of control of people. The Tai Yuan applied both political and social means to control people.

As for the non-Tai minorities who came to Nan with the Lue, they were well-accustomed to living in Tai areas. Their dealings with the rulers of Nan differed little from their dealings with the rulers of Sipsongpanna. There seems to have been few problems between the Tai Yuan rulers of Nan and groups such as the Akha.

Political Means of Control

Ho pen pho, Man pen mae (Yunnanese is father, Burmese is mother) is a phrase referring to the political status of Sipsongpanna, indicating that it was not an independent state but was under both Chinese and Burmese suzerainty. Due to its remote location, however, Sipsongpanna enjoyed periods of autonomy. The ruling class of Sipsongpanna had the King at the top of the pyramid, with members of the royal family, nobles, and officials below him. The King owned all the land and natural resources in his country (Bunchuay 1955: 119). In Nan, the rulers possessed the same status as in Sipsongpanna. After the end of Burmese rule in 1775, Nan became a semi-autonomous state tributary to Bangkok. The Chao Luang of Nan exercised power and rights similar to the King of Sipsongpanna (Saratsawadee 1993: 75).

Landownership provided rulers of both Sipsongpanna and Nan with political and economic power over their subjects whose subsistence relied heavily on the cultivation of fertile valley land. The rulers granted land to everyone working for them. Officials involved included *tamnak chao ban na* (field official grades) in Sipsongpanna, and *na sak* (*sakdina* rank) in Nan, granted to the *chao nai* and *thao phaya* (royalty and nobles) who served the King and who then became a part of the ruling class. These *sakdina* grades differentiated status among officials and separated them from the commoners.

There were seven *sakdina* grades in Sipsongpanna:

1 *na saen luang* (great hundred thousand fields)
2 *na mun luang* (great ten thousand fields)
3 *na roi luang* (great hundred fields)
4 *na sao luang* (great twenty fields)
5 *na sao noi* (lesser twenty fields)
6 *na sip* (ten fields)
7 *na sip noi* (lesser ten fields) or *na han* (soldier fields) (Cao Chengzheng 1990: 79–80).

The *na sak* of Nan was rather similar to the *sakdina* grades applied in Ayutthaya and later in Bangkok, since it included the grades of the families of both Chao and officials (Saratsawadee 1993: 84–86). The similarity was that they indicated rank differentiation and social status, rather than the number of rice fields actually owned by individuals. The basic principle was that the ruling class was granted prebendal land which supported them politically and economically. Upon recognizing *nam chao din chao* (water of the Chao, soil of the Chao), indicating that they acknowledged the authority of the Chao, people were obliged to *het na pa wiak* (farm the land and do corvée).

In Sipsongpanna, relevant officials included the *Pho Lam Ban*, *Pho Lam Hua Sip*, and *Pho Lam Müang*. These *Pho Lam* were granted land or actually benefited from the land in villages and *müang* outside Chiang Rung. *Khun Nua Sanam* (Chao and higher officials) in Chiang Rung appointed *Pho Lam Müang* to act as intermediaries between the Chiang Rung court and the outer *Müang*. Their duties were to inform the *müang* about affairs in Chiang Rung and to provide information on *müang* affairs to the court at Chiang Rung. The *Pho Lam Müang* did not, however, have any administrative functions of their own. The *Khun Nua Kwan* of each *müang* were also appointed to be *Pho Lam Hua Sip* or *Pho Lam Ban*, and gained benefits from their *Luk Lam*. Those people who farmed *na pho lam* or *na chao phaya*, gave rice and provided services to their *Pho Lam*. The *Pho Lam* system of Sipsongpanna implied an attempt to consolidate control of the centre over the outer districts and to set up a close relationship between the Chiang Rung court and other *müang*, as well as to enable the ruling class to control the people's resources.

There were three categories of rice field in Sipsongpanna:

1 *na luang chao*, which belonged to the King and the *Thao Khun* of the *müang*. It consisted of *na tok thawai*, all of the produce of which went to the owners while the farmers who came from various villages received seeds and a supply of food. Holders of *na chao* and *na thao khun* received 30 per cent of the rice each season
2 *na pho lam*, which was the most numerous. This was prebendal and on it the farmers, or *luk lam* accepted the principle of *het na pa wiak*
3 *na hua ban*, which belonged to villages as a whole. Farmers paid a 30–40 per cent tax to the *Thao Khun*. *Na hua ban* land was proportionately smaller than either of the other types (Ratanaporn 1986: 30–31).

Under this *kin na* system (literally, to eat the rice field, i.e. to receive produce from the rice field), land was used to control the people. The ruling class, whether the *Khun Nua Sanam* of Chiang Rung or the *Khun Nua Kwaen* of other *müang* was able to exert control over their subjects. Beside receiving rice from official rice fields, the ruling class received service from villagers. Furthermore, on the traditional Tai new year in April and during the Buddhist rainy season retreat, the *Luk Lam* had to pay their respects to the *Pho Lam*. Villagers who failed in accordance with this patronage system risked the loss of their rights to farm the land (Ratanaporn 1986: 31–32).

The *nangsu phun na Müang Nan* (Book of rice fields in Muang Nan) described a similar *kin na* system in Nan, but used a different means for calculating official land grades. In Nan, the *Chao Buak Nai To* was responsible for the same duties and earned the same rewards as the *Pho Lam* of Sipsongpanna. Corvée provided by different *müang* was also mentioned (Arunrat 1985: 1–6).

The ruling class of Nan consisted of *Chaonai*, *Thao Khun*, *Pho Müang* and *Nai Ban*. The first two groups comprised the *Sanam*, which administered *Wiang Nan* (the city of Nan) and the *Na Ban* ('in front of the village', that is the area just outside the Wiang). *Pho Müang* and *Nai Ban* took charge of distant *müang* and villages (*ban*), respectively.

In Nan, due to the scarcity of manpower, rights to farm land were not sufficient to ensure the obedience of the people; laws and punishment were additionally needed. Since people in Nan could change their *Chao Shu* (master) by moving to faraway *müang*, people were forbidden to change their *Chao Buok Nai To*. This was the case in Müang Len, Müang Chiang Khaeng, Müang Luang, Müang Phu Kha, Müang Chiang Lap, and Müang La (Saratsawadee 1993: 75). To prevent people of various statuses moving about at will – *kha lak pai thai lak ma* (literally non-Tai [Kha] furtively going, freemen [Tai] furtively coming) – Nan, Chiang Mai, Lampang, and Lamphun joined together in issuing an edict stating that people from these four cities travelling to other *müang* had to carry passports indicating the number of people, animals and valuables they were carrying. Those without passports would be arrested and sent to the *sanam* (state assembly). Those visiting their family in another *müang*, and who decided to stay there permanently, were required to pay a sum of money to their *Chao Buok Nai To* as compensation (Saratsawadee 1993: 87–88).

Social Means of Control

The Lue people practised a combination of Theravada Buddhism and animism. Among the Lue, religious belief was used as another social means to control people. By emphasizing the doctrine of karma, Lue Buddhism was used to legitimize the ruling class and to convince the ruled to accept their fate. While the sophisticated belief system of Buddhism remained distant from the people (with the major exception of the concept of karma), spirit worship was very familiar. Nature was personified in order to be understandable, and perhaps controllable, in the form of *phi* ('spirit(s)') which could be contacted by mediators or ritual performers, and propitiated by sacrifices. People felt much relieved and more secure after worshipping spirits before starting economic and social activities. Spirit worship developed into a belief system controlling the people's social behaviour. Strict rules were set up to control people at every level. There were spirits of the state, of *müang*, villages, rice fields, rivers, weirs, forests, and houses. Propitiating the same spirits served to unify the people. Membership in *müang* and villages was confirmed by participation in spirit worship. As a part of this worship, spirits had to be informed when people moved in or out, thus representing another form of social control (Chang 1987: 58).

Similar to administrative levels of the state, there was a hierarchical order of spirits (see Anan 1984). At the top was *phi müang*, the guardian spirit of the *müang*, for which sacrificial rituals were performed by the Chao Luang. This ritual thus enhanced royal status because it emphasized the importance of the ruler by his serving as the mediator between the people and the highest spirit of the state. This ritual function aimed at guaranteeing fertility and state security. In return, people paid respect to him as well as paying taxes and offering tribute and corvée labour. At the village level, every village had a *phi ban*, the village guardian spirit which was 'fed' and celebrated (*liang*) annually by the villagers. These spirits were usually former kings, famous village chiefs, or founder figures who were the common ancestors of the villagers.

These spirits played a crucial role in controlling people and reinforcing the political and economic interest of the ruling class. In Nan, Tai Yuan villages made annual sacrifices to their *phi ban* (Chanan 1984: 58). The Lue who settled in Nan usually did not worship the Tai Yuan spirits, but most often brought their own spirits from their former *müang* or villages. Ban Nong Bua, Ton Hang, and Don Mun, for example, whose people came from Müang La in Sipsongpanna, worshipped the spirit of the Chao Luang of Müang La. Their sacrificial ritual was very strict, exclusive, and sacred. It took place once every three years. During the three-day ritual the villagers closed Ban Nong Bua, where the ritual was performed, preventing anyone from entering or leaving. Those who violated this rule would be severely fined. Only Lue people were allowed to attend the ritual, and the ritual performers were descendants of Chao Müang La and other members of royalty from Müang La (Ban Nong Bua School n.d.). Such exclusivity shows the continuing strength of Lue identity in these villages. More important, though, such a ceremony linked the village leadership with the villagers. Every household had to be present and contribute money or goods for use in the community ritual.

The village of Ban Rong Ngae, in Pua District, performed sacrificial rites to its guardian spirit, entitled Chao Luang Chang Puak Nga Kew, three times annually. This spirit of Ban Rong Ngae was believed to be the Chao of Müang Lin or Müang Len in Sipsongpanna, who had fled fighting there and came to found this village in Nan. After his death, the people erected a spirit house for him and asked him to take care of the village (Chiang Mai University 1987: 46).

Even though the spirits were Lue, people did not escape from the political control of the Tai Yuan rulers of Nan. Since the law of Nan forbade people to kill buffaloes, the Lue who wanted to sacrifice a buffalo to the *phi ban* had to request permission from the Chao Luang or the *Pho Müang* (Saratsawadee 1993: 67). Thus the Nan authority still participated in the belief system of the Lue. After obtaining permission from the Nan authorities, the Lue could perform the ritual, but at the same time they were recognizing the role of the Nan rulers as ritual supporters who benefited from the ritual in terms of fertility and protection.

Comparing the system of control of people as between the Lue in Sipsongpanna and the people of Nan, similarities can be observed between these two Tai-speaking groups, Lue and Tai Yuan. These similarities do not occur so much because the two groups were both Tai, but more because they were both subsistence agricultural societies which made their living off the land in a particular way. When the Lue came to settle in Nan, they fitted in well with the existing system which prevailed among the people who *het na müang lum* (plant rice in the lowland). The ruling class of Nan was thus able to apply the same means of control to the Lue without major difficulty.

Nan rulers were content to let the Lue villages under their control have considerable autonomy. As long as the Lue fulfilled their requirements to pay taxes and perform corvée, they could maintain their cultural distinctiveness without interference from above. The different ethnic *phi ban* did not cause any conflict but rather helped control villagers in each village, thus facilitating the *müang* in exercizing power more efficiently. Similar conditions also applied to non-Tai groups who came to settle in Nan. In return for paying tribute and co-operating with the Nan authorities, they were able to maintain their own cultural distinctiveness.

Observations

After the centralization of Thailand that occurred in the late nineteenth and early twentieth centuries, the nation took on a more unified appearance. The power of the traditional Chao, the rulers of the northern states, declined as the Bangkok government took administrative and financial control from them. At the same time, ethnic differences declined among all groups, the Lue in Nan included. Sacrificial rituals to the *phi müang* fell into gradual neglect due to the decrease in the Chao's power and abolition of the *sakdina* system, the traditional means by which manpower was controlled. Land was no longer the sole property of the Chao Luang. The people who cleared and farmed land now had rights to it as well. A system of law was implemented, and a new administrative apparatus set up with a more comprehensive methodology for controlling people.

The combined effect of these changes was to undercut the political role of the *phi müang* (state spirits), which then declined in importance and status. *Phi ban* (village spirits), on the contrary, survived the changes during the nineteenth century, since their roles were social as well as political. As such, these Lue *phi ban* have helped the Lue identity to endure longer than that of some other groups.

References

Anan Ganjanapan (1984), 'The partial commercialization of rice production in northern Thailand', unpublished Ph.D. dissertation, Cornell University.

Arunrat Wichienkeaw (1985), *Nang Su Phun Na Muang Nan*, Chiang Mai: Wittayalaikhru.

Ban Nong Bua School (Public Relations), *Nae Nam Ban Nong Bua Tambon Phakha Amphoe Thawangpha Changwat Nan*, mimeo, n.d.

Bunchuay Srisawat (1955), *Thai Sipsong Panna*, vol.1, Bangkok: Rabpim.

Cao Chengzheng (1990), 'The Sakdina system in Thailand and the field official grades of the Dai nationality' Proceedings of the 4th International Conference on Thai Studies, 11–13 May.

Chanan Wongwiphat (1984), *Chao Nan*, Bangkok: Amarin.

Chang Kong Ching (1987), *Chon Chat Thai Nai Prathet Chin*, Bangkok: Chalermnit.

Chanta, Pho Ui (1814), Manuscript mulberry paper book (*kadat sa*) kept by Mr Pheng Phrarom, 188 Mu 5, Ban Nong Bua, Tambon Pakha, Tha Wang Pha, Nan.

Chiang Mai University (1987), 'Phithi Buang Suang Chao Luang Chang Phuek Nga Khiew Khong Chao Tai Lue Ban Rong Ngae Amphoe Pua Changwat Nan', *Phithi Buang Suang Duang Winyan Banphachon Chak Sipsong Panna (Phi Puya)*, Chiang Mai: Lan Na.

Collection of Chronicles (1964), PT. 10, Bangkok: Kaona.

Kraisri Nimmanhaeminda (1965a), 'Put Vegetables into Baskets, and People into towns', in Lucien M. Hanks, Jane R. Hanks and Lauriston Sharp (eds.), *Ethnographic Notes on Northern Thailand*, Ithaca, N.Y.: Cornell University, Southeast Asia Program, Data Paper No. 58, 6–9.

Prachakitkorachak (1972), *Phongsawadan Yonok*, Bangkok: Phraepittaya.

Prime Minister's Office (1971), *Tamnan Phun Muang Chiang Mai*, Bangkok: Prime Minister's Office Press.

Ratanaporn Sethakul (1984), *Kan Samruat Thang Chat Phan Khong Chon Phow Tai Nai Lum Maw Nam Ping Changwat Chiang Mai*, Chiang Mai: Payap University.

—— (1991), 'Ekapap Nai Kwam Lak Lai: Sangkhom Lai Chatphan Nai Lan Na', *Journal of Payap University* 5:2 (July-December).

—— (1986), 'Sipsong Panna: Bot Samruat Kan Pokkhrong Lae Sangkhom Kon Kan Plod Ek Pi 1950', *Sipsong Panna: Adit Lae Pachuban*, Chiang Mai: Son Nang Su.

Sai Sam Tip (1976), 'The Lu in Sip Sawng Panna from the earliest times down to A.D. 1644', MA thesis, Rangoon University.

Saratsawadee Ongsakul (1993), *Khomun Lanna*, Chiang Mai: Sathaban Wichai Sangkhom.

Somchet Wimonkasem (1992), 'Thai Lu Muang Nan', paper presented at the seminar on *Tai Lu Textile Heritage and the Social and Cultural Context of Lan Na*, 2–4 September, Rim Kok Resort, Chiang Rai.

Chapter Fifteen

Ethnic Heterogeneity and Elephants in Nineteenth-Century Lanna Statecraft

Katherine A. Bowie

Introduction

Contemporary Thailand is often characterized as having a remarkably homogeneous population with the exception of its Muslim and hill tribe minorities. This view is increasingly challenged by studies of Thai nation-state formation, the process through which the 'geo-body' of contemporary Thailand was forged from historically semi-autonomous tributary statelets (Thongchai 1994). Pioneering studies by Nigel Brailey (1968, 1973–74), Ansil Ramsay (1971), Tej Bunnag (1977), and David Wyatt (1969) of the administrative consolidation of the central Thai state, from the late nineteenth century have been followed by a newer wave of scholarship that has focused on processes involved in the creation of a modern national identity (Barme 1993; Copeland 1993; Jiraporn 1992; Keyes 1966; Reynolds ed. 1991; Streckfuss 1987; Vandergeest 1990).

However, while recent scholarship on nation-state formation has recognized regional variation and the existence of petty states within these regions (currently identified as northern, northeastern, central, and southern Thailand), little attention has been paid to the internal character of these tributary polities. Earlier generations of scholars generally assumed these tributary states were ethnically and culturally homogeneous. Although Anderson laments the lack of research on minorities and national integration in earlier studies of the Thai state, he writes that 'the modern Siamese state in some sense does territorially correspond to a "pre-colonial" kingdom based on a wet-rice agricultural core area dominated by a *single ethnic group*' (1978: 211; emphasis added). As Thongchai notes, many scholars have emphasized 'continuity, homogeneity, and the persistence of traditions as 'the distinct characteristics, or even the unique features, of modern Siam' (1994: 13). The failure to consider the constitution of the population 'leaves us to suppose that the populations which made up such polities may have been homogeneous' (Rajah 1990: 126).

Plate 23. 'Départ de Bassac'

It is becoming clear that the petty states of the nineteenth century were not internally homogeneous. Historians have frequently noted that South East Asian rulers were more interested in control over people than territory. This is epitomized in the expression 'put vegetables into baskets and put slaves into kingdoms (*kep phak sai sa, kep kha sai müang*; Kraisri 1965). In 1376 AD, a census 'enumerated 300,000 male Lao eligible for compulsory labour (military) service each year, in addition to 400,000 non-Tai' (Wyatt 1984: 83 cited in Rajah 1990: 126). There is evidence of considerable ethnic diversity in the nineteenth century resulting from forced resettlements of war captives (Bowie 1988, 1996; Grabowsky 1994; Ratanaporn 1989; Snit and Breazeale 1988; Terwiel 1989).

The consequences of ethnic diversity for understanding the practice of mainland South East Asian statecraft have received little scholarly attention. I suggest that the historical process of transforming an ethnically heterogeneous population into a more homogeneous nation–state requires an understanding not only of recent nation–state formation but also the 'ethnic management' strategies of traditional South East Asian states. Using oral histories and archival sources, I explore the use and ownership of elephants, seeking to reconstruct the ethnic identity of those who cared for the royal lords' elephants in nineteenth century northern Thailand. I have chosen to focus on elephants (a) because of their importance for the political economy of these northern Tai states, and (b) because of their association with specific ethnic groups, notably Karen and Khamu.

This chapter is divided into four sections: the first summarizes evidence concerning the practice of taking civilian war captives and consequences for ethnic diversity; the second considers the political and economic importance of elephants; and the third section looks at elephant mahouts and suggests a dual pattern: ethnic diversity among royal or state mahouts and ethnic specialization among those working for private owners. I conclude by considering whether traditional states contributed to a historical process of ethnic homogenization, if at all, by default or by design.[1]

Ethnic Diversity of Tai States

Although historians have long recognized that obtaining war captives was the motivation of many military campaigns, the numbers of captives and their consequent significance for South East Asian statecraft have not been much considered. Recent work is establishing that war captives were a sizeable portion of the northern Thai population in the nineteenth century (see Bowie 1988, 1996; Grabowsky 1994; Ratanaporn 1989).

Dr. David Richardson, in his diary of his journeys to Chiang Mai in the 1830s (Ms: 143), provides one of the earliest accounts of the number of war captives in northern Thailand:

> 'The *thooghee* of this village [Ban Pasang (Basang) in Lamphun] and of Ban San Kanoy and most of the villagers were captured about 29 years ago [1805–6] and brought here as slaves from the city of Moung Neaung about 45 days march northerly from this, about one month northeast of Ava and about three long days from the Chinese frontier. The mother of Meng Nyot Boo was a sister of this *thooghee's* wife – they say there were about 2,000 people brought away.' (Ms: 56).

Richardson estimated that some three-quarters of the kingdom's population were war captives. Captain McLeod gives a sense of the social impact of the war captives on the kingdom of Chiang Mai in his journal in 1837: 'the greater part of the inhabitants of Zimme are people from Kiang Tung, Muang Niong (Yong), Kiang Then (Tsen or Hsen), and many other places to the northward. They were originally subjects of Ava (Burmah)' (quoted in Hallett 1890: 202). In another passage he writes: 'They, with the Talaings (Peguan Mon), comprise more than two-thirds of the population in the country' (quoted in Hallett 1890: 202). Holt Hallett concurs that a considerable portion of the population of the northern Thai kingdoms were captives:

> 'From the time when Kiang Hsen was captured till 1810, Ping Shan armies frequently raided into the Burmese Shan States – proceeding as far west as the Salween and as far north as the border of China – sacked the towns, and carried away the inhabitants into captivity' (1890: 202).

Some sense of the magnitude of these population relocations was given by the ruling lord of Chiang Saen in an interview with Hallett. In describing the territory he ruled, the lord explained 'that many other cities were scattered about the country, but owing to their having been depopulated during the wars of last and the beginning of this century, most of their names had been forgotten' (1890: 199). The city of Chiang Saen itself was besieged by the Lao of Vieng Chang [sic] and Luang Prabang, together with the Lao of Chiang Mai from 1794 to 1797. When the city fell in 1804 'The city was destroyed; some of the people escaped across the Salween and settled in Mokmai and Monay, and the rest were taken captive to the Ping States, and distributed amongst them' (Hallett 1890: 202).

John Freeman estimated that about half of the population of Lamphun province were descendants of war captives (1910: 100). The devastation caused by repeated warring and raiding was considerable:

> 'In raids as these, whole villages were wiped out, entire valleys depopulated, for not only were many killed by the robbers or carried off as slaves, but the survivors fled to the forests and dared not return' (1910: 99).

Thus there is agreement among several independent nineteenth century observers, ranging from early travellers such as Richardson and McLeod to later observers such as Hallett and Freeman, that at least half of the population of the northern Thai kingdoms were war captives. Northern Thai texts and oral histories tend to confirm these archival accounts (see Bowie 1988, 1996; Grabowsky 1994).[2]

War captives were limited neither to the nineteenth century nor to northern Thailand. King Ramkhamhaeng's thirteenth century inscription records that 'If I went to attack a village or a city and collected some elephants and ivory, men and women, silver and gold, I gave them to my father' (Benda and Larkin, ed. 1967: 40–41). Simon de la Loubère says of late seventeenth century Ayuthaya that: 'They busie themselves only in making slaves. If the Peguins (sic), for example, do on one side invade the lands of Siam, the Siamese will at another place enter the Lands of Pegu, and both Parties will carry away whole Villages into Captivity' (1969: 90). Wales describes such war expeditions as 'the regular occupation of the dry season' (1934: 64); and Crawfurd writes of his visit in 1821 that 'The Siamese equally carry off the peasantry of the open country of both sexes' (1915: 145, cited in Turton 1980: 255). Terwiel summarizes the ethnic diversity of the central plains region in the early nineteenth century:

> 'Hitherto historians have only acknowledged the cosmopolitan character of the capital city, and the fact that the countryside was equally diverse has been ignored. It has been shown here, however, that during the first fifty years of the nineteenth century, tens of thousands of Mo'ns and Laotians, and thousands of Khmers, Vietnamese, Malays and Burmese were distributed throughout the provinces . . . . In the later nineteenth century there is no longer an influx of Khmers, Laotians, or Mo'ns into the central provinces,

and therefore the false impression prevails that in Central Thailand there is such a thing as a relatively homogeneous Thai culture. The data presented above has demonstrated that, on the contrary, early nineteenth century Central Thailand was a heterogeneous "melting pot"'. (1989: 253–254).

In addition to the mass relocation of population as war captives, smaller groups of people were also kidnapped and sold as slaves. These people represented a wide range of ethnic groups, many coming from non-Tai upland populations.[3] Warring led to the voluntary flight of villagers, seeking refuge in more peaceful areas. Long-distance trade further facilitated the migration of people from different backgrounds. Thus a variety of political and economic factors encouraged a considerable mixing of people of different heritages in the Tai kingdoms.

State and Elephants

Elephants provide an opportunity to gain insight into nineteenth century statecraft. They abounded in Thailand, particularly in the northern regions. Edwardes records of his trip to Chiang Mai in 1879 that: 'There are many thousands of these animals in Chiangmai and numbers of these are daily to be seen. They are reared in Chiangmai and are also brought from the northeastern Laos States' (in Nartsupha and Prasartset 1978: 180–181). According to a high-ranking Chao interviewed by Hallett 'elephants were very numerous in the country; there were fully 8000 in both Zimme and Lakon, even more in Nan, and about half that number in Peh' (1890: 104). Bock notes that 'the forests seemed as full of wild elephants as the town was of domesticated ones' (1986 [1884]: 174), observing somewhat quaintly:

'From Raheng northwards, to the boundary of the Ngiou and Lao States (in about 20o N. lat.), may be said to be the centre of the supply of elephants in Siam, and while man's principal work in the country seems to have been the erection of Temples, nature's supremest effort, so far as the animal world is concerned, appears to have been reserved for the multiplication of Elephants.' (1986 [1884]: 144; see also Dodd 1923: 253; Cort 1886: 202).

Albeit in variable numbers, elephants were found throughout the rest of Thailand as well. Thus it is no surprise that elephants figure prominently in Thai symbolism. Siam has often been called the 'Land of the White Elephant' and its form has been used on the country's flags, coins, medals, and temples. Elephants figure strongly in legendary accounts of the founding of the northern kingdoms. Their imposing role in royal ceremonial processions is recorded in an account of the Chief of Chiang Mai's procession which totalled 120 elephants:

'The Chief has left M. Fang, in great state, bugles blowing, drums and gongs beating, and 4 dozen soldiers followed by a magnificent tusker elephant, on which the chief is seated. The elephant is followed by many men on foot carrying spears, then follow his favourite wives, each seated on an elephant.' (Anonymous [1885]: 32–6).

In addition to their much noted symbolic and ritual role, elephants played vital roles in war, in transportation and communication, in agriculture and forestry, and in trade.

Military uses of elephants

Sixteenth century accounts describe the Siamese army at the beginning of the sixteenth century as consisting of '20,000 cavalry, 250,000 infantry, and 10,000 war elephants' (Bowring 1969 [1857] II: 61; see also Bowring 1969 [1857] II: 107, 125; Tachard 1981 [1688]: 164–65). It is not clear how many war elephants were owned by the nineteenth century Thai kings, however apparently over a thousand were used by the Siamese army in the 1854 attack on Chieng Tung (Bowring 1969 [1857] II: 366).

Elephants fulfilled a range of military functions. Some elephants 'were trained to tear down obstacles and, above all, to kill' (Edwardes 1972: 99). Mock battles re-enacted elephants 'charging an intrenchment' (Crawfurd 1987 [1828]: 219) or battling each other (Bowring 1969 [1857] II: 330). Besides men, elephants also carried military equipment into battle. Colquhoun writes that 'One branch of the army consisted of an elephant service, the animals being trained to carry two jingals and four men each', a jingal being a heavy musket fired from a rest (1885: 96). In addition elephants 'were used as a means of transport by the Siamese and Burmese armies in great numbers' (Colquhoun 1885: 96).

Elephants in transportation and communication

Bock describes elephants, together with bullocks, as the 'the beasts of burthen in Lao' (1986 [1884]: 175); the elephant was 'the ship of the forest' (Freeman 1910: 96). 'Owing to the state of the roads, through the jungle, over high mountain ranges, through almost impassable bogs and deep streams, the elephant was almost the only mode of travel for journeys of any distance' (Dodd 1923: 253–254). 'The elephant is an absolute necessity during the rainy season throughout the mountainous districts of Siam and the neighbouring Shan country to the north, the rivers and streams being without bridges' (Colquhoun 1885: 89). 'For what the camel is in the desert, and the dog upon the icefloe, that is the elephant in the forests of

Nan. For hauling teak, for collecting rattans or jungle grass, for carrying tobacco, rice, or cotton, and for any journeying away from home, he is indispensable to his master' (Smyth 1898: 108–109).

> 'According to a member of the ruling family of Chiang Mai "1000 elephants are employed in carrying goods to and from Kiang Hsen, chiefly for transhipment to Luang Prabang and elsewhere".' (Hallett 1890: 104).

Although elephants could carry loads weighing up to 950 pounds, the load in northern Thailand averaged about 300 pounds (Smyth 1898: II; 107; see also Colquhoun 1885: 90; Younghusband 1888: 16; Le May 1926: 70–71).

Elephants in agriculture and forestry

Elephants performed numerous domestic and agricultural tasks for their owners. A long-standing use of elephants was transporting agricultural crops, especially rice. Villagers recall the lords' elephants arriving at harvest time to carry rice from the royal lands back to the royal granaries in town. Elephants were used to plough land and to develop new landholdings, by clearing trees and boulders from fields. They helped in the construction of dams and in clearing irrigation canals.

Elephants were used to haul timber for construction purposes, notably temples and the homes of the well-to-do. While many villagers were able to build homes of bamboo, the wealthier built their houses of teak. Several villagers mentioned that the teak logs for the temple pillars were dragged there by elephants belonging either to lords or to members of the rural élite. Elephants were used to haul firewood, making it easier to cook and maintain an entourage than it would have been for ordinary villagers whose daily firewood had to be sought piecemeal day by day.

Elephants played a major role in the timber-logging industry, most notably teak logging. 'In the deep jungles, elephants exist in a wild state, and are captured and sold to our timber merchants, who use them for the extraction of teak and other woods from the forests, and for the manipulation of the timber at the numerous sawmills existing in the seaport towns' (Colquhoun 1885: 281).

Trade in elephants

Elephants were traded, both as living animals and as body parts. Ivory was an important item of exchange (Bock 1986[1884]: 321; Bowring 1969 [1857] II: 63; Smyth 1898: 117), both as an item of tribute within kingdoms (Younghusband 1888: 46) and of export, for example to India (ten Brummelhuis 1987: 36) and China (Bock 1986[1884]: 269). Not only ivory, but also the hides and bones, teeth and hooves were exported to China from 'the Lao States' – a term by which the writer would have included Chiang Mai – (Crawfurd 1987 [1828]: 429); Bock 1986[1884]: 269).

There was an important trade in the elephants themselves. Seventeenth century accounts record an extensive export trade in elephants, primarily to Coromandel and Bengal (Anderson 1981 [1889: 20, 98, 200). As one traveller to the region in 1695 records:

'All the country of Malacca, Combaya, Siam, Ciampa, Cocincinna, and Tunchin abounds in elephants, of which the Siamese particularly make a great trade, carrying them by land to the opposite coast and port of Tenazarin, belonging to the king of Siam, near the Gulf of Bengala, where merchants buy to transport them by sea into the dominions of Mahometan princes.' (Anderson 1981 [1889]: 20; also 98, 200; see also Gervaise 1989 [1688]: 209); Crawfurd 1987 [1828]: 429; Hutchinson 1985 [1940]: 12; Collis 1982: 57–58).

Elephants were exported to Burma: 'The extensive grassy plains and the wooded country in Northern Siam form a great breeding-ground for elephants, ponies, and cattle, which are carried into British and Upper Burmah, and there bartered for merchandise' (Colquhoun 1885: 278). Younghusband noted that Nan was 'considered a very cheap country for buying elephants; I met several Burmans from Moulmein looking out for them' (1888: 91). 'The export [from Nan] of elephants to Chieng Mai and Burma is said to amount to from two to three hundred animals a year' (Smyth 1898: 117). Hallett was told by a Chiang Mai Chao that 'from 200 to 300 elephants were yearly taken into Burmah' (1890: 104). According to the British trade report of 1858, no fewer than 1,060 elephants and 10,000 head of cattle were purchased from the Chiang Mai region alone (FO 69/30).

Those who bought and sold elephants were generally members of the élite. Figures given in interviews suggest a price range for an elephant at the turn of the century of 3–5,000 baht (Bowie 1988). Edwardes mentions elephants in 1870 costing anywhere from 600 to 2,300 rupees (in Nartsupha and Prasartset 1978: 181) while 'in Chieng Mai a really experienced teak-hauling elephant with good tusks may fetch Rs. 3,000' (Smyth 1898: II: 107). Wages even after the turn of this century were one *win* (14 *satang*) per day, so even at 1,000 baht an elephant cost the equivalent of something like 20 years wages for a hired agricultural labourer. Freeman estimated that the revenue from one elephant hunt in 1908 'would bring five to ten thousand dollars to their captors' (1910: 77).

Ethnicity and Elephants

In other South Asian kingdoms, specific minority groups have come to be associated with elephants.[4]Three ethnic groups are frequently mentioned in association with elephants in Thailand. Writing of northeastern Thailand, Francis Giles notes that 'The most skilled elephant hunters in the Korat region are found amongst the Sue [Sui, Kui] of Surindr [Surin]' (1930: 68). The American Presbyterian missionary Dr. Collins' diary of a journey from Kanburee to Burma in 1867 records that 'The elephants in this part of Siam belong chiefly to the Karens' (quoted in Bacon 1881: 279). Hallett also noted that 'Most of the elephants working in the teak-forests are owned by Karens' (1890: 40–4) while Khamu and other teak workers 'are brought by their masters from their homes in the neighbourhood of Luang Prabang' to work in the northern Thai forests (1890: 21). Hallett reports: 'Our Karen mahouts had been replaced by Shans' (Hallett 1890: 45). Shan or 'Lao', no doubt including Khon Müang, were also involved together with Karen and Khamu as elephant drivers (Colquhoun 1885: 93–94)[5] and hunters (Le May 1923: 196).[6] Giles, who has left us one of the most extensive studies of elephants in Siam, regarded the Sue of the Korat region to be the most skilled elephant hunters, among whom 'this profession' had become hereditary (1930: 2). He notes interestingly that:

> 'This spirit language is used by the hunters on the Korat plateau where the inhabitants are Khmer, Sui, So, Sek, Puthai and Lao, as well as in the Lao provinces of Northern Siam, Nan, Chieng-rai and Chieng-mai where the people are Lao, Yao, Tin, Kha, Miao and Mushu . . . . It will be noticed that most of the command words are of foreign origin and used very generally by all elephant men *irrespective of their race or language.*' (1930: 68–69; emphasis added).[7]

Oral histories can permit a finer-grained analysis than archival sources by providing information about both elephant caretakers and their owners. Out of some 550 oral histories, I have information on 54 elephants owners who can be divided into three main categories: ruling lords (4), lesser lords (21) and commoners (29). The greatest number of elephants was owned by the ruling lords. I conducted interviews in 25 villages where families had had members who served as royal mahouts caring for state elephants. It was not possible to obtain an accurate number of elephants, especially where scores and even hundreds of elephants were being kept in a given village. I therefore assumed, conservatively, that each village cared for a range of 10–20 elephants, a total of 250–500 elephants (see table below). Villagers described ruling lords as owning hundreds of elephants, while the largest number of elephants for a non-ruling lord was estimated at 14 and the usual figure was only one or two. If each of these 21 lesser lords is assumed to own an average of 5–10 elephants, they would have owned a combined total of 105–210 elephants. Thus four individual Chao, or 7 per cent of the total number of elephant owners owned half the total number of elephants. Ruling and lesser lords together owned about three-quarters of all elephants. If commoners were assumed to have owned as many as 5–10 elephants each, the 29 commoner elephant owners owned about 145–290 elephants, or one-quarter of the total number (see Bowie 1988 for a more detailed discussion).

Archival sources suggest that a higher percentage of elephants would have likely been owned by lords, particularly ruling lords, than my own cautious estimate which has tended to under-estimate the number of royal elephants and over-estimate the number of elephants owned by lesser lords and commoners. The *Mengraisat* declared ownership of elephants to be a royal monopoly (Wichienkhiew 1976). As late as the nineteenth century, the northern Thai lords reserved 'to themselves the sole right to hunt the elephant and rhinoceros' (Bock 1986[1884]: 269). Freeman writes of 'the princes who claim ownership in the wild elephants in the mountains' (1910: 76) and refers to wild elephants as 'assets of the princes' (1910: 85). Edwardes records that the ruling lord of Chiang Mai owned 300 elephants (in Nartsupha and Prasartset 1978: 180–81), while Bock notes that 'The Chow Operate [*upparat* Ed.] . . . is very rich, having a good deal of cash, besides some 60 elephants' (1986 [1884]: 322). Colquhoun gives some idea of the relative scale of ownership among the élite:

> 'In the Siamese-Shan states, the chiefs, besides slaves and serfs, are possessed of numerous elephants. The tsobua, at the time of our visit, owned over a hundred and fifty; the kyou-koopone, or sister-in-law of the tsobua, one hundred and thirty-five; the chao hona, a hundred; and every chao, from five to twenty.' (1885: 256).

Whatever the historical strictures on elephant ownership had been, certainly by the latter part of the nineteenth century commoners also owned elephants. Nonetheless, by far the greatest number of elephants belonged to the court.

Table 1: Elephants and Owners

	No. of owners	Percentage of owners	No. of elephants	Percentage elephants
Chao, Ruling	4	7	250–500	50
Chao, Lesser	21	39	105–210	21
Commoner	29	54	145–290	29
Total	54	100	500–1,000	100

By differentiating these categories of elephant ownership we reveal an interesting difference in the ethnicity of the elephant caretakers. Of the 25 villages which provided the ruling lords with royal mahouts, I have information on the ethnic background of 23 villages.[8] In order of frequency, the following ethnic groups were mentioned: [Tai] Khoen (6), [Tai] Khon Müang (4), Lawa (3), Mon (3) Karen (3), [Tai] Yong (2), and Khamu (2).[9] Thus, among these villages of royal mahouts, no single ethnic group predominates. The villages in which Karen and Khamu mahouts predominated were said to be those where elephants were used in logging.

Whereas the royal elephants belonging to ruling lords appear to have been cared for by *khwanchang* (drivers or mahouts) from a range of different ethnic groups, elephants belonging to lesser lords and commoners appear to have been more likely to have had Karen and Khamu mahouts. For example, Chao Mahawong in Saraphi District employed a Karen man to take care of his elephants and timber interests. Mahouts involved in the timber industry seem to have been overwhelmingly Karen and Khamu. Chayan Vaddhanaphuti notes that the teak industry near his fieldwork village of Baan Chang, Mae Taeng, 'was operated by the Khamu and Karen' (1984: 133) and refers to 'Khamu from the vicinity of Luang Phrabang, who were brought, or sold, to work for the [Borneo] teak company' (1984: 206). The forefathers of each of the Karen and Khamu mahouts I interviewed had worked in the teak industry.

This split pattern – ethnic diversity among royal mahouts, and ethnic specialization among non-royal mahouts – may have one of two possible explanations. Perhaps while relatively unskilled villagers could serve as ordinary mahouts who watched over the animals on a day-to-day basis, the more skilled work of capturing and training elephants lay with specialized minorities. After all, elephant-hunting was 'an occupation described to be laborious and somewhat dangerous' (Crawfurd 1987 [1828]: 429; see also Smyth 1898: II: 71; Le May 1923: 196). However, my own interviews with villagers suggest that the specialized knowledge needed for capturing and training elephants could be easily learned, and that daring and physical prowess were important prerequisites. A traditional elephant 'veterinarian', a Khon Müang, insisted that northern Thai were just as involved in all aspects of the elephant business as ethnic minorities.[10] A Shan (Ngio) villager who had owned an elephant told me that 'There were Khamu who were afraid of elephants too' (Lung Noi Taan Bothiryan, age 70. Baan Nam Ton, Tambon Baan Kaat, Sanpatong, Chiang Mai, 28 June 1995). Even the most common technique used to capture elephants involved large numbers of villagers in both building the kraal and driving elephants into it (Bock 1986 [1884]: 70; Thompson 1987 [1910]: 238; Buls 1994 [1901]: 137–40). I interviewed both Khoen and Khon Müang villagers in Thung Phii Sub-district, Sanpatong District who recall their forefathers being conscripted to help with the royal elephant hunt.

A more compelling explanation is based upon understanding elephant owners' differential access to labour. Labour control was in turn dependent on the internal organization of the Thai state and changing international relations. The ruling lords had the right or ability to exact corvée labour to care for their elephants. They also owned large numbers of slaves, many of whom, as we have already noted, were war captives. Royal mahouts were likely to be ethnically heterogeneous because the subordinate population was multi-ethnic. The ruling lords owned the greatest number of elephants, and therefore commanded the labour of a far higher percentage of elephant mahouts. Lesser lords, commoners, and foreigners involved in the teak logging industries would have had to buy or hire their mahouts. The industry grew in importance in the latter half of the nineteenth century as British subjects received a growing number of teak concessions from the northern Thai lords. Faced with labour shortages, European timber companies increasingly relied on imported wage labour. Karen who were British subjects from Burma, and Khamu from Laos were not subject to royal corvée or tribute obligations, and were free to work for wages. Moreover, if given the choice, northern Thai villagers generally preferred not to be mahouts, seeing it as a lonely and dangerous life, with considerable time spent away from village and family. Thus ironically the ethnic groups most closely involved during the nineteenth century in the care of elephants were those most independent of the Thai state.

Rather than viewing the prominent role of Karen and Khamu as mahouts as the continuation of a long-standing position as elephant-specialists to the court, I suggest it was a historically specific response to the growth of the teak industry. The care of state elephants was not restricted to specialized minorities, but ethnically distributed. Consequently, two different ethnic patterns emerge which correspond to two types of ownership of elephants and two types of access to, or control over labour. There is ethnic diversity with regard to the care of the royal elephants and there is ethnic specialization with regard to the care of private elephants.

State Ethnic Policies

State policy necessarily plays a role in accentuating ethnic identity or facilitating assimilation given an ethnically diverse population, as Judith Toland has suggested: 'Although ethnic diversity is a characteristic of all state populations, the nature of that diversity is related to how each state has carried out its building process' (1993: 3). Recent scholarship has tended to focus on the role of the state in the maintenance or intensification of ethnic identities, in contrast to earlier literature on assimilation. Verdery's recent article on 'ethnic demobilization' or the 'unmaking of an ethnic collectivity' in Romania is a rare study of the historical conditions under which ethnic identities become less salient (1985).

Although some sense of historical ethnic identity remains among many villagers in northern Thailand, it is secondary to their identity as 'northern Thai' (Khon Müang) or 'Thai' (see discussion in Moerman 1965; Wijeyewardene 1991: 69; and for the northeast see Keyes 1966, 1967). Many social and cultural practices facilitated assimilation, including sharing temples, attending each other's religious celebrations, intermarrying, long distance trading etc. State policies in turn affected the structure of the Buddhist Sangha, patterns of intermarriage, and economic productivity. The role of traditional South East Asian states in facilitating (or hindering) the ethnic homogenization of their populations remains to be considered. For some scholars, ethnic diversity was either irrelevant or unimportant to South East Asian rulers. Tambiah argues that Thai kingdoms were held together 'not so much by the real exercise of power and control as by devices and mechanisms of a ritual kind' (1976: 125). Ratanaporn concludes that 'All peoples were welcomed in the Northern States due to the lack of population; there was virtually no racial discrimination' (1989: 26), a view earlier suggested by Wales who noted that war captives 'were indeed hardly regarded as foreigners and, in later times, some of them rose to positions of considerable importance in the administration' (1965: 65–66).

More nuanced propositions have been put forward recently. Anderson suggests 'it was relatively easy for Mon, Lao, Persians, Chinese, or Malays to be loyal to the monarch', and that 'Their ethnic identity in no way determined the degree of their access to him' (1978: 213). The court was by no mans passive in this and 'worked hard at integrating their kingdoms – and indeed expanding them – by multi-ethnic polygyny' (1978: 213). Thongchai too claims that the court was conscious of the ethnic diversity of its population and was indeed proud of it: 'the more diverse races and languages of the people under the power of the overlord, the more powerful that overlord would be recognized' (1993: 11). Yet the Siamese élite portrayed themselves as distant and superior rulers over a seemingly homogeneous domesticated populations (*chao ban*), so distant that Thongchai wonders 'to what extent the monarchs saw their place being a part of the whole Siamese people' (1993: 16).

Grabowsky contrasts the situation in central Thailand with that in northern Thailand, and concludes that it was 'fundamentally different'. While in the central region 'non-Siamese populations were considered culturally inferior', 'there were no attitudes of any racial or cultural superiority by the Yuan (Chiang Mai) élite towards most of the war captives' (1994: 87; see also Ratanaporn this volume).

> 'The Khon and Lu resettled by Kawila in territories within the present borders of Thailand were seen by the Yuan not at all as "foreigners" (*khon tang chat*), but were viewed as people belonging to a greater Lan Na cultural zone. Yuan, Khon and Lu speak mutually understandable dialects, and they

use, with minor regional variations, the same "Dharma script" (ibid.: 74). . . . [But] nowhere did captives inhabit large coherent areas. Their villages were always interspersed between Yuan settlements' (ibid.: 83).

Traditional rulers may have generally pursued 'ethnic-blind' policies, but they seem to have sometimes taken deliberate measures to minimize potential political risks of ethnic diversity. Richardson provides two rare glimpses into the early nineteenth century northern Thai statecraft, which suggest that the ruling lords deliberately settled their population in a way to ensure fragmentation. The sister of a captive lord explained to him that: 'As they amounted to 3,000 people, they were afraid to trust them together and they were distributed in small numbers about the different villages in this principality which the Birmans had then only recently left and which was very thinly peopled' (Ms: 58–59).

She explained that she herself had initially been 'sent down as an addition to the King of Siam's harem'. Richardson continues:

'He [the King] had however the humanity . . . to send her back again with instructions to the Chow Thiiwiit to give as little additional cause for sorrow and allow the captives to live as much together as possible . . . . They never made any combined attempts to escape and large proportion are now collected in this vicinity under her brother' (Ms: 58–59).

Thus, by going counter to the norm of dispersion, the King was able to gain the co-operation and gratitude of a subjugated population to good political effect. This apparent exception suggests what normative practice may have been. Interspersing villagers of differing ethnic groups would have impeded intra-ethnic political mobilization.

Ethnic homogenization was one of the consequences of the state's 'ethnic management strategies' of dispersion and ethnic fragmentation. Decreasing intra-ethnic group interaction promoted inter-ethnic integration. The common plight of war captives may have further contributed to their willingness to overcome differences in ethnic background and encouraged them to forge a new identity as Khon Müang or Khon Thai. As long as they did not interfere with state interests, the court appears to have allowed villages to pursue their preferred cultural beliefs and ritual practices.

This chapter has explored the ethnicity of elephant mahouts, an occupation which preliminary evidence indicated was subject to ethnic specialization. Evidence has been adduced that the royal mahouts who cared for state elephants were of diverse ethnic backgrounds, and non-state elephants were cared for by members of specific minority groups. This evidence could be used to argue that traditional statecraft was 'ethnic-blind', but I believe state efforts to minimize the salience of ethnicity were deliberate. Traditional South East Asian statecraft minimized the political relevance of ethnic diversity by following a policy of 'ethnic egalitarianism', that is, of exploiting all subalterns more or less equally and granting special favours to none on the basis of ethnic heritage. Ethnic heterogeneity was the historical reality of the subaltern. The forging of a more homogeneous identity of Khon Müang, and later Thai, is as much the consequence of traditional practices of South East Asian statecraft as of twentieth century processes of nation-state formation.

Notes

1 This chapter has benefitted from discussions with Arjun Guneratne, Thongchai Winichakul, Hugh Wilson, Charles Keyes, Ron Renard, Kevin McIntyre, Surasinghsamruam Shimbhanao, and Andrew Turton. I would also like to acknowledge Megan Sinnott and Minako Kakishita for bibliographical assistance.

2 Although sceptical of western travel accounts, Grabowky concludes that by 1840 '25–40% of the population in the five Northern Thai principalities Chiang Mai, Lamphun, Lampang, Phrae, and Nan were war captives or their descendants' (1994: 84).

3 Colquhoun writes 'there is little doubt that the sparsity of the hill-tribes in the hills neighbouring Zimme [Chiang Mai] has been chiefly caused by their having been, in the olden time, systematically hunted like wild cattle, to supply the slave-market' (1885: 257–58, 70; see also Bowie 1996).

4 For example, in Nepal the Tharus (Guneratne, personal conversation); in South India the Kurumba and Naiker tribes (Stanley-Milson 1991); in Sri Lanka the Pannikayan or Muslim population (Spittel 1944); and in Burma the Karen, are most frequently associated with elephants (Clarke 1944).

5 Hallett and Colquhoun differentiate the treatment of elephants by Karen and Shan respectively. Colquhoun writes 'Karens are much kinder drivers than the natives of India, Burmese, or Shans, and their charges seem more compliant to their soft words, signs, and coaxing than to the cruel hook-hammer used by the others' (1885: 93–94; see also Hallett 1890: 45).

6 English-language writers of the day based in Burma often used 'Shan' to refer to the northern Thai or Khon Müang of today, while writers based in Siam often called them 'Lao'.

7 He notes of the spirit language used in hunting elephants that '[it] does not seem to have much in common with any of the languages used in the surrounding [northeastern] districts such as Khmer, Sue, So, Sek, Puthai, La-wa, Lao, Yao, Tin, Kha, and other aboriginal dialects' (Giles 1930: 68).

8 The majority of royal mahouts appear to have been slaves, in turn primarily war-captives. Additionally, some villagers became mahouts as a punishment. Villagers recall examples of murderers who were given a choice between execution or caring for a rogue elephant in must.

9 Given how few lowland Lawa villages there are in the Chiang Mai Valley, I was surprised that on at least three occasions, the ethnicity of the *khwanchang*, or at least of the village in question, was given as Lawa.

10 Remarkably, he himself suggested that northern Thai were more likely to work for the ruling lords and ethnic minorities such as Karen and Khamu for the timber companies (interview with Poh Naan Lohng Thammalert, age 81, Baan Mae Moh Sarii, Tambon Saket, Amphur Muang, Lampang, 24 June 1995).

References

Anan Ganjanapan (1984), 'The Partial Commercialization of Rice Production in Northern Thailand, (1900–1981)', Ph.D dissertation, Anthropology Department, Cornell University.

Anderson, Benedict R. O'G. (1978), 'Studies of the Thai State: The State of Thai Studies', in Eliezer B. Ayal (ed.), *The State of Thai Studies: Analyses of Knowledge, Approaches and Prospects in Anthropology, Art History, Economics, History and Political Science*, Southeast Asia Program, Athens, Ohio: Ohio University, 193–247.

Anderson, John (1981), [1880] *English Intercourse with Siam in the Seventeenth Century*, Bangkok: Chalermnit.

Anonymous [1895], *An Englishman's Siamese Journals 1890–1893*, Bangkok: Siam Media International Books.

Bacon, George B. (1881), *Siam, the Land of the White Elephant, as it was and is.* New York: Charles Scribner's Sons.

Barme, Scot (1993), *Luang Wichit Wathakan and the Creation of a Thai Identity*, Singapore: Institute of Southeast Asian Studies.

Bock, Carl 1986), [1884] *Temples and Elephants: Travels in Siam in 1881–1882.* Singapore: Oxford, University Press.

Bowie, Katherine A. (1988), 'Peasant Perspectives on the Political Economy of the Northern Thai Kingdom of Chiang Mai in the Nineteenth Century: Implications for the Understanding of Peasant Political Expression', Ph.D dissertation, Anthropology Department, University of Chicago.

—— (1996), 'Slavery in Nineteenth Century Northern Thailand: Archival Anecdotes and Village Voices', in Paul Durrenberger (ed.), *State Power and Culture*, New Haven: Center of Southeast Asia, Yale University.

Bowring, Sir John (1969), [1857] *The Kingdom and People of Siam,* Kuala Lumpur: Oxford University Press.

Brailey, Nigel J. (1968), *The Origins of the Siamese Forward Movement in Western Laos, 1850–92*, Ph.D dissertation, University of London.

—— (1973–74), 'Chiengmai and the Inception of an Administrative Centralization Policy in Siam', two parts, *Southeast Asian Studies* 11/3 (December): 299–320 and 11/4 (March): 439–69.

Buls, Charles (1994), [1901] *Siamese Sketches,* Walter E. J. Tips (transl.), Bangkok: White Lotus Co. Ltd.

Chayan Vaddhanaphuti (1984), *Cultural and Ideological Reproduction in Rural Northern Thai Society.* Ph.D dissertation, Anthropology Department, Stanford University.

Clarke J. A. (1944), 'Are Elephant Kraals Justified?: The Karen Stockade Method of Capturing Wild Elephants in Burma', *LORIS* December, 172–174.

Cohen, Paul (1981), *The Politics of Economic Development in Northern Thailand*, 1967–1978, Ph.D thesis, London School of Economics and Political Science, University of London.

Collis, Maurice (1982), [1951] *Siamese White*, Bangkok: DD Books.

Colquhoun, A. R. (1885), *Amongst the Shans*, London: Field and Tuer.

Conant, S. S. (1874), 'The Land of the White Elephant, *Harper's New Monthly Magazine* 48, (February) 378–389.

Copeland, Matthew P. (1993), *Contested Nationalism and the 1932 Overthrow of the Absolute Monarchy in Siam*, Ph.D dissertation, Australian National University.

Cort, Mary Lovina (1886), *Siam: The Heart of Farther India*, New York: Anson D. F. Randolph & Co.

Crawfurd, John (1987), [1828] *Journal of an Embassy to the Courts of Siam and Cochin China*, Introduction by David K. Wyatt, Singapore: Oxford University Press.

Curtis, Lillian Johnson (1903), *The Laos of North Siam*, Philadelphia: Westminster Press.

Dodd, William Clifton (1923), *The Tai Race: Elder Brother of the Chinese,* Cedar Rapids, Iowa: Torch Press.

Edwardes, Michael (1972), *Ralph Fitch, Elizabethan in the Indies,* New York: Barnes and Noble.

Freeman, John H. (1910), *An Oriental Land of the Free,* Philadelphia: Westminster Press.

Gervaise, Nicholas (1989), [1688] *The Natural and Political History of the Kingdom of Siam,* John Villiers (transl.), Bangkok: White Lotus Co. Ltd.

Glazer, Nathan and Daniel P. Moynihan (1970), *Beyond the Melting Pot: The Negroes, Puerto Ricans, Jews, Italians and Irish of New York City,* 2nd ed., Cambridge, MIT Press.

Giles, Francis H. (Phya Indra Monti Srichandrakumara) (1930), 'Adversaria of Elephant Hunting (together with an account of all the rites, observances and acts of worship to be performed in connection therewith, as well as notes on vocabularies of spirit language, fake or taboo language and elephant command words)', *Journal of the Siam Society* (XXIII): 61–96.

—— (1932), 'An Account of the Rites and Ceremonies Observed at Elephant Driving Operations in the Seaboard Province of Lang Suan, Southern Siam', *Journal of the Siam Society* 25 (2): 153–214.

Gordon, Milton M. (1964), *Assimilation in American Life: The Role of Race, Religion and National Origins*, New York: Oxford University Press.

Gould, Mr (1876), Foreign Office Series, No. 69, vol. 64, Public Records Office, London.

Grabowsky, Volker (1994), 'Forced Resettlement Campaigns in Northern Thailand During the Early Bangkok Period', *Oriens Extremus* 37/1: 45–107.

Graham, W.A. (1924), *Siam*, London: De La More Press.

Hallett, Holt S. (1890), *A Thousand Miles on an Elephant in the Shan States*, Edinburgh: William Blackwood and Sons.

Hutchinson, E. W. (ed.) (1968), *1688 Revolution in Siam: The Memoir of Father de Bèze*, Hong Kong: University Press.

—— (1985), [1940] *Adventurers in Siam in the Seventeenth Century.* Bangkok: DD Books.

Jiraporn Witayasakpan (1992), *Nationalism and the Transformation of Aesthetic Concepts: Theatre in Thailand During the Phibun Period.* Ph.D dissertation, Cornell University.

Keyes, Charles F. (1966), *Peasant and Nation: The Integration of a Thai-Lao Village in the National System of Thailand,* Ph.D dissertation, Cornell University.

—— (1981), 'The Dialectics of Ethnic Change', in Charles F. Keyes (ed.), *Ethnic Change*, Seattle: University of Washington Press, 4–30.

Kraisri Nimmanahaeminda, (1965), 'Put Vegetables into Baskets, People into Towns', in L. M. Hanks J. R. Hanks, and Lauriston Sharp (eds.), *Ethnographic Notes on Northern Thailand,* Southeast Asia Data Paper No. 58, Ithaca: Cornell University.

La Loubère, Simon de (1969), The Kingdom of Siam, Oxford in Asia Historial Reprints, Kuala Lumpur: Oxford University Press.

Landon, Kenneth P. (1940), 'The Problem of the Chinese in Thailand', *Pacific Affairs*, xii/2.

Le May, Reginald (1926), *An Asian Arcady: The Land and Peoples of Northern Siam*, Cambridge: W. Heffer and Sons Ltd.

Lieberman, Victor (1991), 'Secular Trends in Burmese Economic History, c. 1350–1830, and their Implications for State Formation', *Modern Asian Studies* 25/1:1–31.

McGilvary, Daniel (1912), *A Half-Century Among the Siamese and the Lao*, New York: Fleming H. Revell Company.

McLeod, Captain.(1836), *Journal of Captain McLeod*, Manuscript Division, British Museum, London.

Moerman, Michael (1965), 'Ethnic Identification in a Complex Civilization: Who are the Lue', *American Anthropologist* 67:1215–30.

Nartsupha, Chatthip, and Suthy Prasartset (eds.) (1978), *The Political Economy of Siam, 1910–1932*, Bangkok: Social Science Assocation of Thailand.

Natedao Phatkul (1995), 'A State of Nature', *The Nation*, Friday, February 24, C7–8.

Purcell, Victor (1965), *The Chinese in Southeast Asia*, Oxford in Asia.

Rajah, Ananda (1990), 'Ethnicity, Nationalism, and the Nation-State: The Karen in Burma and Thailand', in Wijeyewardene, Gehan (ed.), *Ethnic Groups across National Boundaries in Mainland Southeast Asia*, Singapore: Institute of Southeast Asian Studies, 102–133.

Ramsay, James Ansil (1971), 'The Development of a Bureaucratic Polity: The Case of Northern Siam', Ph.D dissertation, Cornell University.

Ratanaporn Sethakul (1989), *Political, Social and Economic Changes in the Northern States of Thailand Resulting from the Chiang Mai Treaties of 1874–1883*, Ph.D dissertation, History, Northern Illinois University.

Reynolds, Craig J. (ed.) (1991), *National Identity and its Defenders: Thailand, 1939–1989*. Monash Papers on Southeast Asia No. 25, Clayton, Victoria, Australia: Monash University Centre of Southeast Asian Studies.

Richardson, Dr David (1830–1836), *Journals of Dr. Richardson*, Manuscript Division, British Museum, London.

Sanderson, G. P. (1983), [1893] *The Wild Beasts of India*, Delhi: Mittal Publications.

Schomburgk, Sir Robert H. (1863), 'A Visit of Xiengmai, the Principal City of the Laos or Shan States', *Journal of the Asiatic Society of Bengal* 32: 387–399.

Smyth, H. Warington (1898), *Five Years in Siam: From 1891–189,* London: John Murray.

Skinner, G. William (1957), 'Chinese Assimilation and Thai Politics', *Journal of Asian Studies* (Feb 16):237–50.

Snit Smuckarn and Breazeale, Kennon (1988), *A Culture in Search of Survival: The Phuan of Thailand and Laos*, New Haven: Yale University Southeast Asia Studies (Monograph No. 31).

Spittel, R. L. (1944), 'Pannikayan Elephant Noosers of Ceylon', *LORIS*, December, 175–7.

Stanley-Millson, Caroline (1991), 'Asian Working Elephants in South India', *Asian Affairs* 22 (February): 11–19.

Streckfuss, David (1987), 'Creating "the Thai": The Emergence of Indigenous Nationalism in Non-Colonial Siam 1850–1980', MA Thesis, University of Wisconsin-Madison.

Sukumar, R. (1989), *The Asian Elephant: Ecology and Management,* Cambridge: Cambridge University Press.

Tachard, Guy (1981), [1688] *A Relation of the Voyage to Siam, Performed by Six Jesuits, 1685*, Bangkok: White Orchid Press.

Tej Bunnag (1977), *The Provincial Administration of Siam, 1892–1915*, Kuala Lumpur: Oxford University Press.

ten Brummelhuis, Han (1987), *Merchant, Courtier and Diplomat: A History of Contacts between the Netherlands and Thailand*, Lochem-Gent:Uitgeversmaatschappij de Tijdstroom.

Terwiel, B. J. (1989), *Through Travellers' Eyes: An Approach to Early Nineteenth-century Thai History*, Bangkok: Editions Duang Kamol.

Thomas, J. S. (1902), 'The Shan Rebellion in Northern Siam', *Board of Foreign Missions, Presbyterian Church USA. Siam Letters and Correspondence, 1840–1910*, Philadelphia, Pennsylvania, vol. 271, No. 93 (August 28).

Thompson, P. A. (1987), [1910] *Siam: An Account of the Country and the People*, Bangkok: White Orchid Press.

Thongchai Winichakul (1994), *Siam Mapped: A History of the Geo-body of a Nation*, Honolulu: University of Hawaii Press.

Toland, Judth D. (ed.) (1993), Ethnicity and the State Political and Legal Anthropology Series, vol. 9, New Brunswick, New Jersey: Transaction Publishers.

Turton, Andrew (1980), 'Thai Institutions of Slavery', in James L. Watson (ed.), *Asian and African Systems of Slavery*, Oxford: Basil Blackwell.

Vandergeest, Peter (1990), *Siam into Thailand: Constituting Progress, Resistance and Citizenship*, Ph.D dissertation, Cornell University.

Van Vliet, Jeremias (1910), [1692] 'Description of the Kingdom of Siam', L. F. van Ravenswaay (transl.), *Journal of the Siam Society* (VII): 1–105.

Verdery, Katherine (1985), 'The Unmaking of an Ethnic Collectivity: Transylvania's Germans, *American Ethnologist,* 12: 62–83.

Vincent, Frank (1988), [1873] *The Land of the White Elephant: Sights and Scenes in Burma, Siam, Cambodia and Cochin-China 1871–2,* Bangkok: White Lotus Co. Ltd.

Wales, H. G. Quaritch (1934), *Ancient Siamese Government and Administration.* London: Bernard Quaritch Ltd.

Wijeyewardene, Gehan (1990), *Ethnic Groups across National Boundaries in Mainland Southeast Asia.* Singapore: Institute of Southeast Asian Studies.

Wyatt, David K. (1969), *The Politics of Reform in Thailand: Education in the Reign of King Chulalongkorn*, New Haven: Yale University Press.

Younghusband, G. J. (1888), *Eighteen Hundred Miles on a Burmese Tat Through Burmah, Siam and the Eastern Shan States,* London: W.H. Allen & Co.

Part VI

POSTSCRIPT

Chapter Sixteen

A New Stage in Tai Regional Studies: The Challenge of Local Histories

Nicholas Tapp

From the Thai point of view

Since the International Thai Studies Conference started in Bangkok in 1984 (there was a precursor in New Delhi, retrospectively titled the First ICTS, and a later regional workshop specifically on ethnic minorities in Buddhist polities), there has always been an awkwardness (remarked on by many) in the topics of the conference. There have been papers dealing specifically with the Thai majority population of Thailand, Thai (meaning Thailand) ecology and development and history, literature, language, culture and manners. There have been other papers dealing with the broader groups of people speaking languages of the Tai family of which Thai is one, which have included the Northern Thai and the Lao populations of northeastern Thailand, the Lao people of Laos, the Shan of Burma, the Lue and many smaller Tai-speaking groups in China, Laos and Vietnam. And then there have been papers dealing with unrelated (in a cultural/linguistic sense) peoples who form ethnic minority groups within Thailand and neighbouring countries, such as the Hmong and Yao, Akha and Lua'. In effect we have had Thai studies, Tai studies, and studies of other ethnic minorities, within a single conference.

It is my feeling that with this volume, which directly tackles the issue of the traditional 'incorporation' of non-Tai peoples into Tai political systems (Tanabe) and the transformation of these relations under the impact of the nation-state, together with the recent initiation of the International Conference on Tai Studies, a new stage in these sub-regional studies has been reached. We may be finally out of some of the practical dilemmas of the past. It is worth mentioning also that ethnic minority specialists (such as Renard and Alting von Geusau) have fruitfully combined here in a new way with those specialising in Thai/Tai studies to examine the historical legacies of a communal past and some of the inter-relationships and conflicts of the present.

The region spoken of through these papers is a wide and intrinsically fascinating one, as the maps show us, stretching from the plateau of Guizhou in southwest China down through Guangxi to the Malaysian borderlands areas, across Burma and into Assam, and through the former French Indochinese colonies of Vietnam, Laos and Cambodia. Throughout this sub-region Tai-speaking peoples and others have formed states, while Tai-speaking peoples and others have also formed minorities in the states dominated by others. To understand the cultural geography of the area it is essential to take into account the historical conditions under which the borders of modern nation-states were formed, and in particular the impact of colonialism on shaping the frontiers which divide Tai speakers and the speakers of other languages. This is why the combination of historians with anthropologists in this book is constructive, and why so many of the papers here have adopted an explicitly textual viewpoint. For the first time the crucial discourses of nineteenth century and early twentieth century narrative in forming and shaping images of 'the Other' are examined in detail (esp. Thongchai, but also Bowie, Renard, Kobkua and Nishii), and we can see how the processes of classification and hierarchical distancing of early modern scholarship (Thongchai) contributed to the cultural uniformity demanded by modern nation-states.

There is of course a reason why the International Thai Studies Conference has taken the form it has, with ethnic minority studies jostling uneasily with Thailand scholarship. This is to do with a general movement towards Thai cultural studies within the Thai academic world, associated with notions of Thai nationalism, with which many have been uncomfortable. Thailand's recent economic and political hegemony in the region has been accompanied by an enormous expansion of consumerist Thai cultural influence, which can be seen in the Thai television programmes regularly watched in Vientiane, the capital of Laos, or in the Thai-style villas and hostelries built in Kunming and the 'Sipsong Panna' (Xishuang Banna) area of China's Yunnan province.

Among the older generation of Thai scholars, and among political historians in general, Thai Premier Phibun Songkhram's wartime vision of a Pan-Thai League is not easily forgotten. And indeed, historically, there is no very obvious reason why other Tai states rivalling Thailand in present-day importance should not have been formed in the region, or why a vast Tai-speaking empire stretching from China to Malaysia should not have emerged from the dispersed Tai-speaking peoples who formed a honeycomb of smaller states across the region. Yet this did not happen, and the reasons why no larger Tai political body emerged must be sought partly in the nature of Tai feudal political systems themselves, partly in the power of neighbouring cultural influences – of the Burmese, Vietnamese, and Chinese in particular – but above all in the influence of colonialism in shaping the borders of modern Burma, Malaysia and Vietnam.

The papers in this volume amount to a sustained critique of what has until recently often been assumed to be the predominant cultural homogeneity of Thailand's population, as Kathleen Bowie most explicitly points out – the view that 'to be Thai is to speak only Thai, to be Buddhist' (Keyes 1979 in Evans), or as Kobkua puts it, 'speaking Thai, following the teachings of Buddhism, and upholding certain Thai cultural values'. And what emerges, perhaps for the first time in the context of 'Thai' studies, is the extraordinary diversity of cultural identity which the modern nation-state of Thailand has controlled, and which it has largely been able successfully to disguise.

As Kobkua also says, a generally accepted central concept of 'Thai-ness' is now 'gradually disintegrating in the face of the nation's awareness of the multi-racial, multi-cultural components of its population'. Thongchai similarly talks of the 'fragmentation, the ethno-spatial heterogeneity, and tension of diversity within the nation', while Bowie refers to ethnic heterogeneity as 'the historical reality of the subaltern' in pre-modern Thailand. Bowie traces a renewed interest among historians in the cultural diversity of the populations of traditional Tai tributary statelets, reminding us how probably half the population of North Thailand in the mid-nineteenth century were (ethnically diverse) resettled war captives (see Terwiel 1989), and draws attention to the importance of these massive historical displacements of population, and of the policies deliberately aimed at their integration. Putting the 'vegetables into baskets, and the serfs into principalities' (indicatively translated by Ratanaporn as putting 'people' into 'towns', but by Bowie as putting 'slaves' into 'kingdoms'), was an explicit mechanism of population control adopted from 1788 (Ratanaporn).

It is the precise nature of this traditional process of 'incorporation' and the subsequent transformation of cultural identities which concerns many of the contributors, in a way which successfully demonstrates that 'nationalism is not simply ethnicity writ large' (Keyes) and questions 'the assumed congruence between nation-state and culture' (Evans). So Kossikov is concerned with the 'meta-ethnic' nationality policies of the new Laos, which are resulting in a renewed sense of Lao ethnicity; and Mayoury with the 'hegemonic politics of one tribal group' in Laos. Nishii demonstrates a process of the 'emergence and transformation of peripheral ethnicity' and the strength of ideologies of 'local power' prior to the modern development of 'Thai-izing policies' in the case of the 'Sam Sam', the Thai-speaking Muslims on the Malaysian borders.

The issue here is the 'dominant, centralized Buddhist discourse emanating from Bangkok' (Tanabe) which has sought to erase and control cultural differences, and the related Thai 'discourse on civilization' which

Thongchai so clearly shows to have been instrumental in the formation of Siam as a 'geo-body'. Nineteenth-century narratives which represented an explicitly hierarchalizing and homogenising 'classification by more powerful outsiders' (the Thai) of the varied populations of Thailand, served to fortify the now central position of Bangkok in the national and political discourse of modern nationalism, associated with colonialism, transformed the Karen 'from subjects to citizens'. Several papers look at the exact mechanics of how traditional states, by contrast, managed their diverse populations Bowie through the 'ethnic management strategies' which she shows to be associated with different types of elephant ownership, Evans noting the importance of the traditional matrimonial alliances forged with indigenous chieftains.

It has been Condominas' (1990) argument that the 'apparently irreversible Tai-ization' of non-Tai populations was a key element in Tai political expansion (Evans, Tapp); traditional Tai states, in different periods, in fact had complex relations with non-Tai populations, whose differentiation as non-Tai was often (as Renard remarks) more an indication of social status than of ethnic or racial denotation. Ratanaporn (1989, in Bowie) concurs with the view of an absence of racial discrimination in pre-modern North Thailand. Indeed, the diversity of populations controlled was seen as an aspect of the traditional overlord's power (Thongchai 1994, in Bowie). As Tanabe shows, the (constructed) category of certain crucial non-Tai groups was ambivalently viewed by Tai-speakers, as wild or uncivilised on the one hand, and yet on the other hand as 'original holders of the land' on which the royal power of Tai states was based.

This sort of relationship between the Tai and (a particular category of) non-Tai was manipulated and perpetuated through 'devices and mechanisms of a ritual kind' (Tambiah 1976 in Bowie), a 'ritual language' which united people of the *müang*, the realm, with people of the *pa*, the forest (Renard). The importance of this ambivalent relationship (which linked the subjugation of non-Tai peoples with authority over territory) was lost with the advent of modern nationalism and the administrative centralisation of modern Thailand (Renard, Tanabe); even in traditional states, as policies of dispersing the members of particular ethnic groups were pursued, inter-ethnic homogeneity within the kingdom as a whole was increased (Bowie).

There are various processes here, of 'Tai-ization' or the cultural absorption of diverse populations into Tai ethnicities, of the maintenance of ritual and political relations with autochthonous populations, of the classification of war captives as slaves in the complex feudal *kin na* systems of Tai polities, and of the later 'pseudo-ethnographic' differentiation of the 'docile others' from the 'wild others' which Thongchai describes so well. In the process of the centralisation of state control traditional identities have been disguised or transformed, repainted and realigned, as the Karen become – quite inaccurately – the wicked opium-growers of the central Thai imagination (Renard, Thongchai).

What is most important is the shift which these papers represent – towards a concern with deconstructing the centralising discourse of Thai modernism, towards a recognition of the cultural and ethnic diversity and richness of modern Thailand, towards an interest in the mechanics of traditional mechanisms of population control and, above all, towards the possibilities of recognitions of 'the Others within' (Thongchai). Within the context of a general abandonment of the kind of essentialism on which past philosophies of cultural relativism have been based, the volume as a whole does, I think, speak of the power of the periphery in defining the centre and of the challenge of local histories to authoritative central histories (Reynolds 1992) of the type propagated by the nation-state.

It also partly redefines a future ethnographic realm in which it may be possible to speak in both a more open and a more mature way of the historical and current relations of ethnic minorities with the state, and of the Tai with the non-Tai in what remains a unified historical and ecological region; a historical realm surreally populated by King Chulalongkorn as 'King of the Karen' (Renard), riding out in disguise to visit his 'subjects' (Thongchai), while the French in Laos imposed a tax on the size of women's breasts (Mayoury) and the invulnerable, invisible culture hero of the 'Sam Sam' on the Malaysian border dealt in slaves and elephants (Nishii).

From the Minority Point of View

From that point of view it may continue to include discussions of ethnic minorities within the rubric of a conference on 'Thai' studies, dealing with both the Tai as minorities in other states, and with those ethnic minorities (such as the Karen, Hmong, 'Sam Sam' and Akha dealt with here) who are only partially represented in Thailand. Yet as there is now a conference on 'Tai Studies', perhaps there should also be one on the non-Tai minorities who have never formed powerful or lasting states, but who have perpetually been the 'Others' formed by more powerful discourses. There are already Hmong Studies Conferences, Akha/Hani workshops and development projects, Karen National Unions, and International Associations of Yao Studies. But when will these be properly represented in academic discourse?

In the meantime we have to accept the academic mirroring of political realities; Tibet is a part of China, the Hmong are an ethnic minority group within the modern borders of Thailand. That Thai studies as a whole is beginning to reflect on the diversity and fragmentation of the constituted Thai national self can only be a good sign for the continued political repression of the ethnic minority groups represented within Thailand. But it is really now time for the ethnic minority specialists themselves to wake up to the interactionalist, rather than primordial, models of ethnic identity pioneered by Leach (Evans, Tanabe). Thongchai shows how early narrative Thai discourse has mirrored western ethnography in its essentialist divisiveness towards the unacceptable realities of cultural, political, social, religious, linguistic, economic diversity. I feel strongly that ethnic minority specialists, such as myself, in their reaction against the centralised discourse of Thai-ness, which is the focus of so many of these papers, have on the other hand generally attempted to exaggerate and reinforce the distinctiveness of the people they have studied, and to have much underplayed the extent of their historical, cultural, political, ecological, linkages with the peoples (I am thinking of the Thai) who have dominated them. And I know that other minority researchers feel the same.

Here cultural essentialism, the assumed congruence of 'nation' with 'culture', and the identification of nationalism with ethnicity, are directly implicated in the academic discourses and debates which have taken place. Relations between the state and those defined as 'ethnic' minorities have been symmetrically replicated and mirrored in the placement of ethnic minority studies – whether these are of non-Tai cultural groups within the framework of the Thai state, or of Tai-speakers and those who form minorities within Thailand within a larger state such as China within the larger context of 'Thai studies'. Very generally the strength and commonality of social relations between Tai-speakers and speakers of other languages who either were subordinated within Tai states, or who formed states within which Tai-speakers were themselves subordinated (Vietnam, China) has not been recognised, neither in local narrative discourse nor in the academic reportage on particular groups (such as the Lue in Yunnan).

Yet these relations were extensive and not necessarily of an ethnic nature, as Renard shows and Ratanaporn remarks. Culturally, ecologically, the minorities of modern Thailand historically enjoyed particular relations with Tai/Thai peoples which modern scholarship in its concern for the culturally unique, like the discourse of modern nationalism through the blanket extension of an inappropriate notion of 'Thai-ness', has largely disguised. Tanabe shows us some of these relations, at a ritual and symbolic level; and there were more, at an everyday level of comprehension of a common and interdependent ecological region which found reflection in both symbolic and political relations. The extent of influences of the non-Tai on the Tai (suggested by Tanabe), and of the Tai on the non-Tai (Kammerer 1989; Walker 1992) has still not been fully recognised; and the reasons for this lie as much in the conventions of western academic reporting as in those indigenous discourses which from the late nineteenth century onwards sought to disguise and obscure the extent of similarities

Plate 24. 'Trophée magique des Gnia-heuns'

between those classified as 'Thai' and those classified as 'the other' at the same time as new models of Thai cultural identity were extended.

Relations between those who are currently minorities and those who are currently majorities were then in the not-so-distant past far more extensive and particularised than they appear today, and some of the blame for over-emphasising their differences must lie with those non-Thai researchers who, without a clear understanding of the history of Tai political systems, which seem to have been inclusive of cultural difference

357

in a more radical way than has generally been realised, went out determined to prove the differences of 'their' peoples' from that of the dominant Thai majorities who subordinated them. It may be, therefore, that as Thai studies move towards a recognition of the strength of cultural diversity within both traditional Tai states and modern Thailand, studies of the non-Tai ethnic minorities are moving towards a recognition of much more extensive relations with the Tai than have been generally recognised in the past.

One of the clearest indications of the latter is in the history of messianic movements within Thailand (Turton and Tanabe 1984), which clearly showed the uniting of culturally and ethnically diverse populations behind local and regional identities of the type described by Nishii, against the administrative centralisation, reinforced by Buddhism, of modern Thailand (see Keyes 1971). There is, I feel, a common and local understanding, between ethnically diverse populations, which is based on the possession of a common history and common economic circumstances, and which has overriding importance when compared to the effects of national minority policies and the efforts of foreign researchers to prove the ethnic and cultural distinctiveness of their chosen peoples. This has been largely overlooked by modern academic scholarship in its concern with classification and by nationalist rhetoric in its desire to homogenise.

It is the contribution of this volume to have attempted to show that, from the viewpoint of Thai cultural studies, it is now down to the efforts of individual minority specialists to show, in detail, the relations of given populations with the larger state structures and policies which have defined them. In all, this is an indicative and intrinsically interesting case, of how academic discourse has mirrored and reflected political realities, and how it is now attempting to escape some of the constraints posed by its own enmeshment in historical circumstance.

References

Condominas, Georges (1990), *From Lawa to Mon, from Saa' to Thai: historical and anthropological aspects of Southeast Asian social spaces*, Canberra, The Australian National University, (Occasional paper of the Department of Anthropology).

Kammerer, Cornelia (1989), 'Territorial Imperatives: Akha Ethnic Identity and Thailand's National Integration' in John McKinnon & Bernard Vienne (eds.) *Hill Tribes Today*. Bangkok and Paris, White Lotus and ORSTOM.

Keyes, Charles F. (1971), 'Buddhism and National Intergration in Thailand' *Journal of Asian Studies*, 30(3): 551–567.

—— (1979) 'Introduction', in Charles F. Keyes (ed.), *Ethnic Adaptation and Identity: The Karen on the Thai Frontier with Burma*, Philadelphia: ISHI.

Ratanaporn Sethakul (1989), *Political, Social and Economic Changes in the Northern States of Thailand Resulting from the Chiang Mai Treaties of 1874–1883*, Ph.D. dissertation, History, Northern Illinois University.

Reynolds, Craig (1992), 'The plot of Thai history: theory and practice' in G. Wijeyewardene and E. Chapman (eds.) *Patterns and Illusions: Thai History and Thought*. Singapore, Australian National University and Institute of South-East Asian Studies, Singapore.

Tambiah, S.J. (1976), *World Conqueror and World Renouncer: a study of Buddhism and polity in Thailand against a historical backdrop*, Cambridge: Cambridge University Press.

Terwiel, B. J. (1989), *Through Travellers' Eyes: an Approach to early Nineteenth-century Thai History*, Bangkok: Editions Duang Kamol.

Thongchai Winichakul (1994), *Siam Mapped: a History of the Geo-body of a Nation*, Honolulu: University of Hawaii Press.

Turton, Andrew and Tanabe, Shigeharu (eds.) (1984), *History and Peasant Consciousness in South East Asia* (Senri Ethnological Studies No. 13). Osaka, National Museum of Ethnology.

Walker, Anthony (1992), *The Highland Heritage: Collected Essays on Upland North Thailand*. Singapore, Suvarnabhumi Books.

Note

The Regional Workshop on Ethnic Minorities in Buddhist Polities, in Bangkok in June 1985, was organised by the International Council of Ethnic Studies in Kandy, with Chulalongkorn University.

Plate 25. 'Tired'

Appendix:
Illustrations: sources and notes

Note: all captions appearing in the text and in List of Illustrations p. xxi (given here in italics) are original, with the exception of Cover, Frontispiece and Plates 6, 9 and 18, which also involve translations.

Frontispiece *A Prince (Cao Müang) of Nan, probably early nineteenth century*

Sangaroon Kanokpongchai (ed.) 1986 *Wat Phumin and Wat Nong Bua (wat phumin lae wat nong bua)* Mural Paintings of Thailand Series No. 2 (4) Bangkok: Muang Boran Publishing House, p. 70.

page 70: 'It can be assumed that the person was one of the governors of Nan.' Fresco in Wat Phumin, Nan Province, northern Thailand.

1 *Talio, or charm*

Carl Bock, 1884 *Temples and elephants: travels in Siam in 1881–1882*, London: Sampson Low, Marston, Searle, & Rivington, [reprinted OUP, 1986] p. 266.

The 'talio' (*taleo, chaleo*) is a kind of protective sign or 'taboo' indicator which is common to Tai and many non-Tai peoples in the region (see Plate 10 below).

2 *A meal offered by the king of Muong You*

Francis Garnier, 1996, *Further travels in Laos and in Yunnan: the Mekong Exploration Commission Report (1866–1868) – Volume 2*, Bangkok: White Lotus, p. 79.

page 75–6: 14 September 1867 'The palace was vast, constructed in hard wood and with very competent carpentry work. The king received us in a great hall, into which daylight penetrated only through narrow windows hidden by silk wall-hangings. He was a young man of twenty-six years with a distinguished face and infinitely gracious in manner. He was dressed in green satin with red flowers and the lights in the rubies that he was wearing in his ears lit up the silky reflections of his rich dress. He was seated on cushions embroidered with gold. All around him were the mandarins of the palace lined up in respectful poses. At his feet were the insignia of his royal rank, i.e., his saber and richly chiseled golden vases.'

3 *Route from Bangkok to Kiang-Tsen*

Bock (op. cit.), p. 440.

4 *Designs on the borders of [Shan] turbans*

Leslie Milne 1910, *Shans at home*, London: no publisher given [reprinted Paragon, New York, 1970], p. 169.

5 *The library of a Laotian pagoda*

Louis Delaporte and Francis Garnier, 1998, *A pictorial journey on the Old Mekong Cambodia, Laos and Yunnan: the Mekong exploration commission report (1866–1868) – Volume 3*, Bangkok: White Lotus, p. 126.

[parts are from *Le Tour du Monde 1869–71*, and F. Garnier, *Voyage d'exploration en Indo-Chine* (official publication 1873, and 1885 edition, Paris: Hachette.]

6 *Ngo' Pa*
   (i) *Mr. Khanang dressed as a Ngo'*
   (ii) *Mr. Khanang in full dress for attendance on His Majesty*
   (iii) *The Ngo' Pa called 'Khanang': photograph executed by the hand of His Majesty King Chulalongkorn*

H.M. King Chulalongkorn 1997 *Ngo' Pa: a play by His Majesty King Chulalongkorn (bot lakorn ruang ngo' pa: phrajaniphon nai phrabat somdej phracula cormklao cao yuu hua)*, Bangkok: Krom Silpakorn.

   (i) Mr. Khanang dressed as a Ngo' (ruup nai khanang taeng tua pen ngo') p. 42;
   (ii) Mr. Khanang in full dress for attendance on His Majesty (ruup nai khanang taeng tem yos tam sadet) p. 36;
   (iii) The Ngo' Pa called 'Khanang': photograph executed by the hand of His Majesty King Chulalongkorn (ngo' pa 'khanang' phaap thai fii phrahat phrabaat somdet culacomklaocao yuuhua) p. 187.

7 *Lao architecture: the Chow Radjasee's house at Kiang Hai [Chiang Rai]*

Bock (op. cit.), p. 304.

page 303–7: 1882 'I here give a picture of the residence of the Chow Radjasee [governing prince of Chiang Rai, son-in-law of the Vice-Roy (Upparat) at Chiang Mai] not because it is of the most elaborate design, but because it will serve as a type of Lao [here, Khon Müang, Ed.] architecture and domestic arrangements. There are no fine houses or palaces in the country; the houses of prince and peasant are the same in general plan and in mode of construction, the only difference being in the size and in the quality of material and workmanship. A few bits of extra carving on the gables, and the fact that it is constructed throughout of teak, may distinguish a prince's house from that of any ordinary person; . . .'

8 *Karen packmen*

H. Warington-Smyth, 1898, *Five years in Siam: from 1891 to 1896*, London: John Murray, two volumes, Volume 1, p. 297.

9 *Princess Dara Rasmee wearing tribal 'fancy dress'*

Nongyao Kanchanacarii (ed.) 1990, *Dara Rasmii: phraprawat phrarajchaya cao Dara Rasmii, [Dara Rasmee: history of the Royal Princess Dara Rasmee]*, Chiang Mai: Suriwong, plate 18 between pp. xix–1.

'phra rajchaya Dara Rasmii nai chalong phraong faensii chao khao' [Princess Dara Rasmee wearing tribal 'fancy dress']

Princess (Cao) (Raja Jaya) Dara Rasmee (1873–1933) was the eleventh and youngest child of Cao Inthanon (Indavijayanonda) the seventh ruler of Chiang Mai (r. 1870–1897) following its re-establishment in 1780 by his grandfather's elder brother Cao Kawila. From the age of 13 she resided at Court in Bangkok as 'Princess Consort' (Cao Chom) of King Chulalongkorn (Rama 5; r. 1868–1910). Her only child died in infancy. In 1914, at the age of 41 and four years after the death of Rama 5, she was permitted to return to live in Chiang Mai. She travelled extensively throughout the North, from the Salween to the Mekong, visiting peoples of all ethnicities, apart from Khon Müang notably Karen (Hmong and others are also specifically mentioned). In 1926 she was a key local figure in the first ever ceremonial visit to Chiang Mai by a ruling Thai monarch, organised by Prince Damrong. Her brothers Cao Inthawararot (r. 1897–1911) and Cao Kaew Nawarat (r. 1911–1939) were to be the last two rulers of the dynasty.

Apart from the caption, the source gives no further detail of this photograph or the event represented. We can deduce that it was taken probably fairly soon after 1914. This was a time when the religious leader Kuba Srivichai was in lively contact with Karen and other minorities in his mission of an inclusive, Buddhist and Lanna 'cultural revitalisation'. Apart from the Princess (seated centre) it is not clear who if anyone else might be in the costume of another culture, whether they are Thai or Khon Müang, or of a non-Tai minority. There appear to be costumes of more than one people. The picture calls out for detailed analysis. How respectful and/or light-hearted was this 'dressing up'; and when was the practice of 'fancy dress' (*faensii* became a Thai term), and in particular the adoption of 'minority' costume introduced. This may have been a Bangkok conceit introduced or translated to the North by Princess Dara. Or the term *faensii* may be a later interpretation. The resonances with the case of Khanang are poignant (Thongchai this volume).

10 *Ecriture des Khâs*

Harmand, Jules, 1877, Le Laos et les populations sauvages de l'Indo-Chine, pp. 1–48, in Charton, Edouard (ed.) 1879, *Le Tour du Monde: nouveau journal des voyages, Vol. 38,* Paris: Hachette, p. 46.

page 46: 27 March 1877 [near the village Moun-hou-Meuong, Bolovens] 'J'aperçois, pendant la route, à quelques pas de l'amorce d'un petit sentier, une grossière barrière faite de bambous et d'arbres abattus, ornée d'hexagones et de bouquets d'herbes; au-dessus du sentier, se balançait une petite planchette, portant sur chacun de ses bords une série d'encoches régulières, mais les unes grandes, les autres plus petites. Je réunis les cornacs et je leur demande s'ils savent ce que veut dire cet écriteau. Malheureusement je n'avais pas de sauvages avec moi, et les Laotiens d'Attopeu, bien qu'habitués à vivre en pleine forêt, côte à côte avec les Khâs, ne me semblent pas très au fait de ce mode d'écriture. Enfin, après une assez longue discussion entre eux, on me donne l'explication suivante:

A droite, une série de douze petites encoches, une série de quatre grandes, plus une troisième série de douze petites.

Traduisez: "D'ici douze jours, tout homme qui osera franchir notre palisade, sera notre prisonnier, ou nous payera quatre buffles ou (ou bien *et*) douze ticaux de rançon."

A gauche, huit grosses encoches, onze moyennes, neuf petites. Ce qui signifie: "Notre village compte huit hommes, onze femmes et neuf enfants."'

['On the way, at the beginning of a little path, I [Dr Jules Harmand, French traveller and ethnologist, in 1877] noticed a rough barrier made of bamboo and cut down trees decorated with hexagons [probably *'taleo'* see Plate 1, Ed.] and bunches of plants; above the path dangled a little board, on each side of which was a series of regular notches, some large, others smaller. I called together the elephant drivers and asked them if they knew what this notice meant. Unfortunately I had no savages with me, and the Laotians of Attopeu, although they are used to living side by side with the Khâs deep in the forest, seemed not to be well acquainted with this form of writing. Finally, after a long discussion, they explained it to me as follows:

On the right, a series of twelve little notches, a series of four large ones, then a third series of twelve little ones.

Translated as: 'From today, for the next twelve days, anyone daring to pass beyond our fence will become our prisoner, or will pay us four buffaloes or (or perhaps *and*) twelve ticals in ransom.'

On the left, eight big notches, eleven middling size, nine little ones. Which means: 'Our village numbers eight men, eleven women and nine children.']

11 *Village de Khâs Bolovens*

Harmand (op. cit.), p. 41.

12 *The Hanuman or Hoalaman, from a native drawing*

Bock (op. cit.), p. 69.

13 *Phya Nyak, the king of serpents and dragons*

Holt S. Hallett, 1890, *A thousand miles on an elephant in the Shan states,* London: Blackwood, p. 227.

14 *The Rachasee: king of beasts*

Bock (op. cit.), p. 165.

15 *The city of Luang Prabang*

Delaporte (op. cit.), p. 182.

page 32: When you cross the Mékong to the side opposite Luang Prabang, and climb the bank, you can see the river strewn with boats far below; there is a distant view of the city, with its streets at right angles to the river and its twenty pagodas with their roofs half-hidden by a forest of palm trees. A small pyramid erected on a marble rock dominates the city. Behind it, a chain of hills rises and in the background there is a curtain of high calcareous mountains with sharp summits. A little to the left, beneath the pyramid, in the middle of the city is the Nam Hou ravine which runs south to north amid coconut tress and flows into the Mékong, two hundred meters up river.'

16 *Réception chez le prince d'Oubôn*

Harmand (op. cit.), p. 9.

page 6–7: 16 February 1877 'Malgré toute l'antipathie que je ressentis pour le *khiao* d'Oubôn, je dus me décider à aller le voir. Je le fais, suivant l'étiquette, prévenir de ma visite, afin de lui laisser le temps de sortir toute sa friperie européenne, et de passer les magnifiques bas bleus dont il est si fier.

Il me reçut sur un beau tapis de France, sous un vaste hangar établi le long du fleuve à son intention. . .

On me fit passer en revue les armes des râteliers, qui étaient de bons fusils rayés de fabrique anglaise, de belles lances, des sabres de tous les modèles.'

[Despite my strong dislike of the Cao Müang of Ubon, I [Dr Harmand] had to make up my mind to go and see him. I gave him due notice of my visit, as protocol required, so that he would have time to get out all his old European finery, and to put on the splendid blue stockings of which he is so proud.

He received me on a beautiful French carpet, under a huge open shed he had had expressly built along the river bank.

I was obliged to inspect the racks of weapons which were good rifles of English make, fine lances and swords of every description.']

17 *The ancestors Pu Nyoeu and Nya Nyoeu learn to make the salutation to show respect* (wai) *before the dance during the New Year festival at Wat S'ieng T'ông, Luang Prabang [1952]*

Charles Archaimbault, 1959, La naissance du monde selon les traditions lao, in *La naissance du monde*, Sources Orientales, Vol. 1, Paris: Editions du Seuil. [reprinted as La naissance du monde selon les traditions Lao: le mythe de Khun Bulom, in Charles Archaimbault, 1973, *Structures religieuses Lao (Rites et mythes)*, Vientiane: Vithagna, pp. 97–130], p. 27.

page 113–14: 'Phi Seua Muang de Muang Thên, les Pu Nyoeu Nya Nyoeu, comme précise le texte du grand serment, avaient rang spécial parmi les génies gardiens des douze marches du royaume de Khun Bulom. Or à Luang Prabang, ces deux thên occupent, non loin de la colline sacrée, près de la pagode royale de Aham, un des douze autels réservés aux génies protecteurs du territoire. En tant que Devata Luang, ils sont un peu à l'écart des autres divinités, qui doivent les convier à partager les mets qui leurs sont présentés.'

[According to the text of the great oath [of loyalty] the tutelary spirits of Müang Thên [at Dien Bien Phu] the Pu Nyoeu Nya Nyoeu, had a special place among the guardian spirits of the twelve lands of the Kingdom of Khun Bulom. At Luang Prabang these two founding ancestors live in one of the twelve shrines to the guardian spirits of the territory, situated not far from the sacred hill [Pousi] near the royal Wat Aham. As Royal Deities they are somewhat distinct from other divinities, which are obliged to invite them to share the food offerings they receive.]

18 *Convoi de sauvages esclaves*

Harmand (op. cit.), p. 8.

page 6: 15 February 1877 'Il paraît que, lorsque les temps sont durs, que la rentrée de l'impôt n'a pas été fructueuse, qu'une épizootie a sévi sur les buffles ou sur les éléphants, en un mot qu'il faut se "remonter un peu", les mandarins laotiens [at Bassac Ed.] organisent des expéditions contre les sauvages . . . . Il faut ajouter que ces razzias ne se font d'ordinaire que contre les sauvages indépendants, qui ne reconnaissent pas l'autorité des chefs laotiens et n'acquittent aucun tribut . . . . Quand le nombre de captifs de tout âge et de tout sexe paraît suffisant, on les mène chargés de liens à Bassac, à Stung-treng, à Attopeu; des marchands indigènes ou des Chinois, mais surtout des Malais du Cambodge [probably Cham Ed.], les achètent pour en former des convois, qui sont expédiés principalement à Bang-kôk, à Korât, et à Phnôm-penh.'

[It seems that when times are hard, when tax collection has not been fruitful, when disease has been raging among the buffalo or elephants, in a word when there's a need to 'restock a bit', the Lao officials [at Bassac] mount expeditions against the savages . . . . It must be said that these raids are usually only against the independent savages, who do not recognise the authority of the Lao chiefs and pay no tribute . . . . When they have a sufficient number of captives, of all ages and sexes, these are taken bound to Bassac, to Stung-treng and to Attopeu; local or Chinese merchants, and especially Malays from Cambodia [probably Cham Ed.] buy them and put them in convoys which are then sent mainly to Bangkok, Korat and Phnom Penh.]

19 '. . . *les aborigènes par l'offrande d'une jarre d'alcool, renouvellent le contrat ancien . . .*'

Charles Archaimbault, 1964, Structures religieuses au Laos, in his *Structures religieuses Lao (Rites et mythes),* 1973, Vientiane: Vithagna, pp. 77–95 [see also his Religious structures in Laos, *Journal of the Siam Society,* 52.1, 1964.], p. 82.

page 82: 'Au moment de la course de pirogues [at Bassac or Campasak], le quatrième jour de la cérémonie, les aborigènes par l'offrande d'une jarre d'alcool, renouvellent le contrat ancien avec le descendant de ceux qui furent chargés de maintenir l'ordre dans le pays.'

[At the time of the boat race, on the fourth day of the ceremony [at Campasak], the aboriginal people renew the contract, by means of a jar of rice alcohol, with the descendant of those who were charged with the obligation to maintain order in the country.']

20 *A Yak*

Hallett (op. cit.), p. 57.

21 *Phya In or Indra*

Hallett (op. cit.), p. 187.

22 *'Khattha Kumara . . . in royal costume with a man'*

Sangaroon (op. cit.), p. 58.

Khattha Kumara was an incarnation of the Bodhisattva whose life of many adventures was spent relieving human suffering, using superhuman powers. Scenes from his life are represented in the frescoes in Wat Phumin, Nan Province, in northern Thailand.

page 58: 'Khattha Kumara is in royal costume with a man carrying bags. The prince wears a hat with pointed top, which could have been painted in red lacquer and gilded. . . . He is adorned with various ornaments on top of the dress. He also wears a pair of exquisite shoes. In contrast, his man wears much simpler costume. But his thighs have intricately tattooed designs.'

23 *Départ de Bassac*

Harmand (op. cit.), p. 13.

24 *Trophée magique des Gnia-heuns*

Harmand (op. cit.), p. 35.

page 35–6: 'Je visite plusieurs cases et cahutes [of the 'Gnia-heun' people – Nya Hön – of the Bolovens Plateau Ed.]. Dans toutes je trouve une réduction de maison, haute de vingt centimètres, placée sur une sorte de petit autel, puis, à côté, une espèce de petite panoplie extrêmement curieuse.

On y voit, disposé avec un certain art, sur une monture de bambou, tout ce qui constitue la vie du sauvage: un petit sac ou une petite arbalète avec un carquois de flèches microscopiques, un mortier à riz de la grosseur d'un dé à coudre avec son pilon, une pirogue de poupée, pourrais-je dire, munie de ses pagayes, une nasse et une hotte à l'avenant; le tout est couronnée par un oeuf de poule et un paquet de plumes. Enfin, on voit encore, sur cet étonnant simulacre, des graines de riz et quelques houppes de coton, etc., collés avec de la résine ou de la cire.'

['I visited a number of huts and cabins [of the Nya Hön people]. In each of them I found a scale model of a house, about twenty centimetres high, placed on a little altar of sorts, and by it a highly interesting trophy.

This consisted of everything that goes to make up the life of the savage, arranged with some artistry on a bamboo frame. There was a little bag, a cross-bow with a quiver of tiny arrows, a rice mortar the size of a thimble with its pestle, a dugout canoe and oars, as if made for a doll, a fish trap and matching creel; the whole thing is topped off with a chicken's egg and a bundle of feathers. And for the final touch to this amazing image, are grains of rice and tufts of cotton stuck on with resin or wax.]

25 *Tired*

James McCarthy 1900, *Surveying and exploring in Siam*, London: John Murray, p. 145.

Index

Abdul Hamid, Sultan 187
Abdul Rahman, Tunku 165, 167, 168,
  170, 171, 184
Aberle, D. 105
Adzaw, A. 137
Ahai and Liuqia 141
Aijmer, G. 295
Akha Society for Culture and Art 125
Akha/Hani peoples 15, 35-6, 66, 122-3;
  archaic oral texts of migration 132-4;
  in Burma 125; conclusions concerning
  inter-ethnic relations 150-3; Corvée
  and slave trade 135; diaspora 123-8;
  ethno-linguistic characteristics of sub-
  groups 127-8; Euleubiue/Latseubieu
  songs 134; genealogical practices as
  ethnic alliance system 146-50;
  geographical dispersal 123; Guidzuiei
  133-4; hermeneutics of texts/histories
  131-2; historical context from external
  sources 128-30; hunger, poverty, loss
  of irrigated lowland 135-6; internal
  records of marginalization/inter-ethnic
  relations 130-8; internal/external
  history discussed 138-42; Kajehjeheu
  135; landlessness, poverty, oppression,
  marginalization 134-7; line of alliances
  144; line of diagnostics/healing 145-6;
  line of knowing customary law 145;
  line of leadership 144; line of life 144;
  line of taking care of rice-fields 145;
  line of teaching 144; line of technical
  knowledge 145; and lines of survival/
  transmission of traditional knowledge
  143-6; loss of lowland to the Tai
  134-5; Misang laweu 134-5; in
  northern Laos 125-6; in northern
  Thailand 126-7; related peoples in
  northern Vietnam 126; Sjhazizieu
  songs/Tjiditjieu ceremony 133; stories
  of oppression/exploitation 136-7;
  texts describing inter-ethnic relations
  137-8; traditional knowledge/
  unification of diaspora 142-3; in
  Yunnan 124-5
Allton, I. 91
Alting von Geusau, L.G.M. 15, 35, 66,
  122, 123, 126, 132, 134, 135, 138,
  143
Anderson, B.R. O'G. 54-5, 109, 208,
  284, 337, 342
animality 18
Annandale, N. and Robinson, H. 165,
  169-70, 182, 184
Anou, King 208, 210
anthropology 35
Aram Khirirak 74
Archaimbault, C. 7, 9, 17, 166, 168, 182,
  184, 298, 302
Arong Suthasasna 168, 173
Arunrat Wichienkeaw 326
assimilation 25-8, 33-4
Astri Shurke 173
autochthonous peoples 17, 295-9, 304
Awang Poh 171
Axang Laoli 252
Ayutthaya 6, 68

Backus, C. 126, 128, 129, 139, 140, 147
Bai Yu 142